# ACCESS
# SAN FRANCISCO

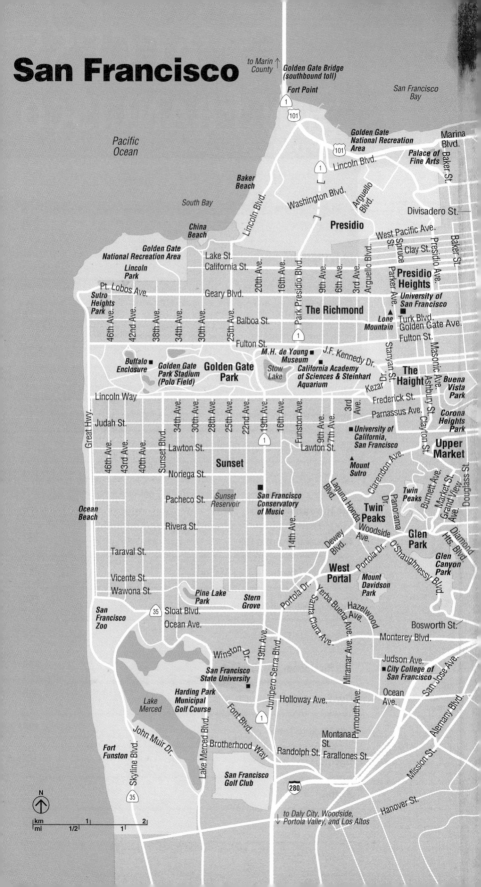

# San Francisco

to Marin County ↑

**Golden Gate Bridge**
**(southbound toll)**

Fort Point

San Francisco Bay

Pacific Ocean

Golden Gate National Recreation Area

Marina Blvd.

Palace of Fine Arts

Baker St.

Lincoln Blvd.

Baker Beach

Washington Blvd.

Divisadero St.

South Bay

**Presidio**

West Pacific Ave.

China Beach

Presidio Ave.

Spruce St.

Clay St.

Golden Gate National Recreation Area

Lake St.

California St.

20th Ave.

16th Ave.

9th Ave.

6th Ave.

3rd Ave.

Arguello Blvd.

Parker Ave.

Baker St.

**Presidio Heights**

Lincoln Park

Pt. Lobos Ave.

Geary Blvd.

**The Richmond**

University of San Francisco

Sutro Heights Park

46th Ave.

42nd Ave.

38th Ave.

34th Ave.

30th Ave.

25th Ave.

Balboa St.

Lone Mountain

Turk Blvd.
Golden Gate Ave.

Masonic Ave.

Fulton St.

Fulton St.

**Buffalo Enclosure**

**Golden Gate Park Stadium (Polo Field)**

**Golden Gate Park**

M.H. de Young Museum

Stow Lake

J.F. Kennedy Dr.

Stanyan St.

**The Haight**

Buena Vista Park

California Academy of Sciences & Steinhart Aquarium

Kezar Dr.

Ashbury St.

Clayton St.

Corona Heights Park

Lincoln Way

3rd Ave.

Frederick St.

Parnassus Ave.

**Upper Market**

Great Hwy.

Judah St.

34th Ave.

30th Ave.

28th Ave.

25th Ave.

22nd Ave.

19th Ave.

16th Ave.

Funston Ave.

9th Ave.

7th Ave.

University of California, San Francisco

Burnett Ave.

Market St.

Grand View Ave.

Douglass St.

Lawton St.

Lawton St.

Mount Sutro

**Sunset**

Clarendon Ave.

Twin Peaks

Diamond Hts. Blvd.

46th Ave.

43rd Ave.

40th Ave.

Sunset Blvd.

Noriega St.

Panorama Dr.

Pacheco St.

Sunset Reservoir

**San Francisco Conservatory of Music**

14th Ave.

Laguna Honda Blvd.

**Twin Peaks**

**Glen Park**

Ocean Beach

Rivera St.

Dewey Blvd.

Woodside Ave.

**Glen Canyon Park**

Taraval St.

Portola Dr.

O'Shaughnessy Blvd.

Vicente St.

Wawona St.

Pine Lake Park

Stern Grove

**West Portal**

Mount Davidson Park

Bosworth St.

San Francisco Zoo

35

Sloat Blvd.

Winston Dr.

19th Ave.

Portola Dr.

Yerba Buena Ave.

Santa Clara Ave.

Hazelwood Ave.

Monterey Blvd.

Ocean Ave.

Judson Ave.

City College of San Francisco

San Jose Ave.

Lake Merced

**San Francisco State University**

Juniper Serra Blvd.

Holloway Ave.

Miramar Ave.

Ocean Ave.

Alemany Blvd.

Harding Park Municipal Golf Course

Fort Funston

John Muir Dr.

Skyline Blvd.

Lake Merced Blvd.

Brotherhood Way

Font Blvd.

1

Montana St.

Randolph St.

Plymouth Ave.

Farallones St.

Mission St.

**San Francisco Golf Club**

280

Hanover St.

N

35

to Daly City, Woodside, Portola Valley, and Los Altos

km

mi

1/2

1

1

2

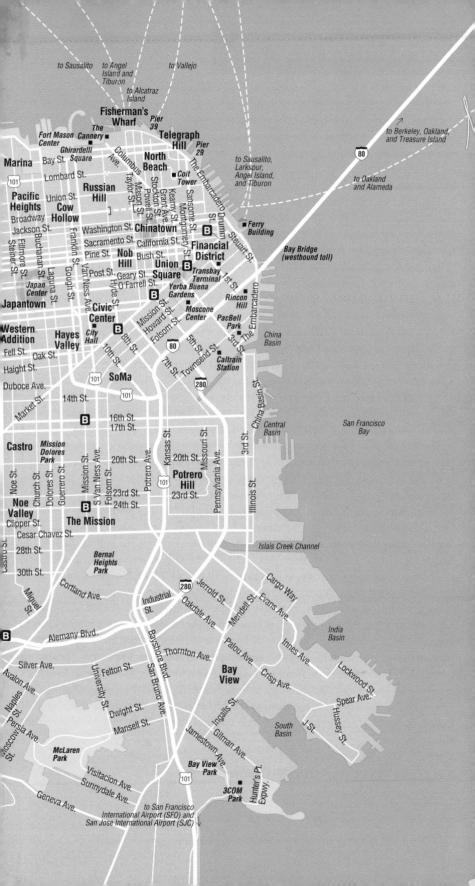

# ORIENTATION

The City by the Bay's stature as one of the US's most attractive, welcoming destinations is well deserved. Honeymooners continue to be lured by San Francisco's romantic charm, seasoned travelers like the civilized pace and dramatic views, families appreciate the many attractions for children, gays and lesbians flock to this tolerant town for its vibrant subculture and executive types *love* to have their conventions here year after year. In light of the recent demand for housing, driven by the influx of dot-com millionaires, real estate prices have soared.

San Francisco covers only 47 square miles; it is situated on a peninsula, with the **Pacific Ocean** to the west, the **Golden Gate Strait** to the north, and the **San Francisco Bay** stretching north to east. Its 728,921 inhabitants make it the second-largest city in the nine-county **Bay Area,** a region that continues to thrive. Owing to the booming Internet industry located near San Jose, the city is flush with cash. As a result, many new civic projects and improvements are underway.

Originally inhabited by the Ohlone Indians and reputedly visited by British admiral Sir Francis Drake in 1579, the region saw five flags fly—representing England, Spain, Mexico, the Republic of California, and the United States—from 1579 through 1850. This part of the West Coast has been the subject of curiosity ever since gold was discovered at Sutter's Mill in 1848. San Francisco became known as a place to get rich quick—and a place to spend it all, as the miners and other high rollers flooded to the pleasure palaces of the Barbary Coast. When the city was largely demolished by the 1906 earthquake and fire, attention was again riveted on the region. But San Francisco was quickly rebuilt, sowing the seeds of the indomitable image that persists today.

Since then, San Francisco has cultivated its freewheeling reputation and made news on different fronts, from the kitchens of famous restaurants to the violent scenes of labor unrest on the docks and the 1978 assassinations of mayor George Moscone, along with Harvey Milk, a gay member of the board of supervisors (known to many as "The Mayor of Castro Street"). The city has been in the forefront of social movements since the arrival of the flower children and the "summer of love" in 1967; and today the large gay and lesbian community presses for change as it continues to lobby for homosexual rights. San Francisco ranks in the front lines of culture, with a world-class opera house, symphony, and ballet company, as well as some of the best Asian, European, and modern art museums in the country. Europeans love San Francisco because, in many respects, it is the most European of American cities. Hispanics gravitate to the Spanish-speaking Mission district, and Asians also feel at home, since the city has one of the largest Chinese populations in the country, a substantial Japanese community, and increasing numbers of Vietnamese, Cambodian, Laotian, and Filipino immigrants. Even New Yorkers are comfortable in San Francisco, frequently comparing it to the Big Apple. Locals have been accused of being smug about their city, and the charge is probably valid. San Franciscans know and love the Bay Area, and enjoy sharing its attractions. And, as the visitor quickly discovers, the city they take such pride in is one that reveals its many treasures over the course of time.

**AREA CODE 415 UNLESS OTHERWISE NOTED.**

# How To Read This Guide

ACCESS SAN FRANCISCO° is arranged by neighborhood so you can see at a glance where you are and what is around you. The numbers next to the entries in the following chapters correspond to the numbers on the maps. The type is color-coded according to the kind of place described:

Restaurants/Clubs: **Red**

Hotels: **Purple** | Shops: Orange

**◗ Outdoors: Green** | Sights/Culture: Blue

♿ Wheelchair accessible

## WHEELCHAIR ACCESSIBILITY

An establishment (except a restaurant) is considered wheelchair accessible when a person in a wheelchair can easily enter a building (i.e., no steps, a ramp, a wide-enough door) without assistance. Restaurants are deemed wheelchair accessible *only* if the above applies, *and* if the rest rooms are on the same floor as the dining area and their entrances and stalls are wide enough to accommodate a wheelchair.

## RATING THE RESTAURANTS AND HOTELS

The restaurant ratings take into account the quality, service, atmosphere, and uniqueness of the restaurant. An expensive restaurant doesn't necessarily ensure an enjoyable evening; however, a small, relatively unknown spot could have good food, professional service, and a lovely atmosphere. Therefore, on a purely subjective basis, stars are used to judge the overall dining value (see the star ratings at right). Keep in mind that chefs and owners often change, which sometimes drastically affects the quality of a restaurant. The ratings in this guidebook are based on information available at press time.

The price ratings, as characterized at right, apply to restaurants and hotels. These figures describe general price-range relationships among other restaurants and hotels in the area. The restaurant price ratings are based on the average cost of an entrée for one person, excluding tax and tip. Hotel price ratings reflect the base price of a standard room for two people for one night during the peak season. Expect a 40 percent discount on hotel rates January and February.

## RESTAURANTS

| | |
|---|---|
| ★ | Good |
| ★★ | Very Good |
| ★★★ | Excellent |
| ★★★★ | An Extraordinary Experience |
| $ | The Price Is Right (less than $10) |
| $$ | Reasonable ($10-$15) |
| $$$ | Expensive ($15-$25) |
| $$$$ | Big Bucks ($25 and up) |

## HOTELS

| | |
|---|---|
| $ | The Price Is Right ($100-$150) |
| $$ | Reasonable ($150-$180) |
| $$$ | Expensive ($180-$250) |
| $$$$ | Big Bucks ($250 and up) |

## MAP KEY

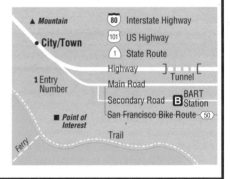

# Getting to San Francisco

## Transportation

## Airports

### San Francisco International Airport (SFO)

Fourteen miles south of San Francisco on the peninsula is **SFO,** the fifth busiest airport in the country, seventh in the world. Most transatlantic flights, as well as many domestic flights, arrive and depart from **SFO.** Fifty major carriers serve the airport. The International Terminal opened September 26, 2000. The signature, wing-like building holds two new international concourses and connecting corridors to domestic terminals. If time allows, visit the Louis A. Turpen Aviation Museum. A BART station linking the airport to downtown opens fall 2001. Travel time between downtown and SFO will be 30 minutes. A new AirTrain also debuts fall 2001 moving passengers to nine stations and a proposed 10th station at the site of a future hotel.

Currently, transportation between terminals is provided by airport shuttles located on the upper level. There is service between terminals every 5 to 7 minutes from 6AM to midnight, and every 10 to 15 minutes, midnight to 6AM.

### AIRPORT SERVICES

| | |
|---|---|
| Airport Police | 650/876.2424 |
| Currency Exchange | 650/266.9420 |
| Currency Exchange | 650/877.0264 |
| Customs | 650/876.2816 |
| First Aid Station | 650/877.0444 |
| Ground Transportation | 800/736.2008 |

Information .............................................650/761.0800
Lost and Found ...................................650/876.2261
Parking .................................................650/877.0227
Traveler's Aid.......................................650/877.0118
Website .............................................*www.flySFO.com*

## AIRLINES

Aeroflot ...............................................888/340.6400
Air Canada ..................650/876.7461, 800/776.3000
Air China (CAAC)..........650/877.0750, 800/986.1985
Air France..............................................650/877.0308,
..........................800/237.2747, www.airfrance.com
AirTran Airlines....................800/AIRTRAN, www.ata.com
Alaska Airlines ............650/875.8600, 800/426.0333
Alitalia Airlines................800/223.5730, www.alitalia.it
America West Airlines .........877.0458, 800/235.9292
American Airlines ...................................650/877.6118,
.....................800/433.7300, www.americanair.com
American Eagle............650/877.6453, 800/433.7300
American Trans Air ......650/877.0412, 800/225.2995
Asiana Airlines ............650/877.3010, 800/227.4262
ANA ...............................800/235.9262, www.ana.co.jp
British Airways ...........................................................
....................800/247.9297, www.british-airways.com
Canadian Airlines International .......................................
..............................650/877.5905, 800/426.7000
Cathay Pacific ............................................................
....................800/422.9626, www.cathaypacific.com
China Airlines ..............650/877.8578, 800/227.5118
Continental Airlines ....650/876.2612, 800/525.0280,
...............................................www.flycontinental.com
Delta Air Lines ............650/877.1017, 800/221.1212,
.....................................................www.delta-air.com
Eva Airways..................650/876.7422, 800/695.1188
Finnair ......397.5540, 800/950.5000, *www.finnair.com*
Frontier Air Lines .....................................800/432.1359
Hawaiian Airlines....................................800/367.5320
Japan Airlines ..................800/525.3663, www.jal.co.jp
KLM Royal Dutch Airline ......................800/374.7747
Korean Air....................650/737.5600, 800/438.5000
LASCA (airlines of Costa Rica)................800/825.2272
Lufthansa....................650/876.7332, 800/645.3880,
....................................................www.lufthansa.com
Mexicana Airlines ........650/877.4905, 800/531.7921,
.....................................................www.mexicana.com
Midwest Express ..........650/877.0170, 800/452.2022
National Airlines.....................................888/750.5387,
....................................................www.nationalairlines.com
Northwest Airlines
    (Domestic) ......................................800/225.2525
    (International) ........650/877.6913, 800/447.4747,
.....................................................www.nwa.com

Quantas ....................800/227.4500, www.qantas.com
Philippine Airlines ........650/877.4800, 800/435.9725
Singapore Airlines ......650/876.7372, 800/742.3333,
...............................................www.singaporeair.com
Southwest Airlines ......650/877.0112, 800/435.9792,
.....................................................www.southwest.com
Swiss Air ..................800/221.4750, www.swissair.com
TACA International Airlines ...........650/650/877.8412,
...............................................................800/225.2272
Thai Airways ........................................800/426.5204
Tower Air................................................800/221.2500
TWA ......650/877.4112, 800/221.2000, www.twa.com
TW Express ..................650/877.4112, 800/221.2000
United Airlines/United Express, Shuttle by United ..........
........650/876.3069, 800/241.6522, www.ual.com
USAirways/USAirways Express ..............650/877.5543,
.....................................800/428.4322, www.usairways.com
Virgin Atlantic Airways.........................800/862.8621,
...............................................................www.fly.virgin.com
Western Pacific Airlines .........................800/930.3030

## Getting to and from SFO

### BY BUS

**SamTrans** buses No. 7B and 7F leave from the airport's upper level every 30 minutes between 6AM and 12:30AM and travel north to the bus terminal at **First** and **Mission Streets. SamTrans** also operates bus 3B between the airport and the **Daly City BART** station. For information, call 650/508.6200 or 800/660.4287 elsewhere in California. Door-to-door shuttle service is generally reasonably priced. Shuttle operators include the **Bay Area Super Shuttle** (558.8500) and the **Yellow Airport Shuttle** (282.7433). Catch them on the upper level. **Lorrie's Airport Service** offers door-to-door service from the upper level of **SFO** and has group rates. For more information, call 334.9000. The **SFO Airporter** offers service to all major hotels on **Union Square,** with departures every 20 minutes (between 6:15AM and 11:30PM) from the lower level. For information, call 495.8404. Also www.airportride.come and www.transitinfo.org.

### BY CAR

The most direct way to get from the airport into San Francisco is by **Highway 101** (also called **Bayshore Freeway**). Depending on traffic and weather conditions a typical ride into town will take 30 to 45 minutes; it takes longer during rush hour.

### RENTAL CARS

Most national and local car-rental agencies are located at and around **SFO,** and most major hotels have car-rental counters. Options run the gamut—everything from your basic Ford to a Rolls-Royce, Ferrari, or a classic two-seater T-Bird. Weekly (a minimum of five days) or three-day weekend rates are usually the best deals, but you should always shop around. Contact the following major companies for their current rates:

Avis.............................650/877.3156, 800/331.1212

Budget .......................650/877.0998, 800/527.0700

Dollar ........................650/244.4130, 800/800.4000

Hertz...........................650/877.1600, 800/654.3131

National .....................650/877.4745, 800/328.4567

Thrifty .........................650/788.8111, 800/367.2277

Or, for the extremely budget-conscious:

Reliable ......................................(downtown) 928.4414

## BY LIMOUSINE

A luxurious transportation alternative, limousine or town car service between **SFO** and downtown San Francisco can cost approximately $55 to $70 (not including tax and tip), depending on the size of the car. Contact one of the following companies for further information:

Associates Limousines of San Francisco ........563.1000

Atlas Limousine ..............................................681.9400

Gateway Limousine ...............................800/486.7077

Quicksilver Town Car Service ..........................431.1600

RLM Executive Limousine......431.1993, 800/431.1993

Regency Limousine .......................................922.0123

Uptown Limousine, Inc. ...............................................
...............................650/589.7373, 800/669.5466

## BY TAXI

Taxis are available on the lower level of the airport to downtown San Francisco. The flat rate fare of $30 is standard for all airport transfers.

## Oakland International Airport (OAK)

Located five miles south of downtown Oakland on **Highway 880,** this airport is smaller than **SFO,** making it less confusing to navigate. The airport's two terminals are linked by a moving indoor corridor. A convenient shuttle service is also available between both terminals.

## AIRPORT SERVICES

Airport Information and paging ..............510/577.4000

Airport Police.........................................510/577.4900

Customs .................................................510/273.7706

Lost and Found .......................................510/577.4095

Parking ...................................................510/633.2571

Website ....................................www.oaklandairport.com

## AIRLINES

Alaska Airlines ......................................800/426.0333

Aloha Airlines ........................................800/367.5250

American West ......................................800/235.9292

American Airlines ..................................800/433.7300

Corsair/New Frontier.............................800/677.0720

Delta Air Lines .......................................800.221.1212

Martinair Holland ..................................800/627.8462

Mexicana ..............................................800/354.2562

Southwest Airlines..................................800/435.9792

SunTrips ................................................800/786.8747

United Airlines ......................................800/241.6522

## Getting to and from Oakland International Airport (OAK)

### BY BUS

**AirBART** (510/577.4294) runs approximately every 15 minutes to the **Coliseum/Oakland BART** station. The bus picks up passengers at **Terminals 1** and **2** and at **Airport Drive and Neil Armstrong Way.** The fare is $2. AC Transit (510/817.1717) operates in the East Bay.

### BY CAR

The easiest way to reach downtown San Francisco from the Oakland airport is to take **I-880** at the airport to **I-80** west across the **San Francisco–Oakland Bay Bridge** into San Francisco.

### RENTAL CARS

Most national car-rental agencies are located at and around **Oakland International Airport.** Weekly (a minimum of five days) or three-day weekend rates are usually the best deals, but you should always shop around. Contact the following major companies for their current rates:

Avis ......................................................510/577.6370

Budget ..................................................510/568.4770

Dollar ...............................................510/638.2750/1/2

Hertz.....................................................510/639.0200

National .................................................510/632.2225

### BY LIMOUSINE

Limousine services are also available; the cost ranges from $40 to $70 depending on the size and type of car.

Expresso Limousine Service............................421.6422

Airport Meridian Limousine and Sedan Service ..............
................................................................737.8500

## San Jose International Airport (SJC)

This airport is located about 2 miles from downtown San Jose and approximately 50 miles south of San Francisco via Highway 101. Although farther from the city than either **SFO** or **OAK,** it often offers less expensive flights to some destinations.

### AIRPORT SERVICES

Airport Administration ............................408/277.5366

Airport Information and Paging ..............408/277.4759

Airport Police .......................................408/227.5400

Business Service Center .......................408/993.9844

Currency Exchange ......408/287.0748, 408/287.3748

Customs ................................................408/291.7388

Lost and Found......................................408/277.5419

Parking ..................................................408/293.6788

Travelers' Information Booths .......................................
................................408/287.9849, 408/277.4500

## AIRLINES

Alaska/Horizon Air........408/277.5677, 800/426.0333

American......................408/291.3808, 800/433.7300

America West .............408/295.4171, 800/235.9292

Delta ...........................408/286.6981, 800/221.1212

Mexicana....................408/293.8474, 800/531.7921

Northwest/KLM ............408/282.1903, 800/225.2525

Reno Air .....................408/291.5861, 800/736.6247

Skywest......................408/993.9063, 800/221.1212

Southwest...................408/283.5910, 800/435.9792

TWA............................408/292.5010, 800/221.2000

United ....................................800/241.6522

### Getting to and from San Jose International Airport

### BY BUS

Several companies provide direct transportation to downtown San Francisco. **South and East Bay Shuttle** (800/548.4664) and **M&M** (800/286.0303) can be found opposite **Terminal C.** The fare will run from $35 to $44 per person.

## BY CAR

The easiest way to reach downtown San Francisco from San Jose is to exit the airport on **Airport Boulevard** going northeast to **Bayshore Freeway** (Highway 101). This highway becomes I-80 which leads directly into San Francisco.

## RENTAL CARS

Most national car-rental agencies at **San Jose International Airport** are in **Terminal C.** Weekly (a minimum of five days) or three-day weekend rates are usually the best deals, but you should always shop around. Contact the following major companies for their current rates:

Alamo ........................408/288.4650, 800/327.9633

Avis .......................................408/993.2224

Budget .................................408/286.7850

Dollar ..................................408/280.2200

Hertz .....................................408/437.5725

## BY LIMOUSINE

A luxurious transportation alternative, limousine service between San Jose and San Francisco can cost anywhere from $70 to $95.

Expresso Limousine Service ..........................421.6422

Airport Meridian Limousine and Sedan Service................
....................................................................737.8500

## Getting around San Francisco

### BAY AREA RAPID TRANSIT (BART)

A clean, reliable, easy-to-use underground transportation system serving parts of San Francisco, **Daly City,** and the **East Bay.** The system operates Monday through Friday from 4AM to 1:30AM, Saturday from 6AM to 1:30AM, and Sunday from 8AM to 1:30AM. On weekdays, trains run on all 4 routes approximately every 15 minutes, and extra service is offered during rush hours. After 7PM and on Sunday, trains run on only 2 routes every 20 minutes, and you may have to transfer to another train to get to your final destination. On Saturday, they run on 4 routes every 20 minutes until 6PM; after 6PM they run on 2 routes every 20 minutes. Brochures about using the system and train schedules are available at all **BART** stations. All stations have facilities for people with disabilities.

To buy a ticket, check the prominently displayed information chart to determine your destination and the ticket value required for a one-way trip. Ticket machines sell tickets for any amount between $1.10 and $40. One ticket, therefore, can be good for many rides. *Note: Save the ticket to exit the station.*

Discount tickets are available for senior citizens (age 65 and older), people with disabilities, and children ages 5 to 12. You can also buy discounted high-value tickets. All discounted tickets are sold *only* at participating institutions (for information call 992.2278), and *not* at **BART** stations. An excursion-ride ticket allows you to tour the entire system, visiting any of the 34 stations for up to 3 hours as long as you enter and exit at the same station. If you get out en route, the fare gate will compute the normal fare (obviously, this is a good deal for hard-core train buffs only). For information about **BART** and connecting bus service, call 510/465.BART.

### BICYCLES

Bicycles in San Francisco, with its infamous steep streets, may seem overly ambitious for all but the most physically fit, but if you plan your route to avoid the hills a bicycle can be one of the best ways to see the city. San Francisco's Department of Parking and Traffic has a bicycle program that sets out these routes. Even numbered routes travel east/west and odd numbered routes north/south. (See "Plum Paths for Pedal Pushers in the City by the Bay" on page 142 and the individual chapter maps for the designated routes.) **The Embarcadero** and the **Golden Gate Promenade** both provide breathtaking views of the bay. **The Presidio** and **Golden Gate Park** are also bicycle-friendly. Bicycles can be rented from **American Bicycle Rental** (2715 Hyde St, at Fisherman's Wharf, 931.0234) and **Blazing Saddles** (1095 Columbus, at Francisco St, and Pier 41, 202.8888). Cyclists *with permits* are allowed to take their bikes on trains during non-commute hours only (weekdays from 4AM to 6:30AM and 6:30PM to 1:30AM and all day on weekends and holidays).

### DRIVING

Driving in San Francisco's **Downtown** and **Financial Districts** is suitable only for extremely patient people

who can handle the frustration of slow-moving traffic. **North Beach, Chinatown,** and **Telegraph Hill** are also congested, and parking is very difficult. Many parking meters are timed to provide only a half hour of parking, and traffic cops patrol frequently. Unless otherwise posted, meters operate Monday through Saturday, usually from 7AM to 6PM (check to be sure).

Some curbs are painted colors that have specific meanings, and those who violate the color code will incur costly fines. A **white curb** indicates a drop-off zone for passengers. This code is in effect only when the facility it fronts (a restaurant, theater, or other enterprise) is in operation. If nothing is going on, it's OK to park. A **green curb** signifies parking for 10 minutes only. **Yellow curbs** are for loading and unloading commercial vehicles, and **blue curbs** are reserved for drivers or passengers with disabilities who have an official placard prominently displayed in their car window. Unless information is otherwise posted, it's usually legal to park in green or yellow zones after 6PM.

When parking on San Francisco's hilly terrain always turn the tires toward the street when facing uphill, and toward the curb when facing downhill.

## FERRIES

Ferries still are popular means of transportation to and from the city for commuters from the East Bay and **Marin.** And though they do not have recorded commentary describing the sights, ferries are a less expensive alternative to sightseeing cruises. The landmark **Ferry Building** on The Embarcadero (at Market Street) is one terminus for the **Golden Gate Ferries** (925.5567, www.goldengate.org) while the **Blue & Gold Fleet** (705.5444 or -5555) and **Red & White Fleet** (447.0591) dock at **Fisherman's Wharf/Pier 39.**

## MUNICIPAL RAILWAY (MUNI)

This railway was first called the "Muniserable Railway" by *San Francisco Chronicle* columnist Herb Caen, and he definitely had a point. Drivers working for this citywide transportation system can be gloriously courteous or sadistically unpleasant. The nicest drivers often are on the cable-car lines, where they often entertain the tourists. The **MUNI** system consists of all cable cars, streetcars, trains **(MUNI Metro),** conventional buses, and electric buses that run within the city limits; all operate daily until 1AM. (**BART,** the regional system, connects San Francisco proper to the East Bay and south of the city. You can, however, transfer between the two systems at a few points.) From 1AM to 5AM, nine **Owl** lines operate throughout the city. The fare on

all conveyances except cable cars is $1 for adults and 35¢ for senior citizens (age 65 and older), disabled passengers with a valid Regional Transit Connection Discount Card, and youths ages 5 to 17 (children under 5 ride free). On cable cars the fare is $2 (kids under 5 are free). One-dollar bills are accepted on most buses; however, drivers do not give change. Be sure to request a transfer as soon as you board the bus; it's free and is valid for one and a half to two hours and a maximum of two rides in any direction. One-day, three-day, weekly, and monthly "passes" offer unlimited rides on buses only, while one-day, three-day, and weekly "passports" provide unlimited rides on the buses *and* cable cars. Both passes and passports are sold at the **City Hall** information booth in the **Civic Center** (401 Van Ness Ave, at McAllister St) at **MUNI** headquarters (949 Presidio Ave, at Geary Blvd), and at other locations around the city. There also are discounted passes for children, seniors, and people with disabilities, and tokens are sold in rolls of 10, 20, or 40 (tokens are good on all buses, but you must pay a surcharge using a token on the cable cars).

Maps of the **MUNI** system can be purchased at the City Hall store (in the lobby), bookstores, and magazine stands (a partial **MUNI** map is featured on the inside back cover of this book). Routes are also displayed on bus-stop kiosks, and the "Public Transportation" section of the telephone directory's yellow pages features a map. For information on schedules, passes, and fares, call 673.MUNI or write to **MUNI** (949 Presidio Ave, Room 238, San Francisco, CA 94115).

## TAXIS

In San Francisco they tend to be expensive and are often scarce. Downtown, it's sometimes possible to hail a moving cab, but in general it's best to call and make arrangements for a pickup. It's also relatively easy to get a cab at any of the major hotels; however, plan on waiting a long time for one during the rush hours and when the weather is foul. Taxi companies include **Yellow Cab** (626.2345), **Luxor** (282.4141), and **Veteran's Cab** (552.1300).

## WALKING

Exploring the city on foot reveals the richness and detail that make San Francisco special. The main tourist areas are within a half-hour walk of each other, making walking practical. The steep streets of **Telegraph Hill, Russian Hill,** and **Nob Hill** leave many pedestrians gasping for breath, but the views from the top are stupendous and worth the climb.

# FYI

## ACCOMMODATIONS

San Francisco offers a wide variety of places to stay, from inexpensive motels to charming bed-and-breakfast inns to world-class luxury hotels. Rooms should be reserved at least two months in advance from July through October.

## CLIMATE

San Francisco's mild marine climate boasts temperatures that seldom rise above 70 degrees or fall below 40 degrees. Morning and evening fogs are common from June through August, and rain is not unusual from November through March.

| Months | Average Temperature |
|---|---|
| January-March | 59-48 |
| April-June | 62-50 |
| July-September | 65-54 |
| October-December | 62-51 |

## DRINKING

The legal drinking age is 21. Bars stay open until 2AM. Wine and liquor can be purchased in most grocery stores and supermarkets.

## HOURS

Most shops in San Francisco are open from 10AM to 6PM Monday through Saturday. The large department stores, as well as some shops, are open on Sunday.

## MONEY

**Deak International, Foreign Exchange, Associated Foreign Exchange,** and many major banks handle currency exchanges. Traveler's checks are available at banks and at **American Express** and **Thomas Cook Travel** offices. Banks are open Monday through Friday, generally until 4PM, and often on Saturday morning (usually until 1PM).

## PARKING

There are some relatively inexpensive city-owned parking garages, particularly for short-term parking, but parking in congested areas tends to be costly. Here are some low-cost 24-hour parking facilities:

**Ellis-O'Farrell Garage** 123 O'Farrell St (between Powell and Stockton Sts), 986.4800

**Fifth & Mission Garage** 833 Mission St (between Fourth and Fifth Sts), 982.8522

**North Beach Garage** 735 Vallejo St (between Stockton and Powell Sts), 397.5102

**Portsmouth Square Garage** 733 Kearny St (between Clay and Washington Sts), 982.6353

**Sutter-Stockton Garage** 444 Stockton St (between Sutter and Bush Sts), 982.8370

**Union Square Garage** 333 Post St (enter on Geary Street between Stockton and Powell Sts), 397.0631

## PERSONAL SAFETY

Drugs and crime are unfortunate components of urban living, and San Francisco is no exception. In general, neighborhoods that could be troublesome look it (of course, there are exclusions). In **Golden Gate Park,** stay on well-populated paths and avoid walking there after dark. Surrounding the downtown side of the **Civic Center** is a high-crime neighborhood called the **Tenderloin** that's often a way station for undesirable types. Toward the west side, the neighborhood is improving, but caution is still advised. Once you're past the busy downtown area (from about **Fifth Street** and going west

to **Gough Street), Market Street,** San Francisco's main thoroughfare, is distressingly seedy. At night there's a virtual parade of vagrants. The **South of Market** area is in a state of transition; although there are many upscale shops, restaurants, and businesses, at night it helps to be cautious. The **Mission District** is another part of town that calls for extra caution, particularly after dark. And the Haight-Ashbury neighborhood, still filled with its share of panhandlers and lost youth, can be somewhat intimidating.

## PUBLICATIONS

The city's morning newspaper is the *San Francisco Chronicle.* The afternoon paper, the *San Francisco Examiner,* tends to offer more in-depth investigative reports than its competitor. At press time, the sale of the Examiner is pending and the staffs of the two papers may be merging. *San Francisco Magazine,* a monthly magazine for public television station **KQED,** covers everything from politics and personalities to fashion and food. *S.F. Weekly* and the *Bay Guardian* are both liberal, free, alternative newspapers that provide good listings of entertainment events. *BAM* (Bay Area Music), a free tabloid published twice a month, covers the local music scene. The *San Francisco Independent* is a community newspaper published daily, and the *Nob Hill Gazette* is a monthly that covers the society scene. The weekly *Sun Reporter* serves the black community, *Hokubei Mainichi* is a daily Japanese-English publication, and the daily *Chinese Times* is the largest of several Chinese newspapers. The *Jewish Bulletin* is published every Friday. Gay and lesbian newspapers include the weekly *Bay Area Reporter,* the *San Francisco Sentinel,* and *Bay Times.* The weekly *San Francisco Business Times* is the business-oriented publication. All are available on newsstands.

## RESTAURANTS

There are over 3,200 restaurants and drinking establishments in San Francisco offering a variety of cuisine at a wide range of prices. Fresh local produce, especially seafood, has contributed to the city's well deserved reputation as a culinary capital whose multiethnic citizens bring an international flavor to the dining scene.

## SHOPPING

Some of the best cutting-edge fashions can be found at boutiques along **Geary, Powell, Post,** and **Stockton Streets.** This area, known as **Union Square,** caters to every taste and budget and includes such fine department stores as **Macy's, Nordstrom, Saks Fifth Avenue,** and **Neiman Marcus.** Bloomingdales is expected to occupy the old Emporium space on Market St. **The Embarcadero Center, Pier 39, The Cannery,** and **Ghirardelli Square** showcase everything from museum-quality artifacts to the latest designer wear. Other shopping areas include **Japan Center,** noted for art galleries and bookstores.

## SMOKING

San Francisco has stiff antismoking regulations. Minors cannot buy cigarettes. It's illegal to light up in offices,

public buildings, banks, lobbies, stores, sports arenas, stadiums, and theaters, restaurants and on public transportation. The smoking ban has recently been extended to bars, cocktail lounges, nightclubs.

## STREET PLAN

With the exception of certain residential neighborhoods, most of San Francisco is laid out on a grid plan, with Market Street dividing the north and south segments of the city. Each block increases its numbering by 100, so buildings on the first block of a street might start with number 1, the second block with 100, and the third with 200. Newcomers may be confused by the numerical streets and avenues, which are in two different neighborhoods. When San Franciscans speak of "the avenues," they are referring to the numerically named avenues— **Second Avenue, Third Avenue,** etc.—that extend through the **Richmond** and **Sunset** districts. But other numerical streets, **First Street** to **30th Street,** span the **South of Market** area.

## TAXES

An 8.5 percent sales tax is added to purchases in San Francisco. If your purchases are shipped to a destination outside of California, you will be exempt from the sales tax. Foreign visitors may have to pay duty in their home country. An 8.5 percent tax is added to restaurant bills, and hotels tack a 14 percent room tax to the bill.

## TELEPHONES

Calls from pay phones within the 415 area code cost 35¢.

## TICKETS

The main source for tickets to concerts, theater, and sports events is **City Box Office** (392.4400) and **BASS (Bay Area Seating Service),** located in **Tower** and **Wherehouse** record shops. Tickets can also be charged by phone (there is a small charge for each ticket) or purchased at the theater box office. **BASS** charge by phone: 510/762.2277

## TIME ZONE

San Francisco is in the Pacific Time Zone, three hours earlier than New York City.

## TIPPING

A 15 percent tip is standard for taxi fares and restaurants (although a 20 percent tip for a good service is becoming more common). Hotel porters and station porters expect $1 per bag. Concierges expect tips based on the quality of their service and the generosity of the guest. If you've used the concierge's advice a lot and he or she has recommended places that made your stay more pleasurable, tip at least $5.

## TOURS

There's something here for everyone. Here's a sampling of what's offered:

One of the largest operators of tours, **Gray Line** (reservations 558.9400) runs from two locations: at Union Square, opposite the **Westin St. Francis Hotel** (Powell St, between Geary and Post Sts); and from the bus terminal (First and Mission Sts).

**All About Chinatown** (982.8839) offers daily two-hour visits to the city within a city. Discover an herbal pharmacy, a fortune cookie factory, and the **Stockton Street** food markets, and enjoy a dim sum lunch. Also in Chinatown, cooking instructor and food writer Shirley Fong-Torres conducts cooking classes and leads the **Wok Wiz Chinatown Tours,** (981.8989). Highlights include area history, plus visits to an herbal emporium, a fortune cookie factory, and produce markets and food stores.

**Cruisin' the Castro** (550.8110) features insights into gay contributions to the city. Historian and longtime resident Trevor Hailey leads four-hour visits to the Harvey Milk camera shop, Castro Theatre and Victorian homes.

**The Flower Power Haight Ashbury Walking Tour** (221.8442) celebrates the 1960s. Former hippie Rachel Heller provides two-hour tours to favorite haunts of flower children: the Grateful Dead house on **Ashbury Street,** Janis Joplin's favorite crash pad, psychedelic shops, and the old **Nickelodeon.**

**Victorian Home Walk** (252.9485, www.victorianwalk.com) is a 2.5-hour tour by Muni and walking where you learn to distinguish Queen Anne, Italiante, and Stick-style Victorians. You'll see more than 200 Victorians.

Let **Roger's Custom Tours** (650/742.9611) provide a closer look at San Francisco. Roger F. Erickson guides visitors to all the high points of the city, as well as to specialized destinations such as small museums off the beaten path.

For a unique look at San Francisco's nightlife join **3 Babes and a Bus** (552.CLUB, www.threeBabes.com) on Saturday. Party-goers can dance the night away at four hot clubs and then be whisked back to their hotel.

The gray whale migration can be witnessed June through November off the Pacific coastline; **Oceanic Society Expeditions** (474.3385) conducts trips to the Farallones from Fort Mason pier January through April.

Travel in comfort by van to uncrowded wilderness areas with **California Nature Treks** (337.7143). Small group adventures focus on wildlife viewing and natural history.

## VISITORS' INFORMATION CENTER

Visitors' information center, open Monday through Friday from 9AM to 5:30PM and Saturday and Sunday from 9AM to 3PM. The **San Francisco Convention and Visitors Bureau** (1 Hallidie Plaza, Lower level, at Powell and Market Sts, 391.2000, 974.6900) provides maps, information on lodging, and various discounts. The San Francisco City Pass booklet contains discounted admission tickets to six museums and a seven-day MUNI Passport valid on all MUNI vehicles and cable cars. The mailing address is PO Box 429097, San Francisco, CA 94142-9097.

Visitor information
on the web:

www.sfvisitor.org .............................................................
..............San Francisco Convention & Visitors Bureau.

www.flysfo.com ........San Francisco International Airport

www.thinker.org ........M.H. de Young Museum in Golden
Gate Park, and Califonia Palace of the Legion of
Honor in Lincoln Park at 34th Ave and Clement St

www.fishermanswharf.org ................Fisherman's Wharf

www.sfmuseum.org ............San Francisco City Museum

## Phone Book

### EMERGENCIES

Ambulance/Fire/Police ...........................................911

AAA (road service) .................................800/222.4357

Highway Patrol .............................................557.1094

Auto Theft.............................................707/648.5550

Children's Emergency Services ......................558.2650

Handicapped Crisis Line ........800/426.4263 (CA only)

Hospitals

California Pacific Medical Center, Pacific Heights ......
...............................................................923.3333

San Francisco General Hospital, Potrero ....353.6300

UCSF Medical Center, Parnassus ..............476.1037

Pharmacy (open 9-6) ................................392.4137

Poison Control Center (Northwest CA only) ...............
.....................................................800/523.2222

Police (Non-Emergency) ...............................553.0123

### VISITORS' INFORMATION

AC Transit Bus Lines (East Bay Area) ....510/839.2882

Amtrak....................800/872.7245, www.amtrak.com

Bay Area Rapid Transit (BART) ..............650/992.2278

Better Business Bureau ...............................243.9999

Caltrain Peninsula Commuter Rail Service (Bay Area)....
...............................................................800/660.4287

Greyhound Bus Lines ...........................800/231.2222

MUNI Bus Lines (San Francisco) .................673.6864

Road Conditions ..................................800/427.7623

SamTrans Bus Lines (South Bay) ..........800/660.4287

Time.............................................................767.8900

US Customs ................................................782.9210

US Passport.................................................538.2700

Visitors Information Center ...........................391.2000

24-hour Hotline:

English........................................................391.2001

French ........................................................391.2003

German .......................................................391.2004

Japanese .....................................................391.2101

Spanish .......................................................391.2122

Weather.......................................................364.7974

Youth Hostels............................788.5604, 771.7277

# MAIN EVENTS

San Francisco, always abuzz with activity, hosts a wide variety of special events and festivals throughout the year. The following is a sampler of the many treats available in and around the city. The dates for some events vary from year to year; for up-to-the-minute information call the **San Francisco Convention and Visitors Bureau** (391.2000).

## January

**San Francisco Sports and Boat Show** presents large floating toys for affluent adults during two weekends in mid-January at the **Cow Palace.**

**Ballet season** begins at the **War Memorial Opera House.**

## February

The **Chinese New Year** takes place sometime between late January and late February.

The **Golden Gate Kennel Club Dog Show,** considered the largest dog show west of the Mississippi, is held the first weekend in February at the **Cow Palace.**

## March

**St. Patrick's Day Parade** marches down **Market Street,** where the bars are filled with merrymakers.

The **San Francisco Flower and Garden Show** transforms the Cow Palace into a five-acre gallery of 23 astonishing gardens, complete with waterfalls, metal sculpture mermaids, and a miniature Tuscan village. Tickets to the preview party 750.5441. Tickets to the garden show 771.6909.

The last week of the month heralds the **Cherry Blossom Festival,** which is observed in the **Japanese Tea Garden at Golden Gate Park.**

## April

Sunrise services are held at dawn on **Easter Sunday** on **Mount Davidson,** the highest hill in the city.

The **San Francisco International Film Festival** (931.FILM) presents cinema at various venues around the city through mid-May.

## May

**Cinco De Mayo Parade and Celebration,** commemorating Mexico's defeat of French troops in 1862, takes place throughout the **Mission** district during the first week of the month.

Latin American and Caribbean cultures blend in the **Mission** district for the very festive **Carnaval** on the last weekend of the month.

## June

Take the kids to the **Pier 39 Street Performers Festival.** Comedians, jugglers, unicyclists gather the first weekend in June at Pier 39 to do their zany acts. 705.5500

The annual **Father's Day Kite Festival** enjoys a perfect (and windy) setting at **Marina Green,** at the edge of San Francisco Bay (956.3181).

Summer concerts at **Stern Grove** (www.sterngrove.org) bring San Franciscans with picnic baskets for free performances of opera, ballet, and music from classical to jazz, bluegrass and African beat (252.6252).

With more than 300,000 participants, the **Lesbian/ Gay Freedom Day** parade and celebration is the biggest show in San Francisco and the largest of its kind in the US. Annual events are held at the **Civic Center** and the Market Street parade route in late June (864.3733).

## July

Fireworks explode during the **July 4th** celebration along the waterfront from the **Ferry Building** to **Fisherman's Wharf.**

**San Francisco Symphony Pops** concerts are summer events at the **Civic Auditorium** (974.4060).

A **Summer in the City** popular music series is held at **Davies Hall** three weeks in July (864.6000). Concerts feature artists such as Bobby McFerrin, Johnny Mathis, Audra McDonald, and Little Richard.

The last Sunday in July is the **San Francisco Marathon.** Over 6,000 athletes race from the **Golden Gate Bridge** to **Golden Gate Park.**

## August

Early August is the popular **Nihonmachi Street Fair** at **Japantown** where Japanese-style fun and games are the order of the day.

The **Ringling Brothers and Barnum & Bailey Circus** is presented at the **Cow Palace** for five days in late August, ending on Labor Day.

## September

**Piers 30** and **32** come alive with the **San Francisco Fair** during Labor Day weekend.

**Shakespeare in the Park** (Saturday and Sunday from Labor Day weekend through the last Sunday in September) is performed at the temporary outdoor theater in the **Liberty Meadow** of **Golden Gate Park.**

**Opera Season** begins with a gala formal ball on opening night at the **War Memorial Opera House.**

**Symphony Season** begins in **Davies Hall** and runs until June. (864.6000)

**San Francisco's Blues Festival** attracts some of the world's best blues stars to the **Great Meadow** at **Fort Mason** for two days the last weekend of September. (979.5588)

## October

**Castro Street Fair,** one of the city's largest and longest running street celebrations, is held the first week of the month.

**Fleet Week** floats into the city with its parade of ships under the **Golden Gate Bridge.**

Head to **North Beach** and **Fisherman's Wharf** for the annual **Columbus Day** celebrations and parade.

**Halloween Night** is among the city's more colorful celebrations, with thousands of costumed revelers converging on Market and the **Civic Center.**

The last week of October and the first week of November the **San Francisco Jazz Festival** takes place in venues throughout San Francisco and Oakland. Free noon concerts of world-class jazz take place at Justin Herman Plaza, at the Embarcadero Center during the festival. (788.7353, 800/850.7353, www.sfjazz.org)

## November

**Dia de los Muertos** (Day of the Dead), held in the Mission district at the beginning of November. It commences with the celebration of life procession leading to ornately decorated altars. (826.8009)

The annual **Holiday Lights Celebration** at **The Embarcadero** includes the illumination of the waterfront with more than 17,000 lights.

**Kristi Yamaguchi Embarcadero Center Holiday Ice Rink** opens at Justin Herman Plaza, offering skating sessions, classes, and birthday parties. (956.2688)

## December

**Huntington Park Tree Lighting Ceremony** takes place the first week in December atop Nob Hill. Festivities begin at Grace Cathedral at California and Taylor Sts at 5:30PM then move to the park where over 10,000 twinkling lights adorn the park's trees. Christmas carols sung by the San Francisco Girls Chorus. Complimentary hot chocolate. (474.5400)

**Christmas at Sea** is held the second weekend at Hyde Street Pier. Caroling, storytelling, hot cider, kids crafts, and a visit from St. Nick aboard a historic ship. (561.6662)

**Sing-It-Yourself Messiah** is held in early December at **Davies Symphony Hall** with the audience performing under the direction of various conductors.(864.6000)

The **Dickens Christmas Fair** depicts a Victorian holiday with entertainment, food, and drink. It runs through the last weekend of December at **Pier 39.**

# CIVIC CENTER

S an Francisco's **Civic Center** is acclaimed by critics everywhere as the complex with the finest collection of Beaux Arts buildings in America. **Daniel Burnham,** the architect commissioned to design the city's master plan, combined a highly developed aesthetic sense with the know-how of a skilled politician. He was invited to the city for consultation by millionaire and former mayor James Phelan, who, along with other prominent citizens, had become concerned about the ugliness of the building construction that was blighting the city. **Burnham** came with his young assistant, **Willis Polk** (himself a westerner), and was immensely impressed with the potential of the natural

setting. In 1904 he set up a cottage office on Twin Peaks so he could look down on the terrain as he worked out his vision of the city's future. He was generations ahead of his time in suggesting such ideas as one-way streets, downtown subways, and residential areas where backyards would be merged into a common park. **Polk** wished to preserve the crest of the hills with access roads that curved to follow the contours of the land rather than conventional gridiron patterns. He designed a huge park for Twin Peaks with landscaped slopes and a special watercourse that would carry the city's water supply from reservoirs. But before any real action could be taken, much of San Francisco, including the old City Hall, collapsed in the 1906 earthquake and fire, literally burying **Burnham**'s plans. However, he was not ready to give up. With his enthusiastic supporters (John McLaren, first superintendent of **Golden Gate Park**; Phelan; sugar czar Claus Spreckels; and others), he set a campaign in motion to rebuild the city. Political scandal delayed their plans, but **Burnham** finally salvaged part of his project and convinced the supervisors to finance the monumental **Civic Center**. Alas, it was not until after his death that his recommendations were acted upon.

The man largely responsible for actually getting **City Hall** built was "Sunny" Jim Rolph. He was the mayor for two decades, and he considered the hall his proudest achievement. (Other projects launched by Rolph were the first San Francisco Public Library, **Civic Auditorium, Hetch Hetchy Aqueduct,** the yacht harbor, and the campaign to build the **Bay Bridge**.) **City Hall**'s architect was **Arthur Brown Jr.,** a designer who had what colleague **Bernard Maybeck** admiringly called "perfect taste." **Brown** attended the Ecole des Beaux Arts in Paris along with his fraternity brother **John Bakewell Jr.,** and garnered more prizes than had ever been received by an American. Upon their return, the two young men set up the architectural firm of **Bakewell and Brown.** They soon won a contest for designing the City Hall in Berkeley, and though they felt they had no chance of winning, they competed for the greater prize: the key building in San Francisco's **Civic Center** master plan, **City Hall.** Ignoring sensible restrictions, they produced a plan for a spectacular structure that even by today's standards was exorbitant in design and expense. The new team won out over established stars in the field, and their victory catapulted **Brown** to the front ranks of American architects. By 1936, when the **War Memorial Opera House** and **Veteran's Building** were in place, a unified square of stately and ornate Beaux Arts architecture had been built. And it was in this opera house that the charter creating the United Nations was signed nine years later.

One of the more recent additions to the complex—which breaks completely with this design tradition—is the modern **Louise M. Davies Symphony Hall,** inaugurated in 1981 and renovated in 1992. Two blocks away, the **San Francisco Public Library** took up residence in 1996 in its contemporary new headquarters, designed by **James Indigo Freed** of **Pei Cobb Freed and Partners.**

The building, with its gray granite facade, is a modern-day interpretation of the classic Beaux Arts style. West of the **Civic Center,** Hayes St bustles with many fine restaurants, galleries, and antiques shops. East and north of the Civic Center is a portion of the **Tenderloin,** a former crime- and poverty-ridden area where Asian immigrants, many from Vietnam and Cambodia, have settled, opened small businesses, and brought the neighborhood a respectability it hasn't enjoyed for years.

## 1 RICHELIEU

$$ An early 1900s ambience pervades this 150-room hotel, where children under 12 stay free when sharing a room with a parent. The coffee bar serves continental breakfast and is open daily. ♦ 1050 Van Ness Ave (at Geary St). 673.4711, 800/296.RICH; fax 673.9362 ♿

## 2 MONARCH HOTEL

$$ Modern conveniences are combined with 1920s charm in this attractive hotel, which is close to Fisherman's Wharf and other activities, but located on the fringes of a questionable neighborhood. The 101 rooms have the feel of a European hostelry— there are canopied beds, shuttered windows, and an open courtyard. The lower lobby has facilities for meetings. The hotel's restaurant serves a hearty breakfast. ♦ 1015 Geary St (between Polk St and Van Ness Ave). 673.5232, 800/777.3210; fax 885.2802 ♿

## 3 MITCHELL BROTHERS O'FARRELL THEATRE

This infamous sex palace was rendered even more infamous a few years back by the slaying of one Mitchell brother by the other. As the sign warns, "Admission is limited to adults who will not be offended should they observe any type of sexual activity." The innocent mural outside belies the steamy action within. ♦ Cover. Daily. 895 O'Farrell St (at Polk St). 441.1930 ♿

## 4 GREAT AMERICAN MUSIC HALL

Top talent appears at this premier music club, which showcases rock, pop, jazz, and comedy. Robin Williams, Leon Russell, Buddy Rich, and Count Basie have all performed here. It's a large place with a balcony, but the sights and sounds are excellent from almost any table. A dinner menu offering "hip bar food" such as french fries, California-style quesadillas, spareribs, pizza, and salads is available. There is a full bar and a new coffee bar. ♦ Cover. Box office: M-Sa (Su if there is a show). 859 O'Farrell St (between Larkin and Polk Sts). 885.0750

---

Dense afternoon and evening fogs are common in San Francisco during the summer months, sometimes causing the temperature to drop by as much as 30 degrees in a matter of hours.

---

Poet Maya Angelou was San Francisco's first black female street-car conductor.

---

## 5 THE PHOENIX HOTEL

$$ The 44-room urban inn is a one-acre oasis of respectability in a downscale neighborhood. It has a resortlike feel, with a pool, outdoor cafe, garden, and massage and other bodywork services on site. Popular with the artistic and celebrity sets, the hotel has hosted such exalted personages as Linda Ronstadt, Faye Dunaway, Ziggy Marley, and JFK Jr. The bedrooms and grounds feature original art from Bay Area artists, and the hotel has its own video channel featuring movies made in San Francisco. On-site parking and continental breakfast are included. ♦ 601 Eddy St (at Larkin St). 776.1380, 800/CITY.INN; fax 885.3109 ♿

Within The Phoenix Hotel:

### BACKFLIP

★★$$ A Miami-esque restaurant and bar in blue and chartreuse, this slightly tacky restaurant offers flambé cocktail-style cuisine, such as mussels lit with dark rum. A clever bridge connects the restaurant to the circular bar in the back. ♦ American ♦ Tu-Su cocktails and dinner. Reservations recommended. 771-3547 ♿

## 6 CALIFORNIA CULINARY ACADEMY

★★$$ The students at San Francisco's best-known cooking school may change, but standards remain uncompromisingly high. You have a choice of two restaurants: The **Academy Grill** offers a lunch menu of sandwiches, salads, and other straightforward fare, as well as a buffet dinner; the more formal **Careme Room,** surrounded by a glass-enclosed kitchen, serves a prix-fixe three-course lunch and dinner on most weekdays and a classic European buffet dinner on Friday (the menu reflects what students are learning to make that week). Be forewarned: Prices are not as low as many diners think they ought to be for student labor. ♦ Continental ♦ M-F lunch and dinner. Reservations recommended for the Academy Grill, required for the Careme Room. 625 Polk St (at Turk St). 771.3500 ♿

## 7 VIVANDE Ristorante

★★★$$$ Carlo Middione, who draws raves for his wonderful **VIVANDE Porta Via** in Pacific Heights, branched out by opening this impressive trattoria in the Opera Plaza complex. The rustic menu features winning pastas, risottos, fish, and meat dishes. Highlights include tagliatelle tossed with oyster and shiitake mushrooms; sweet shrimp and fresh lemon risotto; and a buttery sea bass served on a lightly charred wedge of cabbage, drizzled with lemon oil, and surrounded by roast potatoes. Be sure to peek in the rest room to see the intricately painted, vaguely bawdy scenes—they're the talk of the town. ♦ Italian ♦ M-F lunch, and Tu-Sa dinner until midnight.Reservations recommended. 670 Golden Gate Ave (between Van Ness Ave and Franklin St). 673.9245 &

## 8 A Clean Well-Lighted Place for Books

This shop is popular with bibliophiles looking for the latest good read. Signings and readings by authors are often held. ♦ Daily; F-Sa until midnight. Opera Plaza, 601 Van Ness Ave (at Golden Gate Ave). 441.6670 &

## 8 Max's Opera Café

★$$ Jeans and evening gowns mix in this upscale New York-style deli and bar, a popular pre- and post-performance haunt for those attending events at the nearby **Performing Arts Center.** Specials include ample portions of barbecued brisket of beef—enough for two. Calorie counters can choose from such low-fat—but equally large—selections as salads with an oil-free mustard dressing, broiled chicken breast with tomato vinaigrette, and a turkey salisbury steak. The wait staff also provides entertainment, breaking into song throughout the evening. Takeout is available. ♦ American/Deli ♦ Daily lunch and dinner. Opera Plaza, 601 Van Ness Ave (at Golden Gate Ave). 771.7301 &

## 9 Federal Office Building

This building was constructed in 1959 by **Albert F. Roller, Stone/Marraccini/Patters,** and **John Carl Warnecke.** The bland face of the federal government building—a Miesian slab block set back from the street—offers a somber contrast to the ornate designs of the Civic Center. ♦ 450 Golden Gate Ave (between Larkin and Polk Sts)

## 10 Stars

★★★$$$ Stars still attracts movers and shakers, socialites, and visiting glitterati as it did under Jeremiah Tower's rein. Chef Christo-pher Fernandez embarks on a new era for the Stars kitchen, creating farm fresh, seasonal dishes. He uses wild mushrooms from the forests of Mendocino, line-caught fish from the Pacific and farmstead meat and produce from Sonoma County, and turns out the trendiest dishes in town—de rigueur for his high-profile patrons. Menu includes grilled beef tenderloin with spinach, mashed potatoes and black truffle; wood-roasted mussels; grilled Pacific swordfish with asparagus, fingerling potatoes and green garlic; and for dessert, an impressive selection of soufflés. ♦ Californian ♦ M-F lunch; daily dinner. Reservations recommended. 555 Golden Gate Ave, (between Polk St and Van Ness Ave). 861.7827 &

## 11 Edmund G. Brown State Office Building

**Skidmore, Owings & Merrill** were the architects for this complex, which was built in 1986. Their design complements the **Louise M. Davies Symphony Hall** down the street by facing diagonally toward **City Hall** and completing the Beaux Arts composition of civic buildings along this stretch of Van Ness Avenue. Clad in white precast concrete, it has a large seal of the State of California above the entry to the courtyard, which is disappointingly institutional in scale. ♦ Van Ness Ave (at McAllister St) &

## 12 Sunny Jim's City Grille

★$$$ With its proximity to City Hall and the Opera House, this restaurant caters to politicos by day and performing art patrons by night. If you come with a party of six you can sit in a plush booth and dine behind drawn velvet curtains. It's the kind of secrecy Sunny Jim, San Francisco's mayor from 1912 until becoming governor in 1930, would have appreciated. The menu also reflects tastes of the early twentieth century: pot au feu, shepherd's pie, chicken pot pie, chicken and dumplings. Chef Joe Jack researched cookbooks and restaurant menus from the reign of James "Sunny Jim" Rolph, Jr. and created a few of his own. Try the cornmeal fried oysters and chopped salad for starters and the Dungeness crab pot or crackling skin pork shank with apple-fennel sauerkraut for a taste of the times. ♦ American ♦ Daily lunch and dinner. 500 Van Ness Ave (at McAllister St). 546.7050 &

## 13 Abigail Hotel

$$ Built in 1926 to house members of visiting theater groups, this hotel was remodeled in 1990 in an arty European style. Gone are the smiling moose head and family of

stuffed elk; now there's a cozy, British feeling, complete with antiques, down comforters, and turn-of-the-century English art. While still not exactly luxurious, the 60-room hotel is a good value and conveniently located. ♦ 246 McAllister St (between Hyde and Larkin Sts). 861.9728, 800/243.6510; fax 861.5848

Within the Abigail Hotel:

## MILLENNIUM

★★$$ The cheerful setting here boasts a black-and-white tile floor, wall sconces, and sponge-painted walls. Main courses include a saffron and corn risotto, topped with a smoky stew featuring three beans and chunks of butternut squash; and chanterelle purse—phyllo dough filled with chanterelle and shiitake mushrooms, braised leek tofu "ricotta," and a barley-millet pilaf—served over a roasted shallot sauce and asparagus. Desserts are low-fat takeoffs on all-American favorites, including a nondairy butterscotch custard with an apple and cranberry compote. ♦ Vegetarian ♦ M-F lunch; Sa dinner; Su brunch and dinner. 487.9800

## 14 HIBERNIA BANK

At the time of its construction in 1892, **Willis Polk** described **Albert Pissis**'s design as "the most beautiful building in the city." He'd take back his claim if he could see it today. Now in use as a police administration center, the tightly sealed building has certainly lost its luster. Notice how it turns the corner of Jones and McAllister Streets at Market Street with a domed vestibule. ♦ Jones St (at McAllister St)

## 15 VETERAN'S BUILDING

Built in 1932 to honor World War I soldiers, this Beaux Arts-style edifice has a near identical twin in the **War Memorial Opera House.** In addition to housing the **Herbst Theater** (see below), the building is home to the offices of veterans' groups. ♦ 401 Van Ness Ave (at McAllister St). 621.6600. City Hall: 554.4000 ♿

Within the Veteran's Building:

## HERBST THEATER

Built in 1932, this minor component of the **Performing Arts Center** was refurbished in 1978. But the orchestra seats are raked, and the balconies sit too far back in this 923-seat theater. It's best for small theatrical

performances, dance groups, lectures, and recitals. The hall is adorned with murals depicting Earth, Water, Air, and Fire, the four elements of the ancient world. They were executed by British painter Frank Brangwyn for the Panama-Pacific Exposition of 1915. ♦ First floor. 392.4400 ♿

## 16 INN AT THE OPERA

$$$ This 47-room hotel was built in 1927 to house visiting opera stars. Elegantly restored, its luxuries include queen-size beds, large bathrooms, wet bars, small refrigerators, microwaves, 24-hour room service, concierge services, and parking. Just a few steps away are the **Opera House** and **Davies Symphony Hall.** ♦ 333 Fulton St (between Franklin and Gough Sts). 863.8400, 800/325.2708; fax 861.0821 ♿

Within the Inn at the Opera:

## OVATION AT THE OPERA

★★$$$$ Filled with wonderful oil paintings and flower arrangements, an ornate bar, dark wood appointments, an oversize fireplace, and deep, plush banquettes, it's appealing at any time, and the perfect spot for a nightcap and a light bite after a concert or evening on the town. Chef Victor Franco creates a seasonal menu that might include roasted free-range chicken breast with chicken and pistachio sausage, butter whipped yams, and caramelized apples; or seared Maine scallops with blood orange glaze and braised greens. Free valet parking. ♦ Californian/American Grill ♦ Daily dinner. Reservations recommended. 553.8100 ♿

## 17 JARDINIÈRE

★★★$$$ Traci Des Jardins' restaurant does more than just fill the need for dinner before a performance or after an afternoon on trendy Hayes Street. Warm weathered brick both help create a backdrop for a classy celebration at this two story restaurant. Backlit champagne buckets were built into a ribbon-like railing on the mezzanine level and the dome over the oval bar is fitted with fiber optics, tiny champagne-bubble lights to make you remember that nothing sets a celebratory tone better than champagne. Extensive by-the-glass wine selections include Billecart-Salmon Brut Rosé, or California sparkling wines such as Iron Horse Brut or Gloria Ferrer Brut. Chef Des Jardins, who was "born into a family that took pride in eating well," changes the menu daily. Starters can include lobster-leek-chanterelle strudel, and entrees range from pan-roasted squab with baby turnips and tatsoi, to lamb loin with squash blossoms, cranberry beans and tomato confit. An inventive cheese course features more than 50 choices that are kept in a temperature controlled "cave." For dessert try the bittersweet Scharffen Berger chocolate torte, or brown butter walnut cake with creme fraiche and caramel ice cream, or sip a glass of Bonny Doon Vin de Glacière Muscat. There's also a five-course tasting menu. ♦ French-Californian. ♦ Daily dinner. Late-night menu until midnight. Reservations recommended. 300 Grove Street (at Franklin Street). 861.5555. &

## 17 SAN FRANCISCO BALLET ASSOCIATION BUILDING

Architect **Beverly Willis** designed this modest addition to the **Civic Center** composition in 1984. It contains administrative offices, a ballet school, and state-of-the-art rehearsal studios. The facilities are not open to the public. ♦ 455 Franklin St (at Grove St). 861.5600

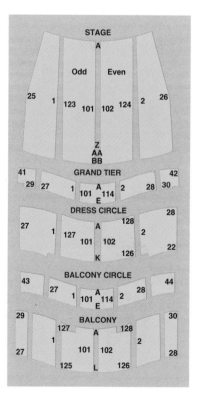

## 18 WAR MEMORIAL OPERA HOUSE

This splendid and ornate house is the crown jewel of San Francisco's **Performing Arts**

**Center.** With seating for 3,176 (see the plan left), it opened on 15 October 1932, and like the **Veteran's Building** it is dedicated to the memory of World War I soldiers and is now home to the city's renowned opera and ballet companies. The opera season opens in September with a gala—replete with splendidly gowned and bejeweled patrons—and runs through December. The ballet season immediately follows. ♦ 301 Van Ness Ave (at Grove St). 861.4008 &

## 19 CITY HALL

The focal point of the **Civic Center** complex was designed in 1915 by **Bakewell and Brown.** This magnificent symbol of government has a huge dome (modeled after St. Peter's in Rome), Baroque stairs, and echoing marble-clad corridors. The building underwent a $175-million seismic renovation. Visit the City Hall Store in the lobby. The plaza in front of the building has gardens and playgrounds; and is often used for fairs and festivals. ♦ Van Ness Ave (at McAllister St). 554.4000

Within City Hall:

**Museum of the City of San Francisco** Exhibits feature the history of the city, including mementos from the 1906 earthquake and fire, the celebration at the end of World War II, and photos of the 1989 earthquake. The 22-foot tall *Goddess of Progress* statue once crowned the old City Hall that was demolished in the 1906 earth-quake. ♦ Free. ♦ Lobby. 928.0289 &

## 20 SAN FRANCISCO PUBLIC LIBRARY

Opened in April 1996, San Francisco's library, designed by **Pei Cobb Freed and Partners** with **Simon Martin-Vegue Winkelstein Morris Associated Architects,** has double the capacity of the former library across the street, housing more than two million books and audiovisual materials. Note that the gray granite facades on Larkin and Fulton Streets blend with the Beaux Arts style of the **Civic Center,** while the stark geometric formation along Grove and Hyde Streets complements the modern commercial buildings on nearby Market Street. The library's interior is organized around two major spaces: a great open staircase and a five-story skylit open space that connects the library's various divisions. The library is divided into several centers, including **Art and Music, Business and Technology,** the **Environmental Center,** the **Government Information Center,** and **Humanities and General Collections.**

There are also centers for the blind and visually impaired, and for the deaf and hearing impaired; a **Chinese Center;** an **African-American Center;** a **Gay and Lesbian Center;** the **Children's Center,** which features a storytelling room and the **Children's Creative Center** with live performances and crafts programs. The **Exhibit Gallery** showcases rare artwork and artifacts from the library's own collection, as well as those on loan from other institutions such as the Smithsonian and the Library of Congress. A cafe offers beverages and light snacks.
♦ 100 Larkin St (at Fulton St). 557.4400 ♿

Within the San Francisco Public Library:

## SAN FRANCISCO HISTORY ROOM AND SPECIAL COLLECTIONS DEPARTMENT

In this combination document-and-photograph museum and research library you'll find glass cases filled with memorabilia, including photos of some of the city's classic buildings that no longer exist and of historic events such as the opening of the Golden Gate Bridge. ♦ Free. Tu-W, F afternoon; Th, Sa morning and afternoon. 557.4567 ♿

## 21 ORPHEUM THEATER

**B. Marcus Priteca** designed this 2,503-seat theater in 1926. In bygone days, it was an important part of the vaudeville scene. Today, the huge space is used for large-scale theatrical productions. The theater will temporarily host performances of the **San Francisco Opera** until renovations are completed. ♦ 1192 Market St (at Hyde and Eighth Sts). 474.3800, San Francisco Opera 861.4008 ♿

## 22 UNITED NATIONS PLAZA

This plaza memorializes the fact that the UN Charter was written and signed in this city in 1945. The plaza has become a hangout for panhandlers. ♦ Market St (at Fulton St) ♿

In United Nations Plaza:

## HEART OF THE CITY FARMERS' MARKET

Fresh fruits and vegetables, direct from the growers, are sold at low prices. ♦ W, Su.

Market St (between Grove and Fulton Sts). 558.9455 ♿

## 23 SAN FRANCISCO PERFORMING ARTS LIBRARY AND MUSEUM

Exhibitions related to the performing arts of the Bay Area are featured here.
♦ Free. Tu-Sa. 399 Grove St (at Gough St). 255.4800 ♿

## 24 ABSINTHE BRASSERIE AND BAR

★★$$ Popular with a diverse clientele, this attractive restaurant has an interesting menu that changes daily. Showstoppers include grilled chicken stuffed with herbs in a Champagne sauce. Excellent oyster bar. ♦ French/Mediterranean ♦ M-F lunch and dinner; Sa dinner; Su brunch and dinner. Reservations recommended. 398 Hayes St (at Gough St). 551-1590 ♿

## 25 E.F. DORIAN, INC.

Unique ethnic folk art and jewelry from around the world are sold here. ♦ Daily. 388 Hayes St (between Franklin and Gough Sts). 861.3191

## 25 AMPHORA WINE SHOP

Under the same ownership as Absinthe, this shop specializes in small-production handcrafted wines from Europe and California such as Pahmeyer Winery from Napa, Alban Vineyards from the Central Coast, and Didier Dageneau from Loire Valley. Discuss your taste preferences with the sommelier at the desk. They stock a wall of $10 or less bottles for neighborhood patrons as well as a good selection of half-bottles that fit hotel mini-bars. Tu-Su. 384-A Hayes St (between Franklin and Gough Sts). 863-1104

## 25 SAN FRANCISCO WOMEN ARTISTS GALLERY

The work of Bay Area women artists is showcased in this nonprofit, volunteer-run sales and rental gallery. ♦ Tu-Sa. 370 Hayes St (between Franklin and Gough Sts). 552.7392 ♿

## 26 HAYES STREET GRILL

★★$$$ One of the city's most renowned seafood houses, it has built a reputation for serving the freshest fish with a choice of a half-dozen sauces. Salads all have unusual twists, such as grilled calamari with fennel, red onion, and arugula, or shrimp with grapefruit and lime. The 1930s-style light fixtures, bentwood chairs, white walls, and white tablecloths give the place a comfortable look. The service is erratic—anywhere from grill-room-surly (heaven help you if you want to send anything back!) to diner-friendly. ♦ Seafood ♦ M-F lunch and dinner; Sa-Su dinner. 320 Hayes St (at Franklin St). 863.5545 &

## 26 VICOLO PIZZERIA

★★★$ Consistently good cornmeal-crusted, California-style pizzas with unusual toppings, as well as tasty salads, are produced at this pleasant little side-street restaurant with a galvanized metal-and-glass exterior. It's a great spot for pre- and post-theater snacking. ♦ Californian/Italian ♦ Daily lunch and dinner. 201 Ivy St (at Franklin St). 863.2382 &

## 27 EVELYN'S ANTIQUE CHINESE FURNITURE

For a good selection of Chinese pieces, this is the place. ♦ M-Sa. 381 Hayes St (at Gough St). 255.1815 &

## 28 EC STUDIO STORE

Paper products never looked so handsome as they do here, all gussied up in colorful packages trimmed with big bows. Owner Hal Brandes designs and manufactures everything he sells: journals, sketch pads, stationery sets, cards and photo albums in leather, suede, and fabric. It's a good place for desk accessories. ♦ Tu-Sa. 347 Hayes St (between Franklin and Gough Sts). 621.1015 &

## 29 RICHARD HILKERT, BOOKSELLER, LTD

This cozy shop filled with old and new books specializes in interior design and architecture,

but also has a good selection of general interest reading. Call ahead to make sure it's open, as hours tend to be irregular. ♦ M-Sa; Su at owner's discretion. 333 Hayes St (between Franklin and Gough Sts). 863.3339 &

## 29 COULARS BOUTIQUE

Whimsical clothing – shoes, ties, earrings, dresses – for women and children is hand-painted by owner Maryke Coulars. ♦ M-Sa Jan-Nov; daily Dec. 327 Hayes St (between Franklin and Gough Sts). 255.2925

## 29 NUTS ABOUT YOU

All kinds of nuts, teas, baskets, coffees, and confections tempt irrepressible snackers. The store will also pack and ship orders. ♦ Daily. 325 Hayes Street (between Franklin and Gough Sts). 864.6887

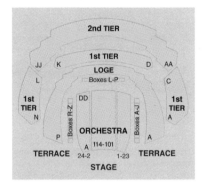

## 30 LOUISE M. DAVIES SYMPHONY HALL

Designed by **Skidmore, Owings & Merrill,** this hall, which is named after arts patron Louise M. Davies, who contributed $5 million toward its construction, opened in 1980 after more than a decade of squabbling. It cost $33 million to build (all but $5 million of it was raised privately), and in 1992 the hall underwent a $10-million acoustical and architectural face-lift (see the plan shown above). The renovations included a new sound and video system as well as a computer-assisted resculpting of the walls to improve acoustics. The hall is the official home of the **San Francisco Symphony,** whose season runs from September through May. Besides the symphony, the 2,743-seat **Davies** regularly books other musical and touring groups. ♦ Admission charge for tours. Tours of the Performing Arts Center (Louise M. Davies Symphony Hall, War Memorial Opera House and Herbst Theatre meet at the Grove Street entrance M. on the hour 10AM to 2PM. Van

## TROLLEYS TO YESTERYEAR

Matt Morrow/NORTH MARKET STREET GRAPHICS '98

The cheerful clang of historic trolleys once again sounds on Market Street, thanks to the donations of vintage cars from various US cities and other countries. Originally introduced in 1935 at a time when a fleet of 1,000 electric cars plied Market Street, a hundred streetcars were brought back into operation in 1995 to launch MUNI's new F-line service. These Presidential Conference Cars (PCCs), affectionately called "green torpedoes," run from Castro Street, past the Civic Center area, through the Financial District to the Ferry Building, then rumble north along the Embarcadero to Pier 39, with its terminus at Fisherman's Wharf.

Some examples of trolleys from other places include Car 351 from Johnstown Pennsylvania; the popular "boat" car of the English seaside resort of Blackpool; two 1927 trams from Japan and a 1928 tram all the way from Australia. As a result, no city comes close to matching San Francisco's collection of Art-deco era streetcars. So hop aboard one for a riotous ride through the scenic heart of the city.

Ness Ave (at Grove St). Tours 552.8338, box office 431.5400 &

### 31 BILL GRAHAM CIVIC AUDITORIUM

Designed by architect **John Galen Howard,** the auditorium was completed in 1915 during the architectural renaissance that followed the destruction of the 1906 earthquake and fire. In 1993 the **Civic Auditorium**'s name was changed to honor Bill Graham, the local rock music impresario who promoted such legends as the Grateful Dead, Miles Davis, and Jimi Hendrix. The auditorium serves as the city's main conference center and has seating for 7,000 people. ♦ 99 Grove St (between Larkin and Polk Sts). 974.4000. &

### 32 ARTS COMMISSION GALLERY

Indoor and outdoor exhibitions of work by both emerging and established Bay Area artists are presented here. ♦ Tu-Sa. 25 Van Ness Ave (between Oak and Fell Sts). 252.2590 &

### 33 BISTRO CLOVIS

★★$ The setting is pure Parisian wine bar, where classic country flavors come alive in the

## THE BEST

**Dianne Feinstein**
United States Senator

I'm a native San Franciscan and terribly in love with my city. Selecting a favorite place is consequently very difficult, since there are simply miles and miles of pleasures and delights packed into our 47-square-mile area.

However, caveats aside, I always recommend that visitors stroll through **Golden Gate Park,** with its more than 1,000 acres of magnificent trees, plants, and greenswards. The park also houses our renowned **Japanese Tea Garden,** a special park within a park whose ambience is unmistakably Eastern—a wonderful place to reflect and relax.

Some of San Francisco's finest museums are also located within **Golden Gate Park**—the **Asian Art Museum,** the **M.H. de Young Memorial Museum,** the **Academy of Sciences,** and the **Steinhart Aquarium.**

I also highly recommend visiting San Francisco's **Chinatown**—one of the largest outside of Asia—where you can eat exquisitely for very low prices and shop for virtually anything.

And don't forget to ride one of San Francisco's cable cars. The city, with tremendous support from the private sector, has rehabilitated this century-old transportation system—America's only moving national monument—and it remains a great way to see San Francisco's incredibly hilly streets and spectacular views.

Visit **Fisherman's Wharf,** too, and sample our incomparable Dungeness crab, sourdough bread, and succulent seafood. Be sure to take a boat ride on **San Francisco Bay,** one of the world's most beautiful deep-water bodies. You can sail right under the **Golden Gate Bridge**—as well as the equally impressive **Bay Bridge.** Views of San Francisco from the bay are breathtaking.

As for restaurants, we have more per capita than any city in America and they range fully across the world's most exciting cuisines. We have food for literally every palate!

Shopping is also excellent, particularly in **Union Square,** one of the nation's leading retail centers, located in the heart of downtown San Francisco.

My final recommendation is probably the most important one: Be sure to meet our citizens. San Francisco is a cultural cornucopia of the world's people, most of whom are friendly, helpful, and eager to share their insights about life in San Francisco.

---

onion soup gratinee, sweetbread and scampi casserole, and duck filet with green peppercorn sauce. Be sure to do some wine sampling, too: Three two-ounce tastes of different wines are available at a modest fee. ♦ French ♦ T-Sa dinner. 1596 Market St (at Franklin St). 864.0231 &

**34 GRAND CENTRAL STATION ANTIQUES**

Two floors are filled with French, English, and Belgian furniture and collectibles from the 18th to 20th centuries. ♦ Tu-Su. 1632 Market St (between Franklin and Gough Sts). 252.8155.

**35 ZUNI RESTAURANT & BAR**

★★★$$$ Since opening 15 years ago with a menu of Southwestern fare (hence the name), this cafe has developed a Mediterranean style of cooking that includes a grand selection of oysters, roast chicken with bread salad (bread and greens in a Champagne vinaigrette), juicy ground-to- order hamburgers on house-baked focaccia, and frosty espresso granita (coffee-flavored shaved ice). ♦ Californian/Mediterranean ♦ Tu-Su breakfast, lunch, and dinner. Reser-

vations recommended. 1658 Market St (at Rose St, between Franklin and Gough Sts). 552.2522 &

**35 RED DESERT**

A fine collection of succulents and cacti is attractively displayed in a sandy habitat. ♦ Daily. 1632 Market St (at Rose St, between Franklin and Gough Sts). 552.2800

**36 PENSIONE SAN FRANCISCO**

$ This pleasant European-style hotel has 36 small, cheerful rooms with shared bathrooms (there are 9 rooms and 4 bathrooms on each floor). ♦ 1668 Market St (between Franklin and Gough Sts). 864.1271; fax 861.8116

**37 BEAVER BROS. ANTIQUES & PROP RENTALS**

This is the largest prop-rental shop in San Francisco, so, theoretically, you can try the merchandise before buying. Victoriana, bric-a-brac, and an eclectic assortment of other stuff from bygone eras are presented on two jam-packed floors. ♦ Daily. 1637 Market St. 863.4344 &

---

Restaurants/Clubs: Red | Hotels: Purple | Shops: Orange | Outdoors/Parks: Green | Sights/Culture: Blue

# SOUTH OF MARKET (SOMA)

**P**opularly known as SoMa, but familiar to an earlier generation as "South of the Slot," the South of Market area has evolved into one of San Francisco's most eclectic, artsy frontiers. It incorporates gay bars, trendy restaurants, a wholesale flower market, outlet shops, bus terminals, a convention center, warehouses, and rock, comedy, and jazz clubs. Artists, dancers, and musicians like the relatively modest rents for huge spaces they can convert into studios and living quarters, although rising real-estate prices have made truc bargains a thing of the past.

Close to **The Embarcadero** and the bay, SoMa has always been home to industry. Several foundries were located here in the 1850s, along with row after row of tiny houses, many prefabricated in the East, occupied by the city's first industrial population. Author

Jack London, who was born on **Third Street** in 1876, reflected the rough-and-ready nature of the neighborhood in his work. But when it became apparent that the climate was warmest on this side of town, **Rincon Hill,** long since blasted away and buried under the approach to the **Bay Bridge,** became a very prestigious address. Small, elegant shops filled **Second Street.** Adjacent **South Park** was a pioneer real-estate development promoted by George Gordan, an Englishman who set out to model an exclusive community for 64 families on the plan of terraces in London—stately Georgian houses that were built around an enclosed park to which only the residents had a gate key. Here, among others, lived cattle king Henry Miller, Senator William McKendree Gwin, and Hall McAllister, until he lost his mansion in a poker game.

But before the park was half built, the decline of Rincon Hill set in because of the persistent industrialization of the neighborhood. Its residents fled to Nob Hill, abandoning their homes to Japanese immigrants. Rooming houses and machine shops took over, although remnants of grandeur can still be seen here and there, especially on Third Street between **Bryant** and **Brannan Streets.** To the delight of citizens, signs of rebirth continue to appear throughout the neighborhood, as creative types buy, move into, and gentrify structures that have suffered decades of neglect.

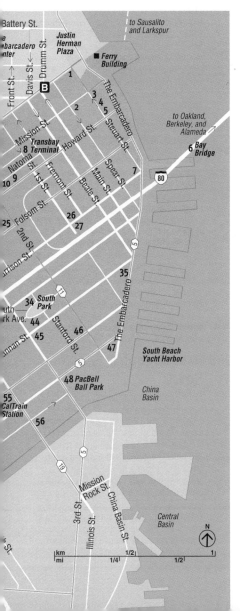

In October 1993, **Yerba Buena Gardens**—the spectacular $87- million arts and cultural center—opened its doors, making the South of Market area San Francisco's artistic hot spot.

The center's striking visual-arts building was designed by renowned Japanese architect **Fumihiko Maki;** its theater, by highly acclaimed New York architect **James Stewart Polshek;** and its massive brick **Museum of Modern Art** designed by Swiss architect **Mario Botta.**

These buildings, along with five and a half acres of gardens, join the **Moscone Convention Center**—northern California's largest meeting facility—in transforming what was once an area lined with skid-row flophouses into an impressive complex with numerous satellite restaurants, shops, and hotels that have forever changed the face of SoMa. PacBell Park baseball stadium recently opened at China Basin. And plans are underway to build a new cruise ship terminal at South Beach.

## 1 ONE MARKET RESTAURANT

★★★$$$ Celebrity chef Bradley Ogden has once again created a hit restaurant that, despite its grand size, gets so packed you often have to make reservations weeks in advance. The view and the sounds set the mood: The airy dining room lined with huge windows overlooks the side of **Justin Herman Plaza** and the end of bustling Market Street, and jazz piano music dominates the attractive bar in the evenings. Ogden is in the process of making his menu more casual, with such dishes as meat loaf, pork chops, roasted vegetables, and grilled beef tenderloin. This venture is every bit as successful as the others, but the food quality is more variable—sometimes marvelous, sometimes just okay. ◆ Californian ◆ M-F lunch and dinner; Sa dinner; Su jazz brunch and dinner. Reservations recommended. 1 Market St (at Steuart St). 777.5577 ⑤

## 2 RINCON CENTER

The old **Rincon Annex Post Office Building**, built here in 1940 by **Gilbert Stanley Underwood**, is one of the city's masterpieces, and was incorporated into a massive complex of offices, shops, restaurants, and apartment towers in 1989 by **Johnson, Fain, and Pereira Associates.** The historic murals that were in the annex lobby are the centerpiece of the 85-foot-high skylighted atrium from which falls a magnificent cascade of water. The post office has moved to 2 Rincon Center. ◆ Spear St (at Mission St) ⑤

## 3 AUDIFFRED BUILDING

Built in 1889 by Hippolyte d'Audiffred, this brick building was the only one south of Market to survive the fire after the 1906 earthquake. Ironically, it burned down in 1981, but has since been restored. ◆ Mission St (at Steuart St)

Within the Audiffred Building:

## BOULEVARD

★★★$$$ Chef and restaurateur Nancy Oakes, who has been called one of the 10 best chefs by *Food & Wine* magazine and chef of the year by *San Francisco Focus* magazine, joined forces with acclaimed restaurant designer Pat Kuleto in creating this handsome restaurant. Here Kuleto has created a room with three distinct areas: the bar, defined by a domed brick ceiling and an intricate peacock-patterned tile floor; the informal central section, with an open kitchen and a counter; and the dramatically lit, more formal dining area. Oakes is known for her lusty combinations and innovative presentations. The menu changes often, but try anything that includes quail, or the vanilla-cured pork loin. The wine list is a little pricey, but features some excellent, hard-to-find California wines. ◆ Italian ◆ M-F lunch and dinner; Sa-Su dinner. Reservations recommended. Entrance on Steuart St. 543.6084 ⑤

## 4 HOTEL GRIFFON

$$$ Originally built in 1907, making it the oldest hotel on the waterfront, this 63-room place is part of the expanding Financial District, which has moved south of Market Street. It is a block from the **Ferry Terminal** and a scant two blocks from the **California Street Cable-Car Line. The E-Line** passes right in front. The rooms have minibars, and complimentary services include morning coffee and daily newspaper delivery. ◆ 155 Steuart St (between Howard and Mission Sts). 495.2100, reservations only 800/321.2201; fax 495.3522 ⑤

Within the Hotel Griffon:

## BISTRO RÔTI

★★★$$ Any seat in the house offers a good view of the action here: There's a lively bar scene up front; in the middle, a chef tends a rotisserie at an open brick fireplace; and, in the back, counter seats overlook an open kitchen and tables have views of the Bay Bridge. The food has a French twist, as evidenced by such offerings as french fries with lemon aioli, or the grilled duck breast salad with peaches and a port vinaigrette. Dessert offerings include cherry-and-apricot brioche pudding, and an excellent crème brûlée. ◆ Californian/French ◆ M-F lunch and dinner; Sa-Su brunch and dinner. Reservations recommended. 495.6500 ⑤

## 5 HARBOR COURT HOTEL

$$ When the much-hated Embarcadero Freeway was torn down due to damage caused by the 1989 quake, this hotel gained some great bay views. Housed in a 1907 building, it has 131 small guest rooms (30 have the views) and a magnificent lobby with a stone fireplace. Patrons are entitled to half-price entry into **Harry Denton**'s nightclub (and don't have to wait in line), plus gym privileges at the adjacent **YMCA,** complimentary wine every evening from 5 to 7PM, and daily limousine service to the Financial District. ◆ 165 Steuart St (between Howard and Mission Sts). 882.1300, 800/346.0555 ⑤

# THE LONG AND WINDING ROADS

**Lombard Street** has long laid claim to being the crookedest street in the world, but it seems the famed San Francisco roadway has a little competition. The good citizens of Burlington, Iowa, insist the honor belongs to their own Snake Alley, a brick-laid street that was constructed in 1894 and consists of seven curves on a 16 percent grade. They say that although Lombard boasts more switchbacks and an 18.2 percent grade, it is broken up into a series of short increments, whereas Snake Alley maintains a sinuous stretch of continuous curves. Then again, some San Franciscans claim that the crookedest-street title may really belong to yet another curvaceous roadway: **Vermont Street,** in San Francisco's **Potrero Hill District.** The street has only 6 curves and a measly 14.3 percent grade, but its muscle-straining, hair-raising turns are much sharper than those of the other contenders.

San Francisco has other winding ways worth exploring, including the following favorites:

**Twin Peaks Drive** up the hill at the intersection of **Clarendon Avenue** and **Twin Peaks Boulevard,** then wind down the 12 curves (in a 9,000-foot stretch) to **Portola Drive.** The view, 910 feet above sea level, is spectacular.

**O'Shaughnessy** and **Teresita Boulevards** Begin at the intersection of Portola Drive and O'Shaughnessy Boulevard, heading southeast. Arrows shaped like C's warn you of the curves—20 of them in 12,000 feet. Turn right on **Brompton Avenue** and again on **Joost Avenue.** Then turn right on **Foerster Street** for two blocks and again at Teresita Boulevard. The following block—which alone has nine curves—is lined with charming, colorful houses.

**Telegraph Hill** Four curves—and, unfortunately, a passel of traffic jams—in 2,400 feet lead to the landmark **Coit Tower.** On a clear day, the view of **Alcatraz** and the city is tremendous and worth the effort.

**Russian Hill** Named after a graveyard (long since removed) for Russian seamen.

---

## 6 BAY BRIDGE

Charles H. Purcell was chief engineer for this bridge, which eliminated the isolation between the cities of San Francisco and Oakland. The longest steel high-level bridge in the world, and one of the most costly structures ever built, it took three years to construct. The eight-mile span from approach to approach is, in fact, two bridges separated by a tunnel through Yerba Buena Island. The foundations of one of the piers extend 242 feet below water, deeper than those of any other bridge ever built. The pier is bigger than the largest of the world's pyramids and required more concrete than the Empire State Building in New York City. The San Francisco side consists of a double-suspension bridge; the Oakland side is a cantilever bridge. The bridge has two levels, with five lanes in each direction. Originally, electric trains and trucks ran on the lower deck and cars on the upper deck, but the tracks were removed in the late 1950s when the trains were replaced by buses. During the October 1989 quake, an upper section of the bridge collapsed onto the lower one, sending motorists fleeing from their cars and killing one person; the damage was repaired in just one month. Today it's the busiest thoroughfare in the area. Tolls have raised enough revenue to pay for other means of public transportation, including the **BART** tube, the **San Mateo/Hayward Bridge,** and most of the **Dumbarton Bridge.** The best views of the bridge are from Yerba Buena Island and from below on **The Embarcadero** in San Francisco. ♦ Toll westbound.

## 7 GORDON BIERSCH

★★$$ This branch of the popular Palo Alto–based brewery-restaurant was a word-of-mouth success even before it opened. Beer, brick, and business suits dominate the ground floor, while diners herd upstairs to sample the sparse but tempting menu. Visually stimulating but acoustically devastating, this place—located in the old Hills Brothers coffee factory—seems to reach rock-concert decibel levels even at lunch. ♦ Californian ♦ Daily lunch and dinner. Reservations recommended. 2 Harrison St (at Steuart St and The Embarcadero). 243.8246 &

## 8 TRANSBAY TERMINAL

When the Bay Bridge was opened, this austere, functional 1939 building by Timothy Pflueger (with consulting architects Arthur Brown Jr. and John L. Donovan) replaced the Ferry Terminal as the gateway to the city.

---

Restaurants/Clubs: Red | Hotels: Purple | Shops: Orange | Outdoors/Parks: Green | Sights/Culture: Blue

Buses to the Amtrak station in Oakland and bus tours to Lake Tahoe and Reno leave from here. ♦ Mission St (at First St) &

Within the Transbay Terminal:

## GRAY LINE TOURS

Day tours to Muir Woods, Sausalito, Yosemite, the Wine Country, Carmel, and Monterey— as well as city tours of San Francisco— depart from this bus terminal. ♦ Reservations required for some tours.   Scheduling information 558.9400

## 9 CARIBBEAN ZONE

★$$ The airplane cabin suspended above the dining room is not just for decoration— it's a cocktail lounge that serves drinks with names like Sex in the Jungle, Goomba Boomba, and Belize Breeze. Not surprisingly, food isn't the major draw here, but it's pretty good. The tropics-inspired menu lists lots of munching options: conch fritters with a lime-mustard mayonnaise, grilled prawns with chipotle and orange juice, and panfried green plantains with salsa. Those who stick around for a main course can order paella, jerk chicken, salmon with sesame seeds, or smoked pork loin with grilled pineapple and rum. ♦ Caribbean ♦ Daily lunch and dinner. Reservations recommended for lunch. 55 Natoma St (off Second St between Mission and Howard Sts). 541.9465 &

## 10 MR. RALPH'S CAFE

★★$ Behind this unassuming cafe's bright green facade, architects and artists from the neighborhood lunch on a creative selection of sandwiches such as chicken, spinach, and sun-dried tomato; grilled eggplant; and mozzarella, roasted red pepper, and basil. ♦ Californian ♦ M-Th breakfast, lunch, and dinner until 7PM; F until 8PM; Sa breakfast

and lunch. 90 Natoma St (off Second St between Mission and Howard Sts). 243.9330

## 11 ARGENT HOTEL

$$$$ This sleek hotel was built in 1983 by Air France and features 667 rooms and suites, many with sweeping city views. Within walking distance of Union Square, the Financial District, and the **Moscone Convention Center,** it offers guests valet parking, a health club, room service, and a business center. The hotel caters to allergy sufferers and the environmentally conscious by offering "green suites": Special air- and water-filtration systems are featured in 19 rooms along with toiletries which have not been tested on animals. ♦ 50 Third St (between Mission and Market Sts). 974.6400, 877/222.6699; fax 543.8268; www.argenthotel.com &

Within the Argent Hotel:

## CAFE 53

★$$$ This revamped Art Deco restaurant features American fare. Unfortunately, the food does not match the elegant ambience. Specialties include prime rib, pasta primavera, and fried bass with soy sauce. ♦ American ♦ Daily breakfast, lunch, and dinner. 974.6400 &

## 12 FRIENDS OF PHOTOGRAPHY/ ANSEL ADAMS CENTER FOR PHOTOGRAPHY

Works by the gallery's namesake, one of California's greatest photographers, are always on display. Other exhibitions focus on vintage to contemporary photography. ♦ Admission; children 12 and under free. Tu-Su. 655 Mission St (between New Montgomery and Third). 495.7000 &

## 13 PACIFIC TELEPHONE BUILDING

One of the most beautiful skyscrapers in San Francisco, this 1925 building, by **Miller & Pflueger** and **A.A. Cantin Architects,** owes much to **Eliel Saarinen**'s celebrated design proposed for the Chicago Tribune Tower, particularly in the building's profile, detailing, and vertical emphasis. Notice the modern entrance lobby with its Chinese decorated ceilings. ♦ 130-140 New Montgomery St (between Howard and Mission Sts)

## 14 HOTEL PALOMAR

$$$$ This sleek boutique hotel brings a welcome urbanity to bustling south of Market. Secluded five floors above Market St in a refurbished 1907 landmark building is a 198-room hotel. You'll find a clean, artful design that includes walnut parquet floors, hand-tufted wool carpets, and headboards with

green velvet panels. ◆ 12 Fourth St (at Market St). 348.1111, 877/294.9711; www.hotelpalomar.com

Within the Palomar Hotel:

## 14 FIFTH FLOOR

★★★★$$$$ Guinea hen with classic sauce chausser, roasted poussin with foie gras jus, and suckling pig a la orange are a few of the highlights of Chef George Morrone's menu. The restaurant has received accolades and a four star rating within months of opening. Decorated like a Parisian nightclub, the dining room is located on the fifth floor of Hotel Palomar. ◆ French ◆ Reservations recommended. M-Sa breakfast, dinner. 348.1555

## 15 OLD NAVY

This four-story flagship store has a fun, energetic atmosphere throughout. The ground floor contains the menswear line, the Old Navy General Store, and Torpedo Joe's 61-seat submarine inspired restaurant. ◆ 801 Market St (at Fourth St). 344.0375

## 16 THE JEWISH MUSEUM OF SAN FRANCISCO

Another of **Willis Polk**'s masterpieces, this 1907 building was originally the Pacific Gas and Electric Substation. It was restored as part of the Yerba Buena Redevelopment Project, and was completed in 1999. ◆ 222 Jessie St (bounded by Third and Fourth Sts, and Mission and Market Sts.)

## 17 MARRIOTT HOTEL

$$$$ This controversial hotel close to the **Moscone Convention Center** went up in 1989 amid considerable architectural acrimony. Critics lambasted **Anthony J. Lumsden**'s design, comparing its 40 stories to a jukebox. The hotel opened ahead of schedule after the October 1989 earthquake, when it sprang into use as an emergency shelter, thereby muting some critical voices. The imposing structure has 1,500 rooms and suites, an indoor swimming pool, a spa and health club, a 40,000-square-foot ballroom,

and more than 85,000 square feet of meeting and exhibition space. Food and beverage facilities on premises include the **Kinoko Japanese Restaurant,** the **Garden Terrace, Allie's American Grill,** the **Atrium Lobby Lounge,** and the **View Lounge** (on the 40th floor). ◆ 55 Fourth St (at Mission St). 896.1600, 800/228.9290; fax 896.6176 ⅙

## 18 THE MOSSER VICTORIAN HOTEL OF ARTS AND MUSIC

$$ This landmark hotel's small rooms are more than made up for by its prices (which border on the philanthropic) and its superb location near Union Square and the **Museum of Modern Art.** The 165 rooms are decorated with rattan furniture and floral fabrics, and the restaurant features a cabaret show in the evenings (hence the hotel's rather misleading name). Hotel guests receive a complimentary continental breakfast. Beware—some floors have shared baths. Ask about reduced weekly rates. ◆ 54 Fourth Street (between Mission and Market Sts). 986.4400; 800/227.3804; fax 495.7653 ⅙

## 19 THE CARTOON ART MUSEUM

This second-floor exhibition space is devoted to art that tickles the funny bone. There is a children's gallery where budding artists can get hands-on experience using markers and crayons. Classes and tours are available. ◆ Admission; reduced for children 5 and under. W-Su. 814 Mission St (at 4th St). 227.8666 ⅙

## 20 METREON

This Sony entertainment complex has 12 movie screens, an IMAX, and various attractions, including The Way Things Work-in Mammoth 3D, Where the Wild Things Are, the Sony store, and an upscale food court. ◆ 101 4th Street (Between Mission and Minna Sts). ⅙

Inside Metreon:

**M**ON**TAG**E

### MONTAGE

★★$$$ This restaurant has a menu as vibrant as its colors. Montage has sleek booths, and four TV monitors play videos of current art exhibits. The wide-ranging menu includes Moroccan chicken wings, pork chop with spaetzle and caramelized apples, and lamb shank with creamy fromage blanc

---

**Restaurants/Clubs: Red | Hotels: Purple | Shops: Orange | Outdoors/Parks: Green | Sights/Culture: Blue**

polenta. If you decide to stop by for a late-night dessert after a movie, try the mocha float wth Scharffenberger chocolate ice cream. ♦ Californian ♦ Daily lunch, M-Sa dinner. Metreon, second level. 369.6111

## 21 Yerba Buena Gardens

This $87-million arts and cultural center is the result of 30 years of public planning and debate and is intended to feature the work and talents of San Francisco's diverse ethnic and artistic communities. Many of the major structures were designed by internationally acclaimed architects, including the 55,000-square-foot **Center for the Arts Galleries and Forum** by Japanese architect **Fumihiko Maki; James Stewart Polshek and Partners'** 755-seat **Center for the Arts Theater;** and the home of the **San Francisco Museum of Modern Art,** designed by Swiss architect **Mario Botta,** which opened in January 1995 to commemorate the museum's 60th anniversary. The five-and-a-half-acre Esplanade, bordered by Howard and Mission Streets, and Third and Fourth Streets, features a memorial to Martin Luther King Jr., a 20-foot-high, 50-foot-wide waterfall made of Sierra granite; the **Sister City Garden,** which is planted with flowers and plants from San Francisco's 13 sister cities from around the world; and a number of public artworks. Arts organizations both traditional and "on the fringe," have a welcome home at the Yerba Buena Center for the Arts. Dance companies who perform here include Smuin Ballets/SF, Margaret Jenkins Dance Company. ODC/SF and Alonzo King's Contemporary Ballet. Tickets 978-ARTS. ♦ Bounded by Folsom and Mission Sts, and Third and Fourth Sts. Program information 978.ARTS

## 22 San Francisco Museum of Modern Art (SFMoMA)

In January 1995, in celebration of its 60th year, the museum relocated its collection from the Veteran's Building in the Civic Center to larger quarters in **Yerba Buena Gardens.** Its handsome brick box home was designed by internationally acclaimed Swiss architect **Mario Botta** and features a 125-foot cylindrical skylight which channels light down to the first-floor atrium court. More than 17,000 works of art are housed on the museum's four floors of gallery space. The permanent collection contains works by Pablo Picasso, Henri Matisse, Wassily Kandinsky, the Abstract Expressionists (including large holdings of Clyfford Still), Josef Albers, Isamu Noguchi, Alexander Calder, and distinguished California artists. Among the contemporary international works are Anselm Kiefer's *Osiris and Isis,* Sigmar Polke's *The Spirits That Lend Strength Are Invisible III (Nickel/Neusilber),* Cody Noland's *Dance Hall Doors,* and Nam June Paik's *Egg Grows.* The museum functions as a cultural center for contemporary art, films, and live music. The active photography department presents frequent exhibitions from its extensive permanent collection and temporary shows of 20th-century photography. **MuseumStore,** on the main floor, is open daily and has the city's best selection of modern-art books and catalogs, gifts and jewelry. A pleasant, inexpensive cafe is located on the fourth floor (open during museum hours). The **San Francisco Museum of Modern Art Rental Gallery** (see page 105) is located at Fort Mason, Building A. ♦ Admission; free first Tuesday of the month. M-Tu; F-Su; Th until 9PM. Tours daily. 151 Third St (between Howard and Mission Sts). 357.4000

Within the San Francisco Museum of Modern Art:

### Caffè Museo

★$ The eye-catching decor consists of wooden pegboards, a slatted ceiling, a striped granite floor, and leather directors' chairs. Sandwiches, including an excellent grilled vegetable version, are made with focaccia, and the salad choices range from barley with mushrooms and artichokes to saffron rice studded with bits of zucchini and whole rock shrimp. ♦ Mediterranean ♦ M-Tu, F-Su breakfast, lunch, tea, and dinner until 6PM; Th until 9PM. 357.4500 ♿

## 23 Crown Point Press Gallery

This gallery prints and publishes etchings and woodblock editions by artists who work here by invitation. It is known internationally for its high quality and standards. ♦ Tu-Sa. 20 Hawthorne La (second entrance at 657 Howard St (between Second and Third Sts). 974.6273 ♿

## 23 Hawthorne Lane

★★★$$$ A hot place for daring California cuisine since it opened in 1995, this establishment has a menu that features boldly flavored American fare with a few Asian accents mixed in. Try grilled tenderloin of beef with spicy greens in fresh spring rolls; seared Maine scallops with mâche, Cabernet sauce, and horseradish crème fraîche; or slices of Sonoma lamb with artichoke risotto and tomato tarragon sauce. Desserts also have an artistic bent: A light cheesecake, topped with a rich lemon curd, is accompanied by swirls of blueberry sauce and berries. ♦ Californian

◆ M-F lunch and dinner; Sa-Su dinner. Reservations recommended. 22 Hawthorne Lane (at Howard St). 777.9779 ᕦ

## 24 CHEVYS

★★$$ This popular restaurant has found a formula for success and repeated it many times throughout the Bay Area. Tortillas are made on the premises, along with terrific fajitas and other Mexican fare. They're offered in substantial portions in a deliberately funky setting, where beer cases serve as room dividers. It's a casual dining experience that's especially enjoyable when everything is washed down with a pitcher of the slushy (although not too potent) margaritas. ◆ Mexican/Takeout ◆ Daily lunch and dinner. Reservations required for eight or more. 201 Third St (at Howard St). 543.8060. Also at: Two Embarcadero Center, Promenade level (between Clay and Sacramento Sts). 391.2323; Stonestown Galleria (at 19th Ave and Winston Dr). 665.8705 ᕦ

## 25 THE FLY TRAP

★★★$$ Named after a long-closed, but once popular Financial District restaurant, this is one of the area's more upscale spots, with a mirrored, casually elegant interior and a menu that borrows some culinary inspiration from its namesake. Main courses include sautéed sweetbreads with mushrooms, calves' liver with bacon and onions, and chicken Jerusalem (with artichoke hearts). ◆ Californian/Italian ◆ M-F lunch and dinner; Sa-Su dinner. Reservations recommended. 606 Folsom St (at Second St). 243.0580 ᕦ

## 26 SAILORS' UNION OF THE PACIFIC BUILDING

**William S. Merchant**'s 1950 building symbolizes the power that unions gained after the bitter struggles and strikes of 1934. It is reminiscent of European Constructivist buildings of the 1930s. ◆ 450 Harrison St (at First St)

## 27 76 TOWER UNION OIL COMPANY BUILDING

A landmark on top of Rincon Hill, the triangular-shaped tower designed in 1941 by **Lewis P. Hobart** is directed toward the approach ramp to the Bay Bridge. It is clad in white porcelain enamel—a material that architects have rediscovered. ◆ 425 First St (at Harrison St)

## 28 HOTEL MILANO

$$$ Originally constructed as a hotel in 1920, this building's latest incarnation was conceived to play host to movie production companies filming on location in San Francisco. It contains a private screening room and other facilities for film crews. Most business travelers who come here enjoy the convenience of walking to the nearby **Moscone Convention Center.** The 108 spacious, airy rooms have picture windows, fax and computer connections, and a two-line speakerphone with voice mail. Other amenities include a two-story fitness center and the hotel's restaurant (see below), which provides 24-hour room service. ◆ 55 Fifth St (between Mission and Market Sts). 543.8555, 800/398.7555; fax 543.5885 ᕦ

Within the Hotel Milano:

## M POINT

★★$$$ The light wood appointments, modernistic ceiling mural, and arched windows overlooking the street all add to the fresh-scrubbed ambience at this place. The menu features 10 starters and about 10 main courses. Best bets are chicken egg drop or miso soup; tamari marinated organic chicken with mushroom risotto. For dessert, try the gooey warm chocolate cake with Kaluha chocolate sauce and housemade vanilla bean ice cream. ◆ Californian/Asian ◆ Daily breakfast, lunch, and dinner. 543.7600 ᕦ

## 29 THE PICKWICK HOTEL

$$ This 192-room hotel is well located— mere footsteps from Market Street shopping, and just a block away from the **Moscone Convention Center** and the **Museum of Modern Art** and has recently been renovated. It's a terrific value and has already been discovered by many European visitors. The hotel restaurant serves breakfast and a light lunch. ◆ 85 Fifth St (at Mission St). 421.7500, 800/227.3282; fax 243.8066 ᕦ

Restaurants/Clubs: Red | Hotels: Purple | Shops: Orange | Outdoors/Parks: Green | Sights/Culture: Blue

## 30 MOSCONE CONVENTION CENTER

This 1.2-million-square-foot facility anchors the vast **Yerba Buena Gardens** complex. It's named after assassinated mayor George Moscone and was designed by **Hellmuth, Obata & Kassabaum.** The city's premier meeting and exhibition facility was expanded in 1992 by **Gensler & Associates** and **DMJM** to the tune of $200 million. Although largely underground, the center's imaginative use of skylights and other light-maximizing features keeps conventioneers from feeling like troglodytes. Alas, it is too small. A new building, Moscone West, at Fourth and Howard Sts, will add 300,000 square feet of function space. ♦ 747 Howard St (between Third and Fourth Sts). 974.4000 &

## 31 MAX'S DINER AND BAKERY

★$ A sign on one side of the door reads "This is a good place for a diet." A sign on the other side says "This is a bad place for a diet." Both are true. Sandwiches are huge, big enough to feed two people. There are also traditional blue-plate dinner specials, low-fat dishes, and lots of salads. Cakes, pies, and crisps—in huge portions—are fine desserts. ♦ American ♦ Daily lunch and dinner; F-Sa until midnight. 311 Third St (at Folsom St). 546.6297 &

## 32 YERBA BUENA SQUARE

With lots of discount and outlet shopping for men, women, and children under one roof, this is a bargain hunter's heaven. The largest store in the complex is the **Burlington Coat Factory Warehouse** (495.7234), which carries a huge supply of coats and just about everything else. **The Shoe Pavilion** (974.1821), with last season's styles from well-known manufacturers at 30 to 70 percent off, is also worth checking out. ♦ Daily. 899 Howard St (at Fifth St). 543.1275

## 33 LuLu

★★★$$ One of the best meals in San Francisco can be had at this recently expanded spot. Formerly three separate eateries, they are now connected throughout and serve the same menu. Fish and tender cuts of meat come slow-cooked from a rotisserie or a wood-burning oven. The food, presented on Italian pottery platters, is served family style. For entrées, consider the roast chicken or the grilled rib eye for two, served over a bed of thinly sliced potatoes and artichokes. Don't miss the fire-roasted chestnuts with white truffle honey. Warm chocolate cake, with a gush of molten chocolate in the center, is the most popular dessert. The dramatic Main Room has a soaring ceiling with a skylight, seating on two levels, and an open kitchen. ♦ French/Italian ♦ Daily lunch and dinner. Reservations recommended. 816 Folsom St (at Fourth St). 495.5775; fax 495.7810 &

## 34 SOUTH PARK CAFE

★★$$ Here's a little bit of Paris overlooking the urban oasis of **South Park.** With the long, narrow room painted in ocher, the cozy bar, and the brief menu, the atmosphere is French cafe all the way. There's blood sausage, steamed mussels, roast pork tenderloin with potato puree, and duck breast with honey, ginger, and cinnamon. Desserts include a classic crème brûlée, profiteroles, and a bittersweet chocolate cake. ♦ French ♦ M-F breakfast, lunch, and dinner; Sa dinner. 108 South Park Ave (between Third and Second Sts). 495.7275

## 35 DELANCEY STREET RESTAURANT

★★$$ This self-described "ethnic American bistro" makes a social statement as well as a culinary one. It's run by residents of the Delancey Street Project, a residential community and training program for former down-and-outers. The handsome copper bar, handcrafted by the residents, and the wood and brass appointments create a modern bistro look. The outdoor patio provides a lovely view of the Bay Bridge and the water-front area. On any given day, the menu might include matzo-ball soup, Szechuan noodles with peanut sauce, Moroccan vegetable stew, or salmon mousse in phyllo. The American fare includes such staples as meat loaf, pot roast, barbecued baby back ribs, and chicken. ♦ American ♦ Tu-F lunch and dinner; Sa-Su brunch and dinner. Reservations recommended. 600 Embarcadero (at Brannan St). 512.5179 &

## 36 US COURT OF APPEALS BUILDING

This Neo-Classical federal building boasts a stone-clad facade and a fine marble-faced postal lobby. The structure by **James Knox Taylor** sustained serious damage in the 1989 earthquake and has been undergoing exten-sive renovations by the architectural firm **Skidmore, Owings & Merrill.** It was sched-uled to reopen by late 1997. ♦ Seventh St (at Mission St)

## 37 CLUB 1015

This is the place to go on weekend nights if you're young and hip and love to dance. The three dance floors each have their own theme (1970s disco, modern, jazz). Underclad, libid-inal dancers hover in wrought-iron cages above the dance floors. It is straight on Friday, gay on Saturday. ♦ Cover. F-Sa 10PM to 7AM. 1015 Folsom St (between Sixth and Seventh Sts). 431.1200

## 38 Brain Wash

★$ This combination laundromat and cafe makes great sense for busy singles who want to accomplish something while they socialize. The 49-seat cafe, separated from the washers and dryers, offers simple foods such as sandwiches, pasta, and chili. The last call for dryers is 9:30PM, but the merriment continues for another hour and a half in the cafe. ♦ Californian ♦ Daily. 1122 Folsom St (at Seventh St). Cafe 861.3663. Laundromat 431.WASH

## 39 Julie's Supper Club

★$$ The deliberately funky retro decor, heavy on 1950s icons that might have come from a pine-paneled rec room of that era, attracts an upwardly mobile crowd of singles to this noisy restaurant and bar with a courtyard. The food aims to be interesting: Try fried wontons, fried calamari, and chicken brochettes. For the main event, the grilled New York steak, leg of lamb, or pork chops will provide the fuel for partying the night away. ♦ American ♦ M-Sa dinner. Reservations recommended. 1123 Folsom St (at Seventh St). 861.0707

## 40 Rainbow Grocery and General Store

Collectively owned and operated, these two-stores-in-one reflect strong environmental positions and countercultural tastes. The grocery stocks a sizeable assortment of organic produce and health foods, while the general store carries a staggering variety of items, from housewares, toiletries and natural-fiber clothing to toys and gemstones. Vitamins and cast-iron ware are offered at particularly attractive prices. ♦ Daily. 1145 Folsom St (between Seventh and Eighth Sts) 863.9200 ♿

## 41 Antonio's Antiques

Very fine 17th- to 19th-century French, English, and continental antiques, including furnishings and accessories, fill three floors here. ♦ M-Sa. 701 Bryant St (at Fifth St). 781.1737

## 42 Fringale Restaurant

★★$$$ Loosely translated, fringale means "I'm starving" in French. Well, anyone who's feeling a mite peckish is in for a treat at this intimate, soothing restaurant. The Basque owners describe their food as "Gallic exotic," and although it's far removed from nouvelle cuisine, the kitchen has an equally light hand with sauces, turning out intriguing dishes such as sautéed sweetbreads and split Basque sausages. ♦ French ♦ M-F lunch and dinner; Sa dinner. Reservations recommended. 570 Fourth St (between Brannan and Bryant Sts). 543.0573

## 43 Bizou

★★★$$ In a romantic old fashioned bistro with hanging light fixtures and glazed mustard-colored walls, Loretta Keller prepares such favorites as tempura-fried green beans, Catalan shrimp, and fresh grilled sardines. The slow-simmered and gently baked dishes are just the thing on a foggy day. Desserts are memorable, especially the summer berry pudding, with its dense, moist, cakey texture and plenty of fruit. ♦ French ♦ M-F lunch and dinner. Reservations recommended. 598 Fourth St (at Brannan St). 543.2222 ♿

## 44 Ristorante Ecco

★★$$ Though changes in the kitchen have caused the food to falter a bit, an always reliable choice, *linguine al Ecco,* is one of the best dishes on the menu—an unlikely mix of linguine, pears, pecans, gorgonzola, and parmesan (ask to have it split into two portions for an appetizer). Another option for starters is the deep-fried squid with fennel and red onion. Main courses include *poussin* (baby chicken) stuffed with olives, salmon served on white beans, and rabbit braised in red wine with mushrooms. ♦ Italian ♦ M-F lunch and dinner; Sa dinner. Reservations recommended. 101 South Park Ave (between Second and Third Sts). 495.3291

## 45 Jack London's Birthplace

A plaque on the Wells Fargo Bank marks the birthplace of this legendary writer. ♦ Brannan St (at Third St)

## 46 San Francisco Fire Department Pumping Station

This stripped-down Classical building houses pumps for the city's elaborate water system designed after the 1906 earthquake and fire. It was built in 1920 by **Frederick Meyer** to

ensure that the city would never again be left without adequate means of fighting a massive fire, even if the water mains from outside were ruptured. ♦ 698 Second St (at Townsend St)

## 46 IT'S TOPS COFFEE SHOP

★$ Breakfast or lunch at this family-run enterprise is like a trip down memory lane. The 1940s influence is everywhere. ♦ American ♦ Daily breakfast and lunch. 1801 Market St (at McCoppin St). 431.6395

## 47 SEA CHANGE

This welded steel sculpture by international artist Mark di Suvero is the entrance to **South Beach Yacht Harbor** and marks the southern end of The Embarcadero. The seventy-foot-tall bright red object, standing on four legs that converge at the top, contains a kinetic piece that moves with the wind. Columnist Herb Caen has likened the sculpture to chopsticks impaling a giant dim sum. ♦ King St (between The Embarcadero and Second St)

## 48 PACBELL PARK

A new baseball stadium opened its doors April 11, 2000 when the San Francisco Giants played their season opener against the Los Angeles Dodgers. Known as "the Miracle on Third Street," PacBell Park combines the feel of an old-fashioned ball park with splendid bay views. It is located beside the bay at China Basin. Most of the 40,800 are taken, except for the upper deck. One-hour tours take place daily. 10a-2p. $10 per person. Buy your tickets online or through Bass. April to October. ♦ King and Third Sts. 972.2000, 800/734.4268, www.sfgiants.com ♿

## 48 TWENTY FOUR

★★★$$$ The Giants may be striking out overhead, but you can be scoring some delicious food from Twenty Four's winning menu. Named after Willie Mays's baseball number, this restaurant features new American cuisine in a smart deco interior directly below the stadium. The aroma of spit-roasted meat and slick upscale interior are the first surprises. You'll enjoy creamy Dungeness crab chowder and seared halibut on cannellini beans, and roasted chicken. Desserts don't hit a home run, but the kitchen is working to improve them. Outdoor seating on warm days. ♦ American ♦ Daily lunch and dinner. 24 Willie Mays Plaza (at Third and King Sts). 644.0240.

## 49 LIMELIGHT

This bookstore specializes in film and theater books. ♦ M-Su. 1803 Market St (between McCoppin and Guerrero Sts). 864.2265 ♿

## 50 BELL'OCCHIO

All kinds of things you never knew you needed but suddenly can't live without, such as imported ribbons, silk roses, unusual toiletries, curious trinkets—mostly European—are here to tempt you. ♦ Tu-Su. 8 Brady St (off Market St, between 12th and Gough Sts). 864.4048

## 51 BEAVER BROS. ANTIQUES AND PROP RENTALS

This is the largest prop-rental shop in San Francisco so, theoretically, you can try the merchandise before buying. Victoriana, bric-a-brac, and an eclectic assortment of other stuff from bygone eras are presented on two jam-packed floors. ♦ Daily. 1637 Market St. 863.8391

## 52 NEW LANGTON ARTS

This nonprofit gallery specializes in experimental (and sometimes controversial) works by American and international artists. The theater presents performance art, literary readings, and jazz in the evenings. ♦ W-Sa. 1246 Folsom St (between Eighth and Ninth Sts). 626.5416 ♿

## 53 THE STUD

Rock, funk, oldies, New Wave, and world-beat music draw a crowd your mother might not approve of. There are some women, but the clientele is mostly male, mostly gay. ♦ Cover on some nights. M-Sa until 2AM. 399 Ninth St (at Harrison St). 863.6623

## 54 THE FLOWER MARKET

This area is fragrant with blossoms and abloom with activity when most of the city sleeps. It's the wholesale center for the floral trade, but some shops also sell retail at very attractive prices. ♦ M-Sa mornings. Sixth St (at Brannan St). 392.7944, 781.8410 ♿

## 55 TRAIN DEPOT

The terminal for the former **Southern Pacific Railroad** line now houses the commuter trains to San Jose. Originally this was the starting point for the famous *Coast Starlight* and *Daylight Express* trains to Los Angeles. The old mission-style station was demolished in 1979 to make way for the current utilitarian structure. ♦ At Fourth and Townsend Sts

## 56 CHINA BASIN BUILDING

If this 1922 warehouse/office building by **Bliss & Faville** were put on end, it would be

## The Best

**Joan Jeanrenaud**

Cellist, Kronos Quartet

**In the morning:**

**North Beach:** Get up and head for **Caffè Puccini** on **Columbus Avenue** for cappuccino, orange juice, and pastries, then wander around, maybe going all the way up to **Coit Tower** for a great walk and vista of beautiful San Francisco.

**In the afternoon:**

**Marin Headlands:** Going north over the **Golden Gate Bridge** are the Marin Headlands. Take the

**Stinson Beach** exit and make a left on **Tennessee Valley Road.** Make sure to stop at the fruit stand on the corner. Go as far as you can until you come to a parking lot. Get out and walk to the beach—even as far as Stinson Beach, or anywhere on the beautiful headlands. Coming here always reminds me of why we live in the Bay Area.

**In the evening:**

**Chez Panisse:** In **Berkeley,** world-renowned, and worth the trip across the bay or halfway around the world! Another choice would be dinner at the **Hayes Street Grill** and an evening at the **San Francisco Opera.**

---

850 feet high and one of the city's tallest structures. In 1988, it was repainted in blue with white stripes to resemble an ocean liner. ♦ 185 Berry St (between Third and Fourth Sts)

## 57 Manora's Thai Cuisine

★★★$$ Many cognoscenti think this is one of the best Thai restaurants in the city. Try the Pooket Skewer—vegetables, scallops, prawns, calamari, mussels, and other seafood served with spicy lemon-garlic and sweet chili sauces; the pork infused with garlic and pepper; or the minced fish steamed in banana leaves. ♦ Thai ♦ M-F lunch and dinner; Sa-Su dinner. 1600 Folsom St (at 12th St). 861.6224. Also at: 3226 Mission St (at Valencia St). 550.0856 ♿

## 58 Hamburger Mary's

★$ Bikers, artists, socialites—in fact, just about every facet of San Francisco's varied population eventually turns up at this noisy, funky, well-entrenched restaurant where ear-splitting music makes conversation almost impossible. The crowd seems to like it that way, and the hamburgers are an undeniable hit. ♦ American ♦ daily lunch and dinner. 1582 Folsom St (at 12th St). 626.5767 ♿

## 59 Paradise Lounge

There's live music seven nights a week and two performance spaces in this counter-cultural hot spot. Downstairs, the "lounge stage" fits audiences of 200, while a larger performance area on the same floor holds up to 450 moving bodies. In **Above Paradise,** the acoustic lounge upstairs, activities include everything from poetry readings to musical performances. The dress code is relaxed. ♦ Cover F-Sa. Daily until 2AM. 1501 Folsom St (at 11th St). 861.6906

## 59 El Bobo

★★$$ This popular, dress-down meeting place for the SoMa set serves dinner seven nights a week. The Venus Chocolate Cake is the "best there is." Live music—from jazz to rockabilly to blues—turns the place into a nightclub. 1539 Folsom St (between 11th and 12th Sts). 255.8552 ♿

## 60 Slim's

Rocker Boz Scaggs is a part owner of this live music-and-dance club, which bills itself as the "home of roots music." Country, jazz, and blues musicians, some well known, some up-and-coming hopefuls, have played here, as has Scaggs himself. ♦ Cover. Daily to 2AM. 333 11th St (between Harrison and Folsom Sts). 522.0333

## 61 Gift Center

Formerly a warehouse, this 1917 **Maurice Couchot** building was renovated in 1984 by **Kaplan/McLaughlin/Diaz** with the construction of a large atrium in place of the original light well. Designed in Art Deco style, its shops are open to wholesalers only (although the restaurants are open to the public); the center is often used for large parties. ♦ 888 Brannan St (at Eighth St). 861.7733

## 62 Diamond and Jewelry Mart

This glass-block building was designed in 1985 by **Tanner, Leddy, Maytum, Stacy Architects** to house showrooms for the computer industry, but Silicon Valley went into an economic decline by the time it was completed. Never used for its intended purpose, it now houses wholesalers catering to the jewelry trade, and it's not open to the public. The building often appears in TV commercials. ♦ 999 Brannan St (at Division St). 255.2718

---

Restaurants/Clubs: Red | Hotels: Purple | Shops: Orange | Outdoors/Parks: Green | Sights/Culture: Blue

# UNION SQUARE

**S**an Francisco's most famous shopping district is the nearest thing to a crossroads you'll find in the city. Union Square, the park for which the area is named, is filled with chess players, trysting lovers, street performers, flowers, and flocks of greedy pigeons. On bordering streets are most of the legendary chic shops, including **Tiffany**, **Hermès**, and **Cartier**, that lure browsers and buyers. It's all here, from the sublime to the sleazy—whether you want high-fashion clothing, an inexpensive souvenir, jewelry, perfume, books, household items, antiques, Oriental rugs, or art.

Musicians, some of outstanding caliber, enliven the area. Many, in fact, play professionally in the evening and use their street time for practice and pocket money. There are street artists with a wide range of talents as well. Adding to the local color, both literally and figuratively, are the curbside flower stands selling whatever blooms

are in season for a bit less than the florists. The flower stands owe their beginning to civic leader and publisher Michael de Young, who in the late 1800s allowed the vendors—usually youngsters of Italian, Belgian, Irish, or Armenian descent—to sell their flowers in front of the de Young building and protected them from the police. They were licensed in 1904, and, as with the cable cars, any attempt to suppress the stands has been halted by a sympathetic public.

**Maiden Lane** is an elegant, tree-lined alley that extends two blocks east of Union Square from **Stockton** to **Kearny Streets.** Once known as **Morton Street** and considered a disreputable area, it now features exclusive shops and sidewalk bistros.

## 1 PETITE AUBERGE

$$ Just a few doors up Bush Street from the **White Swan Inn** is another offspring of the Four Sisters. This one has a French country theme and is more understated, a bit less spacious, and slightly less expensive. But if you can get past the vast collection of teddy bears inhabiting the 26 rooms and the lobby, you'll find the same kind of warmth and family hospitality that characterize its neighbor. A full breakfast is served, but there is no restaurant. Evening turndown service includes a chocolate and a rose on your pillow. ♦ 863 Bush St (between Mason and Taylor Sts). 928.6000; fax 775.5717

## 2 WHITE SWAN INN

$$$ In this era of bustling hotels, this is an exciting and romantic find. The Four Sisters Inns group has managed to turn a 1900 hotel on downtown Bush Street into an English garden retreat that epitomizes charm and quiet good taste. There are 26 rooms, each with a bath, a fireplace, and a refrigerator, all furnished in handsome antiques and lovely fabrics. There's a stunning common room adjacent to a tiny garden, where a bountiful breakfast and tea, including home-baked breads and pastries, are served (there is no restaurant). You may also have sherry and wine by the fireplace and browse through the latest periodicals. Most important of all, the feeling of a real family welcome surrounds every service. ♦ 845 Bush St (between Mason and Taylor Sts). 775.1755; fax 775.5717

## 3 HOTEL TRITON

$$$ The 140 smallish rooms here are stocked with playful and sophisticated modern furniture decorated in a pink-and-gold color scheme. The hotel works hard to ingratiate itself with the fashion and entertainment industry, so expect to rub shoulders with some glitzy folk. They have just added to its celebrity suite collection the Sarah & Vinnie "On-Air" Suite. Other suites include Suite Judy Blue Eyes by Graham Nash, the J. Garcia Suite, the Black Magic Bedroom by Carlos Santana, and the EcoChic Suite by Wyland. Cafe de la Presse serves breakfast, lunch and dinner. ♦ 342 Grant Ave (at Bush St). 394.0500, 800/433.6611; fax 394.0555 &

## 4 LE CENTRAL

★★$$$ Regularly patronized by San Francisco Mayor Willie Brown, this place turns out hearty, tasty fare. The grilled steak topped with roquefort sauce is great, though the provencale cassoulet is even better. ♦ French ♦ M-Sa lunch and dinner. Reservations recommended. 453 Bush St (between Mark La and Grant Ave). 391.2233 &

## The Irish Bank
### Bar & Restaurant

## 4 THE IRISH BANK BAR & RESTAURANT

★★$$ San Francisco's most authentic Irish Bar serves Irish and California cuisine outdoors in warm weather when the alley fills with tables and canvas umbrellas, becoming a great spot for Saturday and Sunday brunch. ♦ Irish ♦ Daily lunch and dinner. 10 Mark La (off Bush St between Claude La and Grant Ave). 788.7152 &

## 5 OBIKO

One-of-a-kind high fashion, most of it created by Bay Area designers, is offered at this cutting-edge shop. ♦ M-Sa. 794 Sutter St (between Taylor and Jones Sts). 775.2882 ♿

## 6 FLEUR DE LYS

★★★★$$$$ Flowered fabric is fashioned into a room-size tent over an impressive arrangement of fresh flowers at the center of the dining area, making a perfect setting for the stunning French/Californian menu. In addition to the impressive à la carte selections, there is a four-course tasting menu beginning with a spectacular "Symphony of Fleur de Lys Appetizers" (which may include a crab cake, a sushi roll slice prepared with quinoa, and a slice of foie gras studded with pecans), followed by an entrée such as venison tournedos on braised endive, herb-crusted rack of lamb, or sautéed veal medaillon. The setting is beautiful and the food is some of the best in the city. ♦ French/Californian ♦ M-Sa dinner. Reservations and jacket required. 777 Sutter St (between Taylor and Jones Sts). 673.7779 ♿

## 7 HOTEL BERESFORD

$ This modest, European-style hotel is located downtown near the theater district. The 114 rooms are small but pristine and comfortable. It's a good value, and family rates are also available. ♦ 635 Sutter St (between Mason and Taylor Sts). 673.9900, 800/533.6533 ♿

Within the Hotel Beresford:

## THE WHITE HORSE TAVERNE

★★$$ This place replicates an Edinburgh pub, and as might be expected, the cooks do a splendid job with grilled meats. Portions are large: The hamburger is a challenge to finish, and the corned beef and cabbage consists of a half-dozen thick slices of meat and half a head of cabbage cut into wedges and arranged on the plate with a boiled potato. ♦ American ♦ Daily breakfast and lunch; Tu-Sa dinner. Reservations recommended for dinner. 673.9900 ♿

## 8 HOTEL SHEEHAN

$ A good location and a decent price here are combined with such amenities as an Olympic-size swimming pool, a reading room, and a large lobby (but no restaurant). This low-budget hotel was formerly a **YWCA;** the

60 rooms have been pleasantly refurbished. ♦ 620 Sutter St (at Mason St). 775.6500, 800/848.1529; fax 775.3271 ♿

## 9 THE ORCHARD

$$$ A full-service European-style hotel in a gracious building dating back to 1907, this hostelry offers a high standard of personalized service. The 94 elegant rooms are equipped with private baths, direct-dial telephones, and minibars. Room service and special secretarial assistance are available around the clock, and there is a daily wine hour. Another plus: It's located just one block from Union Square. ♦ 562 Sutter St (between Powell and Mason Sts). 433.4434, 800/433.4434; fax 433.3695 ♿

## 10 CARTWRIGHT HOTEL

$$ This is yet another downtown hotel that has been redone and prides itself on personal touches. The lobby incorporates large arched windows, giant plants, Oriental rugs, and comfortable seating and reading areas. The 114 rooms are homey, each decorated with antiques and vases of fresh flowers. A continental breakfast is available for a modest price. Complimentary afternoon tea and cakes are served, and there is a wine hour daily. ♦ 524 Sutter St (between Powell and Mason Sts). 421.2865, 800/227.3844; fax 421.2865 ♿

## 11 PASQUALE IANNETTI GALLERY

An extensive collection of prints by old masters up through the 20th century, including Goya, Daumier, Picasso, Miró, and Klee, is housed in this gallery. It also presents changing exhibitions of graphic art. ♦ M-Sa. 531 Sutter St (between Powell and Mason Sts). 433.2771 ♿

## 12 SIR FRANCIS DRAKE HOTEL

$$$ To preserve some of the flair of its namesake, this newly renovated hotel keeps a doorman in full yeoman-of-the-guard attire. The lobby, with murals, crystal chandeliers, mirrors, sweeping marble staircase with bronze balustrade, and vaulted gold-leaf

ceiling, reflects the splendor and romance of the 1930s. Because it is small by the standard of many of its neighbors (435 rooms and suites), it is able to integrate the luxurious advantages of a larger hotel with a more personal approach to hospitality. For the business traveler, there are special rooms available with a desk and seating area for interviews or briefings. **Scala's** bistro offers Italian fare and **Harry Denton's Skylight Room** offers martinis at sunset and dancing to live music. ♦ 450 Powell St (at Sutter St). 392.7755, 800/227.5480; fax 391.8719 &

### 13 CROWNE PLAZA AT UNION SQUARE

$$$ One block from the square, this 400-room hotel offers an ideal location as well as fabulous views of the city. ♦ 480 Sutter St (at Powell St). 398.8900, 800/465.4329; fax 989.8823

### 14 450 SUTTER STREET OFFICE BUILDING

This medical/dental office building clad in undulating terra-cotta was designed by **Timothy Pflueger** and built in 1930. It is a good example of Art Deco architecture. Notice the elaborately designed entrance lobby with its Pre-Columbian styling. ♦ Between Stockton and Powell Sts

### 15 WILKES BASHFORD

Beautiful and expensive designer clothes for men and women are sold in lush surroundings complete with music and wine. Even if your budget can't take the strain of shopping here, stop by to see the witty and surreal window displays. ♦ M-Sa. 375 Sutter St (between Grant Ave and Stockton St). 986.4380 &

### 16 MÉTIER

This elegant boutique sells women's clothing by European and American designers such as Peter Cohen, and Alberto Biani. The jewelry cases display unique works of local artists along with some vintage baubles and bangles. ♦ M-Sa. 355 Sutter St (between Stockton St and Grant Ave). 989.5395

### 17 TEUSCHER CHOCOLATES OF SWITZERLAND

Expensive and delectable Swiss chocolates will tempt the most discriminating sweet tooth. ♦ M-Sa. 255 Grant Ave (between Campton Pl and Sutter St). 398.2700 &

### 17 KRIZIA

Many swear by this boutique, which sells the famed Italian designer's fashions. The sweaters and scarves are as beautiful as they are pricey. ♦ M-Sa. 253 Grant Ave (between Campton Pl and Sutter St). 433.5550

### 18 BANANA REPUBLIC

This specialty chain of shops got its start selling safari-style clothing in an atmosphere that's a lot more comfortable than any jungle. Now much of the Indiana Jones-style gear has been replaced by well-crafted, reasonably priced contemporary fashions. ♦ Daily. 256 Grant Ave (at Sutter St). 788.3087 &

### 19 WINGS AMERICA

Amateur pilots rub shoulders at this emporium, stocked with Aloha shirts, aviator jackets and model planes, including the legendary "Gooney Bird" DC-3. ♦ M-Sa. 262 Sutter St (between Kearny St and Grant Ave). 989.9464 &

### 19 HACKETT FREEDMAN GALLERY

This fourth-floor gallery displays modern American paintings and sculpture. ♦ Tu-Sa. 250 Sutter St (between Kearny St and Grant Ave). 362.362.7152 &

### 20 CAFÉ CLAUDE

★★$ The menu revolves around typical bistro fare, with a few specials chalked on a blackboard. Grazers will love the charcuterie platter, which includes pâté. If cassoulet is on the menu, don't pass it up, and wash it down with a Côtes du Rhône. And for dessert, what else but chocolate mousse? ♦ French ♦ M-Sa lunch, and dinner. 7 Claude La (between Sutter and Bush Sts). 392.3505

### 20 MARGARET O'LEARY

The Irish farm girl-turned-designer who says "A good sweater is like an old friend" shows her stunning collection of soft, elegant chenille sweaters and knitwear. ♦ M-Sa. 1 Claude La (between Sutter and Bush Sts). 391.1010

---

## 21 THE ANDREWS HOTEL

$$ In a city rife with the posh and chic, the principal charm of this small, 48-room hotel lies in its atmosphere of civilized informality. For example, the complimentary breakfast can be carried back to bed on trays from hallway buffets. The cozy rooms are decorated in floral chintz, and each one has a desk, upholstered armchair, and remote control television. The staff is knowledgeable about the city and happy to recommend many favorite places known only to locals. ◆ 624 Post St (between Taylor and Jones Sts). 563.6877, 800/622.0557 in CA, 800/9.ANDREWS; fax 928.6919

Within The Andrews Hotel:

### FINO

★★$$ The arched windows and blazing fireplace make this a romantic place to dine, although the Italian fare is only so-so. Each dish is a variation on a theme: Piccata (lemon-caper) sauce is served on veal, chicken, scallops, salmon, and even beef. Many of the pastas have three too many ingredients; the simpler ones are by far the most successful. One reliable menu choice is the *contadini* (seafood, chicken, or both, served with sausage, prawns, whole garlic cloves, mushrooms, peppers, and other vegetables). ◆ Italian ◆ Daily dinner. 928.2080 &

## 22 THE PRESCOTT HOTEL

$$$ This 166-room hotel is close to Union Square. The Edwardian-era decor features deep jewel tones; amenities include minibars, dryers, and terry-cloth robes. Complimentary evening wine, hors d'oeuvres, coffee, and tea are served. The hottest attraction, however, is that guests have an easier time than ordinary mortals getting a table at **Postrio,** the exciting hotel dining room. There is also room service (provided by the restaurant), and limousine transportation to the Financial District can be arranged. ◆ 545 Post St (between Mason and Taylor Sts). 563.0303, 800/283.7322; fax 563.6831 &

Within The Prescott Hotel:

### POSTRIO

★★★★$$$ Wolfgang Puck's northern California outpost looks like a slice of LA. However, although the ambience is influenced by Hollywood, the inventive food is rooted in San Francisco's strong Italian and Asian heritage. Chefs (and brothers) Steven and Mitchell Rosenthal have put their own spin on Puck's signature cuisine with such creations as garlic lamb stir-fried with mint and fresh chilies, smoked salmon served on a giant blini, and grilled quail accompanied by a soft egg ravioli (pierce the pasta, and the yolk of a quail egg oozes forth). While everyone seems to come here for lunch or dinner, most people don't realize it's also a great downtown breakfast spot. ◆ Californian ◆ M-F breakfast, lunch, and dinner; Sa-Su brunch and dinner. Reservations recommended. 776.7825 &

## 23 DONATELLO HOTEL

$$$ This is indeed a polished jewel. Throughout the hotel there is a tasteful blend of Italian marble, Murano glass, European antiques, and contemporary art. The 95 rooms and 9 suites are larger here than in any other hotel in the city, although some of them could do with new furnishings. Especially appealing are the fifth-floor rooms, which open onto a private terrace. The hotel is the creation of A. Cal Rossi Jr., the hotelier who masterminded the **Stanford Court Hotel,** but here, in the absence of a Nob Hill view, the staff compensates with extraordinary service. ◆ 501 Post St (at Mason St). 441.7100, 800/792.9837 in CA, 800/227.3184; fax 885.8842 &

Within the Donatello Hotel:

### ZINGARI

★★$$$ Owner/chef Giovanni Scorzo of this place, named for the Italian word for "gypsies," has chosen to feature dishes from all over Italy, presented in an elegant, refined style with such menu offerings as broiled calamari topped with fresh tomatoes and basil, grilled and smoked mozzarella cheese served with portobello mushrooms and radiccio (which the menu calls "wild chicory"), and veal loin stuffed with truffles and Fontina cheese, as well as risottos, pasta dishes, and salads. The intimate dining room boasts Venetian marble accents. ◆ Italian ◆ Daily breakfast, lunch, and dinner. Reservations recommended. 885.8850 &

# Streetcars of Desire

San Francisco's beloved cable-car system made its maiden voyage on 1 August 1873. With its Scottish inventor, Andrew Hallidie, at the grip, the car successfully tackled five hilly blocks along **Clay Street** to **Portsmouth Square** in **Chinatown.**

Hallidie, a mine-cable designer during the Gold Rush days, decided to invent the system after witnessing an unfortunate accident on a steep hill: A horse-drawn wagon had rolled backward, dragging the helpless horses behind. Hallidie's system was safer, and it opened up areas in the city previously thought unsuitable for building homes.

Just before the 1906 earthquake, cable cars had reached their peak, with 600 cars traveling a 110-mile route. But the system sustained heavy damage during the quake and fire, and many lines were not rebuilt. Electric trolleys took over some of the lines, and the number of cable cars dwindled over the next 50 years. But in 1955 the city voted to preserve the famed hill-climbers, and in 1964 they became the first moving National Historic Landmark in the United States.

Starting in 1984, at a cost of more than $60 million, the system underwent two years of head-to-toe renovations. Old track and cable vaults were pulled up and replaced. For extra strength, deeper grooved rails and more flexible curves were installed. The track was also realigned or moved to avoid interfering with traffic, and the pulleys and depression beams that guide each cable were replaced. The historic Washington-Mason car barn was completely renovated and its traditional appearance preserved. The cars themselves were given a shiny coat of maroon, blue, and gold paint, as well as new brakes, seats, and wheels.

Today you can choose from three lines: the **Powell-Mason Line;** the **Powell-Hyde Line,** which is said to offer the best views and the most thrilling curves; and the **California Line.** There are 44 cable cars in all, with 27 used at peak times. An average of 13 million passengers travel on the 17 miles of track in a year—about 35,616 people a day.

Each six-ton car attaches itself to a cable beneath the street, moving along at a steady 9.5 miles per hour by the turning of 14-foot wheels located in barns. A cable-car operator starts and stops the car by mechanically gripping the cable to make the car go forward and by releasing it to stop the car. Tension can be adjusted if necessary to keep the cable from slipping.

## 24 THE PAN PACIFIC HOTEL SAN FRANCISCO

$$$ Formerly the **Portman,** this 338-room hotel was designed and built in 1987 by well-known architect **John C. Portman Jr.** The bathrooms are marble with large dressing areas, built-in cabinetry, and telephones. One personal valet is provided for every 7 rooms, and room service is available 24 hours a day. Exemplary personal service, such as having a private car waiting at the airport to drive you into town, is stressed here, but the hotel staff doesn't always live up to this reputation. Business facilities include four conference suites and a boardroom with a private dining facility that provides continuous buffet service for all meetings. Secretarial, translation, and audiovisual services are offered, and computers are available. In addition, there is a solarium, a ballroom, and a rooftop club with breathtaking views for breakfast, tea, or cocktails. ♦ 500 Post St (at Mason St). 771.8600, 800/327.8585; fax 398.0267 &

Within The Pan Pacific Hotel San Francisco:

### PACIFIC

★★★$$$ Located in the hotel lobby, this restaurant features an imaginative selection of the best of each season's produce, offering sautéed lobster accented with the earthy perfume of truffles and the crunch of barely cooked cabbage, and squab touched with truffles, this time in a creamy, rich risotto. In another inspired combination, pheasant is paired with braised cabbage and mashed potatoes with truffles. ♦ Californian/ Asian ♦ Daily breakfast, lunch, and dinner. Reservations recommended for dinner. 929.2087 &

## 25 RUBY SKYE

Featuring art nouveau architecture and plush modern furnishings, this nightclub is one of the most elaborate clubs in the Union Square area. Dance on the main floor or socialize in the Jungle Room. ♦ Nightclub ♦ 420 Mason St (at Geary St) 693-0777. www.rubyskye.com

## 26 THEATRE ON THE SQUARE

Just a half block from Union Square, this 800-seat house has enlivened San Francisco theater by bringing in quality Off-Broadway shows. ♦ 450 Post St (between Powell and Mason Sts). 433.9500 &

## 26 KENSINGTON PARK HOTEL

$$ This former **Elks Lodge** has 84 spacious rooms and one elegant suite with traditional English furniture, damask fabrics of rose and blue, Chippendale-style armoires, and bath-

rooms in marble and brass. Amenities include complimentary breakfast, and tea and sherry are served among the palms every afternoon in the beautifully restored lobby with its hand-painted Gothic ceiling. The views of the city and bay are especially good from the upper corner rooms. ♦ 450 Post St (between Powell and Mason Sts). 788.6400, 800/553.1900; fax 885.3268 &

## 26 FARALLON

★★★★$$$$ From Bristol Bay salmon to Willapa Bay oysters, diners indulge in some of the world's finest piscean pleasures. You will find fish imported from as far away as New Zealand. Since the cuisines of the Americas, Europe, and Asia have influenced seafood cookery, the menu extends to all parts of the globe. Try the Spanish mackerel tartare as an appetizer and continue with pan-seared Alaskan sea scallops. Desserts, particularly the passion fruit cake, are first-rate. In keeping with this high-styled coastal cuisine, the restaurant's illuminated pillars simulate sea kelp and the hand-blown lighting, jellyfish. ♦ Seafood ♦ M-Sa lunch and daily dinner. Reservations required. 450 Post St (between Powell and Mason Sts). 956-6969 &

## 27 THE INN AT UNION SQUARE

$$$ This Georgian-style hotel with excellent personal service offers complimentary continental breakfast, as well as wine and hors d'oeuvres (but no restaurant). There are 30 rooms and suites, all individually decorated with an emphasis on a cozy English-country look, and all equipped with minibars. The concierges have a good inside track on the city. ♦ 440 Post St (between Powell and Mason Sts). 397.3510, 800/288-4346; fax 989.0529 &

## 28 BORDERS BOOKS AND MUSIC

If you can't find it here, it probably isn't in print: This mammoth store carries over

160,000 book titles and an extensive music and video selection. There's also an espresso bar. ♦ Daily. 400 Post St (at Powell St). 399.1633. Also at Stonestown Galleria, 19th Ave (at Winston St). 731.0665; www.borders.com ♿

## 29 CHANCELLOR HOTEL

$$$ A fixture on Union Square since 1914, this hotel has an intact Edwardian exterior, which is both solid and soundproofed. Its 137 rooms are fresh and contemporary. The Art Deco **Clipper Ship** lounge—once a popular meeting place for World War II servicemen—has been restored to serve as a party and meeting room. It still contains an 85-foot aerial-photo mural of San Francisco from 1935. Rates, always a bargain for those in the know, have not changed much and are definitely moderate for this prime location. There's a restaurant, **The Chancellor Cafe,** which serves Californian/Italian cuisine, and room service is also available. ♦ 433 Powell St (between Post and Sutter Sts). 362.2004, 800/428.4748; fax 362.1403 ♿

## 30 SAKS FIFTH AVENUE

**Hellmuth, Obata & Kassabaum** designed this building in 1981. The upscale store has escalators that can drive shoppers to distraction, forcing them to walk halfway around the store on each floor to ascend or descend, take the elevator if you're in a hurry. On the fifth floor is a pleasant, sunny restaurant with sometimes good, sometimes so-so food, popular with ladies-who-lunch. ♦ Daily. 384 Post St (at Union Sq). 986.4300 ♿

## 31 TIFFANY & CO.

Bluebloods come here for their blue-ribbon baubles. ♦ M-Sa. 350 Post St (at Union Sq). 781.7000 ♿

## 32 GRAND HYATT HOTEL

$$$$ Rising 36 stories above Union Square, this 693-room hotel is in the heart of the city and offers extensive services for business travelers, including language translation, business-equipment rental, and shipping and mailing, plus all the latest news on business and investor services. Within the hotel is the elegant **Grandview Restaurant and Lounge,** with a breathtaking view. The **Regency Club** comprises floors set aside for guests who pay a surcharge. These smartly decorated rooms include honor bars, concierge services, and complimentary breakfasts. There are also six penthouse suites serviced by trained butlers. ♦ 345 Stockton St (between Post and Sutter Sts). 398.1234, 800/233.1234; fax 392.2536 ♿

Within the Grand Hyatt Hotel:

## GRANDVIEW

★★★$$$ This 36th floor restaurant offers incredible views of Golden Gate Bridge, Alcatraz, Coit Tower, Nob Hill and to the west dramatic sunsets. Chef Chad Minton's cuisine is as visually arresting. Some of his more creative creations include heirloom tomato ceviche, salmon confit, truffle fettuccine, and rack of lamb. Try the sorbet tasting for dessert. ♦ California/French ♦ Daily breakfast, lunch, dinner. 398.1234

In the Grand Hyatt Hotel plaza:

## RUTH ASAWA FOUNTAIN

Created by and named for the noted San Francisco artist, a bronze-relief frieze made up of 41 plaques covers the circular wall of the fountain bowl. Thousands of sculptured figures on the plaques charmingly depict different aspects of the city, from the swaying palms of Mission Dolores to Victorian houses with gingerbread trim. The plaques were modeled from bread dough before being cast in metal, expressing the artist's philosophy that art and everyday life are interrelated.

## 33 CAMPTON PLACE

$$$$ This small and luxurious hotel a half block from **Union Square** used to be the **Old Drake Wilshire.** Although the ambience and decor are stunning, it is the service and extra touches usually found only in Europe's top hotels that the staff likes to emphasize. Professional valets pack and unpack for you, a French laundry and dry-cleaning service is available in-house, secretarial assistance is immediate, shoes are shined every night, and each of the 136 rooms contains a desk and fresh flowers. Corner suites are cozy. Tea is served daily from 2:30 to 4:30PM in the bar. ♦ 340 Stockton St (at Campton Pl). 781.5555, 800/647.4007 in CA, 800/426.3135; fax 955.8536 ♿

Within Campton Place:

## CAMPTON PLACE RESTAURANT

★★★$$$$ The hotel's dining room is the epitome of conservative elegance: quiet, understated, and comfortable. Head chef Todd Humphries presents familiar dishes in interesting new ways. The result is gourmet Californian cuisine. Recommended are the duck breast with baby turnips, kumquats, and kafir lime leaves or pork chops with cardamon, cabbage, apples, bacon, and chestnuts. The wine list is extensive and is considered one of the best in town. ♦ Californian ♦ Daily breakfast, lunch, and dinner. Reservations recommended. 955.5555 ♿

---

Restaurants/Clubs: Red | Hotels: Purple | Shops: Orange | Outdoors/Parks: Green | Sights/Culture: Blue

### 34 ANJOU

★★$$$ Enjoy a charming French ambience in this two-level dining room. The menu created by chef-owner Pierre Morin strikes a balance between tradition and innovation: There's tender duck confit on portobello mushrooms and herb polenta; asparagus with puff pastry in a morel-studded cream sauce; and a casserole of prawns and artichokes. On the classic side, consider the thin-cut New York steak with extra-crisp fries or the calves' brains sautéed with sage, with the *tarte tatin* (upside-down apple tart) for dessert. ♦ French ♦ Tu-Sa lunch and dinner. 44 Campton Pl (off Stockton St, between Post and Sutter Sts). 392.5373

### 35 JAEGER

Fine woolen sportswear imported from England is stocked in this store. ♦ M-Sa. 272 Post St (between Grant Ave and Stockton St). 421.3714 &

### 35 NIKETOWN

Opened in 1997, this athletic-ware shop offers Nike shoes and apparel on 3 shopping levels. ♦ Daily M-Sa 10AM-8PM; Sun 11AM-7PM. 278 Post St (at Stockton St). 392.6453 &

### 36 ERIKA MEYEROVICH GALLERY

Works by the biggest names in the art world—including Pablo Picasso, Henri Matisse, Marc Chagall, David Hockney, Frank Stella, and Andy Warhol—are shown by this sleek gallery owned by Russian émigrés. ♦ M-Sa. 251 Post Ave (between Grant Ave and Stockton St). 421.7171 &

### 37 ALFRED DUNHILL OF LONDON

Famous for its pipes, cigars, humidors, and lighters, this firm sells leather goods as well. ♦ Daily. 250 Post St (at Stockton St). 781.3368 &

### 38 CARTIER

The jewelry, watches, and other trinkets from this renowned French firm are for those who don't have to look at price tags. ♦ M-Sa. 231 Post St (between Grant Ave and Stockton St). 397.3180 &

### 39 SHREVE & CO.

Established in 1862, this retailer showcases fine jewelry, crystal, and silver in a setting suffused with grand architectural touches from a bygone era. ♦ Daily. 200 Post St (at Grant Ave). 421.2600 &

### 40 JOHN BERGGRUEN GALLERY

This prestigious gallery occupies three floors and handles some of the most celebrated names in American art. ♦ M-Sa. 228 Grant Ave (between Post and Sutter Sts). 781.4629 &

### 40 MALM

Established by a leather craftsman who arrived in San Francisco in 1856, this is one of the city's oldest businesses. It's still operated by the same family, which caters to the carriage trade with fine luggage and travel accessories. ♦ M-Sa. 222 Grant Ave (between Post and Sutter Sts). 392.0417. Also at: The Galleria at Crocker Center (Montgomery St at Kearny St). 391.5222.

### 41 COACH LEATHER

This chain store offers a wide variety of sturdy leather bags and accessories. ♦ M-Sa. 190 Post St (at Grant Ave). 392.1772 &

### 42 MAXMARA

Prices are steep here at the first US retail store opened by this Italian manufacturer of high-quality women's clothing. But fashionables swear the values are terrific when compared with other big names in the garment business. ♦ M-Sa. 177 Post St (between Kearny St and Grant Ave). 981.0900 &

### 43 BROOKS BROTHERS

Classic clothes for men and women are the stock in trade at this refined haberdashery. ♦ Daily. 150 Post St (between Grant Ave and Kearny St). 397.4500 &

### 44 WILLIAMS-SONOMA

The well-known cookware chain got its start almost 40 years ago, when it was launched by Chuck Williams. (Williams originally owned a hardware store in Sonoma, hence the name.) The merchandise at this flagship store, beautifully displayed on two floors, offers the serious cook the best in equipment, as well as domestic giftware, and gourmet foods. ♦ Daily. 150 Post St (between Kearny St and Grant Ave). 362.6904. Also at: 2 Embarcadero Center (at Clay and Sacramento Sts). 421.2033 &

## 45 GUMP'S

S.G. Gump & Company was founded in 1865 by German immigrants and former linen merchants, and is now world-famous for jade and pearls, Asian treasures, and the largest collection in the country of fine china and crystal, including such prestigious names as Baccarat, Steuben, and Lalique. There is a bridal registry. ♦ M-Sa. 135 Post St (between Kearny St and Grant Ave). 982.1616 &

## 46 RIZZOLI BOOKSTORE

The West coast branch of this exclusive New York bookstore carries the largest collection of hard cover bestsellers and art books. It's like browsing the library of an Italian count. ♦ M-Sa. 117 Post St (between Kearny St and Grant Ave). 984.0225 &

## 47 BROOKS CAMERAS

In business for more than 50 years, this firm deals in new and used cameras and does video transfers and camera repairs. ♦ M-Sa. 125 Kearny St (between Post and Sutter Sts). 362.4708 &

## 48 SAVOY HOTEL

$$ Renovated by the same couple who revamped the Sherman House in Pacific Heights, this 83-room hotel in a 1915 building now has the feel of a country inn in Provence, with down comforters, old-fashioned etchings, and other homey touches. A continental breakfast is served every morning, and the hotel prides itself on excellent service. ♦ 580 Geary St (at Jones St). 441.2700, 800/227.4223; fax 441.2700 ext 297 &

Within the Savoy Hotel:

### BRASSERIE SAVOY

★★★$$ Some of the best casual French food in the city is offered here. The three-course pretheater dinner is a good value, generally beginning with a simple salad and ending with rich crème brûlée. On the à la carte menu, the duck confit is perfectly highlighted by French lentils, *frisée* (curly endive) and a red wine vinaigrette. The roast chicken set on a bed of mushrooms and garlic mashed potatoes is comfort food at its best. ♦ French ♦ Daily dinner. Reservations recommended. 441.8080 &

## 49 SHANNON COURT HOTEL

$$ This landmark Spanish-style building has 169 large rooms and 5 suites, many with views. The hotel often offers special rates that make the already reasonably priced rooms an extraordinarily good value. ♦ 550 Geary St (between Taylor and Jones Sts). 775.5000; fax 928.6813 &

Within the Shannon Court Hotel:

### LITSU

★★$$ This Art Nouveau bistro turns out some excellent straightforward food. The open kitchen is dominated by a rotisserie. One of the top main-course choices, and by far the best value, is the roast chicken, served with crunchy double-cooked fries. Wine prices are excellent, but the service can be a little disjointed. ♦ Californian ♦ M breakfast and dinner; Tu-Su breakfast, lunch, and dinner. 441.4442 &

## 50 HAROLD'S INTERNATIONAL NEWSSTAND

Magazines and newspapers from abroad and out-of-state are sold to those who want to keep in touch with hometown happenings. ♦ Daily. 524 Geary St (between Taylor and Jones Sts). 441.2665 &

## 51 THE CLIFT HOTEL

$$$$ It's been a San Francisco landmark for almost 80 years. As always, its high standards and individualized attention bring its loyal following back time and time again. Guests call their own shots here. If celebrities wish to come and go so no one knows they are in town, the hotel protects them. If they want a press conference, the hotel can arrange that, too. There are 329 guest rooms furnished simply and elegantly, with many suite combinations. The amenities include extraordinary service and a fine afternoon tea served in the **Redwood Room.** Another plus is the location—two blocks from Union Square, two blocks from the airport bus terminal, and adjoining the theater district. ♦ 495 Geary St (at Taylor St). 775.4700, 800/332.3442; fax 441.4621 &

Within the Clift Hotel:

*The French Room*

### THE FRENCH ROOM

★★$$$$ It's hard to imagine a prettier place to eat. The Caesar salad is superb, as are the veal and fish, particularly the grilled to order Norwegian salmon. This is also the place to splurge on dessert—the chocolate obsession is impossible to resist. ♦ Californian/French ♦ Daily lunch; Tu-Sa dinner; Su brunch. Reservations recommended. 775.4700 &

---

Restaurants/Clubs: Red | Hotels: Purple | Shops: Orange | Outdoors/Parks: Green | Sights/Culture: Blue

## REDWOOD ROOM

★$$ Soaring 22-foot fluted columns and an elegant 75-foot bar decorated with fine Italian marble highlights and Klimt reproductions complete the magnificent Art Deco look. The "bistro" menu lists a nice selection of snacks and light lunch choices. Start with a traditional French onion soup or a Caesar salad, and move on to a Clift burger with crisp Canadian bacon and melted Swiss cheese, smoked turkey club sandwich with avocado, or chicken or shrimp stir-fry with Shanghai noodles. ♦ Californian/French ♦ Daily lunch and dinner (unless closed for a private party). Reservations required. 775.4700 &

## 52 THE WARWICK REGIS HOTEL

$$$ This hotel offers 80 rooms and suites in the heart of the theater district, and within strolling distance of Union Square. The decor is a mix of French and English antiques, including canopied beds and armoires. Some suites offer fireplaces. There are facilities for business travelers, 24-hour room service, and a concierge. ♦ 490 Geary St (between Mason and Taylor Sts). 928.7900, 800/82REGIS; fax 441.8788

Within The Warwick Regis Hotel:

## LA SCENE CAFE AND BAR

★★$$$ A pleasant spot before or after the theater, this richly appointed room is graced with sketches of performers who have appeared at the **Curran Theatre.** The ever-changing à la carte menu features such dishes as apple and fennel salad with gorgonzola and walnuts dressed with a pear vinaigrette; spicy calamari dipped in lemon-caper aioli; polenta napoleon with goat cheese, pesto, and mushroom ragout; and grilled salmon in butternut squash sauce with roasted Peruvian potatoes. The pretheater three-course fixed-price menu is a great deal. ♦ Mediterranean ♦ Tu-Sa dinner. 292.6430 &

## 53 HOTEL DIVA

$$ This hotel's leather, marble, glass, and chrome Euro-tech look often lures the style-conscious business traveler, but there are also classic creature comforts like down comforters and VCRs in all of the 110 rooms and suites. Each minifridge is stocked with refreshments, and original art adorns the walls. Valet parking and an in-room continental breakfast are also provided. The choice location, opposite the **Curran** and **Geary Theaters** and two blocks from Union Square, and the accommodating staff make it a most rewarding stay. The hotel's restaurant, the **California Pizza Kitchen,** provides the room service. ♦ 440 Geary St (between Mason and Taylor Sts). 885.0200, 800/553.1900; fax 885.3268 &

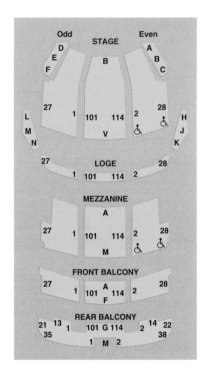

## 54 CURRAN THEATRE

Coproducers Carole Shorenstein Hayes and James M. Nederlander advertise this 1,678-seat theater (see the seating plan above) as the chief pit stop for their *Best of Broadway* series. The live and sometimes lively productions can be worth the hefty ticket price. Avoid the rear balconies unless you're a lip reader—the acoustics are impossible. ♦ 445 Geary St (between Mason and Taylor Sts). 474.3800 &

## 55 GEARY THEATER

Home to the renowned **American Conservatory Theater (ACT),** this Edwardian-style theater opened in 1910 during the city's renaissance after the devastating earthquake and fire of 1906. The theater regained its lost glamour after a $27.5-million restoration and seismic upgrade. ♦ 415 Geary St (at Mason St). ACT box office 749.2228 &

## 56 THE MAXWELL

$$ America's jazz age was the inspiration for this newly restored hotel with midnight colors, plush bedding and hand-painted lamp shades in 153 rooms. **Max's Cafe,** the hotel's American restaurant, serves breakfast, lunch, and dinner in a 1940's interior. Try the lemon meringue pie. ♦ 386 Geary St (at Mason St). 986.2000, 888/SF-4-MAXX; fax 397.2447

## 57 KING GEORGE HOTEL

$$$ This quaint hotel lives up to its billing as a unique antique in the center of the city. Its

location is superb—in the theater district and within walking distance of the many restaurants and shops on Union Square. The hotel, built in 1914 for the Panama-Pacific Exposition, is tall and narrow, much like an Amsterdam canal house. Its nine floors house 143 rooms, all with private baths and in-room safes. Continental breakfast is available daily, and English high tea is served Wednesday through Sunday, complete with scones, crumpets, and finger sandwiches (but there's no restaurant). ◆ 334 Mason St (between O'Farrell and Geary Sts). 781.5050, 800/288.6005; fax 391.6976 ⑤

## 58 HANDLERY UNION SQUARE

$$$ Some poetic license has gone into the naming of this 375-room hotel, which, strictly speaking, is near but not on Union Square. There is a heated outdoor pool and a multilingual staff. Traditional Italian-style food, as interpreted in San Francisco, is served in **New Joe's Restaurant.** There is also a cocktail lounge. ◆ 351 Geary St (between Powell and Mason Sts). 781.7800, 800/843.4343; fax 781.0269 ⑤

## 59 WESTIN ST. FRANCIS HOTEL

$$$$ The second-oldest hotel in the city, this has been a focal point for the social events in San Francisco's history for many years. Royalty, political leaders, literati, and theatrical stars have all made it their headquarters. The hotel was built in 1904 by Charles T. Crocker and his friends to cope with what they felt were inadequate accommodations for the new class of bonanza kings and their entourages. Much effort was made to initiate new ideas for better service: electric grills that cooked a steak in five minutes, perambulators that brought food to the tables, a pneumatic tube that sent service orders to the dining room instantly, and pipes that dumped ocean water into the Turkish baths. After severe earthquake damage in 1906, the reconstructed hotel was so successful that an addition brought the room total to 750, making it the largest hotel on the Pacific Coast. Presently, the newly renovated hotel has 1,192 rooms, 83 suites, and a **Grand Ballroom** that can handle 1,500 revelers, plus 3 restaurants and a lounge. The St. Francis Health Club (774.0357) offers La Stone therapy at this new full-service spa. The fitness center is stocked with Cybex machines and training equipment. Outdoor glass elevators offer a stunning view of the city at a spritely 1,000 feet per minute. ◆ 335 Powell St (at Union Sq). 397.7000, 800/228.3000; fax 774.0200 ⑤

Within the Westin St. Francis Hotel:

## COMPASS ROSE

★★$$ Adjoining the lobby is this luxurious room with an antique-like decor. The menu offers typical Californian cuisine presented with somewhat inconsistent quality. Start your meal with crispy shrimp tempura or a plate of assorted vegetables with basil-yogurt dip, then move on to pan-seared salmon with fried capers, ahi tuna, or broiled Black Angus tenderloin. At the bar, you can munch on some of the appetizers from the regular menu, as well as pizza topped with smoked chicken. A full tea is still served in the afternoon. ◆ Californian ◆ Daily lunch, afternoon tea, and dinner. Reservations recommended. 774.0167

## DEWEY'S

★$$ This sports bar is a fun place to grab a bite and catch your favorite team on one of the many TV sets. Decent cappuccino and excellent house-baked pastries hit the spot at breakfast, while pizzas and sandwiches step up to the plate for lunch and dinner. Decorated in traditional pub style, with wood paneling, scattered tables, and bar stools, the bar features over 50 different beers. ◆ American ◆ Daily breakfast, lunch, and dinner. 774.0169 ⑤

## 60 UNION SQUARE

Since 1850, this plaza has been the heart of downtown San Francisco. The 2.6-acre park,

---

filled with flowers, trees, box hedges, benches, and crisscrossing paths, is in the midst of the city's most bustling shopping area. Its name commemorates a Civil War rally during which demonstrators pledged their loyalty to the Union. A granite shaft celebrating the victory of Admiral Dewey's fleet at Manila Bay during the Spanish-American War marks the center of the square. The face of the bronze statue of *Victory* (pictured on p. 47) atop the monument was modeled after a well-known San Francisco benefactor, Mrs. Adolph de Bretteville Spreckels. ♦ Bounded by Stockton and Powell Sts, and Geary and Post Sts

On Union Square:

## San Francisco Ticket Box Office Service

Nicknamed **STBS** (which is pronounced "stubs" by the locals), this nonprofit facility offers half-price tickets (plus a nominal service charge) on the day of the performance to selected cultural events. Also offered are full-price advance tickets, **BASS (Bay Area Seating Service)** tickets to events throughout the region, and **MUNI** bus passes. ♦ Tu-Sa. Stockton St (at Union Sq, between Geary and Post Sts). 433.STBS &

## Gray Line Tours

Tickets are sold here for local and out-of-city bus tours. Night tours of the city depart from this location, while day tours leave from 425 Mission Street. ♦ Tickets sold daily 8AM-7PM. Powell St. Schedule information 558.9400 &

## 61 Bally of Switzerland

This upscale manufacturer sells footwear, leather goods, and clothing for men and women. ♦ Daily. 238 Stockton St (across from Union Sq). 398.7463 &

"One day if I do go to heaven. . . I'll look around and say, 'It ain't bad, but it ain't San Francisco.'"

—Herb Caen

In 1985 a confused whale that the public named Humphrey hogged the headlines. The great humpback mammal swam beneath the Golden Gate Bridge and then got lost in the Sacramento-San Joaquin River Delta, where he remained until underwater loudspeakers coaxed him back to the open sea by emitting sounds of prey. Humphrey left, but he must have enjoyed all the attention—he's returned several times.

## 62 Gucci

The expanse of brass, marble, and fine woodwork at this world-renowned retailer creates a luxurious environment for those with lots of money to spend on clothes, leather goods, and accessories. ♦ Daily. 200 Stockton St (across from Union Sq). 392.2808 &

## 62 Hermès of Paris

The prices are heart-stopping at this internationally based boutique, where finesse and quality reign supreme in leather goods, scarves, gloves, ties, and clothing for men and women. It is also one of the few places in town where equestrians can purchase a saddle. ♦ Daily. 212 Stockton St (between Geary St and Maiden Lane). 391.7200 &

## 63 Neiman Marcus

**Philip Johnson** and **John Burgee**'s architecturally underwhelming design—both inside and out—has provoked heated debate among San Franciscans since it was built in 1982. Many opposed the destruction of the **City of Paris,** a popular store occupying the site since 1896. A compromise stipulated that the building should incorporate the enormous glass dome that surmounted the old store. At Yuletide, the store erects the most dramatic Christmas tree in the city. ♦ Daily. 150 Stockton St (at Geary St). 362.3900 &

Within Neiman Marcus:

## The Rotunda

★$$ The centerpiece of this elegant restaurant on the fourth floor is the impressive stained-glass dome from the **City of Paris** department store, the site's former occupant. The dome lends a warm, romantic glow to the tiered dining room that wraps around the atrium. Popular dishes include the lobster club sandwich, the oven-roasted chicken with mustard sauce, and the smoked-salmon salad. This is one of the most elegant places for afternoon tea. They serve popovers warm from the oven with strawberry butter. ♦ Californian ♦ Daily lunch. Reservations recommended. 362.4777 &

## 64 Joan & David

Fine footwear for men and women, handbags, and accessories are sold in a dramatic chrome-and-black environment. ♦ Daily. 172 Geary St (between Grant Ave and Stockton St). 397.1958 &

## 65 Maiden Lane

When this exclusive lane was known as Morton Street, it enjoyed a less-than-chic reputation. Up until 1906, when a fire gutted the area, prostitutes sat at open windows and solicited passersby, and there was an average of two murders a week. Gradually, shops took the place of bordellos, and as entrepreneurs struggled to change their street's image, Morton was changed to Maiden in the hopes of sparking a new era—and it has. Except for the occasional delivery truck, today it is a pedestrian-only way lined with fashionable boutiques. On nice days, tables are set out in front of the **Nosheria** and other luncheonettes for alfresco dining. ♦ Between Kearny and Stockton Sts

## 65 CHANEL

One of Maiden Lane's most elegant and exquisite boutiques has three floors of women's clothing and cosmetics by the famous French design house. Some men's accessories are sold here as well. ♦ Daily. 155 Maiden La (between Grant Ave and Stockton St). 981.1550 &

## 66 BRITEX FABRICS

Everything for the seamstress and tailor is offered at this huge store, from exquisite designer fabrics and notions to a whole floor filled with drastically reduced remnants. ♦ M-Sa. 146 Geary St (between Grant Ave and Stockton St). 392.2910 &

## 67 BOTTEGA VENETA

Handmade and pricey leather bags and shoes, scarves, ties, and luggage are available from this famed Italian manufacturer. ♦ M-Sa. 108 Geary St (between Grant Ave and Stockton St). 981.1700 &

## 68 CRATE & BARREL

You'll find great values in well-designed contemporary glassware, dishes, and gifts for the home. ♦ Daily. 125 Grant Ave (at Maiden Lane). 986.4000 &

## 69 FRANK LLOYD WRIGHT BUILDING

This exquisite building designed by **Frank Lloyd Wright** in 1948 has a spiral ramp leading to the upper floor; it was one of the prototypes for the architect's Guggenheim Museum in New York City. The brick exterior has a superbly detailed arched entrance. The gallery within features folk art from around the world. ♦ Daily. 140 Maiden La (between Grant Ave and Stockton St). 392-9999 &

## FOLK ART INTERNATIONAL, XANADU TRIBAL ARTS AND BORRETTI AMBER & DESIGN

These galleries offer a collection of ethnographic and tribal art form from around the world. Ceramics, textiles, furniture and jewelry are the draws here. ♦ M-Sa; Su noon-6PM in summer. &

## 70 CHRISTOFLE

Merchandise from the Paris-based silversmiths (purveyors to the courts of Louis Philippe and Napoléon III) is offered for those with a taste for fine things. ♦ M-Sa. 140 Grant Ave (at Maiden La). 399.1931 &

## 71 BISTRO 69

★$$ Oversize sandwiches, salads, and espresso draw regulars to this unpretentious cafeteria with alfresco dining. ♦ American ♦ M-Sa breakfast and lunch. 69 Maiden La (near Grant Ave). 398.3557 &

## 72 GALLERY PAULE ANGLIM

Celebrated contemporary American artists as well as emerging artists are showcased. ♦ Tu-Sa. 14 Geary St (between Kearny St and Grant Ave). 433.2710 &

## 73 871 FINE ARTS GALLERY AND BOOKSTORE

Contemporary and modern artists are represented here. The gallery was originally at 871 Folsom Street until earthquake damage in 1989 forced a move but not a change of

---

Restaurants/Clubs: Red | Hotels: Purple | Shops: Orange | Outdoors/Parks: Green | Sights/Culture: Blue

name. ♦ Tu-Sa. 49 Geary St, Suite 513, (between Kearny St and Grant Ave). 543.5155

### 73 FRAENKEL GALLERY

This gallery exhibits 19th- and 20th-century fine photography exclusively, including the work of Diane Arbus, Garry Winogrand, Carleton E. Watkins, and Edward Weston. ♦ Tu-Sa. 49 Geary St (between Kearny St and Grant Ave), Fourth floor. 981.2661

### 74 N. PEAL CASHMERE

This shop is cashmere heaven for men and women and includes one of the largest selections of cashmere socks in the world. ♦ M-Sa. 40 Grant St (between Geary and Market Sts). 421.2713 &

### 75 PACIFIC BAY INN

$ Simple, unpretentious, and very inexpensive, this family-owned, European-style inn with 84 rooms is located a few blocks from Union Square. Amenities include 24-hour desk and concierge service, and free in-room videos. For the price, location, and quality, this is one of the best deals in the city. ♦ 520 Jones St (at O'Farrell St). 673.0234, 800/343.0880 in CA, 800/445.2531; fax 673.4781 &

Adjoining the Pacific Bay Inn:

### DOTTIE'S TRUE BLUE CAFE

★★★$ Pancakes and house-baked breads are the lure of this breakfast and lunch spot. A recent change in ownership has brought an increase in vegetarian offerings, especially at lunch, like the roasted eggplant sandwich with goat cheese and tomatoes, black bean chili, and vegetable-filled tarts. ♦ American ♦ Sa-Su breakfast. 522 Jones St (at O'Farrell St). 885.2767 &

### 76 NAPA VALLEY WINERY EXCHANGE

This retail wine boutique features hard-to-find wines, mostly from (surprise!) the Napa Valley. It will ship them, too. ♦ M-Sa. 415 Taylor St (between O'Farrell and Geary Sts). 771.2887 &

### 77 PONZU

★★★$$ From Bangkok to Beijing, diners can snack their way around the Pacific Rim on the chef's selection of small plates. These may include Saigon shrimp with green papaya and chile-mint sauce; rice paper crab and green mango spring rolls with tamarind dip; and red curry clay pot with kaffir lime and green sauce. The restaurant's velvet drapes and table lighting is dramatic and as seductive as the menu. Californian/Asian. Daily dinner. Reservations recommended. 401 Taylor St (at O'Farrell St). 775.7979 &

### 78 SAN FRANCISCO HILTON AND TOWERS

$$$$ Popular with conventioneers, this block-square hotel is the largest on the West Coast (2,000 rooms total, of which 156 are suites). Forty-four guest rooms are equipped for guests with disabilities, and 110 nonsmoking rooms are available. Some rooms are located poolside. The **Towers** form a hotel within a hotel, with seven floors of exclusive services, including a private lounge with complimentary continental breakfast and a cocktail hour. A health club, four ballrooms, and several restaurants are among the facilities. Don't miss the **Cityscape** restaurant and bar, which offers a stunning 360° view of the city. ♦ 333 O'Farrell St (between Mason and Taylor Sts). 771.1400, 800/HILTONS; fax 771.6807 &

### 79 VILLA FLORENCE

$$ This is a princess of a hotel only a few yards from Union Square. The lobby is pretty, with wood-burning fireplaces, murals of Florentine scenes, and fresh flowers abloom everywhere. The 183 bedrooms are gracious, with high ceilings and country-house chintz. Amenities include complimentary morning limousine service to the Financial District and coffeemakers and refrigerators in every room. ♦ 225 Powell St (between O'Farrell and Geary Sts). 397.7700, 800/553.4411; fax 397.1006

Within the Villa Florence:

### KULETO'S ITALIAN RESTAURANT

★★$$ Crowds and a large open kitchen makes this trattoria boisterous yet a seat at the counter can be fun: watch the always-harried chefs pull wonderful pizzas from the oven and exceptional roasted meats from the rotisserie. Pastas are good, too—especially the penne with lamb sausage and red chard in a marinara sauce—though on particularly busy nights the food can be lackluster. The adjoining **Caffè Kuleto** serves espresso drinks, focaccia, panini, and gelato at outdoor tables during the day. ◆ Italian ◆ Daily breakfast, lunch, and dinner. Reservations recommended. 397.7720 &

# Macy's

## 80 MACY'S

A wide variety of merchandise, mostly in the middle-to-high price range, can be found in two buildings across the street from each other. The store that extends to Union Square includes mini-boutiques of designer fashions for women, cosmetics, and home furnishings. The food court in the basement has outlets for **Boudin's Bakery and Café, Ben and Jerry's Ice Cream, Jamba Juice,** and **Wolfgang Puck.** The other structure focuses on menswear, children's clothing, and electronics, and has **Fresh Choice** for more leisurely dining. ◆ Daily. 170 O'Farrell St (at Stockton St). 397.3333 &

Within Macy's:

## CHEESECAKE FACTORY

★★$$ A huge hit with locals and visitors, the restaurant has a terrace overlooking Union Square for outdoor dining. The menu features over 200 items (salads, pizza, chicken) and 40 varieties of cheesecake. ◆ American ◆ 391.4444. &

## 81 F.A.O. SCHWARZ

This three-story branch of the world-famous toy emporium has a live red-coated soldier on duty at the front door to enchant pedestrians of all ages. Don't miss touring the store during the holiday season in November and December—the place puts on quite a display for kids of all ages. ◆ Daily. 48 Stockton St (at O'Farrell St). 394.8700 &

## 82 EMPORIO ARMANI BOUTIQUE

This opulent mini-emporium is the product of a multimillion-dollar renovation of the former **Security Pacific Bank,** built in 1911 and designed by **Bliss & Faville.** The result is breathtaking—racks of beautiful clothes

surrounding a beautiful cafe staffed by an army of beautiful people. If you're hungry (and if you have any money left), take a seat at the counter and share a platter of antipasta misto (assorted appetizers) with a glass of merlot. ◆ Shop: daily. Cafe: daily lunch. 1 Grant Ave (between Market and O'Farrell Sts). 677.9400 &

## 82 PHELAN BUILDING

One of San Francisco's best flatiron buildings, designed by **William Curlett** and built in 1908, this cream-colored, terra-cotta-clad building may have been the inspiration for more recent flatirons, such as the one at 388 Market Street. ◆ 760 Market St (at Grant Ave)

## 83 WELLS FARGO BANK BUILDING

**Clinton Day**'s Beaux Arts design presents a gently curved facade on Market Street. The building complements its classical neighbor, the former **Security Pacific Bank** across the street (now the **Emporio Armani Boutique**). ◆ 744 Market St (at Grant Ave)

## 84 RAMADA INN AT UNION SQUARE

$$$ Formerly the **Hotel Mark Twain,** this hotel has a pleasant lobby and 119 comfortable rooms, all appointed with refrigerators and coffeemakers. Its historical distinction is that it was where the late jazz singer Billie Holiday was arrested for drug possession in 1949. A suite has been named in her honor. The restaurant serves breakfast, lunch, and dinner. ◆ 345 Taylor St (between Ellis and O'Farrell Sts). 673.2332, 800/2RAMADA; fax 398.0733 &

## 85 HOTEL NIKKO SAN FRANCISCO

$$$$ The luxurious expanse of white marble in the vast two-story lobby, punctuated by the lulling sound of water falling from a fountain, may remind some visitors of a mausoleum, but the management believes it calls forth a sense of serenity. Accommodations include 522 guest rooms, including 22 suites, and two authentic Japanese tatami suites. A

fitness center, which the public may patronize, has the city's only glass-enclosed indoor pool. Other amenities are Japanese soaking tubs, the **Fountain Lobby Lounge,** and the **Nikko Lounge,** which is reserved for guests on floors 23 to 25. The restaurant, **Anzu,** serves California cuisine. ◆ 222 Mason St (near Ellis St). 394.1111, 800/NIKKOUS; fax 394.1159

## 86 PARC FIFTY FIVE

$$$$ Part of the Park Lane group, this imposing 1,005-room hotel is the third-largest in town, and is mere footsteps from the **San Francisco Shopping Centre** and the **Powell Street cable-car** turntable. Facilities include a fitness center, two lounges, a business communications center, a **Concierge Club** level, and two restaurants. The intimate **Piazza Lounge** offers grand piano music and cocktail service. The hotel boasts a million-dollar art collection, including vases, custom-made mirrors, sculpture, weavings, and paintings that recall an elegant Italian Renaissance theme. A handsome pair of Italianate lions stand guard in the travertine-marble lobby. At the carriage entrance is a seven-panel bas-relief sculpture by San Francisco artist Ruth Asawa, chronicling San Francisco's past, present, and future. ◆ 55 Cyril Magnin St (between Eddy and Ellis Sts). 392.8000, 800/338.1338; fax 392.4734 &

Within the Parc Fifty Five:

### THE VERANDA

★$$ The inspired garden setting, with its lovely pastel hues, thriving plants, urns, and fountain, delights the eye and makes this an exceptionally pleasant place to have lunch. Order the cioppino (this tomato-and-white wine-based shellfish stew is a San Francisco specialty), fresh broiled salmon, or rack of lamb. ◆ Californian ◆ Daily breakfast, lunch, and dinner. 392.8000 &

### BARLEY 'N HOPS

★$ This convivial sports bar and grill serves up a great half-pound hamburger, and, as the name suggests, features locally brewed beer. ◆ American ◆ Daily lunch and dinner. 392.8000 &

## 87 MONTICELLO INN

$$ Thomas Jefferson never slept here, but he might have felt at home in this country-colonial inn with 91 rooms. Complimentary breakfast and evening wine are included. ◆ 127 Ellis St (between Powell and Cyril Magnin Sts). 392.8800, 800/669.7777; fax 398.2650 &

Within the Monticello Inn:

## PUCCINI AND PINETTI

★★$$ This casual dining spot presents a menu that emphasizes straightforward pasta dishes, a few salads, and well-prepared panini, all at reasonable prices. Chef Adriano Paganini's menu includes angel hair pasta with summer vegetables and basil oil, spicy *penne arrabiatta,* and grilled half-chicken with rosemary potatoes. ◆ Italian ◆ M-Sa lunch and dinner; Su dinner. Reservations recommended. Entrance at 88 Cyril Magnin St (at Ellis St). 392.5500

## 88 HOTEL UNION SQUARE

$$ A haunt of Dashiell Hammett in the 1930s, this 131-room hotel has been remodeled into a modern hostelry with Art Deco influences. It includes three nonsmoking floors, complimentary coffee, tea, and croissants delivered to your floor each morning, and a Mexican bar and lounge called **Carmen's Taqueria.** ◆ 114 Powell St (between Ellis and O'Farrell Sts). 397.3000, 800/553.1900; fax 885.3268 &

## 89 JOHN'S GRILL

★★$$ Established in 1908 and much favored by businessmen, this place was immortalized by author Dashiell Hammett, who made it a hangout for his best-known fictional character, detective Sam Spade. The restaurant is a repository for Spade/Hammett lore. The dark-wood and brass decor is pure men's club, and meals, such as Sam Spade's favorite pork chops with a baked potato, are hearty. Steak and seafood are the specialties. Many dishes feature some Italian influence, though the menu covers a broad range of culinary tastes. ◆ American/Italian ◆ M-Sa lunch and dinner; Su dinner. 63 Ellis St (between Stockton and Powell Sts). 986.0069 &

## 90 VIRGIN MEGASTORE

Modeled after its London flagship sister, this three-story megastore is stocked with more than 150,000 music titles (on CD and cassette), 15,000 video titles, and a well-stocked bookstore. Listening stations with headphones allow customers to hear before they buy, and the *Virgin Megastore Cafe* offers simple sustenance such as soups, sandwiches, and pastries. ◆ Daily. 2 Stockton St (at Market St). 397.4525 &

management put a lot of money into refurbishing the house, and it shows in the gleaming interior. Unfortunately, sight lines in the orchestra remain poor, so try the mezzanine. The 2,400-seat theater books popular musical attractions such as *Beauty and the Beast.* ♦ 25 Taylor St (between Market St and Golden Gate Ave). 474.3800 &

## 90 PLANET HOLLYWOOD

★★$$ Numbered 25 in this worldwide chain of eateries owned by Sylvester Stallone, Arnold Schwarzenegger, and Bruce Willis, this spot delights the fanatical movie buff. It is cluttered with movie photos, costumes, and artifacts (including set pieces from *The Titanic,* one of the half-human robots from the *Terminator* series, and a representation of Stallone's *Demolition Man* character frozen in a block of ice). The theme park ambience aside, recent improvements in the menu have made this a good place for lunch. Salads, soups, burgers are all excellent. ♦ American ♦ Daily lunch and dinner. 2 Stockton St (at Market St). 421.7827 &

## 91 HALLIDIE PLAZA

As part of the **BART**/Market Street Renewal Program, this downtown plaza was created in 1973 by **Mario Ciampi, Lawrence Halprin & Associates,** and **Carl-Warnecke and Associates.** The subway entrance allowed the design to take the form of a terraced amphitheater. Within is a busy office of the **Convention & Visitor's Bureau,** with a wealth of material for tourists provided free or for a nominal charge. Avoid the plaza after dark, as it's often overrun by unsavory characters. ♦ Daily. Between Powell and Market Sts. 391.2000. Recordings about weekly events: English 391.2001, French 391.2003, German 391.2004, Japanese 391.2101, Spanish 391.2122 &

## 92 MCDONALD'S BOOKSTORE

More than one million used and out-of-print books, magazines, and records in good and questionable taste are heaped throughout this overstuffed store, in business since 1926. Management correctly describes the place as "a dirty, poorly lit place for books" (spoofing the name of "A Clean, Well-Lighted Place"— a popular bookstore on Opera Plaza in the **Civic Center** area). ♦ M Sa. 48 Turk St (near Market St). 673.2235 &

## 93 GOLDEN GATE THEATRE

This 1922 **G. Albert Lansburgh**-designed theater (see the seating plan) is part of the Shorenstein Nederlander empire. The

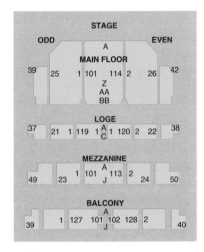

## 94 WARFIELD THEATER

Originally built in 1922 by Marcus Loew to showcase the latest vaudeville and silent-screen productions, this theater now houses a full-service nightclub, restaurant, and bar. G. Albert Lansburgh's conservative facade design belies its flamboyant interior. The ceiling fans out like a peacock tail, and murals can be found downstairs, where a speakeasy was reportedly operated. You can catch modern musical acts in an intimate setting that appears much as it has for over 70 years. ♦ 982 Market St (at Golden Gate Ave and Sixth St). 775.7722; 775.9949 &

San Francisco's visitors total 16.4 million annually.

The San Francisco airport is the fifth-busiest in the nation and the seventh-busiest in the world.

"If it could be well settled like Europe, there would not be anything more beautiful in the world."

—Father Pedro Font, about the hills and bay of San Francisco, 1776

---

Restaurants/Clubs: Red | Hotels: Purple | Shops: Orange | Outdoors/Parks: Green | Sights/Culture: Blue

# FINANCIAL DISTRICT

Often called the "Wall Street of the West," the Financial District, with its **Pacific Coast Stock Exchange**, several corporate headquarters, and elaborate commercial architecture, comprises an area bordered by **The Embarcadero** and **Market, Third, Kearny,** and **Washington Streets.**

When thousands of gold diggers were brought to the muddy shores of a shallow indentation known as **Yerba Buena Cove,** they began to grade the sand dunes along present-day Market Street, dumping sand into the mud flats of the cove. Before that was completed, they also started to build a seawall so ships could unload their cargo directly upon the wharves. For its time, this was a stupendous project, taking decades to complete. Meanwhile, the reclamation of the mud flats continued, with some of the city's smaller hills sacrificed to fill the area between the old waterfront and the new wall until, finally, the Financial District that's here today—everything east of **Montgomery Street**—arose from the sea. Within five years of the first news of the gold strike, Montgomery Street was lined with several bankers' offices. As the gold dust filtered down from the city of Sacramento, some means of handling it had to be found, and since the shopkeepers had scales for weighing the gold and safes for storing it, they were the first to become bankers.

Paradoxically, though rich in gold, San Francisco was poor in money. A pinch of gold subbed for one dollar, and a dollar's length of gold wire was divided into eight parts to serve as smaller coins, referred to as "two bits," "four bits," and so on. Coins from around the world were pressed into service at a rate of exchange based on their size. The Gold Rush boom ended in 1854, resulting in Black Friday's panic, which forced many banks

to close. Not until the colossal riches began to flow from the Nevada silver mines was San Francisco firmly established as the financial center of the West. The Great Fire in 1906 precipitated the rise of another financial giant, A.P. Giannini, a food broker who had retired at age 32 to try out his banking theories with the Bank of Italy, founded by Giannini and his stepfather. Before the advancing flames reached his bank, he removed the assets and records and hauled them home in wagons from his warehouse, well camouflaged with heaps of fruit and vegetables. Consequently, the Bank of Italy—later renamed Bank of America—was the first in the city to reopen.

It's difficult to imagine Montgomery Street or Kearny Street—the heart of the Financial District—when they were paved with sticks, stones, bits of tin, and old hatch coverings.. Today, Montgomery Street is both sleek and imposing, with walls of stone, glass, and marble lining its sides. It awakens before daybreak, when trading begins on the "Big Board" in New York. By 9AM, the skyscrapers are filled with thousands of brokers, bankers, dot come executives, and clerical workers. By dark, its canyons are largely deserted, except for cleaning crews, security guards, and a smattering of restaurant-goers and barhoppers.

"Monkey Block" was the nickname for **Montgomery Block,** a four-story building that for a century stood on the present site of the **Transamerica Pyramid.** It was the first office building of any significance in San Francisco, and the first to be fireproof. Much of the city's important business was carried on here. When business moved out, an amazing group moved in that included some of the most important names in American literary circles: Mark Twain, Bret Harte, Robert Louis Stevenson, Rudyard Kipling, Jack London, Ambrose Bierce, and William Randolph Hearst. All either had office space in the building or regularly hung out at the Bank Exchange, the building's legendary bar. In a second-floor office, a young doctor named Sun Yat-sen plotted the successful overthrow of the Manchu dynasty and later wrote the Chinese constitution. Although they would have mourned the destruction of Monkey Block, these legendary characters probably would be somewhat cheered to know that the site is now graced by the pyramid, one of the city's most prominent landmarks.

## 1 655 MONTGOMERY STREET

Completed in 1984, architects Kaplan/McLaughlin/Diaz's mixed-use tower contains condominiums above offices. ♦ At Merchant St

Within 655 Montgomery Street:

### TOMMY TOY'S

★★★$$$ The owner of this luxurious dining establishment describes the food as "haute cuisine *chinoise*"—and, indeed, it does represent an East/West melding of tastes presented in a palatial setting. The main dining room is fashioned after the 19th-century Chinese empress dowager's reading room, with ancient powder paintings framed in sandalwood. Dishes include such cross-cultural offerings as breast of duckling smoked with camphor wood and tea leaves served with a plum-wine sauce, whole fresh Maine lobster shelled and sautéed with pine nuts and mushrooms in a peppercorn sauce, and prawns in vanilla-flavored sauce with raisins and fresh melon. ♦ Chinese ♦ M-F lunch and dinner; Sa-Su dinner. Reservations recommended. 397.4888

## 2 TRANSAMERICA PYRAMID

**William Pereira and Associates**'s 853-foot-tall building has become a landmark because of its unusual shape and location at the end of Columbus Avenue. It caused great controversy when it was built in 1972 and, until it gained acceptance, gave credence to the belief that California architecture couldn't be taken seriously. (San Franciscans always hastened to add that a Los Angeles firm designed it.) It's the headquarters of the

Transamerica Corporation, founded in 1928 by A.P. Giannini. A public observation area on the 27th floor provides excellent views of such landmarks as the Golden Gate Bridge, **Coit Tower,** and Alcatraz Island, and is open to the public weekdays. The adjoining half-acre **Transamerica Redwood Park** is a pleasant place to sit and gaze up the pyramid's walls or at the lighthearted bronze Puddle Jumpers sculpture. Overlooking the park is the pyramid's restaurant **Vertigo.** ♦ 600 Montgomery St (between Clay and Washington Sts)

### 3 WASHINGTON/ BATTERY STREET BUILDING

Built in 1985, **Fee and Munson**'s narrow office block is only 25 feet deep; bay windows capture additional space for tenants. The facade facing east has a large clock. ♦ Washington St (at Battery St) ♿

### 4 PUNCH LINE

They sure don't have to turn on any laugh tracks when the jokes start flying at this comedy club. Part of the "Bill Graham Presents" empire, it has a slick, urbane look. Snacks and meals are served, but food is certainly not the reason for coming. Aspiring comedians are showcased every Sunday night. You must be 18 years of age or older to attend. Seating is on a first-come, first-served basis. ♦ Cover and two-drink minimum. Shows daily. Reservations required for dinner on weekends. Tickets available at **BASS** outlets or at the door. 444 Battery St (between Clay and Washington Sts), Upstairs. 397.7573 ♿

### 5 YANK SING

★★★$$ One of the best dim-sum houses of San Francisco, this place just happens to be in the Financial District. Were it not for the food, you'd never guess from the high-tech decor that this is a Chinese restaurant. All the dishes arrive on carts, and virtually everything is delicious. Don't miss the Peking duck, steamed pork buns, chicken wrapped in foil, or the petite custard tarts for dessert. At the end of the meal, they count your plates to tally up the bill. ♦ Chinese ♦ Daily lunch. Reservations required. 427 Battery St (between Clay and Washington Sts). 362.1640. Also at: 49 Stevenson Pl (between First and Second Sts). 495.4510 ♿

### 6 ONE MARITIME PLAZA

**Skidmore, Owings & Merrill**'s 25-story slab block with exposed diagonal-steel bracing, built in 1967, is one of the few buildings that visually demonstrates its ability to withstand the forces of an earthquake. The entrance lobby is two floors above the street. ♦ Battery St (between Clay and Washington Sts)

### 7 BANK OF CANTON OF CALIFORNIA

The present building, designed by **Skidmore, Owings & Merrill,** was erected in 1984 to replace the bank's original headquarters, a Financial District fixture since the 1930s. The architects, who strove for a modern update of the lines and detailing of the adjacent stone buildings, commissioned the use of Texas pink granite on the facade of this 17-story structure. ♦ 555 Montgomery St (at Clay St)

Within the Bank of Canton of California:

### PACIFIC HERITAGE MUSEUM

This delightful museum, hidden on a side street on the south side of the bank, offers an impressive look at Oriental culture through art and ceremonial objects, murals, photographs, and clothing. ♦ Free. M-F; closed on bank holidays. 608 Commercial St (off Montgomery St, between Sacramento and Clay Sts). 399.1124 ♿

### 8 PALIO D'ASTI

★★$$ Regional Italian specialties are prepared by chef Craig Stoll in open-display kitchens at this handsome restaurant owned by Gianni Fassio. Many of the pastas are housemade; they're all dressed creatively with such flourishes as artichoke hearts, parmesan cheese, mint, and Italian parsley. The restaurant is open for lunch and the wine bar, with murals depicting Palio pageantry and the famed Italian horse race, is open evenings. The restaurant can be rented in the evening for special functions. ♦ Italian ♦ M-F lunch only. Reservations recommended. 640 Sacramento St (between Montgomery and Kearny Sts). 395.9800; fax 362.6002 ♿

### 9 JACK'S

★★$$$ One of San Francisco's best-known restaurants since 1864, Jack's has been recently renovated, though eating here makes you feel as if you're in a dining room untouched by time. Daily specials may include rib-eye steak, spring lamb stew, salmon tartare. And where else can diners still find such age-old staples as jellied consommé (kind of like a beefy Jell-O) and celery? ♦ American ♦ M-F lunch and dinner; Sa dinner. Reservations recommended. 615 Sacramento St (between Montgomery and Kearny Sts). 421.7355 ♿

### 10 505 MONTGOMERY STREET

**Skidmore, Owings & Merrill**'s Neo-Deco tower houses several offices and the Tokai Bank. Step inside the lobby for a look at the striking pattern of the inlaid-marble floor; the lobby is particularly pretty when it's all decked out during the Christmas season. ♦ Between Sacramento and Commercial Sts

Within 505 Montgomery Street:

## Paninoteca Palio d'Asti

★★$ For a great panino, stop at this offshoot of the popular **Palio d'Asti** restaurant (see p. 56). Assorted salads, pizzas, weekly specials, pastries, and sweets are also available to savor here or to go. ◆ Italian ◆ M-F breakfast and lunch. 362.6900; fax 362.0700 &

## 11 Rubicon

★★★$$$ Owned by Robert De Niro, Francis Ford Coppola, and Robin Williams, this is one of the most popular new dining spots in the city. The dramatic loftlike space has huge windows crossed with earthquake-protection beams, white walls, and dark wood accents. Chef Scott Newman's French-inspired menu features such dishes as seared tuna paired with ragout of root vegetables. Inventive desserts truly satisfy, including apple tart with apple sorbet, red-wine-poached fruit tart, and satiny Black Forest cake. ◆ Californian/French ◆ M-F lunch and dinner; Sa dinner. Reservations required; jacket required. 558 Sacramento St (between Sansome and Montgomery Sts). 434.4100 &

## 12 London Wine Bar

$$ This establishment, which opened in the mid-1980s, claims to be the oldest wine bar in California. It has a classic look, with dark wood, racks and boxes of wine lining the walls, and a clientele that likes to swirl wine, nibble on bread sticks, and discuss the day's events in relaxed surroundings. More than three dozen wines are offered by the glass and are well complemented by light lunches and snacks. ◆ Californian ◆ M-F lunch. 415 Sansome St (between Sacramento and Clay Sts). 788.4811

## 13 353 Sacramento Street

Handsomely clad in teal- and blue-metal panels, **Skidmore, Owings & Merrill**'s low-scale corner office building is a 1984 reconstruction of a building that previously occupied this location. The result is a strange juxtaposition of styles and forms. The rotated plan of the tower ignores the grid of the street and street wall. ◆ At Battery St

## 14 Embarcadero Center

This flashy eight-block complex of retail and office space stretches from Clay, Battery, and Sansome Streets to Justin Herman Plaza and the **Hyatt Regency Hotel** at the foot of Market Street. Four slender, interconnected high-rise towers by **John Portman and Associates** are staggered to allow sunlight to penetrate and to break up what might easily have been a wall-like appearance; each has a triple-level shopping area that houses a total of 125 shops and restaurants. You'll find everything here from **The Gap** (391.8826), **Banana Republic** (986.5076), and **Liz Claiborne** (788.5041) to beauty shops, bookstores, and the **Boudin Sourdough Bakery** (362.3330)—enough to keep the most avid shopper busy for at least a full day. Since the four original towers went up in 1982, three buildings have been added to the center: the **Embarcadero Center West** and the restored **Old Federal Reserve Bank** at Sansome and Sacramento Streets, and the **Park Hyatt Hotel** at Clay and Battery Streets (see the illustrations above). Public areas include sculpture courts, bridges, and walkways within garden settings. The abstract *Vaillancourt Fountain* in the plaza is the center's most controversial sculpture (many think its convoluted metal shapes make it look as if it has weathered an earthquake). But the Canary Island palms swaying in the sea breeze at the new Harry Bridges Plaza, gives the area an appeal akin to a tropical island. Parking at the center is free with validation Monday through Friday 5PM to 3AM and all day Saturday, Sunday, and major holidays; it's discounted with validation Monday through Friday 10AM to 5PM. ◆ Bounded by The Embarcadero and Sansome St, and Sacramento and Clay Sts. 772.0550 &

---

Restaurants/Clubs: **Red** | Hotels: **Purple** | Shops: **Orange** | Outdoors/Parks: **Green** | Sights/Culture: **Blue**

Within the Embarcadero Center:

## CHEVYS

★$$ This popular restaurant has found a formula for success and repeated it many times throughout the Bay Area. Tortillas are made on the premises, along with terrific fajitas and other Mexican fare. Although the blended margaritas tend to taste more like non-alcoholic Slurpees, if you follow some patrons' remedy of ordering a shot of tequila on the side, you'll wind up with a mighty fine drink. Sun worshipers may dine on the patio except when it's reserved for "Happy Hour" imbibing on Friday evenings. ◆ Mexican ◆ Daily lunch and dinner. 2 Embarcadero Center, Promenade level. 391.2323; fax (for take-out orders) 391.4404. Also at: 150 Fourth St (at Howard St). 543.8060; 3251 20th Ave (at Stonestown Galleria). 665.8705 &

## SPLENDIDO

★★$$$ Evoking the look of a centuries-old Mediterranean village, this exciting restaurant unites the talents of design genius Pat Kuleto and successful hotelier/restaurateur Bill Kimpton. Sophisticated, innovative cuisine beguiles diners amid a dizzying potpourri of pan-Mediterranean architectural styles and textures that range from aged brick and stone to pewter and tile. All dishes are made to order and may vary from seared peppered tuna with chive potatoes to grilled lamb served with fried shallots and white bean-garlic flan. Chef Christopher Majer opts for food presentations that look "architectural" and don't just lie flat on a plate. Award-winning desserts and breads are baked on the premises. Patio dining is available. ◆ Mediterranean ◆ Daily lunch and dinner. Reservations recommended. 4 Embarcadero Center, Promenade level. 986.3222

## HARBOR VILLAGE RESTAURANT

★★★$$$ Crystal chandeliers, etched glass, and lacquered chairs accent an interior that's more upscale than many Asian restaurants. Though more traditional entrées are offered, the dim-sum selection here is extensive and especially good. Other popular choices include the minced squab and Peking duck, but ask about any seasonal or chef's specialties. There's a patio area for those who prefer the outdoor take-out dim-sum kiosk. Executive chef Andy Wai of Hong Kong also prepares grand-style Chinese banquets. ◆ Chinese ◆ Daily lunch and dinner. Reservations recommended. 4 Embarcadero Center, Lobby level. 781.8833 &

## LAVASH

★$$ One of the best-located lunch spots around, Lavash has white cloths on the tables and a patio area overlooking Embarcadero Plaza. The food—which includes meze, sandwiches made with organic lavash bread, kebabs and distinctly Middle Eastern desserts like house-made baklava and pomegranate gelatin—is tasty, and the congenial ambience draws an enthusiastic crowd. ◆ Mediterranean ◆ Daily lunch. 4 Embarcadero Center, Street level. 982.2233 &

## HYATT REGENCY HOTEL

$$$$ The silhouette of this quite impressive 803-room hotel is an unmistakable part of the San Francisco skyline. **John Portman and Associates**' 1973 design has received national recognition for outstanding and innovative architecture. The 17-story atrium lobby is filled with artificial plants, trees and greenery toppling from the tiered balconies; and the four-ton Eclipse sculpture by Charles Perry soars from a reflecting pool. The **Eclipse Cafe** serves California cuisine for breakfast, lunch, and dinner in a parklike setting, and the sweeping 60-foot-long **13 Views** watering hole is a full bar offering salads and sandwiches in the afternoon and hot appetizers in the evening. **The Equinox,** the very popular and romantic revolving-rooftop restaurant and bar, provides an incredible view of the Bay Area and serves continental cuisine for lunch and dinner daily and a Sunday brunch. **The Regency Club** offers a business center, bar, and lounge for the luxury-minded business traveler. ◆ 5 Embarcadero Center. 788.1234, reservations only 800/233.1234; fax 398.2567 &

## PARK HYATT HOTEL

$$$$ This 360-room hotel is way up on the list of best places to stay in the city, especially if you are in town on business and need such standard extras as two phones and 24-hour room service. Two Mercedes are also available to shuttle you through the downtown area, and the hotel offers a full business center and 14 meeting rooms. Afternoon tea and caviar are served in the lobby lounge. Entertainment runs nonstop daily from 3 until 11PM. ◆ 333 Battery St (at Clay St). 392.1234, 800/233.1234; fax 421.4233 &

Within the Park Hyatt Hotel:

## PARK GRILL

★★$$$ Chef Charles Lewis offers American fare at this elegant restaurant adorned with rare Australian lacewood, teak and ebony marquetry, and fantastic floral arrangements. Favorite dishes include horseradish-crusted halibut with mashed potatoes and a flurry of crispy leeks, mustard roasted chicken with whipped sweet potatoes, and grilled lamb chops accented with dates and a roasted-garlic flan. ◆ American ◆ Daily breakfast, lunch, and dinner. 296.2933 &

## FEDERAL RESERVE BANK OF SAN FRANCISCO

Sierra-white marble covers three sides of **George Kelham**'s 1924 building, part of the Embarcadero Center complex. The Commercial Street side, which was finished later, is made of glazed terra-cotta brick. The building was renovated as law offices and retail space by **Kaplan/McLaughlin/Diaz** and reopened in 1989. The interior features both real and hand-painted faux marble. Stand across the street for a good view of the eight eagles perched above the entrance. ♦ 400 Sansome St (at Sacramento St)

## 15 FERRY BUILDING

Modeled after the Cathedral Tower in Seville, Spain, this building was designed by architect **Arthur Page Brown** in 1894. It was, in fact, known for many years as the tallest building in San Francisco with its 235-foot-high clock tower. Today it serves as the headquarters of the San Francisco Port Authority and the World Trade Center. Before the bridges were built, it was the gateway to the city, with ferries transporting as many as 50 million passengers a year from all over the bay. Its fine arcades and internal galleria are unfortunately filled with rather undistinguished-looking offices. The once-neglected Embarcadero is undergoing a massive revitalization that includes plans for the renovation of the building. A conceptual building plan by **James Polshek and Partners** features a center atrium opening out onto the bay. There already is evidence of improvements to the dock and berths to accommodate vessels and plans to extend ferry service to Berkeley, **San Francisco International Airport,** and **3Com Park.** ♦ The Embarcadero (at Market St)

In front of the Ferry Building

## FERRY PLAZA FARMERS' MARKET

This festive outdoor Saturday market offers the cream of the crop of several farmers—everything from apples and almonds to radicchio and rhubarb. This fresh food sells at prices lower than any supermarket's—*plus* you get to shop to the beat of a live band of the week. At 10AM, a free "Shop with the Chef" tour begins when a chef from a popular Bay Area restaurant (a different one each week) leads a group around the market and shows participants how to assemble a family basket of the best produce available. At about 11:30AM, the chef demonstrates how to cook some of the foods, followed by tastings. On the second Saturday of each month from April through November, the market hosts such events as a fruit festival, a chili celebration, and a family pumpkin party. There are also other cooking demonstrations and tastings, and about a half-dozen local restaurants assemble booths that sell snacks and meals. ♦ Free. Sa 8AM-2PM. The Embarcadero (in front of the Ferry Building). 981.3004 ♿

## 16 580 CALIFORNIA STREET

Architects **Philip Johnson** and **John Burgee**'s Pseudo-Classical 1984 high-rise is topped by 12 blank-faced statues that surround the glass mansard roof; the figures allegedly represent the mayor and the 11 members of the board of supervisors. Classically, the design is incorrect: The front facade is divided into an equal number of bays, resulting in a column in the middle of the entry. ♦ At Kearny St

## 17 BANK OF AMERICA WORLD HEADQUARTERS

Completed in 1969 by **Wurster, Bernardi & Emmons Inc.** and **Skidmore, Owings & Merrill,** with **Pietro Belluschi** as design consultant, this is one of the best high-rise office towers ever built—52 stories clad in dark-red carnelian marble. The faceted facade and flush glazing create a changing image depending on the season or time of day. At sunset, the reflection of the sun on the windows makes the building look like a towering inferno; at other times it disappears like a black monolith into the fog. Its asymmetrical profile at the top creates sufficient variety to prevent it from becoming boring. The large lump of abstract black marble at the entryway has been dubbed "Banker's Heart" by irreverent locals. ♦ 555 California St (at Kearny St)

Within the Bank of America World Headquarters:

## CARNELIAN ROOM

★$$$$ The stupendous view through the floor-to-ceiling glass wall at this spot high above San Francisco is a sight you'll never forget. The food is not memorable, but stop here for a drink—especially when the sun is setting or the fog is rolling in. If you're bent on having a meal here, however, lovers and those who want to be very, very private may reserve the fabulous **Tamalpais Room,** a hideaway within the restaurant seating just two to six; waiters come only when summoned by a bell. ♦ French ♦ M-Sa, cocktails and dinner; Su brunch and dinner. Reservations recommended. 52nd floor. 433.7500 ♿

---

Restaurants/Clubs: Red | Hotels: Purple | Shops: Orange | Outdoors/Parks: Green | Sights/Culture: Blue

# WELLS FARGO

## 18 WELLS FARGO HISTORY MUSEUM

On display in a renovated and expanded 4,400-square-foot space are artifacts from the Gold Rush days, including old mining equipment, gold nuggets, early banking articles, and period photographs documenting Wells Fargo and early state and local history. The star attraction is an authentic 19th-century Concord stagecoach that was once used on old California trails. A reference

library is open to the public and tours can be arranged, both by appointment only. ♦ Free. M-F; closed on bank holidays. 420 Montgomery St (between California and Sacramento Sts). 396.2619 &

## 19 SECURITY PACIFIC BANK HALL

In **George Kelham**'s impressive old banking hall, the giant granite Ionic columns outside are matched by faux-marble columns inside. Completed in 1922, the hall's spacious volume is appropriate in scale and grandeur to the traditional forms of banking. ♦ Montgomery St (at California St)

## 20 BANK OF CALIFORNIA

Built in 1908 shortly after "The Big One," **Bliss & Faville**'s Corinthian-columned temple contains a grand main banking hall. ♦ 400 California St (at Sansome St)

# SAN FRANCISCO ON TAP

The strong aroma wafting down city streets may signal a welcome break from sightseeing. Trace it to its source and you may arrive at a brewpub thronged with fans of local-brewed ale. To obtain its distinct aroma and characteristic bitterness, the beer is painstakingly produced following a more costly method than that used for commercial beer, in which hops is added to boiling malted barley. On tap may be the city's Anchor Brewing Company which brews Anchor Steam; Liberty Ale; Old Foghorn Ale, a barleywine-style ale; and Anchor Porter, an old-fashioned dark brew with a smoky-toasty aroma and rich flavor.

The brewmasters handcrafting the beer are the city's current celebrities, though they were once a dying breed. In the early 1970s, San Francisco's Anchor Brewing Company wanted to distinguish itself from the light, simple suds put out by corporate breweries. In returning to the richer, full-bodied classic beers, the company helped launch the microbrewing industry, which 15 years later has grown from 50 microbreweries to more than 1,000.

Each pub has its signature brews. You'll find British style ales, Guinness-style stout, porter, bitters. And since this is California, fruit-flavored beers are making a splash with Marin Brewing Company producing some of the best. Blueberry Flavored Ale and Raspberry Trail Flavored Ale both have appealing aromas and a subtle hint of fruit.

If you have an adventurous palate, and want to try some of the city's skillfully crafted beers, here's a few to get you started. Most are open for lunch and dinner where you'll notice great food and beer pairings. Some welcome visitors to view their operations, though **Anchor Brewing Company** (1705 Mariposa St, 863.8350) has the best tour, offered afternoons Monday through Friday by reservation.

**Beach Chalet Brewery & Restaurant** (1000 Great Highway, Golden Gate Park at Ocean Beach, 386.8439) offers a panoramic ocean view with its signature ales.

**Golden Gate Park Brewery** (1326 Ninth Ave near Irving, 665.5800) Brewer Tim O'Day presides over this 125-seat brewery and restaurant in the heart of trendy Irving Street, the city's most upscale brewery.

**Gordon Biersch Brewery Restaurant** (2 Harrison St at The Embarcadero, 243.8246) Stunning views are the draw here where you can enjoy award-winning German-style beer on the waterfront deck. and tour the brewery on the premises.

**Irish Bank Bar & Restaurant** (10 Mark La off Bush St between Grant Ave and Claude La, 788.7152) is San Francisco's most authentic Irish bar tucked away on a hidden alley. Here you can sip a Guinness or Anchor Steam in a confessional salvaged from a church.

**Magnolia Pub & Brewery** (1398 Haight St at Masonic St, 864.7468). Dave McLean brews traditional British-style ales, and features five British hand pumps for cask-conditioned beers served at cellar temperature, a common practice in England.

**San Francisco Brewing Company** (155 Columbus Ave at Pacific Ave, 434.3344) has the most historic location: inside a Barbary Coast saloon with 1907 paddle fans, and a mahogany bar. Allen Paul pours his own brews (you can visit his cellar brewery) as well as those from small specialty breweries.

**ThirstyBear Brewing Company** (661 Howard St, between Second and Third Sts, 974.0905) has a two story state-of-the art-microbrewery on view behind glass. Seven microbrews and a seasonal ale are on tap every day, though the Spanish tapas garner as much praise as the brew.

## 21 FIRST INTERSTATE CENTER

This twin-towered building by **Skidmore, Owings & Merrill** houses a luxury hotel above offices. It was skillfully inserted into the center of the block in 1986 and has an arcade linking Sansome, Battery, and California Streets. The two towers are connected by bridges and capped by two stainless-steel-clad flagpoles. The design represents one of the best examples of modernism and is a stunning addition to the city skyline. ♦ California St (between Battery and Sansome Sts)

Within First Interstate Center:

### MANDARIN ORIENTAL SAN FRANCISCO

$$$$ Stunningly set atop the twin towers and connected by glass sky bridges, this is the Mandarin Oriental Hotel Group's first US palace. Small and beautifully furnished, it has 158 select rooms and suites with outstanding views of the city and bay; those with marble bathtubs looking out picture windows 40 floors up are incredible. The **Oriental Suite,** on the 38th floor, is a home-away-from-home in grand-luxe style, with a parlor, two bedrooms, two and a half bathrooms, a pantry, and an open-air terrace with a 180° view of the bay. The **Taipan Suite,** across the hall, also boasts the same wide vista, as well as a luxurious bedroom, two bathrooms, and a dining room. The secret at this hostelry lies in the personalized service, with a ratio of one staff member to each guest. Particular attention is paid to visiting executives at the lobby-level **Business Center,** which is filled with the latest high-tech office equipment. The sky bridges connecting the towers are worth the admission price. Adjoining the lobby is the Mandarin Lounge, where cocktails and hors d'oeuvres are served. ♦ 222 Sansome St (between Pine and California Sts). 885.0999, 800/526.6566; fax 433.0289 &

Within the Mandarin Oriental San Francisco:

### SILKS

★★★★$$$ Silks unique wall-treatments, hand-painted silk chandeliers evoke the odyssey of Marco Polo and his discovery of silk. The excellent East-West fare here draws a good lunch crowd, and a growing number of evening patrons. Chef Dante Boccuzzi presides over the kitchen where his signature tasting menu features dishes such as red snapper with roasted tomato bouillon of Dungeness crab and baby clams, and Hawaiian tuna and French foie gras terrine with a ruby port reduction. Other options include succulent pan-roasted squab complemented by warm cornbread cake and caramelized apples and onions. ♦ Asian/French ♦ M-F breakfast, lunch, and dinner; Sa-Su dinner. 986.2020 &

## 22 INDUSTRIAL INDEMNITY BUILDING

Formerly the **John Hancock Building,** this 1959 structure by **Skidmore, Owings & Merrill** is contemporary with the **Crown Zellerbach Building** (designed by the same architects), but demonstrates more traditional attitudes toward the street and context. It is clad in polished gray granite and has a retail base with a second-level walkway above. ♦ 255 California St (at Battery St)

## 23 TADICH GRILL

★★★$$ This is the most famous of the San Francisco fish houses that trace their lineage back for decades, and one of the first to grill fish over charcoal. Order the sand dabs, if on the menu, or the petrale sole. Better yet, ask which fresh fish they received that day; all are served with the now-legendary potato-based tartar sauce. For dessert, nothing's more soothing than the creamy rice pudding. Unless you eat in mid-afternoon, be prepared for a long but usually pleasant wait. ♦ American ♦ M-Sa lunch and dinner. 240 California St (between Front and Battery Sts). 391.2373

A Q U A

## 23 AQUA

★★★$$$ Embraced by the see-and-be-seen crowd, this refined restaurant offers lovely-to-behold fish dishes that are imaginatively prepared by executive chef Michael Mina. Try the black mussel soufflé, grilled lobster salad, or rare tuna topped with a meltingly tender slice of foie gras. The desserts taste as spectacular as they look, and the wine list is expertly matched to the imaginative menu. ♦ Seafood ♦ M-F lunch and dinner; Sa dinner. Reservations recommended. 252 California St (between Front and Battery Sts). 956.9662 &

---

Restaurants/Clubs: **Red** | Hotels: **Purple** | Shops: **Orange** | Outdoors/Parks: **Green** | Sights/Culture: **Blue**

## 24 101 CALIFORNIA STREET

With the **Bank of America** building and the **Transamerica Pyramid,** this cylindrical structure by **Philip Johnson** and **John Burgee** acts as the third major landmark in the Financial District. Completed in 1983, its silvery reflective glass looks especially beautiful when seen from the bay at dusk. Although the entrance lobby is rather ungainly, a sloping glass wall slicing across the 90-foot-tall columns makes a dramatic sight. The north-facing plaza on California Street is flanked by two mid-rise blocks cut on the diagonal. ◆ Between Davis and Front Sts

At 101 California Street:

### THE ATRIUM

★★$$$ Off the open plaza is this sophisticated restaurant with a menu that changes daily to reflect the freshest offerings of the marketplace. Sample entrées include spicy Creole jambalaya, a grilled thick-cut pork chop with turnip gratin and Gravenstein applesauce, and *ancho* (dried *poblano*) chili-glazed breast of chicken with garlic mashed potatoes. The sleek dining room, established on several elevated levels, is decorated with black granite, pastel desert colors, and plantation shutters. On sunny days, many diners opt to lunch alfresco. ◆ Californian ◆ M-F lunch and dinner. Entrance on Front St. 788.4101 ♿

## 25 250 MONTGOMERY STREET

**Heller and Leake**'s attractive 1986 office tower is clothed in fiberglass, reinforced concrete, and green granite. ◆ At Pine St

## 26 ROYAL GLOBE INSURANCE BUILDING

Note the elaborate sculpture in **Howells and Stokes**'s 1909 white-marble building with a fine entrance and base. ◆ 201 Sansome St (at Pine St)

At 853 feet, the Transamerica Pyramid is San Francisco's tallest structure.

Use the Ferry Building at the foot of Market Street as your guide to the piers; even-numbered piers are south of the building and odd-numbered piers are to the north.

On New Year's Eve in the Financial and Downtown Districts, it's a tradition to toss calendars out of office windows. The cleanup operation is costly, but locals seem reluctant to give up the practice.

## 27 PACIFIC COAST STOCK EXCHANGE

This structure, once home to the US Treasury, was renovated in 1930 by **Miller & Pflueger** and features two granite sculptures by Ralph Stackpole flanking its entrance. This classically inspired structure is the heart of the Financial District and a little sister to those on Wall Street and in London. ◆ Tours by appointment only. 301 Pine St (at Sansome St). 393.4133

## 28 235 PINE STREET

Note the bronze work above the entrance of this impressive 25-story limestone-clad high rise designed by **Skidmore, Owings & Merrill** in 1990. The 20 relief portrait sculptures, entitled Called to Rise, feature individuals who have contributed significantly to the history of San Francisco, including Juan Bautista De Anza, Phoebe Apperson Hearst, Amadeo Peter Giannini, and **Timothy Pflueger.** For more information about these bronze castings and biographies of the people portrayed, ask the person at the front desk in the lobby for a brochure. ◆ Between Battery and Sansome Sts

## 29 BELDEN PLACE

The Financial District's proletarian version of Union Square's Maiden Lane (a tiny pedestrian way filled with umbrella-covered tables during the lunch hour) has a ways to go yet before it catches up to the cachet of its rival. Still, the brick-walled alley provides a welcome respite from the hustle and bustle at lunchtime. Closed to traffic from 11AM to 3PM, it offers a melting pot of kitchens to choose from, including **Buddha Bistro** (Chinese/Italian), **Café Tiramisù** (Italian), **Cafe Bastille** (Mediterranean), **B44** (Spanish), and **Oh la la!** (sandwiches and great espresso drinks). Many have alfresco dining during the summer. ◆ Between Bush and Pine Sts

Within Belden Place:

### CAFE BASTILLE

★$ The first restaurant to venture out of doors on Belden, it attracts a loyal following with its simple, well-prepared brasserie fare. Choose from salads, soups, crepes, sandwiches, and entrées that range from roasted chicken breast with *pommes frites* (french fries) to *andouillette* (pork sausage) with sautéed onions. Live jazz is featured three nights a week. ◆ French ◆ M-Sa lunch and dinner. 22 Belden Pl. 986.5673 ♿

### CAFÉ TIRAMISÙ

★★$$ The open kitchen at this stylish Italian restaurant turns out fresh pasta, including risotto with earthy mushrooms, osso buco with soft polenta, and roasted whole fish. Save room for the namesake dessert. The walls were decorated by the same muralists who left their mark on the city's popular **Stanford Court Hotel.** ♦ Italian ♦ M-F lunch and dinner; Sa dinner. Reservations recommended. 28 Belden Pl. 421.7044 ⅃

## B44

★★$$ Spanish dining has come to this Parisian cafe scene. The interior is homey with a video of a festival in the chef's hometown of Vilafranca del Penedes. Paella served in small skillets is the dish to order. Varieties include seafood, chicken and vegetarian. Save room for the classic Spanish desserts, such as cinnamon and rice ice cream, and fresh cheese drizzled with honey, walnuts, and sherry. ♦ Catalan ♦ M-F lunch and dinner. 44 Belden Place (between Bush and Pine Sts.). 986-6287 ⅃

## 30 Sam's Grill

★★$$ This Old Guard San Francisco restaurant features polished wood, private rooms, and a menu specializing in sweetbreads served on toast points with crisp slices of bacon and roasted potatoes, minute steak, celery, French pancakes (thin crepes drizzled with lemon juice and powdered sugar). If you've never eaten here, you've got to try it at least once, and be willing to forgive the indifferent service. Jammed for lunch, it's less crowded at dinner if you arrive early. ♦ American ♦ M-F lunch and dinner. Reservations accepted for six or more only. 374 Bush St (between Montgomery and Kearny Sts). 421.0594 ⅃

## 31 Kelly's on Trinity

★★$ Kelly Mills, who won acclaim as chef at the **Clift Hotel,** gave up the fast track to open this cafeteria-style lunch spot several years ago. Chili and three types of soup are offered each day, and the salads range from steak with mushrooms, green beans, and croutons to Asian chicken with celery and eggplant.

♦ Californian ♦ M-F breakfast and lunch. 333 Bush St (at Trinity Plaza, between Kearny and Montgomery Sts). 362.4454 ⅃

## 32 Russ Building

**George Kelham**'s 1928 Gothic high-rise was modeled after the winning entry for the Chicago Tribune Tower competition. Until 1964, it was the tallest building in the city. ♦ 235 Montgomery St (between Bush and Pine Sts)

## 33 Mills Building and Mills Tower

A rare example of the Chicago School west of the Rockies, this 10-story **Burnham and Root** building, completed in 1892, suffered only interior fire damage during the 1906 earthquake. Notice the fine Richardsonian entrance archway on Montgomery Street, the subtly delineated brick planters and strong cornice, and the multifloor frieze. **Willis Polk** supervised the postfire reconstruction and also designed the adjacent **Mills Tower** on Bush Street. ♦ 220 Montgomery St (at Bush St). 421.1444

## 34 130 Bush Street

Ten stories high and just 20 feet wide, **George Applegarth**'s 1910 building is surely one of the narrowest high-rises ever built. This office building has slender Gothic lines and a defined top, middle, and bottom. ♦ Between Battery and Sansome Sts

## 35 The Shell Building

One of the city's most beautiful Art Deco towers, **George Kelham**'s structure, built in 1929, was strongly influenced by **Eliel Saarinen**'s entry for the Chicago Tribune Tower competition. Because of its fine proportions—tripartite division of top, shaft, and base—distinctive silhouette, and contextual relationship to the urban fabric, it is now considered an important source of inspiration for the next generation of skyscrapers. The exterior is sheathed in glazed terra-cotta. ♦ 100 Bush St (between Battery and Sansome Sts)

## 36 Specialty's Cafe and Bakery

This take-out lunch spot is packed at noontime. Everything's made from scratch—even the sandwich bread comes straight from the oven—and the cookies are heavenly. Try their peanut-butter, banana, and wheat-germ sandwich for a change of pace. Catering services are available. ♦ M-F 6AM-6PM. No credit cards accepted. 22 Battery St (at Market St). Daily specials 896.BAKE; catering, delivery, and customer service, all locations 512.9550. Also at: 312 Kearny St (between

---

Restaurants/Clubs: Red | Hotels: Purple | Shops: Orange | Outdoors/Parks: Green | Sights/Culture: Blue

Bush and Pine Sts); 150 Spear St (between Howard and Mission Sts); 1 Post St (at Market St)

## 37 444 MARKET STREET

Architects **Skidmore, Owings & Merrill**'s 38-story, aluminum-panel-clad office tower, completed in 1981, has a sawtooth profile. The building steps back on the 33rd, 34th, and 35th floors, opening out onto gardens that overlook the bay. ♦ At Front St

## 38 388 MARKET STREET

One of **Skidmore, Owings & Merrill**'s most refined buildings is this mixed-use, flatiron office tower, completed in 1987. The triangular site is occupied to the property lines, in contrast to the **Crown Zellerbach Building** two blocks away on Market Street, designed by the same firm. The building's form consists of a cylinder attached to a triangle. The apartments at the top have deeply recessed windows, while the offices below have flush windows. The facade is a dark-red polished granite, which contrasts with the green window mullions. ♦ Between Pine and Front Sts

## 39 GALLERIA PARK HOTEL

$$$ One of the small, renovated hotels springing up around town, this has a superb location, adjacent to the **Crocker Galleria** and two blocks from Union Square and the cable cars. The 177 rooms and suites are equipped with bars and refrigerators, and the grand suite offers the comfort of a fireplace and whirlpool. Meeting rooms are available, and there's even a rooftop jogging track and a small fitness facility equipped with a few exercise machines. ♦ 191 Sutter St (at Kearny St). 781.3060, 800/792.9639; fax 433.4409 ♿

## 39 PERRY'S DOWNTOWN

★★$$ In a clubby mahogony-paneled atmosphere inspired by the original **Perry's** on Union Square, this bustling New York-style pub features hearty American fare. Two standout sandwiches are the lobster club and the New York steak with onions and mushrooms. Main dishes are just as good: Try the grilled pork chops with potato pancakes and applesauce or risotto with chicken and toasted garlic. Leave room for the creamy cheesecake or the apple brown betty with vanilla ice cream. ♦ American ♦ Daily lunch and dinner. Reservations recommended. 185 Sutter St (between Montgomery and Kearny Sts). 989.6895

In 1987, the fireworks for the Golden Gate Bridge's 50th birthday celebration cost nearly $500,000.

# John Walker & Co.
### WINE AND SPIRITS SINCE 1933

## 39 JOHN WALKER & CO. LIQUORS

This is the largest specialty and import liquor store in the area. If you have questions or need to find that rare cognac, the staff is ready to help. Gift wrapping and shipping are available. ♦ M-Sa. 175 Sutter St (between Montgomery and Kearny Sts). 986.2707 ♿

## 40 HALLIDIE BUILDING

**Willis Polk and Company**'s 1917 building is an architectural favorite. Claiming to be the world's first curtain-wall glass facade, it was built for the **University of California** and named after Andrew Hallidie, the inventor of the cable car, who was also a university regent. The glass facade is projected a few feet beyond the floor edge and structure. Decorative railings integrate the fire-escape balconies and stairs and create a wonderful silhouette at the top of the building. The sixth floor is the home of the San Francisco chapter of the **American Institute of Architects,** which usually has an exhibit on display in its entryway (free and open to the public). The **US Post Office** occupies most of the ground floor. ♦ 130 Sutter St (between Montgomery and Kearny Sts)

## 41 HUNTER-DULIN BUILDING

With the revival of interest in Premodern architecture, this 1926 **Schultze and Weaver** building has come to be recognized as one of the finest in the Financial District. Its tripartite division of top, shaft, and base and its rich terra-cotta detailing contrast well with the banality of its more recent neighbors. The style is French château/Romanesque capped by a tile mansard roof. Medieval motifs adorn lobby walls. ♦ 111 Sutter St (at Montgomery St)

## 42 CITICORP CENTER

The best aspect of this 1984 building designed by **William Pereira and Associates** is the conversion of the old **Banking Hall** (built in 1910 by **Albert Pissis**) into an atrium space that's open to the public during the day. The **Citicorp Cafe** (362.6297) and a number of colorful flags help to enliven the space, which previously had an echoing mausoleum-like quality. **Pereira**'s tower is clad in precast concrete. ♦ 1 Sansome St (at Sutter St)

## 43 CROWN ZELLERBACH BUILDING

Following the example of Lever House in New York City, this 1959 design by **Hertzka and**

# THE TOAST OF THE CITY: CHEFS CUISINE

Chefs like Dante Broccuzzi are the reason dining out in San Francisco has reached a zenith of pleasure. Chef de Cuisine at Silks at the Mandarin Oriental hotel and Rising-Star-Chef-of-the-Year, Broccuzzi finesses an incredible tasting menu from the season's best ingredients. He likens his artistry to music. "Different ingredients are notes to complete a song. It's how you play those notes to produce the final piece. When the flavors are off even a little bit, it throws everything out of key." His artful prepara-tion of seared venison with braised swiss chard and chanterelles with port wine-glazed pears won a prize at a cooking competition. Like many of the city's culinary masters, his résumé includes stints at five-star restaurants in Italy, France, London, Manhattan, and Washington D.C. His tasting menu without wine is $52 for 4 courses and $75 for six courses; paired with wine is another $30. Silks at the Mandarin Oriental, 222 Sansome Street. 986.2020. www.mandarinoriental.com

**Knowles** and **Skidmore, Owings & Merrill** represented the then-current fashion for treating buildings as isolated objects withdrawn from the street by a belt of landscaping and clad in thin curtain walling. It's ironic to think that in 1981—in a mere 22 years after it was constructed—a suggestion that the building might be demolished to make way for a taller building prompted discussion about listing the building as a historic landmark. ♦ Market St (between Battery and Sansome Sts)

## 44 88 KEARNY STREET (CALIFORNIA FEDERAL BANK)

Clad in white concrete and embellished with blue tiles, this 1986 **Skidmore, Owings & Merrill** building has one of the finest entrance lobbies and banking halls in the city. The detailing, materials, and lighting evoke an Art Deco flavor. Also take notice of the recon-struction of the old facade on the building located right next door. ♦ At Post St

## 45 PACIFIC TELESIS CENTER

Whereas the **Bank of America World Head-quarters** represented the then-latest ideas (in 1969) about high-rise towers and their relationship to the urban fabric, **Skidmore, Owings & Merrill**'s design (completed in 1982) embodies a change in architectural thought. It rises sheer from the street without a plaza, and its surface consists of flush two-tone granite panels and mirror glazing. The corners are beveled, emphasizing the wraparound smoothness of the cladding. The matte/glossy granite and mirror glass create changing patterns at different times of the day or night. ♦ 50 Post St (at Kearny St)

Within the Pacific Telesis Center:

## CROCKER GALLERIA

This ornate, three-level, glass-barrel-vaulted shopping arcade is modeled after Milan's vast Galleria Vittorio Emanuele. Dozens of shops grace this pretty center, including boutiques ranging from **Gianni Versace** to **Polo/Ralph Lauren.** You'll also find home furnishings, fresh flowers, cookies, cards, and a range of restaurants, most of them small fast-food places catering to workers in the area. ♦ M-Sa. Entrances are on Post St and Sutter St. 393.1505 ♿

## FAZ

★★★$$ The business-lunch crowd flocks to this sleek spot where the menu blends the flavors of the Middle East and California: homemade potato chips share top billing with a salad sprinkled with pomegranate seeds and toasted walnuts and drizzled with a pomegranate vinaigrette. Portobello mushrooms on rosemary focaccia make a popular sandwich, and any of the pastas—perhaps riso (rice-shaped pasta) with baby artichokes in a light tomato sauce—are good choices. For dessert there's honey-soaked baklava with three kinds of nuts, and black-and-white chocolate torte with caramel sauce. You may enter from the third floor of the **Galleria** or at street level. ♦ Californian/Mediterranean ♦ M-F lunch. Reservations recommended. 161 Sutter St. 362.0404 ♿

## 46 HOBART BUILDING

**Willis Polk and Company**'s 1914 building is part high-rise tower, part mid-rise street block. For many years it was one of the tallest struc-tures on Market Street; now it is dwarfed by the **Wells Fargo Tower** next door. ♦ 582 Market St (at Second St)

---

Restaurants/Clubs: Red | Hotels: Purple | Shops: Orange | Outdoors/Parks: Green | Sights/Culture: Blue

# CHINATOWN

S an Francisco's Chinatown is the largest Chinese community on the West Coast—and the second largest in the US next to New York City's settlement. The tourist area, bounded by **Broadway, Columbus Avenue,** and **Bush Street,** and **Kearny** and **Stockton Streets,** is home to many of the 120,000 Chinese-Americans living in the Bay Area, but the population extends to North Beach, Russian Hill, and beyond to the Sunset and Richmond districts. Because the pulse of the community remains within the original perimeters of Chinatown—and because traditions are strong—the suburban Chinese come back on Sunday to shop and dine here.

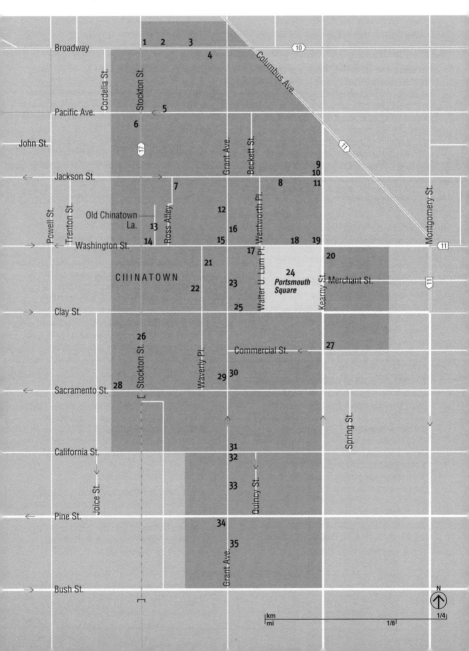

When the first Chinese immigrants arrived, they found a small community huddled around **Portsmouth Square,** which is today still the hub of Chinatown. Once the gold strike was announced, the Cantonese came by the boatload, fleeing famine and the Opium Wars. By 1850 there were more than 4,000 Chinese men (and only seven Chinese women) in the area. Chinese "coolies," a term stemming from the word *kuli* (Chinese for bitter toil), were tolerated as long as they performed the tasks other groups scorned—working the mines, building the transcontinental railroad, and, later, planting the Napa vineyards. But when the work dried up in the 1880s, many Caucasian San Franciscans shared Rudyard Kipling's view of Chinatown: "A ward of the city of Canton set down in the most eligible business quarter of the City." A vicious backlash had set in. When hundreds of unemployed whites tried to run them out of town, the Chinese retaliated by organizing *tongs,* or secret associations, for protection, which soon evolved into warring gangs. These organizations turned to selling opium, running extortion rings, and promoting prostitution, with discipline maintained by squads of hatchet men. It wasn't until the 1920s that conflict was banished from Chinatown's streets.

When the area was totally destroyed by the 1906 earthquake and fire, city politicians planned to relocate the Chinese to less valuable property. Instead, the industrious Asians rebuilt with such dispatch that they reclaimed their district before City Hall could act. And the new Chinatown was just as crowded as the old. By World War II, an average of 20 people shared a bath, and there were about 12 people to a kitchen. This same area— 18 square blocks—is now struggling to absorb the newest wave of immigrants from Southeast Asia.

Chinatown is so much more than the few commercial street-front blocks along **Grant Avenue,** marked by the **Chinese Gate** on Bush Street. It is the back alleys crammed with herb shops; benevolent societies that promote cultural and civic causes; upper-floor residences with balconies; fish hanging on clotheslines; garment sweatshops; the temples; and the action on Stockton Street, which has become the true main street of Chinatown since the tourist trade usurped Grant. Here the food is as much of an attraction as the Grant Avenue trinkets. Fish swimming in tanks, claw-snapping crabs, crate-bound chickens, hanging ducks, exotic greens, and tempting baked goods can all be found here. It doesn't matter if you can't speak any of the myriad dialects swirling around you. Sign language works very well, and shopping in Chinatown can be a remarkable adventure.

## YUET LEE

### 1 YUET LEE SEAFOOD RESTAURANT

★$ Open until 3AM, it's a refueling stop for club prowlers, and the staff is always welcoming. Among the best-sellers are the stir-fry combinations, but these don't show off the kitchen's talents. The salt-and-pepper squid, quickly stirred in a dry wok, is a must-order dish, as are the steamed rock cod and Dungeness crab. For a late-night snack, the shrimp with scrambled eggs will hit the spot. ♦ Chinese/Seafood ♦ M, W-Su lunch and dinner. Reservations required for five or more. 1300 Stockton St (at Broadway). 982.6020 ⴲ

### 2 HING LUNG CHINESE CUISINE

★★$ Fans converge here mainly for the *juk* (a thick rice porridge offered 17 ways). The house special stirs a delicate blend of shellfish and fish into the thick, steaming mixture. Other *juk* dishes include pork liver with sliced pork; fresh clams with abalone, which has a

---

Restaurants/Clubs: Red | Hotels: Purple | Shops: Orange | Outdoors/Parks: Green | Sights/Culture: Blue

clean, fresh flavor; and pork-blood curd, with musty nuances. ♦ Chinese ♦ Daily breakfast, lunch, and dinner. 674 Broadway (between Columbus Ave and Stockton St). 398.8838 &

### 3 CHINESE HISTORICAL SOCIETY OF AMERICA

Rotating exhibitions of the society's collection of artifacts, photographs, and documents trace the history of the Chinese people in America. Displays are captioned in Chinese and English. ♦ Free. Tu-Sa noon-4PM. 644 Broadway St (between Grant and Stockton Sts). 391.1188

### 4 SAM WONG HOTEL

$$ Refurbished in Ming dynasty style, this 81-room brick-front hotel has one of the best locations in town, where Chinatown meets North Beach. ♦ 615 Broadway St (at Grant Ave) 362.2999, 888/595.9188, www.swhotelsf.com

### 5 NEW ASIA

★$ One of the most dramatic dim-sum parlors in the city, this vast restaurant seats more than a thousand. The dim sum taste exceedingly fresh, and the *siu mai* (pork dumplings) are denser than most others, loaded with earthy-tasting cloud-ear mushrooms. One of the most interesting items is the crescent-shaped tapioca wrapper filled with coarsely chopped pork and green peas. ♦ Dim Sum ♦ Daily breakfast, lunch, and dinner. 772 Pacific Ave (between Grant Ave and Stockton St). 391.6666 &

### 6 VALLEJO MARKET

If it swims and it's fresh, it's probably for sale here, and at a reasonable price, too. ♦ Daily. 1145 Stockton St (between Jackson St and Pacific Ave). 433.0403

### 7 GOLDEN GATE FORTUNE COOKIES

In addition to the usual crunchy fortune cookies, this small factory located on a side street produces X-rated versions with declarations that would make Confucius blush. ♦ Daily. 56 Ross Alley (off Jackson St). 781.3956 &

### 8 PEARL CITY SEAFOOD

★★$$ This place looks spiffier than many restaurants in the area, with fashionable tablecloths and black-lacquer chairs. The huge fish tank on a rear wall attests to the freshness of the seafood dishes. Spiced, salted prawns, and prawns with garlic sauce are among the tempting choices. ♦ Cantonese ♦ Daily lunch and dinner. 641 Jackson St (between Kearny and Wentworth Sts). 398.8383 &

### 9 HOUSE OF NANKING

★★★$$ This is one of those hole-in-the-wall Chinese restaurants that are out of this world. Seating is at a half-dozen tables that are crammed together (definitely expect to bump elbows with your neighbors) and at a counter, where you can watch the chef turn the freshest of ingredients (bright purple eggplant, fat green beans, and the like, bought daily at Chinatown markets) into delicious, spicy dishes that never miss. Expect a wait. There's also takeout. ♦ Chinese ♦ Daily lunch and dinner. 919 Kearny St (between Jackson St and Columbus Ave). 421.1429

### 10 DPD RESTAURANT

★★$$ Some of the best Shanghai noodles in the city can be found here. The spicy, thick noodles, which turn mahogany-colored in the wok, are like manna when served with Chinese cabbage and strips of pork. The noodle soups are just as enticing, whether topped with pork chops, beef, or smoked fish. On the seafood menu try the hot braised prawns and the scallops in garlic-and-ginger sauce. ♦ Shanghai ♦ Daily lunch and dinner. 901 Kearny St (at Jackson St). 982.0471

### 10 DAAN ACUPUNCTURE & HERBS CENTER

This shop strives to make Chinese herbs accessible to Westerners. Not only does it stock a complete selection of American ginseng and vitamins, Susan and Lois Yen, certified acupuncturists and American educated, are on hand to counsel and apply needles for a variety of ailments. ♦ Daily. 614 Jackson St (at Kearny St). 433-3278 &

### 11 KAY CHEUNG RESTAURANT

★★$ Crowds line up outside this dim-sum parlor for some of the best dumplings in the city. The fillings are simple and fresh: Try the shrimp dumplings flavored with ginger; the pork steamed buns with red vinegar sauce for dipping; and the shrimp, cilantro, and water chestnut dumplings. In the evenings, when the full dinner menu comes out, the seafood specialties are highly recommended. ♦ Chinese ♦ M dinner; Tu-Su lunch and dinner. 615 Jackson St (at Kearny St). 989.6838 &

### 11 STAR LUNCH

★$ With only 12 seats at the kitchen counter, this eatery is one of the smallest in Chinatown. Diners can feel a blast of heat as the cook turns out popular Shanghai chow mein dishes with either pork or chicken. It's a good place to sample pig's feet in noodle soup or salted cabbage and shredded pork. But stay away from the fermented tofu: even the smell can ruin your appetite. ♦ Shanghai ♦ Tu-Su lunch. 605 Jackson St (at Kearny St). 788.6709

## 12 TEN REN TEA CO., LTD.

More than 40 different teas are available here, as well as Chinese, Korean, and American varieties of ginseng. Many of the teas and ginseng roots are grown on the company's own farms. This is one of the largest such operations in existence, with 60 branches worldwide. Customers may sample whatever tea is being brewed. ♦ Daily. 949 Grant Ave (between Washington and Jackson Sts). 362.0656 ♿

## 13 OLD CHINATOWN LANE

This narrow street was once called the "Street of Gamblers," a reference to Chinatown's mysterious history. ♦ At Washington St (between Ross Alley and Stockton St)

## 14 JADE GALORE

A security officer and two gilded lions guard the entrance to this jewelry shop dealing in Burmese jade and diamonds. ♦ Daily. 1000 Stockton St (at Washington St). 982.4863 ♿

## 15 CHEW CHONG TAI & CO.

The doors opened before 1911, making this the oldest store in Chinatown. It's the place to find calligraphy brushes, ink sticks, and Japanese and Chinese inks. The staff will even mount and frame your completed artwork. ♦ Daily. 905 Grant Ave (at Washington St). 982.0479 ♿

## 16 LI PO

Welcome to one of San Francisco's most bizarre bars. From the minute you walk through the golden cave-mouth entrance, you'll know you're not in Kansas anymore. Kitschy Asian furnishings abound, streetwise waitresses move the booze, and Sinatra serenades on the jukebox. Bottoms up. ♦ Daily 2PM-2AM. 916 Grant Ave (between Washington and Jackson Sts). 982.0072 ♿

## 17 SILVER RESTAURANT

★$$ Though lacking in charm, this place takes its food seriously and is open around the clock. And it's inexpensive, especially during crab season (November through April), when a whole crab is usually priced at about $9; also attractive are the round-the-clock service and friendly, attentive staff. Overall, the food is okay, and the dim sum, the *congees* (rice porridge) or the thin noodles with wontons and a choice of toppings (including excellent barbecued pork or duck) make a fine end to a long night of partying. ♦ Cantonese/Mandarin ♦ Daily 24 hours. 737 Washington St (between Walter U. Lum Pl and Grant Ave). 433.8888 ♿

## 17 OLD CHINESE TELEPHONE EXCHANGE BUILDING

This site used to be home to the *California Star,* the first newspaper in the city and the one that started the rush in 1848 by spreading the cry of "Gold!" The present building, a three-tiered pagoda, once housed the operators for Chinatown's telephone system and later the local **Pacific Telephone and Telegraph** offices. A branch of the **Bank of Canton** is now located here. ♦ 743 Washington St (between Walter U. Lum Pl and Grant Ave)

## 18 BUDDHA'S UNIVERSAL CHURCH

This five-story structure was built by hand using an exotic variety of polished woods. The church contains mosaic images of Buddha, bronze doors, and murals on the roof. ♦ Church: daily. Tours: second and fourth Sunday of June, July, August. 720 Washington St (at Kearny St). 982.6116

## 19 WORLD GINSENG CENTER

This supermarket-size ginseng emporium is a good place to buy the aromatic, gnarled roots of that medicinal herb. There's ginseng from America, China, and Korea in just about every form: extract for tea, tea bags, medicinals, and candies. ♦ Daily. 801 Kearny St (at Washington St). 362.0928

## 20 HOLIDAY INN AT CHINATOWN

$$$ This unique building is the result of an award-winning design by **Clement Chen.** Facilities include 566 rooms with free cable TV, room service until 10PM, a rooftop swimming pool, and 5 floors of underground parking. Altogether, the employees speak 31 languages. ♦ 750 Kearny St (between Merchant and Washington Sts). 433.6600, 800/465.4329; fax 765.7891 ♿

Within the Holiday Inn at Chinatown:

## CHINESE CULTURE CENTER

A valuable resource and communication center for Chinese culture in the West, this facility offers changing art shows and entertainment programs in its 650-seat theater. The center also arranges guided tours. ♦ Free. Tu-Sa. Third floor. 986.1822 ♿

## LOTUS BLOSSOM RESTAURANT

★$ Located on the second floor of the hotel, this restaurant offers an inexpensive all-you-can-eat breakfast and lunch buffet, and the dinner menu features a broad selection of both American and Chinese dishes. ♦ Chinese/American ♦ Daily breakfast, lunch, and dinner. 433.6600 ♿

## 21 THE POT STICKER

★$$ This appealing little side-street restaurant specializes in the fried and steamed meat-filled dumplings for which it is named. ♦ Mandarin ♦ Daily lunch and dinner. 150 Waverly Pl (between Clay and Washington Sts). 397.9985

## 22 TIEN HOU TEMPLE

Located on the fourth floor of a brightly painted building, this temple is dedicated to Tien Hou, Queen of the Heavens and Goddess of the Seven Seas. Flowers, incense, and intricately carved statues fill the small sanctuary. Its hours are unreliable, so your best bet is to take one of the tours arranged by the **Chinese Culture Center** at the **Holiday Inn at Chinatown** (750 Kearny St; 986.1822) every Saturday at 2PM. But if you're walking past and see clouds of incense swirling down from the balcony, you may assume the temple is open. (There's no elevator, only stairs.) The street it's on—Waverly Place—is known as the "Street of Painted Balconies." It's colorful, crowded, noisy, and redolent with the aroma of exotic foodstuffs and incense. ♦ Tu-Sa. 125 Waverly Pl (between Clay and Washington Sts), Fourth floor

## 23 CHINA TRADE CENTER

Three floors of mall-type shops offer jewelry, linens, clothing, watches, souvenirs, and eyeglasses, among many other types of goods. Dangling from the ceiling above the staircase is a large, fierce-looking dragon. ♦ Daily. 838 Grant Ave (between Clay and Washington Sts). &

Within the China Trade Center:

### EMPRESS OF CHINA

★★$$$ This is one of Chinatown's fancy, expensive restaurants, with a celebrity clientele to match. A carved 13th-century panel stands at the entrance, which widens into a "garden pavilion" with an impressive wooden pagoda and a black-and-white marble floor laid in a star-burst pattern. Three romantic and elegant dining rooms, all with beautiful views of the city, are arranged around the pagoda, where the sumptuous food reigns supreme. ♦ Chinese ♦ Daily lunch and dinner. Reservations recommended. 434.1345 &

## 24 PORTSMOUTH SQUARE

Robert Louis Stevenson spent many hours writing in this square, and his recollections of the area can be found in The Wreckers. ♦ Bounded by Clay and Washington Sts, and Kearny St and Walter U. Lum Pl

## 25 ORIENTAL PEARL RESTAURANT

★★$ In this place, one of the city's prettiest dim-sum parlors, customers order from a menu, rather than choosing from a cart. The dumplings aren't the best choices here; instead, go for the salt-baked prawns and the Chiu Chow-style marinated duck, braised in soy sauce and served with a pungent vinegar dipping sauce. The dinner menu is even more enticing. The house special, chicken meatballs, are a mix of chicken, shrimp, water chestnuts, and ham in a delicate, egg-white wrapper. Seafood in a crispy nest of taro is extraordinary in both taste and presentation. ♦ Chinese ♦ Daily lunch and dinner. 788 Clay St (near Grant Ave). 433.1817 &

## 26 STOCKTON STREET

The street of daily life in Chinatown is no longer exclusively Chinese. Other Asian populations, including Vietnamese, Filipinos, and Koreans, have settled and opened businesses here. Chinatown residents buy goods in the grocery and butcher shops, bakeries, and quaint herb-and-spice stores along this thoroughfare and its side streets. Take note of the many handsome brick structures from the 1850s that were once plush private residences. Francis Pioche, a pioneer financier and bon vivant credited with giving San Franciscans an appreciation of fine food, lived at 806 Stockton. Pioche imported many French chefs and cargoes of vintage wines to the city. ♦ Between Sacramento St and Broadway

## 27 HON'S WUN TUN HOUSE

★$ This tiny, bustling, downscale-looking assemblage of Formica tables and limited counter seating is where the cognoscenti gather when they want a great cheap bowl of noodles or dumpling soup. A glass of tea comes with the meal. It's usually crowded, so expect to share a table. ♦ Cantonese ♦ Daily lunch and dinner. 648 Kearny St (at Commercial St). 433.3966 &

## 28 CAMERON HOUSE

This Presbyterian community center was named after Donaldina Cameron to honor her lifetime of work dedicated to freeing singsong slave girls. The women, mostly Chinese and some Japanese, arrived here thinking they would become brides of the mine workers, but instead were used by businessmen as prostitutes and slaves. Cameron came to be known as "Lo Mo," or the mother. Inside the house are old carved cornices, calligraphy, and paintings. ♦ M-F. 920 Sacramento St (at Stockton St). 781.0408

## 29 CHINATOWN KITE SHOP

Stop here to peruse an incredible assortment of all kinds of kites, including windsock and fish kites in cotton or nylon. Some make wonderful decorations for a child's room; all make great souvenirs. ♦ Daily. 717 Grant Ave (between Sacramento and Clay Sts). 391.8217 &

### 30 THE WOK SHOP

Everything you need for creating your own Chinese feast, from cookbooks to utensils, can be found here. ♦ Daily. 718 Grant Ave (between Sacramento and Commercial Sts). 989.3797 &

### 30 EASTERN BAKERY

Try the honey-coated bowties or some of the sweet Chinese cakes, such as black bean, lotus, and melon. ♦ Daily. 720 Grant Ave (between Sacramento and Commercial Sts). 392.4497 &

### 31 OLD ST. MARY'S CHURCH

California's first cathedral now functions as a noontime concert hall, and a neighborhood parish church, though apparently not for the Chinese Catholic community, which favors a different church offering Mass in Chinese. Built of brick in 1854, it survived both the 1906 and the 1989 earthquakes without structural damage. During wartime, it provided social refuge for soldiers on leave. It operated the first English-language school for the Chinese community. Concerts held Tuesday at 12:30. ♦ 660 California St (at Grant Ave). 288.3800

### 32 IMPERIAL FASHION

It's not that the hand-decorated linens and handmade dickeys are any different here than at many other Chinatown shops, but they're particularly well displayed. Prices for the ornate handiwork are less than you'd expect to pay for a lot of machine-sewn tablecloths, guest towels, or napkins. ♦ Daily. 564 Grant Ave (at California St). 362.8112 &

### 33 LOTUS GARDEN

★$$ This vegetarian restaurant beneath a Taoist temple serves familiar Chinese dishes, but without the meat. ♦ Chinese/Vegetarian ♦ Tu-Su lunch and dinner. 532 Grant Ave (between Pine and California Sts). 397.0707

Within Lotus Garden:

### CHING CHUNG TAOIST TEMPLE

Take the stairs to the restaurant's top floor with its lovely stained-glass dome, and you'll find yourself in an ornate temple filled with gilded altars, carved furniture, fruit offerings, and smoking incense sticks. Spend a few minutes in appreciative silent contemplation, then leave refreshed for more sight-seeing. ♦ Daily

### 34 GRANT PLAZA HOTEL

$ This is probably one of San Francisco's most outstanding values. The lobby has glitzy accoutrements such as a crystal chandelier and generation-spanning Victorian and contemporary sofas in shades of pink and plum. The 72 rooms are small but well decorated. Ask for a corner room. On the sixth floor are a marvelous stained-glass dome and panels, legacies from a nightclub that existed on the premises in the 1920s. There's no restaurant, but being in the heart of Chinatown should make dining out a breeze. ♦ 465 Grant Ave (at Pine St). 434.3883, reservations only 800/472.6899; fax 434.3886

### 35 GRANT AVENUE

Chinatown's tourist shopping street is active, crowded, and fascinating. Restaurants and gift stores line the way from the ceremonial gateway located at Bush Street, down Grant Avenue, to Broadway. While many of the stores are virtually identical and most sell similar gifts and souvenirs, it's fun to stroll along and sample several of them. Many shops are open until 9 or 10PM every day, so you can have dinner at one of the many restaurants and then browse. This part of Chinatown is best experienced on foot—don't try driving down Grant (or Stockton for that matter), as traffic is congested and slow. Leaving Grant and wandering among the small, narrow alleys and lanes will allow you to absorb the sights, sounds, and smells of Chinatown. These little passages hold a hodgepodge of businesses: travel services, temples, groceries, laundries, Chinese book and newspaper stores, and benevolent associations. The latter are protective organizations, active in the civic and cultural life of Chinese residents. Note how the brick buildings are decorated with balconies and doorways painted green, red, yellow, and orange. ♦ Between Bush St and Broadway

### 35 TAI NAM YANG

In the furniture business for more than 30 years, the owners of this shop specialize in ornate rosewood pieces, ceramic objects, hand-painted vases and screens, and cloisonné. ♦ M-Sa. 438 Grant Ave (between Bush and Pine Sts). 982.2733

Approximately one in five San Franciscans is a Chinese immigrant.

The flamboyant green-and-ocher Gateway to Chinatown at Grant Avenue and Bush Street serves as the symbolic entrance to the Chinese capital of the Western world. Dragons and lions adorn the gateway, which was erected in 1970.

Early morning, when shopkeepers are busy setting out their wares, is a good time to get a feel for the real (i.e., non-touristy) Chinatown.

**Restaurants/Clubs: Red | Hotels: Purple | Shops: Orange | Outdoors/Parks: Green | Sights/Culture: Blue**

# DIM SUM AND THEN SOME

If you have only one Asian experience in San Francisco, make sure it's dim sum. These delicious tidbits are a local institution; only Hong Kong has more dim-sum parlors, and that's where the tradition originated.

Generally, dim sum are served for brunch; most dim-sum houses open around 10AM and close in the middle or late afternoon. Typically, waiters circle the dining room pushing carts stacked with covered bamboo or stainless-steel containers filled with steamed or fried dumplings, shrimp balls, spring rolls, steamed buns, and Chinese pastries. Just point to the items that look appealing as they roll by; the dim sum won't be listed on a menu, and the waiters often speak no English, so ordering is done by gesture.

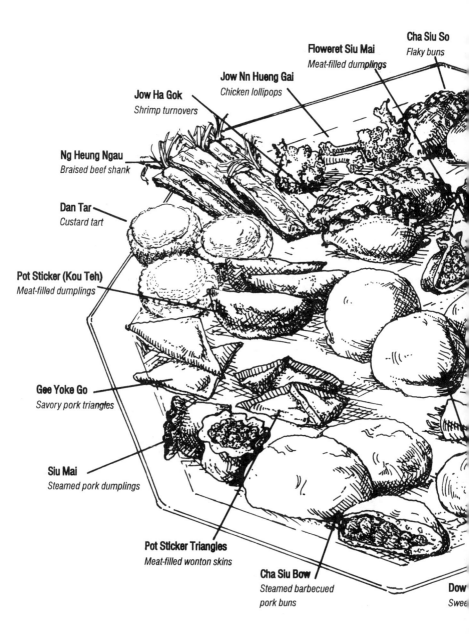

**Cha Siu So**
*Flaky buns*

**Floweret Siu Mai**
*Meat-filled dumplings*

**Jow Nn Hueng Gai**
*Chicken lollipops*

**Jow Ha Gok**
*Shrimp turnovers*

**Ng Heung Ngau**
*Braised beef shank*

**Dan Tar**
*Custard tart*

**Pot Sticker (Kou Teh)**
*Meat-filled dumplings*

**Gee Yoke Go**
*Savory pork triangles*

**Siu Mai**
*Steamed pork dumplings*

**Pot Sticker Triangles**
*Meat-filled wonton skins*

**Cha Siu Bow**
*Steamed barbecued pork buns*

**Dow**
*Swee*

Although dim sum may appear to be exotic, most fillings are pretty straightforward—pork, shrimp, cabbage, mushrooms, and ginger appear in many guises. Such unfamiliar delicacies as duck or chicken feet are sometimes offered, but they are easy to detect and reject, if you so desire. Noodle dishes may also be available, but they will be listed on a menu with English translations, rather than offered from the cart.

The carts circulate continuously, so you can order in stages, taking a few items each time they pass. In the old days, the bill was figured by the number of little plates left on the table, but today, a printed bill is updated by the servers as the meal progresses. It never adds up to much, though—you'll have to eat a lot of food to spend more than $10 a person.

Every dim sum restaurant does things a little differently, but here's a thumbnail guide to some of the most popular items.

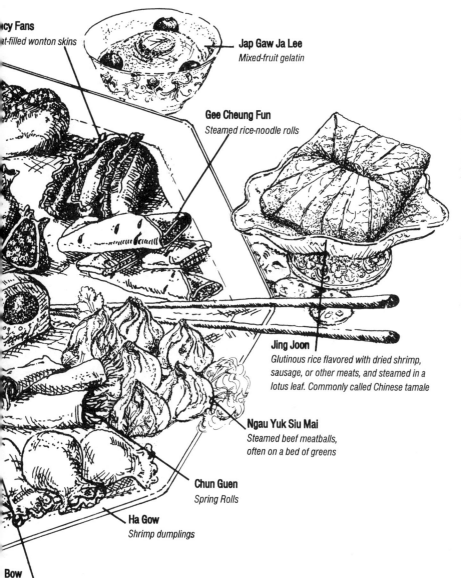

**cy Fans**
*at-filled wonton skins*

**Jap Gaw Ja Lee**
*Mixed-fruit gelatin*

**Gee Cheung Fun**
*Steamed rice-noodle rolls*

**Jing Joon**
*Glutinous rice flavored with dried shrimp, sausage, or other meats, and steamed in a lotus leaf. Commonly called Chinese tamale*

**Ngau Yuk Siu Mai**
*Steamed beef meatballs, often on a bed of greens*

**Chun Guen**
*Spring Rolls*

**Ha Gow**
*Shrimp dumplings*

**Bow**
*an-paste-filled buns*

# NOB HILL/RUSSIAN HILL

**F**ormerly christened the "Hill of Palaces," Nob Hill vies with Telegraph Hill for the honor of being the best known of San Francisco's many hills. The mansions of the rich are gone now, with the notable exception of James Flood's Edwardian brownstone at **1000 California Street;** they've been replaced with luxury hotels, a world-famous cathedral, several exclusive clubs and apartment houses, and upscale condominiums for millionaires.

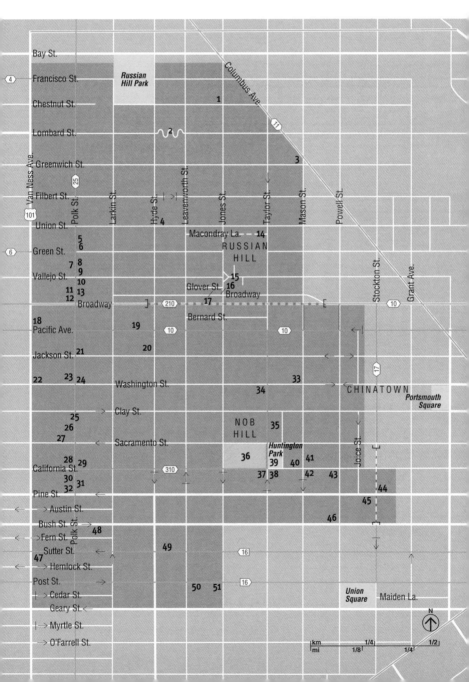

In the late 1850s, at the site of the **Renaissance Stanford Court Hotel,** Dr. Arthur Hayne cut a trail through the chaparral to survey the land and build the first home on the hill for his bride, actress Julia Dean. Within a few years, men of means followed his trail (a steep route that even their horses found difficult to navigate) and began a mass exodus from San Francisco's Rincon Hill and South Park. The advent of the cable car in 1873 encouraged the uphill flow of money, fueling the unbridled ostentatiousness of the homes of the rich and nouveaux riches. Ironically, it was all swept away 30 years later when a massive fire followed the earthquake of 1906.

In a sense, Nob Hill is still the "Hill of Palaces." Fastidious men and women continue to reach their homes or clubs by cable car, though during summer months the riders are almost all tourists. But the reckless display of wealth is gone—the air is more of subdued gentility, although power brokers still make the hill their home. The generally accepted boundaries of Nob Hill are **Bush Street** and **Pacific Avenue,** and **Stockton** and **Larkin Streets.**

Russian Hill, next door, is a neighborhood of contradiction, costly and bohemian at the same time. Studded with sleek high-rise apartments attended by porters, it has its share of the rich and famous. But there are also the working singles, struggling writers, and students from the nearby **San Francisco Art Institute** who share apartments, cramming four or five people into two bedrooms—the only way to afford the high rent. Despite the contrasts, it's the kind of place where customers and shop owners know each other on a first-name basis.

Within walking distance of Union Square, the Financial District, and North Beach, Russian Hill is full of picturesque culs-de-sac, bay views, wooded open spaces, and, of course, that wiggly part of **Lombard Street** that's better known as "the crookedest street in the world." Technically, Russian Hill extends from Pacific Avenue to **Bay Street** and from **Mason** to **Polk Streets,** but its real heart is bordered by **Broadway** and **Chestnut Street,** and **Taylor** and **Larkin Streets.**

## 1 SAN FRANCISCO ART INSTITUTE (SFAI)

This 1871 establishment is the oldest cultural institution in the West. Home to three galleries, the institute has played a central role in the development of contemporary art in the Bay Area. Student work is displayed in the **Diego Rivera Gallery;** the **Walter/McBean Gallery** shows work by professional artists; and the **Still Lights Gallery,** adjacent to the photography studios, has photographic exhibitions. **Paffard, Keatings, Clay**'s 1969 extension to the art institute, designed with great verve, is a rare example of the Corbusian *Béton brut* (concrete in the raw) style in California. It contains a lecture theater, a conference room, studios, workshops, exhibition spaces, and a cafe. ♦ Tu-Su during the school year. 800 Chestnut St (at Jones St). 771.7020 &

## 2 LOMBARD STREET

Nicknamed "the crookedest street in the world," this section of Lombard was designed in the 1920s to respond to the slope's extreme steepness. Faced with brick pavers and landscaped with flowers, shrubs, and hedges, the street is a fine example of the art of road engineering integrated into the urban fabric. Cars are no longer allowed to cruise down the winding road, but it's plenty of fun just to walk down from Hyde to Leavenworth (great exercise for the legs, too). ♦ Between Leavenworth and Hyde Sts

The east end of Lombard Street is considered by most to be the crookedest street in the world, with eight turns in one block.

Lynda Bird Johnson, daughter of the former president, was once asked to leave a cable car for eating an ice-cream cone on board.

Restaurants/Clubs: Red | Hotels: Purple | Shops: Orange | Outdoors/Parks: Green | Sights/Culture: Blue

### 3 BUCA GIOVANNI

★$$$ Buca means "cave" in Italian, and you reach the dining room here by descending a stairway to the lower level. On any given evening, the dishes presented might include ravioli stuffed with eggplant and gorgonzola in a light basil cream sauce or linguine with fresh porcini mushrooms; the restaurant is also known for using home-smoked rabbit in many pasta dishes. ♦ Italian ♦ Tu-Sa dinner. Reservations recommended. 800 Greenwich St (at Mason St). 776.7766 ♦

### 4 ZARZUELA

★★$ With its rough wood, stucco, and brick walls, this charming tapas place has a warm, welcoming look. Among the best hot tapas, lamb tenders are seared to a caramelized crustiness, all the better for the garlic-laced gravy that pools in the bottom of the plate. Scallops are golden outside and still silken inside and surround tender, wilted greens. The shrimp are spiced, cooked, cooled, and drizzled with a tomato-laced mayonnaise. Grilled vegetables, including eggplant and squash, get a boost from the smattering of olive oil and lemon. ♦ Spanish ♦ Tu-Sa dinner. 2000 Hyde St (at Union St). 346.0800 ♦

### 5 LITTLE THAI RESTAURANT

★$ Beneath the spreading branches of a large (fake) coconut tree, diners are served some inexpensive and often memorable dishes. Among the many choices are coconut-milk chicken soup with chilies, lemongrass, and loads of mushrooms and vegetables; *param long srong* (a sliced-pork creation with spinach in a sweet peanut sauce), *larb pad* (ground duck with lemon sauce), and *yum plamuk* (spicy calamari with mint and lemon). ♦ Thai ♦ Daily dinner. 2348 Polk St (between Green and Union Sts). 771.5544 ♦

### 6 LA FOLIE

★★★★$$$$ Without question, this is one of the top Californian/ French restaurants in the city. French-born Roland Passot, his brother George (the sommelier), and his American wife, Jamie, have created a dreamy, casually elegant environment in which puffy white clouds dance across a sky-blue ceiling and rich, yellow print fabric hangs from the French windows and frames the doors. Passot's presentations are breathtaking, and the recently updated menu (which changes seasonally) is better than ever. There might be roast quail leg stuffed with foie gras, backed by a Lyonnaise salad topped with a poached quail egg; *rôti* (roast) of squab and quail; rack of lamb; or fricasseed lobster. Passot also offers an à la carte menu, a five-course Discovery Menu, and a four-course vegetarian menu. You'll enjoy the lighthearted decor: marionettes "Guignol" the owners brought from their hometown of Lyon. ♦ Californian/French ♦ M-Sa dinner. Reservations recommended. 2316 Polk St (between Green and Union Sts). 776.5577 ♦

### 7 YABBIES COASTAL KITCHEN

★★★$$$ People are flocking to Mark Lusardi's relaxing unpretentious restaurant, renowned for its raw bar and grilled fish specialties. Many claim the ex-Vertigo chef is the new seafood king in town. The kitchen turns out wonderful flavorsome yabbies (crawfish in Australian) and other seafood dishes borrowed from various cuisines. Two favorites are pepper-seared ahi with Japanese eggplant and soy-citrus juices, and grilled swordfish with Sicilian capers and green olives. A wide selection of wines by the glass keeps the bar area hopping with locals. ♦ Seafood ♦ Daily dinner. Reservations required. 2237 Polk Street (between Vallejo and Green Sts). 474.4088 ♦

### 7 GREEN'S SPORTS BAR

If you think San Francisco sports fans aren't as enthusiastic as those on the East Coast, just try getting a drink (or getting *in*, for that matter) during a 'Niners game—it's a spectacle worth checking out. Between games, however, this place transforms into a pleasant neighborhood bar. ♦ Daily. 2239 Polk St (between Vallejo and Green Sts). 775.4287 ♦

### 8 ANDREW ROTHSTEIN FINE FOODS

★★$$ Busy business people stop by for pints of curried chicken, Cairo couscous, spicy potatoes and leeks all set for the microwave. Complete take-away meals range from pork loin to beef bourguignon. ♦ Daily. 2238 Polk St (between Vallejo and Green Sts). 447.4094 ♦

### 9 RUSSIAN HILL ANTIQUES

There are two floors of pine furniture, jewelry, and gift items here; most are from early 20th-century America and Europe. ♦ Tu-Su. 2200 Polk St (at Vallejo St). 441.5561 ♦

## 10 THE REAL FOOD DELI

★★★$ Patrons here have come to expect a wide selection of bread from the best bakeries, well-prepared meat and vegetarian dishes, salads, and cheeses. The desserts, however, tend to be uneven. There's seating inside and out for a total of 25 people. Great breads, olives, and cheeses are also sold here, and takeout is available. ♦ Deli ♦ Daily breakfast, lunch, and dinner. 2164 Polk St (at Vallejo St). 775.2805. Also at: 1001 Stanyan St (at Carl St). 564.1117 &

## 11 SWEETHEAT (OAXACA MEXICAN GRILL)

★$ This chic *taquería* has a Russian Hill pedigree but Mission District prices. Specializing in burritos with black beans and brown rice, the restaurant uses no lard and offers several lower-fat options, such as fish tacos and shrimp fajitas. The salsa bar is a plus, and the sangria makes a cool refresher. ♦ Mexican ♦ Daily lunch and dinner. 2141 Polk St (between Broadway and Vallejo St). 775.1055. &

## 12 PASHA

★$$$ Fine Middle Eastern fare and a sensuous, exotic ambience are the drawing cards at this Moroccan restaurant. Don't hesitate to tuck dollar bills into the belly dancer's waistband as she (or he) undulates by. Other temptations include rack of lamb with pomegranate and honey, grilled chicken brochette, or smoky prawns served with basmati rice. ♦ Moroccan/Middle Eastern ♦ Tu-Su dinner. Reservations recommended. 1516 Broadway (near Polk St). 885.4477 &

## 13 THE REAL FOOD COMPANY

This supermarket of organic foods (affectionately referred to by neighborhood residents as "The Real Expensive Food Company") features an excellent produce section. Check the center aisle for fresh bread delivered daily by the Bay Area's best bakeries, and hidden in back is a very good meat-and-fish counter. ♦ Daily. 2140 Polk St (between Broadway and Vallejo St). 673.7420. Also at: 1023 Stanyan St (between Carl St and Parnassus Ave). 564.2800; 3939 24th St (between Noe and Sanchez Sts). 282.9500, 474.8488 &

## 14 MACONDRAY LANE

The condominiums by **Bobbie Sue Hood** fit successfully into the traditional San Francisco bay-windowed residential style on this two-block pedestrian street on the steep north face of Russian Hill. ♦ Between Taylor and Leavenworth Sts, south of Union St

## 15 1000 BLOCK OF VALLEJO STREET

One of the city's most attractive residential neighborhoods, this block consists of three narrow residential streets—Vallejo Street (which is approached from Jones Street by ramps designed by Willis Polk, Polk, Willis), Russian Hill Place, and Florence Street. **Polk** built four Mediterranean-style villas between 1915 and 1916, and **Charles F. Whittlesey** designed the three to the south on Vallejo Street. All are private residences. ♦ Vallejo St (between Taylor and Jones Sts)

## 16 ALLEGRO RISTORANTE ITALIANO

★★$$$ Tucked into an affluent residential area and a favorite of San Francisco politicos and top executives, this pretty place is owned by Angelo Quaranta, who specializes in the foods of central and southern Italy. The most popular dishes are gnocchi, cannelloni, and any of the pastas. *Bruschetta* (thick slices of toasted bread spread with a chopped-tomato mixture) and Cornish hen are our top choices. ♦ Italian ♦ Daily dinner. Reservations recommended. 1701 Jones St (at Broadway). 928.4002 &

## 17 GLOVER STREET DUPLEX

One of the **Dan Solomon–Paulette Taggert** team's beautifully designed San Francisco houses, this consists of two units interlocked one above the other on a 25-foot-wide lot. The front facade is an interesting mixture of traditional bay-window elements and a Classical portico with a severely detailed triangular pediment. The Modernist windows and gateway make the 1982 design of this private residence both Rationalist and Contextual. ♦ 15 and 17 Glover St (between Jones and Leavenworth Sts)

## 18 HARRIS' RESTAURANT

★★$$$ There's no doubt that this steak-and-prime-rib house means business—a glass refrigerator full of its stock is on prominent display to passersby and for sale to those who would rather cook at home. Mrs. Harris herself, who has a cattle-ranching background, presides over the restaurant. Top-quality meats are served in two substantial dining rooms decorated with roomy booths and wood. Lighter suppers (such as soup and salad) are served in the bar. It's reminiscent of a comfortable, old-money ranchers' club. ♦ Steak House ♦ Daily dinner. Reservations recommended. 2100 Van Ness Ave (at Pacific Ave). 673.1888 &

## 19 RISTORANTE MILANO

★★★$$ This small, stylish restaurant serves some of the best Northern Italian dishes in

---

Restaurants/Clubs: Red | Hotels: Purple | Shops: Orange | Outdoors/Parks: Green | Sights/Culture: Blue

town at moderate prices. The waiters are polite and knowledgeable; the contemporary decor is an interesting mix of Japanese woodwork and Milanese design in charcoal gray and off-white. With plenty of repeat customers and reservations limited to parties of four or more, expect a crowd and possibly a long wait unless you dine early or very late. ♦ Italian ♦ Tu-Su dinner. 1448 Pacific Ave (between Hyde and Larkin Sts). 673.2961 &

## 20 HYDE STREET BISTRO

★★★$$ Albert Rainer, the dashing chef-owner, greets and charms customers at the door of his pleasant, modest restaurant. He also produces some outstanding food. His Californian/Austrian approach translates into a captivating vegetable strudel with layers of flaky pastry, excellent roast chicken with the barest whisper of cumin, and rustic veal fricassee with wild mushrooms and spaetzle. Of special note, on this busy street, is the availability of valet parking. ♦ Austrian/Californian ♦ Tu-Su dinner. Reservations recommended. 1521 Hyde St (at Pacific Ave). 292.4415 &

## 21 THE BELL TOWER

★★$ This handsome bar and restaurant is quickly becoming a neighborhood favorite, serving low-priced standards such as burgers, hot dogs, and chicken wings. Also on the menu are inexpensive nontraditional dishes like fried catfish sandwiches; tequila-lime-and-cilantro-marinated Chilean sea bass, served on a bed of black beans; and salmon pasta with herb cream, red onions, and capers. It's the perfect place to take a break and chat with the locals. ♦ Californian/American ♦ Daily lunch and dinner until midnight. 1900 Polk St (at Jackson St). 567.9596 &

## 21 FIORIDELLA

One of San Francisco's most creative (and, yes, expensive) florists; its designs are much favored by the socially prominent. ♦ M-Sa. 1920 Polk St (between Jackson St and Pacific Ave). 775.4065 &

## 21 J. GOLDSMITH ANTIQUES

This cute general store stocks American collectibles—with special emphasis on toys—and sells them at slightly lower-than-market prices. ♦ Daily. 1924 Polk St (between Jackson St and Pacific Ave). 771.4055 &

## 22 HOUSE OF PRIME RIB

★★★$$ A favorite among beef eaters with big appetites, this grill offers handsome decor, comfortable booths, soft lighting, and generous servings of excellent prime rib that are carved at the table. There are even seconds for those who can go the distance.

Good grilled salmon is offered as a non-beef alternative. ♦ American ♦ Daily dinner. Reservations recommended. 1906 Van Ness Ave (between Washington and Jackson Sts). 885.4605 &

## 23 NAOMI'S ANTIQUES TO GO

A paradise for nostalgiaholics, this place stocks lots of American dinnerware, pottery, and china from the 1920s to the 1950s. ♦ Tu-Sa. 1817 Polk St (between Washington and Jackson Sts). 775.1207 &

## 24 BUFFALO EXCHANGE

The young crowd loves the new and recycled clothing stocked here, and many keep their wardrobes going by regularly exchanging what they have for something they like better. ♦ Daily. 1800 Polk St (at Washington St). 346.5726. Also at: 1555 Haight St (between Clayton and Ashbury Sts). 431.7733; 2512 Telegraph Ave (between Blake St and Dwight Way), Berkeley. 510/644.9202 &

## 25 LOWER POLK STREET

The stretch between California and Geary Streets is known as Polk Gulch and was the focus of the city's gay population until most of the action moved to the Castro district. Currently, that portion of Polk is in transition, populated by many drifters and young male hustlers. Much of the gloss the street attained in the 1970s has been lost to a proliferation of shops whose wares are in questionable taste. But as strollers head north, beyond California Street, the area's appeal is alive and well, with a mix of old neighborhood food stores, antiques shops, bookstores, restaurants, and several charming specialty shops. ♦ Between Geary and Lombard Sts

## 26 DOUBLE RAINBOW

Some aficionados claim the rich and creamy ice cream at this shop is the best in San Francisco. The ultrachocolate flavor certainly is tops! ♦ Daily. 1653 Polk St (at Clay St). 775.3220. &

## 27 ACQUERELLO

★★★★$$$ Giancarlo Paterlini and Suzette Gresham, who operate this sophisticated restaurant, serve marvelously inventive contemporary dishes in a soothing, pastel-hued dining room decorated with original watercolors. The small menu, which changes frequently, might include salmon-and-scallop ravioli in dry vermouth, fillet of beef with balsamic vinegar and shallots, or breast of chicken rolled in pancetta with sage and Madeira sauce. ♦ Italian ♦ Tu-Sa dinner. Reservations recommended. 1722 Sacramento St (between Polk St and Van Ness Ave). 567.5432

## 28 BEERNESS BOHEMIA

British beer, darts, pool, and pinball draw Anglophiles and British expatriates to this dark and seedy-looking bar. ♦ Daily until 2AM. 1624 California St (between Polk St and Van Ness Ave). 474.6968 ♿

## 28 SWAN OYSTER DEPOT

★★★$$ This restaurant is a favorite among knowledgeable San Franciscans, although you won't find anything fancier than a lunch counter and stools. But the cold fish dishes are fantastic and the servers among the friendliest around. There is also fish to take home. ♦ Seafood/Takeout ♦ M-Sa breakfast and lunch. 1517 Polk St (between California and Sacramento Sts). 673.1101

## 29 CORDON BLEU

★★$ A perfect choice before catching a movie, this is one of San Francisco's best hole-in-the-wall Vietnamese restaurants, and an unbelievably fine value. Five-spice chicken, a Vietnamese staple, is sumptuous here. ♦ Vietnamese ♦ Tu-Sa lunch and dinner; Su dinner. 1574 California St (at Polk St). 673.5637

## 30 CRUSTACEAN

★★$$ The kitchen turns out flavorful Euro-Asian seafood dishes in this sleek restaurant with its witty, under-the-sea decor. Popular menu picks include "multi-vitamin rolls" (a New Age name for spring rolls), roast Dungeness crab, and royal tiger prawns served over garlic noodles. ♦ Seafood ♦ Daily dinner. Reservations recommended. 1475 Polk St (at California St), Third floor. 776.2722 ♿

## 31 ACORN BOOKS

Used books are bought, sold, and exchanged here. The roughly 30,000 volumes range from rare first editions to paperback mystery thrillers. ♦ Daily. 1436 Polk St (at California St). 563.1736 ♿

## 32 FIELDS BOOK STORE

This shop full of spiritual and esoteric books has been helping its readers solve life's deepest mysteries since 1932. ♦ Tu-Sa. 1419 Polk St (between Pine and California Sts). 673.2027 ♿

## 33 CABLE CAR MUSEUM

The winding house for the underground cables that control the cars, known as the **Cable Car Barn,** was constructed in 1887, then rebuilt after it was badly damaged in the 1906 quake. When the cable-car system was renovated in the early 1980s, the barn was reinforced, but the exterior was left alone. The museum now has an underground viewing room where you may watch the cables work. Photographs and memorabilia are also on display, including three vintage cable cars. ♦ Free. Daily. 1201 Mason St (at Washington St). 474.1887 ♿

## 34 VENTICELLO

★★★$$$ A few years ago, this was probably the best Italian restaurant in the city; changes in the kitchen have dulled its shine a bit, but the food still can be excellent, especially pizzas and anything else from the wood oven, which is the focal point of the two-level dining room. Try the baked mussels, or venison with wild mushrooms, or pizza topped with duck breast, smoked red onions, and tangy goat cheese. ♦ Italian ♦ Daily dinner. Reservations recommended. 1257 Taylor St (at Washington St). 922.2545 ♿

## 35 NOB HILL CAFÉ

★★$ This family-run bistro, where owner Michael Deeb and his friendly staff go out of their way to make you feel at home, is tucked into a charming, quiet corner of Nob Hill. It's a neighborhood favorite, and paintings by local artists adorn the walls. The menu offers traditional Italian cuisine and an array of California-tinged specials at prices uncommonly low for the area. Try the *crostini di polenta* (polenta topped with mozzarella and pesto), a pizza Margherita, or any of the chef's nightly creations. Be prepared to wait— there are only 14 tables and reservations are not accepted.

♦ Italian ♦ Daily lunch and dinner. 1152 Taylor St (between Sacramento and Clay Sts). 776.6500 ♿

## 36 GRACE CATHEDRAL

**Lewis P. Hobart**'s fine Neo-Gothic cathedral, modeled after Notre Dame in Paris, took 53 years to build and was finally consecrated in 1964. Notice the beautiful rose window, completed by Gabriel Loire in Chartres, and the spectacular entry, with its *Doors of Paradise*, taken from the same mold used for the entrance to Ghiberti's Baptistry in Florence. There is also a magnificent organ and a not-to-be-missed boys' and mens' choir. Inside the gift shop is a coffee bar. Parking available. ♦ 1051 Taylor St (bounded by Taylor and Jones Sts, and California and Sacramento Sts). 749.6300 Concert event line 749.6350 ♿

## 37 MASONIC AUDITORIUM

This 3,165-seat auditorium is large, but the sight lines are terrible. Orchestras, dance groups, and lectures appear on the thrust stage. ♦ 1111 California St (between Taylor and Jones Sts). 292.9190 ♿

## 38 THE HUNTINGTON HOTEL

$$$ Small, elegant, impeccably groomed, and located on the peak of Nob Hill, this 140-room hotel is the kind of place that has such a loyal following that advertising is unnecessary. This is partly due to the permanency of its staff, which does much to preserve the Huntington brand of personal hospitality. No two rooms are alike; they all look as if they might well belong in a private residence, and all have a view of either the city or the bay. Suites are equipped with a complete kitchen or a wet bar. Huntington has added the Nob Hill Spa: ten treatment rooms, weight training room and exercise room for yoga, tai chi and Pilates. Complimentary Town Car service to the Financial and shopping districts and tea or sherry served upon your arrival are among the amenities. ♦ 1075 California St (between Mason and Taylor Sts). 474.5400, 800/652.1539 in CA, 800/227.4683; fax 474.6227

Within the Huntington Hotel:

## THE BIG 4

★$$$ Named in tribute to four railroad magnates of San Francisco— Collins P. Hunt-ington, Charles Crocker, Mark Hopkins, and Leland Stanford—this restaurant features decor that brilliantly evokes the late 1800s with such touches as etched beveled-glass panels and polished woods. Chef Gloria Ciccarone-Nehls prepares a combination of French and nouvelle Californian cuisine. ♦ Californian/French ♦ M-F breakfast, lunch, and dinner; Sa-Su breakfast and dinner. Reservations recommended. 771.1140

## 39 HUNTINGTON PARK

This delightful oasis atop Nob Hill has a central fountain that replicates Rome's 16th-century Tartarughe Fountain. ♦ Taylor St (between California and Sacramento Sts)

## 40 THE PACIFIC-UNION CLUB

Remodeled by **Willis Polk** in 1908 after the quake and fire, this Edwardian brownstone was originally built in 1886 for James C. Flood, one of the city's railroad kings. He reputedly spent $1.5 million on the house alone, an enormous sum for the times. Polk added the attic story and the entrance tower, which somewhat mar the original classical lines. The building is now used as a very, very private social retreat for male members of "the Establishment." ♦ 1000 California St (at Mason St)

## TOP OF THE MARK

Dating from 1939, this renowned sky-high lounge, which boasts glorious views from its 19th-floor perch, set the standard for those that came after it. It's an elegant, charming place to watch the sun set or to take in the twinkling lights of the city. On Sundays, when an elaborate, expensive buffet brunch is offered. Cocktails are served all day, and afternoon tea from 2:30PM to 5:30PM. ♦ M-Th 2:30PM-1AM; F-Sa 3PM-2AM; Su brunch 10AM-2:30PM. 392.3434 ♿

## 41 THE FAIRMONT

$$$$ This hotel was constructed on the property of Senator James "Bonanza Jim" Fair, and the foundations of the palace he had planned to build were later incorporated into the hotel. Son-in-law Hermann Oeirichs planned and began construction of the hotel, to the consternation of the city fathers, who could not understand placing any hotel so far from the center of town. New owners took over before the building was completed, hoping to open it in 1906. Although the frame withstood the earthquake, the subsequent fire ate up the interior and work had to begin all over again. When Senator Fair's daughter offered to take the property back, the disheartened owners jumped at the chance. On 18 April 1907, Mrs. Hermann Oeirichs kicked off the opening of the hotel with a magnificent banquet symbolizing the rebirth of the city one year after the earthquake.

Owner Saudi billionaire Prince Alwaleed embarked on a much-needed refurbishing project to return the hotel to its original splendor, beginning with restoration of the Italian marble floor in the grand lobby. With the original building and a 22-story tower, this grand hotel has 600 rooms and suites, six restaurants, six lounges (including the **Fairmont Crown,** the highest public-observation point in the city, and the **New Orleans Room,** with nightly live jazz), two orchestras, international supper-club talent, and an almost one-to-one ratio of guests to employees. ◆ 950 Mason St (at California St). 772.5000, 800/527.4727; fax 789.3929

Within The Fairmont:

## CROWN ROOM TOP OF THE TOWER

★$$$ Sunday brunch, a light lunch, and a buffet dinner are accompanied by what many consider the all-time best view of San Francisco. ◆ American ◆ M-Sa cocktails and dinner; Su brunch and dinner. 772.5131 &

## MASONS RESTAURANT

★★$$$$ One of the most striking rooms in the city, this restaurant on the arcade level of the hotel has an understated elegance—a beautiful wood ceiling and deep chairs upholstered in pastel stripes and patterns. A three-course fixed-price dinner, with choices from the regular menu, is offered before 7PM and is the best bargain. Starters include grilled prawns with couscous, and entrées lean to straightforward grilled preparations such as lamb chops served on soft polenta. For dessert there's chocolate soufflé or warm apple tart with caramel sauce. ◆ Californian ◆ Daily dinner. Reservations recommended. 772.5233 &

## TONGA RESTAURANT AND HURRICANE BAR

$$ Disneyland meets the South Pacific at this funky restaurant on the terrace level; hourly thunderstorms are staged here, with water pouring down over a central pool. A waterfall behind the low-lit bar and artificial orchids and other plants evoke the tropics, as do the funky drinks (such as the Bora-Bora Horror, a mixture of rum, banana liqueur, Grand Marnier, and pineapple juice). ◆ Polynesian ◆ Daily dinner. 772.5278 &

## *The Mark Hopkins*

## 42 MARK HOPKINS INTER-CONTINENTAL SAN FRANCISCO

$$$$ Ever since its opening in 1926, this 392-room hotel (familiarly known as "The Mark") has been well regarded internationally. It was host to officials during the formation of the United Nations, and a vacation site for Presidents Hoover and Eisenhower and countless other celebrities. Major renovations of the famous **Peacock Court** and **Room of the Dons** have restored the ballrooms' historic murals and elegant ambience, and the rooms have once again become favored for society weddings, debuts, and charity parties. Amenities include 24-hour room service, one-day laundry and valet services, terry-cloth robes, in-room movies, video messages posted on the TV screen, minibars, baby-sitting and concierge services, and a health club. There is also a business service center. ◆ 1 Nob Hill (at California and Mason Sts). 392.3434, 800/327.0200; fax 421.3302

Within the Mark Hopkins Inter-Continental San Francisco:

## NOB HILL RESTAURANT

★★$$$$ The atmosphere is formal at this handsome, oak-paneled restaurant, which is largely patronized by hotel guests. The menu changes often and might include consommé of pheasant with poached quail egg and chives, sea bass steamed with fennel and served with a parsnip-caviar mousse and grilled portobello mushrooms, or roast loin of veal with sun-dried-cherry sauce. One of the best deals is a prix-fixe, three-course dinner offered nightly. ◆ Californian/French ◆ Daily breakfast, lunch, and dinner. Reservations recommended. 616.6944 &

## 43 RENAISSANCE STANFORD COURT HOTEL

$$$$ America's top executives often rank this hotel as their favorite in San Francisco. The attractive decor is combined with the

---

amenities of a European-style hostelry. Each of the 402 rooms and suites has individually controlled air conditioning, a marble bath with a dressing room, a color TV well hidden in an armoire, and heated towel racks. Many have canopied beds. Coffee, newspapers, and overnight shoe shines are among the complimentary services. Mercedes and Rolls-Royce limousines are available for hire from 7AM to 8PM. It was built on the site of railroad magnate Leland Stanford's mansion, later the location of a 1912 apartment building, which was gutted to create the hotel. The only remainder from the Stanford days is a 30-foot-high wall surrounding the property, although the design borrows something from the original house. For example, the Stanfords had a circular vestibule illuminated by an amber glass dome three stories above. A similar effect has been achieved in the hotel by covering the central courtyard and fountain with a lofty stained-glass canopy; tea and cocktails are served here. There's also indoor valet parking and a multilingual staff. ♦ 905 California St (at Powell St). 989.3500, fax 391.0513 ♿

Within the Renaissance Stanford Court Hotel:

### FOURNOU'S OVENS

★★★$$$$ The most distinctive places to dine in this multilevel restaurant are in the glass-enclosed conservatory area, which is pleasant for breakfast and lunch, or at the "oven" level, which boasts a magnificent open hearth decorated with Portuguese tiles and a floor-to-ceiling wine cellar. Chef Ercolinio Crugnale's creative menu includes gnocchi with vegetables in a truffle broth, and pasta with rock shrimp and sun-dried tomatoes. The filet mignon, served on a bed of corn kernel-studded mashed potatoes, is topped with a parmesan cheese wafer and a square of foie gras with fried leeks and smokey tomato vinaigrette. One of the best bargains around is the two- or three-course Twilight Supper, served from 5:30 to 6:30PM. ♦ American ♦ Daily breakfast, lunch, and dinner. Reservations recommended. 989.3500 ♿

### 44 THE RITZ-CARLTON SAN FRANCISCO

$$$$ This hostelry occupies a renovated 1909 Neo-Classical building that used to house Metropolitan Life Insurance. Throughout the public areas are fine collections of 18th- and 19th-century artwork and antiques, as well as Aubusson tapestries and Persian carpets. It has 336 beautifully furnished rooms and suites, including a Club Floor with such amenities as private concierge and complimentary continental breakfast and afternoon tea. The multilingual staff offers impeccable, old-fashioned service,

and guests have use of an indoor lap pool and fitness center. An elegant afternoon tea is available daily in the lobby lounge from 2:30PM to 5PM. ♦ 600 Stockton St (between Pine and California Sts). 296.7465, 800/241.3333; fax 986.1268

Within The Ritz-Carlton San Francisco:

### THE DINING ROOM

★★★$$$$ Chef Sylvain Portay presides over the kitchen and turns out some of the most creative Californian/French cuisine in the city. The setting is formal and luxurious, ideal for romance and celebration. The five-course tasting menu, paired with excellent wines, is always available and changes six times a year. It might include such seasonal specialties as glazed oysters with leek fondue, duck breast with crisp potato croutons, rhubarb, lavender, and cracked almonds; or roast squab, the best in town, with sage and pancetta, paired with foie gras and Yellow Finn potatoes. Desserts are heavenly: Leave room for either the blackberry soufflé or the chocolate-hazelnut *croustillant,* crackling with praline. ♦ Californian/French ♦ Tu-Sa dinner. Reservations recommended. 296.7465 ♿

### THE TERRACE

★★$$$ Under the guidance of chef Paul Murphy, the Italian-inspired menu offers such interesting selections as a plate of delicate greens with squares of puff pastry filled with caramelized onions and artichoke hearts, and Tuscan-style chicken with zucchini and roasted potatoes. This spot is perfect for a leisurely lunch; select one of the 15 wines served by the glass to complement your entrée. Located on the courtyard level. ♦ Mediterranean ♦ M-Sa breakfast, lunch, and dinner; Su brunch and dinner. 296.7465 ♿

### 45 NOB HILL LAMBOURNE

$$$ This business-oriented hotel includes a fax machine and a personal computer in all 20 rooms. There also is voice mail, full secretarial support, desktop publishing, and boardroom facilities, but no restaurant. The guest rooms are decorated in contemporary and period styles. ♦ 725 Pine St (between Stockton and Powell Sts). 433.2287, 800/274.8466; fax 433.0975

## THE BEST

**Holly Stiel**

President/Holly Speaks
(Hospitality Consulting and Concierge Training)

Truth be told, I love alternative shopping at consignment shops and flea markets. The best consignment shops are on **Fillmore Street** and upper **Polk Street.**

I love to ride the ferry to **Sausalito,** when I get a lazy 30 minutes to watch the seagulls and take in all the sights and sounds of San Francisco Bay.

If I'm downtown I have breakfast at **Postrio** or **Campton Place Dining Room;** on a nice day, I have lunch at **Cafe Tiramisù** on Belden Place, or eat the warm chicken salad at the **Plaza Restaurant** in the **Grand Hyatt Hotel.**

In the evening it's back to the **Grand Hyatt Hotel** for jazz piano at **Grandview Lounge.**

### 46 CAFÉ MOZART

★★★★$$$$ One of Nob Hill's best restaurants, this refined establishment with intimate dining on three levels produces food that arrives so beautifully arranged on the plate, it's hard to decide whether it should be photographed or eaten. Gourmets who can't make up their minds should choose the *menu dégustation,* which provides samplings of many different dishes that change regularly to reflect the freshest products in the market. Other notable options include tiger prawns champignons and roast duck de Provence. The ambience here is cozy and traditional, with Corots and Monets gracing the walls. A fireplace glows in the main dining room, and only Mozart is played in the background. The wine list is pricey. ♦ French ♦ Tu-Su dinner. Reservations recommended. 708 Bush St (between Powell and Mason Sts). 391.8480 ♿

### 47 GALAXY THEATER

One of the first movie complexes to be built in the city in a generation, this 1984 **Kaplan/ McLaughlin/Diaz** building houses four theaters. It is best seen at dusk, when the neon signs glow rainbow colors. ♦ 1285 Sutter St (at Van Ness Ave). 474.8700 ♿

### 48 ALLIANCE FRANÇAISE

Here's the educational heart of San Francisco's sizable French-speaking community, and an ideal place to learn to *parle français.* ♦ 1345 Bush St (between Larkin and Polk Sts). 775.7755 ♿

### 49 YORK HOTEL

$$ Moderately priced and centrally located, this is one of the many small hostelries that have been spiffed up. The 96 rooms are attractive, and there are trendy extras such as a complimentary wine hour, a complimentary breakfast, and an executive gym. There is no on-premises restaurant. ♦ 940 Sutter St (between Leavenworth and Hyde Sts). 885.6800, 800/808.9675; fax 885.2115 ♿

Within the York Hotel:

### THE PLUSH ROOM

Big-name as well as up-and-coming entertainers play at this unique, aptly named cabaret. Among those who've performed here are Michael Feinstein, Charles Pierce, Jim Bailey, Margaret Whiting, and Andrea Marcovicci. Note the spectacular stained-glass ceiling. ♦ Cover. Hours vary according to show times. 885.6800 ♿

## *Hotel Bedford*

### 50 HOTEL BEDFORD

$$ This 17-story, 144-room inn has a stunning dining room, a friendly lobby, and intimate bedrooms that have the feeling of a private home. Hotel guests are invited to a complimentary wine bar every evening, and room service is available for breakfast and dinner. Another plus: It's just three blocks from Union Square and very close to galleries, theaters, and transportation. ♦ 761 Post St (at Leavenworth St). 673.6040, 800/227.5642; fax 563.6739 ♿

### 51 HOTEL BERESFORD ARMS

$ One of the finest small hotels in the theater district provides a friendly atmosphere and personal service. Many of the 95 rooms have whirlpool baths and wet bars. Senior citizens get discounts and children under 12 may stay free. There is an unusually attractive lobby for entertaining your guests, but no restaurant. ♦ 701 Post St (at Jones St). 673.2600, 800/533.6533; fax 474.0449 ♿

---

Restaurants/Clubs: Red | Hotels: Purple | Shops: Orange | Outdoors/Parks: Green | Sights/Culture: Blue

# NORTH BEACH/FISHERMAN'S WHARF/TELEGRAPH HILL

The North Beach district was named after a beach that once extended from Telegraph Hill to Russian Hill, but has long since been built up by landfill. The community guards its reputation against the creeping encroachment of the neon, skin shows, and drag queens of nearby **Broadway**, as well as the skyrocketing real-estate prices that threaten the stability of its long-standing ethnic mix. But somehow the old ingredients of the melting-pot neighborhood survive, along with certain remnants of the life that made this area the birthplace of the "Beat Generation." Although North Beach is synonymous with "Little Italy," Italians were not the first nor the last to arrive. Chilean prostitutes came first, in the 1850s, attracted by the Gold Rush, only to be chased out by the Irish, who were eventually replaced by more Latin Americans. On a site first occupied

by a Russian Serbian Greek Orthodox Church, the **Washington Square Theater** presented Enrico Caruso in concert. Later this theater became the **Pagoda Palace,** featuring Chinese movies. Supplemented by small colonies of Basques, young working people, and bohemians, the Chinese began crossing Broadway from Chinatown in the 1960s. Today the North Beach population is approximately 50 percent Chinese—and growing—although new Italian immigrants are also settling here once again. The perfect place to sample the tempo of this neighborhood is **Washington Square.** Relax on a park bench here and let the gossip in Chinese and Italian swirl around you while old men and women practice T'ai Chi and kids and drifters hang out on the grass.

Bordering North Beach is Telegraph Hill, with its quaint cottages and vine-covered lanes, flowering gardens, stunning views, and impossible parking. Artists and writers once lived here, but now it's mostly the affluent and established who've made it home. The "Hill," as residents call it, looked quite different in the days of the Gold Rush. Although its height is the same (284 feet), the east slope used to be smooth and round and covered with grazing goats. The barren, jagged cliff you see today was created by sailors digging out ballast for their empty ship holds back when water lapped at the hill's base. The area went through several names, but after the Morse Code Signal Station was set up in 1853, the current name stuck. Although most of North Beach burned in the post-earthquake fire of 1906, the Italians managed to save a number of the old wooden cottages on the hill with a bucket brigade, using barrels of homemade red wine. The tiny shacks, built by early fishermen, now sell for hundreds of thousands of dollars. Crowning the hill is **Coit Tower,** named for Lillie Hitchcock Coit, who provided the funds to build it.

**Fisherman's Wharf,** also bordering North Beach, is one of the city's most popular tourist attractions. Seafood houses stand where crab fishers once hauled in their catch, and there are enough souvenir shops to keep the locals away. At press time, a new ferry landing behind the historic Ferry Arch is under construction. It's best to get to the area by the new streetcar line. An extension of the MUNI F-line starts at the top of Market St travels the palm-tree-lined Embarcadero and ends at Fisherman's Wharf: a total distance of 10.2 miles that provides riders with a dramatic view of the Bay Bridge and waterfront.

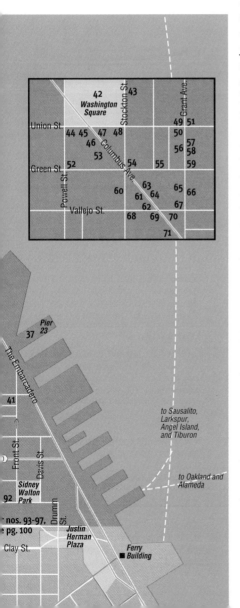

Not much more than a legend remains of the **Barbary Coast,** the once-notorious neighborhood extending between **Washington Street,** and **Pacific Avenue,** and **Montgomery** and **Kearny Streets.** Named after the unsavory pirate headquarters in North Africa, this was where the term "shanghaid" originated, describing the practice of drugging a hapless seaman and shipping him out as a crew member for an understaffed ship. The Barbary Coast was a gathering place for hoodlums—a word coined here during the early 1900s, when the city had a worldwide reputation for viciousness. The area was finally shut down after World War I. In the 1950s it was renamed **Jackson Square** by the decorators who renovated the old buildings, exposing handsome brick walls and restoring the mid-19th-century structures. As a result, these blocks became the city's first designated historic site.

## 1 HYDE STREET PIER

As San Francisco is first and foremost a seaport, no visit to the area would be complete without a tour along the waterfront. Several vessels are docked at this pier (where ferries once carried passengers to Sausalito and Berkeley), which is part of the **San Francisco Maritime National Historic Park System.** The three that are open to the public, the *C.A. Thayer,* the *Eureka,* and the *Balclutha,* hold artifacts, photography collections, and displays that help bring their exciting pasts alive. ♦ Admission; seniors and children under 12 free. Daily. Hyde St (at Jefferson St, at the west end of Fisherman's Wharf) &

At Hyde Street Pier:

### C.A. THAYER

Built in 1895, this schooner (pictured above) was the Pacific Coast's last commercial sailing ship. It transported lumber, served in two wars, and was most recently employed by the fishing industry.

### EUREKA

This was the last diesel-powered ferry to operate in the US. Built in 1890, this vessel hauled freight and passengers for the **San Francisco** and **Northern Pacific Railroads.**

Angel Island, also known as the "Ellis Island of the West," served as an immigration and quarantine station until November 1940. It's the largest island in the bay.

### HERCULES

Berthed beside the *Eureka,* this frigate (pictured above) is under restoration and not open to the public. Built in 1907, the oceangoing tug hauled cargo, crippled ships, barges, and even materials for the Panama Canal.

### BALCLUTHA

A favorite city landmark, this is a classic square-rigged, three-masted sailing ship. Built in Scotland in 1883, it sailed the Cape Horn route for many years, bringing European goods to the West Coast and taking California grains back home. After the turn of the century, it served as a lumber ship, a salmon cannery in Alaskan waters, and finally a carnival ship and Hollywood movie prop.

## 2 LOU'S PIER 47

Everyone from swabbies on shore leave to local blues aficionados checks out the blues, rock, jazz, or whatever's playing at this club. ♦ Shows daily. 300 Jefferson St (between Jones and Leavenworth Sts). 771.0377

## 3 SCOMA'S

★★$$ Believe it or not, this venerable but rundown seafood house is the highest-grossing restaurant in San Francisco, packing people in just about every day of the year. It's the kind of joint where disinterested waiters sling your food at you on the run and present the check before dessert even arrives. Much of the charm of the place is its dockside location. As for the food, the fish is generally very fresh and portions are generous, but the presentation is fatally flawed. Oysters on the half shell, for instance, are mishandled, buried in ice, and sloppily served. Best bets are the grilled fish steaks with simple sauces. ◆ Seafood ◆ Daily lunch and dinner. Pier 47 (at Jones and Jefferson Sts). 771.4383 ♿

## 4 RIPLEY'S BELIEVE IT OR NOT! MUSEUM

Tour two floors of oddities collected by cartoonist Robert L. Ripley. ◆ Admission. Daily. 175 Jefferson St (at Taylor St). 771.6188 ♿

## 5 BOUDIN SOURDOUGH FRENCH BREAD BAKERY

Frenchman Isadore Boudin opened the city's first bakery on Grant Avenue in 1849 and became one of the first to bake sourdough bread. Now there are 10 **Boudin** bakeries in San Francisco, including this one, which provides a glimpse of the mysterious sourdough process. ◆ Daily. 156 Jefferson St (at Taylor St). 928.1849 ♿

## 6 FISHERMAN'S WHARF

The wharf was once the center of San Francisco's commercial fishing fleet, and while the boats are still here, this is now heavy tourist territory. Locals who remember when the business here really was the fishing industry are not pleased with the direction the area has taken and will not be found in significant numbers at the many seafood restaurants, few of which provide much cause for gastronomic rejoicing. ◆ Taylor St (at The Embarcadero)

At Fisherman's Wharf:

## RED & WHITE FLEET

Sightseeing bay cruises circle Alcatraz and point out the sights of the bay . ◆ Admission. Daily. At pier 43 1/3. 447-0591

## PAMPANITO SUBMARINE

This World War II original is docked at the pier. ◆ Admission. Daily. At pier 45. 561.6662

## ALIOTO'S

★★$$$ This is the oldest restaurant in the area known for the spectacular views from the upstairs dining room. The street-side stand offers cracked crab, while the eatery below *Nonna Rose* (359-1200) serves Sicilian homestyle seafood dishes. The upstairs dining room is washed in a quiet brown color scheme that lets the colorful view of gently rocking boats stand out. Sicilian specialties are mixed in with such standard

Cal/Ital dishes as ziti with pine nuts, raisins, tomatoes, and flakes of fresh-tasting fish. ◆ Seafood ◆ Daily lunch and dinner. 8 Fisherman's Wharf (at Taylor St) 673.0183

## 7 HERB CAEN WAY...

Punctuated with historic plaques and pylons recalling events and people of the past, this boardwalk on the bay side of the Embarcadero is named in honor of the late Herb Caen. For more than a half century, the San Francisco Chronicle's Caen was the city's premier columnist, the expert on the city's finest offerings and most titillating gossip. His first column on San Francisco appeared 5 July 1938. It soon evolved into an upbeat blend of news, scandals, vignettes, and thought-provoking dramas, spiced with schmaltz and an occasional thorn in the side of those in power. His wit and flair with words made him one of the most quoted columnists in *Reader's Digest*. The three dots were made part of the promenade's name because Caen always used them to separate items in his column. The Embarcadero (between Berry and Taylor Sts).

## 8 PIER 39

America's third-most-visited amusement attraction (Disney takes the top spots), this two-level shopping street, particularly popular with families, runs along the north waterfront near Fisherman's Wharf (see the map p. 88). It's the northernmost point of the San Francisco peninsula, thus providing superb views of Alcatraz, the Golden Gate Bridge, the bay, and the city skyline. It opened in 1978 after being transformed from a cargo pier into a fictional image of a turn-of-the-century San Francisco street scene, although it resembles a village on Martha's Vineyard more than a West Coast city. It includes shops, waterfront restaurants serving a variety of cuisines (including more than 20 specialty restaurants for families on a budget), the **Blue & Gold Fleet** (sightseeing boats), the Cinemax presentation *The San Francisco Adventure*, a waterfront park, a 350-berth marina, a double-deck carousel, and an amusement area.

Among the pier's stores are those specializing in kites, music boxes, teddy bears, and merchandise for left-handed people. Other attractions include the wildly popular sea lions that have taken over part of the marina on the west side of the pier, and the street performers who play daily free of charge at **Stage I,** at **Center Stage,** or by the carousel. The **Pier 39 Cable Car Company** operates a fleet of motorized trolleys—replicas of cable cars—for city tours and charters.

---

Restaurants/Clubs: Red | Hotels: Purple | Shops: Orange | Outdoors/Parks: Green | Sights/Culture: Blue

## PIER 39

### Upper Level

**A** Chic's Place
Eagle Cafe
House of Joseph
Just for Laughs

**B** Alamo Flags
Fun Stitch
Kite Flite
Lotus Designer Earrings

**C** Skillets

**D** Only In San Francisco
San Francisco Tea & Coffee
  Company

**E** Animal Country
Swing Song

**F** Cartoon Junction
Midsummer Nights
WalkAmerica

**G** Swiss Louis Italian
  Restaurant
Wines of California

**H** The City Store
Krazy Kaps

**J** Dreamweaver
The Marine Mammal Store
National Park Store

**K** Bay View Cafe
Neptune's Palace
The S.F. Gold Co.

**L** The Beat Goes On

**M** Bubba Gump Shrimp Co.
Wyland Galleries
Yet Wah

**N** Dante's Seafood Grill &
  California Wine Bar
Poster Source

**O** Santa's Workshop

**P** Bay Wear
Field of Dreams
Russka Babushka Dolls
S.F. Tops
The Sweater Gallery
US History

**Q** Cinemax Theatre
Mel Fisher's Sunken
  Treasure Exhibit
NFL Shop

**K**

**I** **J**

Double-Deck
Carousel

**G** **H**

**L**

Center
Stage

**E** **F**

**N** **M**

**C** **D**

**A** **O**

**B** **P**

Stage **i**

**Q** Underwater
World

### Lower Level

**A** Burger Cafe
Burrito Wraps
Only in San Francisco
Sal's Pizzeria

**B** Blue Chip Cookies
Conecept
Fantasy Photos
Gold Rush Grill
Swatch
T's Fish & Chips
Trish's Mini Donuts

**D** Chocolate Heaven

**E** Aerosoles
Harry Mason
  Designer Jewely
On the Road Again
San Francisco USA

**F** Le Carousel
The Pier Market

**G** The San Francisco Sock Market
Warner Bros. Studio Store

**H** Barbary Coast Boxes
Leather Blues
The Pearl Factory
Puppets on the Pier
Rice Garden

**I** Behind the Wheel

**J** Beach Bums
Sunglass Hut
Wound About

**K** Crabcakes and Sweets
The Disney Store
The Fudge House
Magnetron

**L** Aunt Fanny's Hot Pretzels
Hollywood USA

**M** Alcatraz Cafe & Grill
Alcatraz Cafe & Grill Gifts
Kitty City
Namcoland
Turbo Ride

**N** The College Shop
Pier 39 Store
Pier 39 Weekend Sports
Poster Source
Shirtique
Sweet Factory

**O** Charms by the Bay
The Crystal Shop
Pacific Time
Smokins' Cigar
We Be Knives

**P** The Cable Car Store
The Pearl Factory
San Francisco City Wear
San Francisco Music Box Co.
Shell Cellar
Victorian Shoppe

**Q** Boudin Sourdough
Dreyer's Grand
  Ice Cream Shop
Namco Cyber Station
NFL Shop
Vlahos' Fruit Orchard

Restaurants include the **Alcatraz Bar & Grill** (434.1818), which gives diners an overview of the rich history of the penal island; **Chic's Place** (421.2442), with its Art Nouveau decor; the **Eagle Cafe** (433.3689), a San Francisco landmark that has been in business since 1928 (it was once a longshoremen's hangout on the site of what is now the garage, until it was lifted and moved to its present location); **Neptune's Palace** (434.2260), a seafood restaurant; the **Skillets,** one of the better places to eat on the pier, with a great view (434.0432); and the **Swiss Louis Italian Restaurant** (421.2913), which was long established in North Beach before relocating here. A parking garage is located across from the pier on Beach Street (the entrance is on Powell Street). The **Blue & Gold Fleet**'s sight-seeing bay cruises depart from the pier; call 705-5444 or 705-5555 for the schedule. The Blue & Gold Fleet Bay Cruise is included in the CityPass booklet, ($33.25 adults, $26.25 seniors, $24.25 youth ages 5 to 17, which also includes museum admissions and unlimited local public transportation. The booklet allows you to substitute the Alcatraz tour, but you must purchase your CityPass booklet from Blue & Gold by calling 705-5555. ♦ Beach St (at The Embarcadero). 981.8030, recording 981.PIER &

Within Pier 39:

## UNDERWATER WORLD

This 707,000-gallon marine attraction, modeled after the original Underwater World in Auckland, New Zealand, transports visitors along a 400-foot-long "journey through the sea" tunnel where they view nearly 200 species of marine life—including sharks and stringrays—in a 12,000-square-foot aquarium. Visitors may step off the moving footpath an anytime during the journey on to a stationary platform to get a closer look. ◆ Admission. Daily. 623.5300

## 9 AQUATIC PARK

This terraced park overlooking the bay sits adjacent to **Ghirardelli Square.** Historic ships managed by the **San Francisco Maritime National Historic Park System** are docked at nearby piers. There is swimming for hardy types, fishing off the scenic **Municipal Pier,** a small beach for wading, and plenty of grass for picnicking with a view. ◆ Beach St (at Polk St)

Within Aquatic Park:

## NATIONAL MARITIME MUSEUM

Part of the **San Francisco Maritime National Historic Park System,** this museum documents maritime history through displays of ship models, photographs, and memorabilia. The fascinating miniatures include passenger liners, freighters, US Navy ships, and a model of the *Preussen,* the largest sail-powered ship ever built. Tours by rangers are available daily. ◆ Free. Daily. Aquatic Park (at Polk St). 556.3002 ⅃

## 10 GHIRARDELLI SQUARE

During the Civil War this was the site of a woolen mill, but it was the famous chocolate factory built here by Domenico Ghirardelli that gave the square its name. The factory was converted into the most attractive commercial complex in the city by **Wurster, Bernardi & Emmons Inc.** and **Lawrence Halprin & Associates** from 1962 to 1967. Their innovative renovation set the stage for retail conversions of Faneuil Hall Market Place in Boston and New York's South Street Seaport, as well as other adaptive-reuse architectural projects around the nation. The location is blessed with views of the bay, and at night the buildings are illuminated with strings of lights. The *Mermaid Fountain* in the central plaza, designed by local artist Ruth Asawa, is a good resting and meeting place. There is usually free entertainment somewhere within the square, which contains dozens of specialty shops, galleries, and restaurants. Among the many interesting places to browse are **Folk Art International** (928.3340); **Operetta** (928.4676) carries Italian ceramics and

tapestries; and **Something/Anything** (441.8003) is a good place to find interesting jewelry and California crafts. The **Information Booth** has a detailed guide to shops and restaurants. ◆ 900 N Point St (across from Aquatic Park). 775.5500 ⅃

Within Ghirardelli Square:

## McCORMICK & KULETO'S

★★$$$ Famed restaurant designer Pat Kuleto has put his distinctive stamp on this fish restaurant. The decor is tasteful and plush, the views are astounding, and the seafood menu is one of the most extensive in the city. The food can be excellent, but with 400 seats plus private receptions and banquets, consistency is a problem. Dozens of fish are featured each day. ◆ Seafood ◆ Daily lunch and dinner. Reservations recommended. 929.1730 ⅃

## THE MANDARIN

★★★$$$ This pricey, pretty restaurant with a view of the bay has exceptional Chinese cuisine. The smoked tea duck is excellent, as is the Beggar's Chicken, which you must order 24 hours in advance. The pot stickers are also of the highest quality. ◆ Chinese ◆ Daily lunch and dinner. Reservations recommended. 673.8812 ⅃

## GAYLORD INDIA RESTAURANT

★★$$$ Part of a worldwide chain, this dining spot is beautiful and elegant, and the food is quite good. Tandoori dishes suspended in a clay oven are its specialty. Ask for a window table for a spectacular view of the bay. ◆ Indian ◆ Daily lunch and dinner. Reservations recommended. 771.8822 ⅃

## GHIRARDELLI CHOCOLATE MANUFACTORY AND SODA FOUNTAIN

This old-fashioned ice-cream parlor and candy store sells luscious hot-fudge sundaes and five-pound chocolate bars. Take a look at the display of some original chocolate-making machinery in the back. ◆ Daily. 474.3938 ⅃

## 11 RESTAURANT GARY DANKO

★★★★$$$$ Having received a five-star Mobil award, Gary Danko is *the* place to go for a meal you'll remember long after you leave. The two dining rooms are wood-paneled and sleek. The menu is divided into sections and prices range from $48 for three courses to $75 for six. Try the lobster salad, or roast lobster, scallop mousse; and guinea hen with cabbage, apples, and fresh chestnuts. Don't pass up the cheese course. ◆ French/Asian ◆ Dinner daily. Reservations required. 800 North Point St (at Hyde St). 749.2060. ᵭ

## 12 THE BUENA VISTA

$$ Always jammed with tourists and locals, this is the place where Irish coffee got started, and it's still a specialty. There's food, too (American fare, such as burgers and chicken), but do a snack tour of nearby **Ghirardelli Square** instead, and have Irish coffee as the finale. ◆ American ◆ Daily breakfast, lunch, and dinner. 2765 Hyde St (at Beach St). 474.5044

## 13 THE CANNERY

Constructed in 1909 as the Del Monte Fruit Company's peach-canning plant, this building was remodeled in 1968 by **Joseph Esherick & Associates** following the successful redevelopment of **Ghirardelli Square.** The three-story complex contains shops, restaurants, a comedy club, galleries, and a movie theater. Its sunken courtyard filled with flowers and century-old olive trees hosts mimes, musicians, and other talented street performers. Treasures from the estate of newspaper tycoon William Randolph Hearst have been installed in some of the facilities. The interior of **Jacks Cannery Bar,** for example, has a 90-foot-long hall, a carved fireplace, and a Jacobean staircase originally built in the early 1600s by **Inigo Jones**—England's first true Renaissance architect—for Queen Elizabeth I's ambassador to France. ◆ 2801 Leavenworth St (at Jefferson St). 771.3112 ᵭ

Within The Cannery:

## COBB'S COMEDY CLUB

Belly laughs are induced here nightly. Patrons get three hours of validated parking at the nearby **Anchorage Garage.** ◆ Cover. Shows nightly. S bldg, courtyard entrance. 928.4320 ᵭ

## CANNERY WINE CELLAR AND GOURMET MARKET

Amidst the clutter of tourist merchandise are stocked more than 300 kinds of beers, 160 single-malt scotches, and a good collection of California wines. Shelves of gourmet products, including mustards, jams, olive oils, and vinegars, round out the food selections. ◆ Daily. N bldg, first floor. 673.0400 ᵭ

## CONFETTI'S

Dazzling cases of chocolates and candies from some of the top purveyors in the Bay Area and elsewhere in the country are the attraction here. For lower-cal treats, walk out the door to the corner, where sister shop **Confetti California Fruits and Nuts** carries a terrific selection of California-grown nuts and dried fruits. ◆ Daily. 474.7377 ᵭ

## 14 THE ANCHORAGE

Heavy on souvenir shops, this complex is downstream from **Ghirardelli Square** and **The Cannery.** ◆ Daily. 2800 Leavenworth St (between Beach and Jefferson Sts). 775.6000 ᵭ

## 15 WAX MUSEUM

This new $15 million museum includes Leonardo de Caprio and Kate Winslet on the bow of the *Titanic,* and San Franciso Mayor Willie Brown. Old favorites have been spruced up. The Chamber of Horrors is back in all its gory detail. Admission. Daily. 145 Jefferson St (between Taylor and Mason Sts). 202.0400

Within the Wax Museum:

## RAINFOREST CAFE

★★$ With its 15,000 gallon aquarium, live birds and two-story waterfall, this entertainment eatery dazzles kids and adults. Amid thunder, lightning, animatronic gorillas, and live macaws, you dine on fresh California pastas, salads, and sandwiches themed to Asian, Caribbean, Southwest, Mexican, and Cajun cuisine (with names like Rasta Pasta and Rumble in the Jungle). You can also enjoy the fun from a giraffe-leg stool under the giant mushroom while sipping organic vegetable juice. Daily lunch, dinner. 440.5610, 440.5355

## 16 THE WHARF INN

$ Granted, it's not the Ritz (and there's no restaurant), but for its location (a block from Fisherman's Wharf) and price (most of the 51 rooms are under $100 a night off-season), this utilitarian hotel is an understated bargain. Add to this free parking and the "no extra person charge," and suddenly one can learn to live with the green-and-mustard decor. ◆ 2601 Mason St (at Beach St). 673.7411, 800/548.9918

## 17 RADISSON FISHERMAN'S WHARF

$$ If you're looking for clean, tastefully decorated rooms at a reasonable price, this above-average chain hotel with 355 rooms is right on the money. Amenities include a pool, restaurant, and lounge, free parking, and, for a few dollars more, a balcony overlooking

Alcatraz Island. It's also within just a few steps of Fisherman's Wharf. ♦ 250 Beach Street (at Taylor St). 392.6700, 877/497.1212; fax 392.6700 &

### 18 SHERATON AT FISHERMAN'S WHARF

$$$ This handsome complex of redwood, brick, and greenery has 525 guest rooms interspersed with courtyards. ♦ 2500 Mason St (at Beach St). 362.5500, 800/325.3535; fax 956.5275

### 19 THE TUSCAN INN

$$$ This 220-room inn, developed by entrepreneur Bill Kimpton who is better known for renovating older properties downtown, follows the successful Kimpton formula, offering style and personal service. Complimentary services include wine every evening and daily coffee or tea by the fireplace in the lobby, and limousines to the Financial District weekday mornings. There's in-house parking, room service, same-day valet/laundry service, and programs for children. ♦ 425 North Point St (at Mason St). 561.1100, 800/648.4626; fax 561.1199

Adjoining the Tuscan Inn:

### CAFE PESCATORE

★★$$ Modeled after a classic Italian trattoria, this attractive, informal restaurant may be the best dining choice in the Fisherman's Wharf area, where pickings are plentiful but culinary excitement is scarce. Diners enjoy classic Italian cuisine featuring fresh pizza from the wood-burning oven and such specialties as *tonna saltimbocca* (seared tuna wrapped in prosciutto) with garlic mashed potatoes and *brodetto,* a hearty fish stew. ♦ Italian ♦ Daily breakfast, lunch, and dinner. Reservations recommended. 2455 Mason St (at North Point St). 561.1111 &

### 20 COST PLUS WORLD MARKET

This warehouse-size store offers reasonably priced imports from all over the world, including baskets, glassware, pottery, tables, specialty foods, and wines. ♦ Daily. 2552 Taylor St (at Bay St). 928.6200 &

### 21 HOLIDAY INN EXPRESS AND SUITES

$$ This new five-story hotel has 240 guestrooms and 20 suites and ample underground parking. No pool but more intimate than the 585-room Holiday Inn-Fisherman's Wharf next door. 550 North Point (between Jones and Taylor Sts). 771.9000.

### 22 SAN FRANCISCO MARRIOTT FISHERMAN'S WHARF

$$$$ One of the most elegant hotels in the wharf area blends apricot marble, comfortable leather, and an abundance of greenery. There are 285 rooms and suites complete with writing desks and cable TV. **Spada**'s, the hotel restaurant, specializes in Angus beef and fresh seafood. The lobby lounge features a complimentary buffet. ♦ 1250 Columbus Ave (at Bay St). 775.7555, 525.0956; fax 474.2099 &

### 23 635 BAY STREET

This apartment building boasts a charming trompe l'oeil exterior that includes painted-on moldings and a giant "keyhole." It's a private residence. ♦ At Jones St

RISTORANTE · ISTRIANO

### 24 ALBONA

★★$$ This is the West Coast's only restaurant serving food of the Istrian Peninsula, the body of land that pokes out below Trieste and is across the Adriatic Sea from Venice. The restaurant is named after a city on the peninsula that was once Italian, then Yugoslav, and now belongs to Slovenia, and the food reflects the Italian and Central European influences of that region. This may be the only establishment in the country that makes cheese-and-nut-filled *crafi Albonesi* (Albonese ravioli). All the desserts, including a knockout apple strudel, are made on the premises. ♦ Italian/Slovenian ♦ Tu-Sa dinner. Reservations recommended. Complimentary valet parking. 545 Francisco St (at Taylor St). 441.1040 &

### 25 ZAX

★★★$$ Husband-and-wife team Mark Drazek and Barbara Mulas share culinary duties at one of the best chef-owned restaurants in the city. This out-of-the-way place has a soothing, modern decor where diners enjoy salmon cooked to a bronze finish and propped on mashed potatoes infused with garlic, served with a warm salad of white corn and baby spinach. ♦ French/Mediterranean ♦ Tu-Sa dinner. 2330 Taylor St (between Columbus Ave and Francisco St). 563.6266 &

---

Restaurants/Clubs: Red | Hotels: Purple | Shops: Orange | Outdoors/Parks: Green | Sights/Culture: Blue

### 26 CAMPBELL-THIEBAUD GALLERY

This gallery specializes in contemporary Bay Area artists. Co-owner Paul Thiebaud is the son of painter Wayne Thiebaud. ♦ Tu.-Sa. 645 Chestnut St (between Columbus Ave and Mason St). 441.8680

### 27 SAN REMO HOTEL

$ The only budget-priced hotel in North Beach, this lovingly restored Italianate Victorian building was constructed in 1906 by A.P. Giannini, Bank of America's founder. With the exception of the penthouse, a cottage on the roof with a brass bed and bay views, the hotel's 62 rooms all share immaculate baths with charming Victorian fixtures. Each of the guest rooms is furnished with antiques or would-be antiques, and some have sinks. There are no telephones or TVs, and the hotel lacks a restaurant, but there is abundant charm. The penthouse, at $125 a night, books months in advance. ♦ 2237 Mason St (at Chestnut St). 776.8688, 800/352.7365

### 28 VANDEWATER STREET

In this short, narrow alley between Powell and Mason Streets are several architectural firms and some interesting housing examples— notably **No. 55**, a condominium development designed by **Daniel Solomon & Associates** in 1981. Its beautifully proportioned facade is adorned with a gently curved arch at the top and a palette of pinks and beiges. **No. 33** next door, designed in 1981 by **Donald MacDonald & Associates**, is a simpler version, painted white. **No. 22** is an apartment block that the architecture firm **Esherick, Homsey, Dodge & Davis** designed in 1976.

### 29 210 FRANCISCO STREET

This 25-foot-wide structure is a modern rein-terpretation of the traditional San Francisco row house. **Backen, Arrigoni & Ross**'s 1985 design has all the essential elements—the curved bay window, the false facade—but is constructed out of contemporary materials, including white porcelain enamel panels, glass blocks, and poured-in-place concrete. It's a private residence. ♦ At Grant Ave

### 30 TELEGRAPH TERRACE

**Backen, Arrigoni & Ross**'s award-winning group of expensive Spanish-style condominiums climbs the steep hillside and looks out over ornamental details that make it fit into its context. The private residences were built in 1984. ♦ Francisco St (at Grant Ave)

### 31 LAPIS

★★$$$ Another fine restaurant has joined the collection along the booming Embarcadero at Pier 33. Guests enjoy breath-taking views of the bay as they feast on Thomas Ricci's Mediterranean dishes from Morocco, Turkey, Spain and southern France. ♦ Mediterranean ♦ The Embarcadero (at Bay St). 982.0203

### 32 GRAFFEO COFFEE ROASTING CO.

You can smell the dark beans roasting several blocks away at this long-established firm, which turns out a daily grind. There's no brewed coffee, however. ♦ M-Sa. 735 Columbus Ave (at Filbert St). 986.2429, 800/222.6250

### 33 MAYBECK BUILDING

This office building was constructed in 1909 around a courtyard with apartments on the upper floors. It was once the **Old Telegraph Hill Neighborhood Center Building** (the oldest neighborhood center in the city). ♦ 1736 Stockton St (between Filbert and Greenwich Sts)

### 34 COIT MEMORIAL TOWER

Located at the top of Telegraph Hill, this 1934 tower (pictured above) by **Arthur Brown Jr.** marks the point where the first West Coast telegraph sent messages notifying the arrival of ships from the Pacific. Messages were then signaled downtown by a semaphore tower. Lillie Hitchcock Coit, who as a girl of 15 had been the mascot of the crack firefighter company Knickerbocker No. 5, left funds to beautify the city in 1929. An incorrect story persists that the tower was shaped to look like a firehose nozzle to commemorate her interest in the fire department. Inside are restored murals depicting California workers. Painted as a Public Works of Art Project during the Depression, the murals, some leaning politi-cally to the left, created a stir when first unveiled. Take the elevator to the top for a spectacular view of the city and bay. The tower's base, from which there are panoramic views, is accessible all day. ♦ Admission for elevator ride. Daily. At the end of Telegraph Hill Blvd

### 35 JULIUS' CASTLE

★$$$$ Even after the owners of this romantic, elegant restaurant perched on the hills near **Coit Tower** refurbished the interior, installed an exhibition kitchen, and hired a new chef, the food here still doesn't match the surroundings. Pasta with broccoli rabe and garlic isn't nearly as special as it should be, and the kitchen insists on using mealy potatoes to showcase sautéed scallops in a refreshing cucumber sauce. Many patrons don't seem to mind, though. With its rich paneled interior, soft lighting, and panoramic vista of the bay, this place has probably kindled more flames than any other dining spot in the city. ◆ French/Italian ◆ Daily dinner. Reservations required. 1541 Montgomery St (at Lombard St). 362.3042

## 36 LEVI'S PLAZA

In 1982 **Hellmuth, Obata & Kassabaum** built this enormous three-building development for the Levi Strauss Company. The architects reduced the vast scale by stepping back the profiles of the buildings so that they would blend into the shape of Telegraph Hill. All the buildings are clad in brick tiles that match the adjoining **Ice House,** a converted office complex. Wander among the Monterey pine, waterfalls, and hop the stepping stones across the creek. Any spot is good for a picnic. ◆ Sansome and Battery Sts (between Union and Greenwich Sts)

Within Levi's Plaza:

### IL FORNAIO

★★$$ This enormously popular restaurant is the last word in trendy decor and dining, and though not each dish the kitchen produces is a roaring success, most are—especially at breakfast, with Italian adaptations of oatmeal and French toast and a knockout fruit-filled calzone. The premises include a pastry shop, pizzeria, *rosticceria* (rotisserie), cafe, and bar, all incorporated into what the management calls *gastronomia Italiana.* Sandwiches at lunch are made with delicious herb breads. ◆ Italian ◆ Daily breakfast, lunch, and dinner. Reservations recommended. 986.0100, 927.4400 &

### FOG CITY DINER

★★$$ The diner concept merely served as design inspiration for this ultrasleek restaurant filled with polished stainless steel, chrome, and neon. A creative, eclectic menu of Californian cuisine offers something for everyone, from crab cakes and grilled sesame chicken to quesadillas and Asian prawns to homemade pickles. It's operated by the same restaurateurs who own the popular **Mustards Grill** in Napa Valley and **Buckeye Roadhouse** in Mill Valley. ◆ Californian ◆ Daily lunch and dinner. Reservations recommended. 1300 Battery St (off The Embarcadero). 982.2000 &

## 37 PIER 23 CAFE

★★$$ "Excuse me, do you mambo?" Well, after a few pitchers of sangria at this bayside restaurant and dance club, you probably will. It's great fun even for people who can't dance (and you know who you are). The food's good, too: Come early and try the spicy meat loaf with mashed potatoes or the crab-and-shrimp quesadilla before squeezing onto the dance floor. When the weather's nice, the alfresco dining is unbeatable. Wednesday is mambo night, and Saturday is reggae. ◆ Californian ◆ Tu-Sa lunch and dinner; Su brunch. Reservations recommended. Pier 23 (near the end of Lombard St). 362.5125 &

## 38 1360 MONTGOMERY STREET

Featured in the Humphrey Bogart movie *Dark Passage,* this 1937 apartment house is designed in the Moderne style, with exterior murals and a fine glass-block facade leading to the entrance lobby. It's a private residence. ◆ At Filbert St

## 38 FILBERT STEPS

Down the east side of Telegraph Hill, the terrain is so steep that Filbert Street becomes Filbert Steps—a series of precariously perched platforms and walkways with some of the city's oldest and most varied housing. A beautifully landscaped walkway climbs down the hill and gives access to the lanes on either side—Darrell Place, Napier Lane. **No. 228** Filbert Steps, built in the 1870s, is a fine example of Carpenter Gothic style. These are private residences. ◆ Between Sansome and Montgomery Sts

## 39 KAHN HOUSE

Similar to his Lovell House in Los Angeles, this 1939 building by **Richard Neutra** steps down the hill and offers its occupants superb views of the bay. Walk to the end of the lane and look over the stone wall. It's a private residence. ◆ 66 Calhoun Terr (between Green and Union Sts)

## 40 REMODELED WAREHOUSES

Some old warehouses in this neighborhood, most built in the 1930s, have been turned into offices for architects, graphic artists, and TV companies. Of particular note are **855 Battery Street,** for **Channel 5/ Westinghouse TV,** remodeled by **Gensler & Associates** (1980-81); **243 Vallejo,** by **Marquis Associates** (1972); **220 Vallejo,** by **Kaplan/McLaughlin/Diaz** (1978); and **101 Lombard Street,** by **Hellmuth, Obata & Kassabaum,** completed in 1979. There are fine old brick warehouses on Battery between Union and Green Streets, plus the old **Ice**

---

**Restaurants/Clubs: Red | Hotels: Purple | Shops: Orange | Outdoors/Parks: Green | Sights/Culture: Blue**

**House,** which is now an office complex, on Union Street between Sansome and Battery Streets. ♦ From Broadway to Lombard St (between Battery and Sansome Sts)

## 41 CAFE DE STIJL

★★$ Started by Assyrian architect **Nilus de Matran** in an old brick warehouse, this hip restaurant serves up Middle Eastern fare including tabbouleh salad with fresh mint and sun-dried tomatoes; turkish lamb salad with toasted almonds, cranberry, and lemon vinaigrette; and a four-spice chicken sandwich with orange-cayenne sauce. ♦ Middle Eastern/Californian ♦ M-W, F-Sa breakfast and lunch. 1 Union St (at Front St). 291.0808 ♿

## 42 WASHINGTON SQUARE

Located halfway along Columbus Avenue, this plaza is the center of the Italian North Beach community. On the north side is the **Church of St. Peter and St. Paul;** on the east, next to the post office, is the **Italian Athletic Club.** Lunching at **Caffè Malvina** (391.1290) on the corner of Stockton and Filbert Streets is a pleasant way to watch the world go by. ♦ Bounded by Union and Filbert Sts, and Stockton and Powell Sts

## 43 THE WASHINGTON SQUARE INN

$$ Each of the 15 rooms at this European-style hostelry, located in the heart of North Beach midway between Fisherman's Wharf and Union Square, is individually decorated and furnished with English and French antiques. Two of the rooms have bathrooms across the hall. The hotel overlooks Washington Square and the **Church of St. Peter and St. Paul.** Continental breakfast, afternoon tea and cookies, and wine are included in the price of a room, but there's no restaurant. ♦ 1660 Stockton St (between Union and Filbert Sts). 981.4220, 800/388.0220; fax 397.7242

For a walk that will literally take your breath away, head over to Filbert Street, the steepest street in San Francisco. It boasts a whopping 31.5 percent grade between Hyde and Leavenworth Streets—enough to make even the most shipshape soul sweat.

The first criminals put behind bars in Alcatraz weren't gangsters like Al Capone or murderers like Robert "The Birdman" Stroud. They were Confederate sympathizers, suspected war spies, and disorderly Native Americans.

## 44 MOOSE'S

★★★$$$ Popular with movers and shakers for power lunches and dinners, it's modern and airy, with windows overlooking the street, an expansive open kitchen, arches separating the bar from the dining area, and live jazz at dinnertime. Try the Mediterranean fish soup with rouille; and gnocchi with smoked salmon, pistou (basil, garlic and olive oil) sauce, crème fraîche, and caviar. The desserts are heavenly. ♦ Italian/Mediterranean ♦ Daily lunch and dinner; Su brunch. Reservations recommended. 1652 Stockton St (between Union and Filbert Sts). 989.7800

## 44 LITTLE CITY ANTIPASTI BAR

★$$ This airy, attractive dining room is a perfect place to meet friends for drinks and a snack. In fact, a whole meal can be made of the antipasti. ♦ Mediterranean ♦ Daily lunch and dinner. 673 Union St (at Powell St). 434.2900 ♿

## 45 GIRA POLLI

★★$ No one does chicken better than this stylish 8-table restaurant, with 18 spits whirling in the wood-fired rotisserie. The Sicilian menu is small, simple, and to the point. Chicken is served with luscious Palermo-style potatoes (boiled in chicken stock and baked with white wine and herbs). The homemade pasta is also richly rewarding, as is the sensational lemony cheesecake. The place does a brisk take-out and delivery business. ♦ Italian/Takeout ♦ Daily dinner. Reservations recommended. 659 Union St (at Powell St). 434.4472. Also at: 590 E Blithedale Ave, Mill Valley, Marin County. 383.6040 ♿

## 45 PASTA POMODORO

★★$ This pasta house offers incredible deals and generous portions. Plus the gnocchi, coated in gorgonzola sauce and spiked with diced tomato, are better than preparations that cost twice as much. The dozen or so pasta dishes include *penne putanesca* (with black and green olives and a slightly spicy tomato sauce); rigatoni with roast chicken, cream, mushrooms, and sun-dried tomatoes; and spaghetti with calamari, mussels, and scallops in a light tomato sauce. ♦ Italian ♦ Daily lunch and dinner. 655 Union St (between Columbus Ave and Powell St). 399.0300 ♿ Also at: 2027 Chestnut St (at Fillmore St). 474.3400 ♿

## 46 VOLARE CAFFE

★★$$ Homemade pastas and carefully grilled meats draw enthusiastic diners to this pleasant, tiled trattoria. ♦ Sicilian ♦ Daily dinner. 561 Columbus Ave (between Green and Union Sts). 362.2774 ♿

### 46 IL POLLAIO

$ Grilled chicken (hence the name which means "chicken coop") doesn't come any better than at this pie-shaped wedge of a cafe. Other entrées—lamb chops, pork chops, and rabbit—are spiced and grilled in the richly flavored and heavily spiced Argentine manner. Soup, a couple of salads, and two desserts round out the short menu. ♦ Italian/Argentine ♦ M-Sa lunch and dinner. 555 Columbus Ave (between Green and Union Sts). 362.7727 &

### 47 MARIO'S BOHEMIAN CIGAR STORE

★$ You'll hear lots of Italian spoken at this tiny, friendly spot, where the clientele hunkers down over a few tables. It's smaller and plainer than other coffeehouses in the area, but many swear it has the best espresso and focaccia sandwiches. It was a cigar store in the 1960s, but you won't find any stogies here anymore. ♦ Coffeehouse ♦ Daily. 566 Columbus Ave (at Union St). 362.0536 &

### 48 FIORE D'ITALIA

★$$$ Opened in 1886, this place claims to be the oldest Italian restaurant in America. Specialties, including risotto, homemade pastas, and veal dishes can be eaten at the bar or in the more formal dining room. ♦ Italian ♦ Daily lunch and dinner. Reservations recomended. 601 Union St (at Stockton St). 986.1886 &

### 49 ITALIAN FRENCH BAKERY

This bakery's breads and breadsticks have won top awards in North Beach culinary competitions. ♦ Daily. 1501 Grant Ave (at Union St). 421.3796 &

### 50 NORTH BEACH PIZZA

★★$ The variety of toppings at this jam-packed pizza parlor is impressive: Ten combinations are offered, including one with pepperoni, mushrooms, and cheese, and another with clams, garlic, and cheese—all smoothed over the slightly doughy crust. You may order your food to go or have it delivered. ♦ Pizza ♦ Daily lunch and dinner. 1499 Grant Ave (at Union St). 433.2444. Also at: 1310 Grant Ave (at Green St). 433.2444

### 51 YONÉ

Sift through a veritable gold mine of beads, buttons, and jewelry; you could even make yourself a necklace or a pair of earrings with what's available here. ♦ Th-Sa. 478 Union St (at Grant Ave). 986.1424

### 52 CLUB FUGAZI

The popular cabaret-style show, *Beach Blanket Babylon,* has been playing here in various incarnations for years. The show's theme changes annually, but it invariably features outrageous costumes, zany hats, and an earnest, high-energy, talented cast bent on making the lowbrow material seem funny. No one under 21 is admitted except for the Sunday matinee. ♦ Admission. Shows daily. Reservations required three to four weeks in advance. 678 Green St (between Columbus Ave and Powell St). 421.4222; fax 421.4817 &

### 52 CAPP'S CORNER

★$ If you have a hungry family or group with not-so-discriminating tastes and not-so-unlimited funds, head for the corner that's belonged to Capp since who knows when. Here you'll learn what Italian "family dining" is all about: back-to-back Sinatra tunes, endless glasses of headache-quality Chianti, and brusque but cheery service. Granted, the food isn't tops, but if you order the mussels marinara, you'll at least leave pleasantly stuffed. ♦ Italian ♦ Daily dinner. 1600 Powell St (at Green St). 989.2589 &

### 53 GOLD SPIKE

★$ Catering to big eaters since 1920, this restaurant, decorated with eclectic clutter, dishes out hearty six-course family-style dinners. There's a crab cioppino feast on Friday. ♦ Italian ♦ M-Tu, Th-Su dinner. 527 Columbus Ave (between Green and Union Sts). 421.4591 &

### 53 L'OSTERIA DEL FORNO

★★★$ This hole in the wall is what you'd expect in North Beach—tables wedged together by the front windows, and friendly and casual service. The kitchen turns out the best focaccia sandwiches, excellent pasta, and a roast of the day, usually beef or a delectable pork that has been marinated and braised in milk. All this for what amounts to small change. ♦ Italian ♦ M, W-Su lunch and dinner. No credit cards accepted. 519 Columbus Ave (between Green and Union Sts). 982.1124

---

**Restaurants/Clubs: Red | Hotels: Purple | Shops: Orange | Outdoors/Parks: Green | Sights/Culture: Blue**

## 54 Caffè Sport

$$ Although the wait may be long, and the service could be a little friendlier, this neighborhood stalwart has lots of charm and character – starting with its roomful of kitschy decor. Popular dishes include cioppino and any of the pastas, which may be paired with lobster, pesto, calamari, shrimp, scallops, or four kinds of cheese. ♦ Italian ♦ Tu-Sa lunch and dinner. 574 Green St (at Columbus Ave). 981.1251 &

## 55 Danilo Italian Bakery

An all-purpose bakery specializing in Tuscan recipes, this shop makes a lot of things very well, among them breads, breadsticks, biscotti, focaccia, and panettone (including the very special anise-flavored *buccelatto*). One of the unique treats is a *torta di verdura*, a dense pie made with Swiss chard, liqueur, raisins, and pine nuts. ♦ Daily. No credit cards accepted. 516 Green St (at Grant Ave). 989.1806 &

## 56 Quantity Postcards

You'll find everything from standard shots of the Golden Gate Bridge to 1950s-type kitsch and some extremely bizarre images (better make sure the folks back home have a sense of humor before dashing off one of these). ♦ M-Th,Su; F-Sa until 1AM. 1441 Grant Ave (between Green and Union Sts). 986.8866. Also at: 570 Columbus Ave (at Green St). 788.1112; 1427 Haight St (at Masonic Ave). 255.1199 &

## 57 Cafe Jacqueline

★★$$ Soufflé's the thing at this cozy, romantic restaurant. Owner Jacqueline Margulis serves savory—albeit costly— selections that might include salmon and asparagus, shiitake mushrooms, or white corn with ginger and garlic. The dessert soufflés are all irresistible. ♦ French ♦ W-Su dinner. 1454 Grant Ave (at Union St). 981.5565

## 58 Savoy Tivoli

$ This long-established, charmingly decrepit North Beach hangout with a sidewalk cafe and recreation room is a great place for meeting the locals. ♦ Italian ♦ Tu-Sat 3PM-2AM. 1434 Grant Ave (between Green and Union Sts). 362.7023

## 59 Bocce Cafe

★$$ One of the better bargains in North Beach, this spacious Italian restaurant serves somewhat respectable cuisine at competitive prices. Try its best dish, the *linguine pescatore* (with a seafood sauce), wash it down with some cheap Chianti, and try not to fall asleep on the sinfully comfortable pillowed booths. Avoid Friday night, when the band shows up and ruins everyone's meal. ♦ Italian ♦ Daily lunch and dinner. 478 Green St (at Grant Ave). 981.2044

## 59 Maykadeh

★★$$ Very popular and very good, this attractive restaurant serves exotic Persian cuisine in a mauve, California-like setting. The lamb dishes are a delight. ♦ Persian ♦ Daily lunch and dinner. Reservations recommended. 470 Green St (at Grant Ave). 362.8286 &

## 60 North Beach Museum

The history of North Beach, Chinatown, and Fisherman's Wharf is presented in old photos and artifacts. ♦ Free. M-F. 1435 Stockton St (between Vallejo and Green Sts), Mezzanine. 626.7070

## 61 Caffè Greco

★$ Ultra-friendly owners Sandy and Hanna Suleiman and their family quickly made this North Beach coffeehouse popular. It's always crowded, and on warm days and evenings conversation spills onto the street through open picture windows. The desserts, including tiramisù and cappuccino cake, are worth every sinful bite. There are also focaccia sandwiches and salads. ♦ Coffeehouse ♦ Daily. 423 Columbus Ave (between Vallejo and Green Sts). 397.6261

## 62 Caffè Puccini

★$ Minimal operatic-themed decor graces this invariably full coffeehouse favored by local residents, who sip their selections while overlooking the Columbus Avenue scene. ♦ Coffeehouse ♦ Daily. 411 Columbus Ave (between Vallejo and Green Sts). 989.7033

## 63 Stella Pastry & Caffe

Try the famous *sacrapantina*, layers of sponge cake brushed with maraschino liqueur and zabaglione. Other noteworthy selections include tiramisù, biscotti, cannoli, and panettone. ♦ Cafe ♦ Daily. 446 Columbus Ave (between Vallejo and Green Sts). 986.2914 &

## 63 Hotel Boheme

$$ Formerly the **Millefiore Inn,** this once-Victorian place has been transformed by interior designer Candra Scott into a hotel that captures the true spirit of North Beach. Look for such touches as handmade light fixtures (some fashioned from parasols found in Chinatown) and bohemian-style furnishings. Each of the 15 guest rooms has a private bath and a queen-sized bed. If you're looking for quiet, be sure to request a room away from Columbus Avenue. ♦ 444 Columbus Ave (between Vallejo and Green Sts). 433.9111

### 64 CALZONE'S

★$$ Savor trendy pizzas from a wood-burning brick oven while people-watching through the large picture windows. For a real winner, try chicken-liver pasta. The management dispatches a free limousine to the Financial District to pick up lunchtime customers. ♦ Italian ♦ Daily lunch and dinner. 430 Columbus Ave (between Vallejo and Green Sts). 397.3600 ♿

### 65 LA BODEGA

★$ Decorated in bright, bold colors, this Spanish restaurant features a lovely abstract brush painting of flamenco dancers. Try the thinly sliced chorizo, and follow it with the paella or the chicken served over vegetable-studded rice. There's live entertainment nightly (after 8PM). ♦ Spanish ♦ Daily dinner. 1337 Grant Ave (between Vallejo and Green Sts). 433.0439 ♿

### 66 MO'S

★$ Some say they turn out the best burgers in the city, or maybe the whole state, here. They might be right. ♦ American ♦ Daily lunch and dinner. 1322 Grant Ave (between Vallejo and Green Sts). 788.3779 ♿

### 67 RISTORANTE IDEALE

★★★$$ True Roman cooking is showcased in Maurizio Bruschi's restaurant, made warm and friendly by the terra-cotta-toned decor and the satisfying dishes such as *pappardelle* (broad noodles) with a tomato-based lamb sauce and penne with a combination of fresh and smoked salmon in a creamy tomato sauce. ♦ Italian ♦ Tu-Su dinner. Reservations recommended. 1309 Grant Ave (at Vallejo St). 391.4129 ♿

### 68 VICTORIA PASTRY CO.

Try the delicious St. Honoré cake here, as well as the biscotti, corcini (chocolate cake), and other types of pastries. ♦ Daily. 1362 Stockton St (at Vallejo St). 781.2015 ♿

### 69 MOLINARI'S

This landmark Italian deli has been a local monument since 1896 and offers a huge selection of Italian sausages, among other typical fare. ♦ M-Sa. 373 Columbus Ave (at Vallejo St). 421.2337 ♿

### 70 CAFFÈ TRIESTE

★$ This quintessential San Francisco coffeehouse is a haven for artists, writers, and gawkers. There are live opera performances and slightly higher drink prices Saturday afternoons. ♦ Coffeehouse ♦ Daily. 609 Vallejo St (at Grant Ave). 392.6739

### 71 THE STINKING ROSE

★$$ You won't find a vampire in sight at this popular restaurant and bar, where *everything*—from the eggs in the morning to the cocktails at night—contains traces of the stinking rose (a nickname for garlic). There's a small store hawking garlic paraphernalia, too. ♦ Italian/American ♦ Daily lunch and dinner. Reservations recommended. 325 Columbus Ave (between Broadway and Vallejo Sts). 781.7673 ♿

### 72 CONDOR BISTRO

$$ San Francisco's moral minority let out a cheer in 1991 when the **Condor Club**'s Carol Doda sign (a larger-than-life rendering of the city's most famous stripper) was torn down and the landmark topless bar became a bistro. It has since been transformed into a sports bar, serving your typical "pub grub." ♦ American ♦ Daily lunch and dinner. 300 Columbus Ave (at Broadway). 781.8222 ♿

### 73 BROADWAY

This brash strip has been a monument to man's mammary fascination since 1964, when Carol Doda first performed her topless act at the **Condor Club.** Once a family street with Italian grocery stores, it became a center for bootlegging in the 1930s, and in the 1940s was dotted with brothels and pool halls. Then, in the 1950s, the strip began to clean up its act when the likes of Lenny Bruce and Barbra Streisand played here at the **Hungry i,** Johnny Mathis sang at **Ann's 448,** and folk musicians strummed at **On Broadway.** The entertainment boom went bust as high-paying Vegas clubs wooed the big names, and by the mid-1960s the street had turned raunchy again. Loud barkers lured leering tourists into the 20 topless clubs, which featured expensive cover charges, lightly liquored drinks, and a parade of breasts. The strip is more subdued now. Most of the surviving topless clubs do not

---

**Restaurants/Clubs: Red | Hotels: Purple | Shops: Orange | Outdoors/Parks: Green | Sights/Culture: Blue**

have liquor licenses, and many of the new businesses are restaurants. ♦ Between Sansome St and Grant Ave

### 73 COLUMBUS BOOKS

Browse through new and used books at discount prices. ♦ M-Th, Su; F-Sa until midnight. 540 Broadway (between Grant and Columbus Aves). 986.3872 &

### 73 ENRICO'S

★★★$$ This lively spot is a saloon, a sidewalk cafe, a gallery for local artists, and a cool jazz venue all rolled into one. The kitchen turns out sophisticated dishes with an emphasis on fresh, organic produce, including an excellent Cobb salad. Also recommended is the Tuscan-style T-bone steak served with white beans. The desserts are great, too, especially "Mickey Mousse," several small chocolate cakes in a pool of crème anglaise. ♦ Italian/Mediterranean ♦ Daily lunch and dinner. Reservations recommended. 504 Broadway (at Kearny St). 982.6223 &

### 74 BRANDY HO'S

★★$ This is one of the best Hunan restaurants in the city, especially for those whose palates are up to the challenge of lots of chili peppers and garlic. The deep-fried dumplings with garlic sauce; onion cakes; smoked ham with garlic; and lamb with crispy rice noodles are but a few of the many pungent temptations available. ♦ Hunan ♦ Daily lunch and dinner. 450-452 Broadway (between Montgomery and Kearny Sts). 362.6268. Also at: 217 Columbus Ave (between Broadway and Pacific Ave). 788.7527 &

### 74 HELMAND RESTAURANT

★★★$$ San Francisco's premier Afghan restaurant has an exotic menu that includes such intriguing choices as *kabuli* (rice baked with lamb tenderloin and raisins), *mourgh challow* (chicken sautéed with spices and yellow split peas), and *theeka kabob* (charbroiled beef tenderloin marinated in yogurt, baby grapes, and herbs). All dishes are deftly prepared and complex in their spicing, but not fiery hot. ♦ Afghan ♦ Daily dinner. Reservations recommended. 430 Broadway (between Montgomery and Kearny Sts). 362.0641 &

### 75 HUNAN

★$$ When San Francisco first fell in love with fiery Hunanese food, this restaurant was here to heat up willing palates. Devotees keep coming back for Diana's specials, a deep-fried pie filled with pork, cheese, and onions; the house-smoked duck; and smoked ham with bell peppers and onions. ♦ Chinese ♦ Daily lunch and dinner. Reservations recommended. 924 Sansome St (off Broadway). 956.7727 &

### 76 CITY LIGHTS BOOKSELLERS & PUBLISHERS

More than any other bookstore, this one, especially beloved by night owls, evokes the atmosphere and accomplishments of literary San Francisco. Owned by poet Lawrence Ferlinghetti, the shop's heyday was the Beat era of the 1950s. Many of the writers who immortalized that time—Allen Ginsberg, Gregory Corso, Michael McClure, Jack Kerouac, and Ken Kesey—are featured, and there's a marvelous poetry section. ♦ Daily until midnight. 261 Columbus Ave (between Pacific Ave and Broadway). 362.8193

### 76 VESUVIO

If it's bohemian atmosphere you're after, this is the place. This landmark North Beach bar is still frequented by artists and poets from the Beat era, in addition to more current representatives of the arts scene. The walls are covered with objets d'art. ♦ Daily. 255 Columbus Ave (between Pacific Ave and Broadway). 362.3370 &

### 77 LITTLE JOE'S

★$ Virtually an institution in North Beach, this is the best of the no-frills, low-cost Italian establishments. The cooks are masters of sautéeing and have been known to sing opera arias as they rattle their pots and pans in view of diners. They do wondrous things with dishes such as squid cooked in its own ink and a simple but superb hamburger served on crusty Italian bread. ♦ Italian ♦ Daily lunch and dinner. 523 Broadway (between Kearny St and Columbus Ave). 433.4343 &

### 78 TOSCA CAFE

★$ Media types, socialites, and a cross section of the city's creative community all love to hang out at this unassuming cafe. Visiting celebrities have been known to pop up as impromptu bartenders. A coffeeless cappuccino made with steamed milk, brandy, and chocolate is the specialty drink. ♦ Cafe ♦ Daily. 242 Columbus Ave (between Pacific Ave and Broadway). 391.1244 &

### 79 TOMMASO'S RESTAURANT

★★$$ *People* magazine proclaimed it one of the country's top three pizza places, but success hasn't spoiled this little spot, which is credited with producing San Francisco's first brick-oven pizza some 60 years ago. All the crisp, thin-crust pizzas are superb. So is the pasta, served with sensible, traditional sauces. ♦ Italian ♦ Tu-Su dinner. 1042 Kearny St (between Pacific Ave and Broadway). 398.9696

### 80 NIEBAUM-COPPOLA WINE STORE AND CAFE

★★$$ This store, cafe and wine bar is an extension of Francis Ford Coppola's Napa Valley winery. You can sample a variety of wines with lunch and dinner. Try the thick grilled vegetables sandwiches for lunch and a hearty risotto for dinner. ♦ Italian ♦ Daily lunch and dinner. 916 Kearny St (at Columbus Ave). 291.1700

### 81 SAN FRANCISCO BREWING COMPANY

$ Allen Paul's brewery, the last of the Barbary Coast saloons, now gets customers who mine their gold in the nearby Financial District. By law, food is served here, but the attraction is the 20 types of domestic and imported beers from small specialty breweries, along with several brewed by the owner on the premises. The interior, dating from 1907, is graced by a solid mahogany bar trimmed with brass, as well as a tile spittoon. Babyface Nelson was captured in what is now the women's room, and Jack Dempsey was a bouncer here for a short time. The management organizes beer tastings and brew-pub crawls sporadically. There's live blues Wednesday and Thursday, and jazz on Monday and Saturday. ♦ American ♦ Daily lunch and dinner. 155 Columbus Ave (at Pacific Ave). 434.3344 &

### 82 CAFFÈ MACARONI

★★$$ This very small, very good, very Italian restaurant has a menu that changes daily to accommodate the market's freshest selections; choices can range from baked stingray to classic pasta dishes. Note: lunch is served across the street at 124 Columbus, (between Jackson and Kearny Sts), 217.8400. ♦ Italian ♦ M-Sa dinner. Reservations recommended. 59 Columbus Ave (at Jackson St). 956.9737

### 83 THOMAS BROTHERS MAPS

Browse through an extraordinary selection of maps, from pocket- to wall-size, as well as globes, atlases, and guides, in this shop that's also known as the Map House. The hanging brass lamps complement the Victorian premises. ♦ M-F. 550 Jackson St (at Columbus Ave). 981.7520 &

### 84 PACIFIC AVENUE

Interesting shops on this street include **Thomas Cara Ltd.** (517 Pacific at Sansome St, 781.0383), an old establishment selling coffee, espresso machines, and kitchenware. ♦ Between Sansome and Kearny Sts

### 85 BIX

★★★$$$ The location on quiet Gold Street, tucked away in the shadow of the **Transamerica Pyramid,** sets the mood for a visit to this posh 1920s-style supper club, where people sip martinis at the elegant bar backed by a bigger-than-life mural, and a torch singer croons in the corner. The menu changes seasonally, but always includes such standbys as Waldorf salad, updated with roquefort cheese, and chicken hash. Other homey dishes might include grilled pork chops with mashed potatoes, grilled lamb chops with mustard and mint, duck confit, and sturgeon with roast vegetables. In these drop-dead surroundings, you might be inclined to splurge on the Russian *osetra* caviar with crème fraîche and toast points. ♦ American ♦ M-F lunch and dinner; Sa-Su dinner. Reservations required. 56 Gold St (between Sansome and Montgomery Sts). 433.6300 &

### 86 WILLIAM STOUT ARCHITECTURAL BOOKS

One of the few great architectural bookstores in America, this shop has grown from a handful of books available at Bill's apartment to a collection of more than 10,000 volumes of rare books, magazines, and portfolios. ♦ M-Sa. 804 Montgomery St (at Jackson St). 391.6757

### 87 JACKSON SQUARE HISTORIC DISTRICT

Designated the city's first historic district, this area contains the only group of downtown business buildings to survive the 1906 earthquake and fire; most date back to the 1850s. Some buildings sustained additional damage in the 1989 quake, but all survived. Most are brick and have been carefully restored and remodeled to become the city's antique showroom center for the prestigious Challiss House, Antonio's Antiques and others. ♦ Bounded by Sansome and Montgomery Sts, and Washington and Jackson Sts

### 87 HOTALING PLACE

This block-long alley leads from Jackson Street, between Montgomery and Sansome Streets, right into the base of the **Transamerica Pyramid.** There are two old warehouses that were distilleries in the Barbary Coast days.

### 88 722 MONTGOMERY STREET

This three-story brick building is registered as a historic landmark. The first meeting of

---

Restaurants/Clubs: **Red** | Hotels: **Purple** | Shops: Orange | Outdoors/Parks: **Green** | Sights/Culture: Blue

Freemasons in California was held here on 17 October 1849. ♦ At Washington St

## 89 ARCH

Drafting instruments and supplies are imaginatively displayed in this beautifully designed architectural-supply store. It's conveniently close to the popular architectural bookstore, **William Stout** (see p. 99) and within easy reach of the many architectural offices in the neighborhood, which explains the crowd at lunchtime. ♦ M-Sa. 407 Jackson St (between Sansome and Montgomery Sts). 433.2724 ♿

## 90 US APPRAISER'S BUILDING

This government building occupies the same block as the **US Custom House,** and both represent contrasting attitudes toward federal architecture. Erected by **Gilbert Stanley Underwood** in 1941, this building represents the aesthetics of the WPA era with its stripped-down Moderne styling. It was reclad in 1988 by **Kaplan/McLaughlin/Diaz** with precast concrete and a new polished-granite base. The same firm redid the windows in 1992. ♦ Battery and Jackson Sts

## 91 US CUSTOM HOUSE

Older than the **US Appraiser's Building** on the same block, this classical Baroque building has a massive rusticated base, an elaborate cornice line, and a generously proportioned entrance hall. It was constructed from 1906 to 1911 by **Eames & Young. Room 504** on the fifth floor houses the US Geological Survey offices, which sell maps of the US and Apollo 11 maps of the moon. ♦ 555 Battery St (at Jackson St)

## 92 KOKKARI

★★★$$$ Mark this spot on your culinary journeys for contemporary Hellenic cuisine. Kokkari also brightens one's dining options around Jackson Square. Entering the restaurant is like coming into a secluded hilltop retreat. A fire blazes in the hearth and makes the old wood gleam. A silver-haired Greek waiter brings a bowl of penne with braised lamb. But the supreme lamb experience is *arnisia paidakia,* three grilled chops with oregano and lemon . For dessert try the poached pear over rice pudding. ♦ Greek ♦ M-Sa lunch and dinner. Reservations recommended. 200 Jackson St (at Front St). 981.0983.

---

In 1907, famous escape artist Harry Houdini put on a show at San Francisco's Aquatic Park. While submerged deep in the frigid waters of the bay, he unshackled himself from chains in just 57 seconds.

## SAN FRANCISCO'S ISLANDS

## San Francisco's Islands

The rocky islands in **San Francisco Bay** are home to a once-notorious prison, naval training stations, and wildlife refuges teeming with sea lions and birds. Tours of **Alcatraz, Angel,** and **Treasure Islands** can be arranged, or you may cruise by them on one of the ferries that dock at **Fisherman's Wharf.**

## 93 ANGEL ISLAND

This square mile of rocky land rising to a summit of 781 feet is the largest island in the bay. It was also the place Lieutenant Juan Manuel de Ayala initially anchored in 1775 during the first European expedition to sail through the Golden Gate. Between 1860 and 1890, the island's **Camp Reynolds** operated as a Civil War outpost and later as a staging area for soldiers engaged in fighting Indians. It is the only remaining garrison of its type from the Civil War. During the Spanish-American War and World Wars I and II, the island served as a debarkation and discharge point for troops. From 1910 to 1940 it was regarded as the "Ellis Island of the West," serving mostly Asian immigrants. It became an internment camp for Italian and German prisoners during World War II.

Today the State Park Service maintains the island, and it's a perfect spot for a day of hiking, bicycling, or beachcombing. Trails meander along rugged slopes on a five-mile route. There are nine environmental campsites on the island. For reservations 800/444.7275). There are also picnic and barbecue facilities, a snack bar during the summer months, and a souvenir kiosk. The **Visitors' Center** offers 20-minute video tours year-round and guided tours of historic sites from April through October. For more information, call 435.1915. ♦ Park: Daily 8AM to sunset. Ferries: Daily in summer, weekends only in winter. The island is accessible by two routes: The Red & White Fleet runs ferries from San Francisco (546.2805, 800/229.2784 in CA), and the Angel Island/Tiburon Ferry Company departs from Tiburon (435.2131)

## 94 FARALLON ISLANDS

In 1872, this chain of craggy islands located 32 miles from Point Lobos was incorporated into the city and county of San Francisco. The name Farallon is derived from the Spanish expression for small, rocky, pointed islands. Inhospitable to humans, these islands today are closed to the public. There is, however, a Coast Guard station on **South Farallon** (the island most visible from San Francisco's shores), and until 1968, a handful of stoic families lived there. Lighthouse keepers had to climb a steep zigzag path 320 feet up to the light, sometimes crawling on their hands and knees during the onslaught of a gale or storm. Today an automated lighthouse and foghorn warn ships to stay away from the treacherous rocks. To many San Franciscans, the significance of the Farallon Islands is mete-orological, demonstrated by the expression "On a clear day you can see the Farallon Islands." They are best viewed from Ocean Beach or Point Reyes in Marin County. You can board a day cruise to the Farallons June through November by calling Oceanic Society Expeditions, 441.1104

## 95 ALCATRAZ ISLAND

When Lieutenant Juan Manuel de Ayala discovered the island in 1775, he named it *Isla de los Alcatraces* (Island of the Pelicans) after the colony of pelicans roosting here. The first lighthouse on the West Coast was installed here in 1854. The island's strategic and isolated position made it ideal for use as a defensive and disciplinary installation. The first cell block was built by the US Army, and from that time on, the island was fated to be a prison facility. Crude stockades held unruly soldiers convicted of crimes in the 1860s, and Indians who proved troublesome were detained here in the 1870s. The island served as a quarantine post for soldiers returning from the Spanish-American War, and after the 1906 earthquake and fire, prisoners from the crumbled San Francisco jails were temporarily held here. In 1934 it became a federal maximum-security prison. The fame of the "Rock" spread as it became home to such notorious criminals as Al Capone, Machine Gun Kelly, and Robert Stroud, who was also known as the "Birdman of Alcatraz." A new section has opened to the public so you can see exactly where the Anglin brothers made their famous escape into the water in 1962. The prison was closed in 1963. Between 1969 and 1971 a political protest and occupation by about a hundred Native Americans put the island in the headlines. Today it is part of the **Golden Gate National Recreation Area** (although some San Franciscans are lobbying hard to turn it into a casino, albeit without much luck so far). An excellent cell-house audio tour (recorded by former inmates and wardens), ranger-led programs, and a slide show are available daily. Dress warmly and plan to stay about two hours. ♦ Fee for ferry. Daily ferry departures. Reservations recommended. Pier 41, Powell St (at Fisherman's Wharf). Blue & Gold Fleet 705-5444, or 705-5555

## 96 TREASURE ISLAND

This artificial island was created to serve as the site of the Golden Gate International Exposition of 1939-40. After the awe-inspiring effort to simultaneously construct two of the largest bridges in the world (the Golden Gate and Bay Bridges, completed within a few months of each other), it seemed fitting to celebrate by building an artificial 400-acre island for the fair. Later it was slated to become the **San Francisco Airport.** Of course, it was found to be too small and much too close to the Bay Bridge, and with the outbreak of World War II, the Navy used the island as a base until 1997. Who will acquire this hotly contested property remains to be seen, but in the meantime it's still worth a visit for the spectacular views of San Francisco and both bridges. ♦ To reach the island, take the Bay Bridge to the Treasure Island exit or take an AC Transit T bus

On Treasure Island:

### TREASURE ISLAND MUSEUM

Located just inside the main gate, the museum has exhibitions on the history of the Navy, Marines, and Coast Guard in the Pacific arena. There is an interesting exhibition on the Golden Gate International Exposition of 1939-40. ♦ Small donation requested. Daily. Bldg 1. 395.5067  も

## 97 YERBA BUENA ISLAND

This island connects and anchors the cantilever and suspension sections of the Bay Bridge. Known in early days as "Wood Island" to seafarers, it was officially named **Yerba Buena** (good herb) after the wild mint that grew here. Historically, Indians used to paddle from the shore in barges made of bundles of reeds and use the island as a fishing station. Remains of an Indian village and cremation pits have been dug up, along with buried contraband from smugglers, portions of a shipwrecked Spanish galleon, and graves of soldiers, pioneers, and goatherds. Today, the island is a **Coast Guard Reservation and Naval Training Station.** It is connected to Treasure Island by a 900-foot causeway. ♦ The Coast Guard offers tours of the island by reservation only. 399.3449

---

Restaurants/Clubs: Red | Hotels: Purple | Shops: Orange | Outdoors/Parks: Green | Sights/Culture: Blue

# PACIFIC HEIGHTS/MARINA

When a cable-car line was built in the Pacific Heights District in 1878, this area quickly became an enclave of San Francisco's nouveaux riches. They moved into huge, gray Victorians, monuments to the bonanza era, and attempted to outdo the wooden castles on Nob Hill with Gothic arches, Corinthian pillars, Norman turrets, Byzantine domes, mansard roofs, and enough stained glass to outfit several cathedrals. Their houses lined **Van Ness Avenue,** which was five feet wider than Market Street and considered the Champs-Elysées of San Francisco.

But the magnificence on **Van Ness Avenue** was short-lived. The earthquake of 1906 reduced the exquisite homes to shambles, and the area never fully recovered. However, eastern Pacific Heights, like Russian and Nob Hills, was rebuilt with luxury apartment houses, and a substantial number of the original Victorians still remain. Today the Pacific Heights and Marina areas, along with **Cow Hollow** and **Presidio Heights,** hold more college graduates, professionals, and families earning upper-middle and higher incomes than any other city district. There are more mansions per city block as well, with handsome examples of the work of architects **Bernard Maybeck, Willis Polk, Ernest Coxhead,** and **William Knowles** on the streets feeding into **Broadway.** One of the oldest is at **2727 Pierce Street.** The city's most photographed group of dainty Victorians is along the south side of **Alta Plaza Park.** The fine collection of Victorian houses on **Union Street** has been turned into a shopper's dream, with more than 300 boutiques, restaurants, antiques stores, and coffeehouses. A drive out Broadway to the **Presidio Gate** will give you a capsule glimpse into the privileged lives of years past and present. Private ownership of such enormous buildings was destined to die out, and many of the more impressive mansions now house schools, consulates, and religious orders, or have been converted into apartments.

Although technically part of the Richmond District, Presidio Heights is philosophically, socially, and economically akin to its neighbor, Pacific Heights. It's a low-density area, filled with elegant private houses. **Sacramento Street,** which starts at **The Embarcadero,** turns into a chic commercial enclave between **Divisadero** and **Spruce Streets.** In this restrained, exclusive neighborhood, more than a whiff

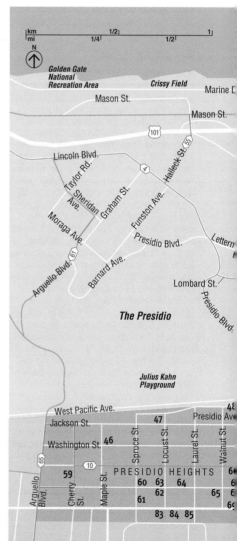

of affluence wafts across the few blocks of expensive specialty shops and antiques stores, some of which are open by appointment only.

Cow Hollow, the area north of Pacific Heights, was named for the 30 dairy farms established there in 1861. A tiny lagoon, **Laguna Pequeña** (also known as **Washerman's Lagoon**), was used as a communal wash basin for the city's laundry. In the late 1800s, tanneries, slaughterhouses, and sausage factories appeared because of the dairies and fresh water from the lake and springs. But pollution from open sewage, industry, and the cows forced the city to banish livestock forever and to fill the putrid lagoon with sand from the dunes on **Lombard Street**.

After the devastating 1906 earthquake and fire, to show the world it was a city that refused to die, San Francisco proceeded to stage one of the most spectacular fairs of all time—the Panama-Pacific International Exposition of 1915. The excuse was the opening of the Panama Canal, and the Exposition was the springboard for a citywide open house that drew more than 18 million visitors. On the bay north of Cow Hollow, 600 acres of marshland were filled in, a seawall was built running parallel to the shoreline, and sand was pumped up from the ocean bottom to serve as fill. The dredging produced enough

deep water to build the **San Francisco Yacht Harbor,** the present site of the **St. Francis Yacht Club,** and enough land to create the Marina District. **Crissy Field** (in The Richmand/The Presidio Chapter) has been returned to marshland and has a good swimming beach. One of the exhibition's buildings, the monumental **Palace of Fine Arts,** is now home to the **Exploratorium,** a very popular family science museum and auditorium. However, the landfill proved to be a dangerously shaky foundation during the 7.1 quake that rocked the city in October 1989. Since then, the recovery has been slow. Some 35 buildings were declared unsafe, with an additional 92 damaged.

The Marina reflects the Mediterranean-revival architecture popular in the 1920s, with mostly pastel, single-family dwellings and large, well-maintained flats along the curving streets. Although **Chestnut Street** offers fine neighborhood restaurants and interesting shops, Lombard Street, or "Motel Row," is generally considered a blight on the cityscape from Van Ness Avenue to the entrance to the **Golden Gate Bridge.** The **Marina Green,** which borders the harbor, is often full of kite flyers, volleyball players, sunbathers, joggers, and boaters. Nearby **Fort Mason,** planned by the Spanish in 1797 as a gun battery for the protection of **La Yerba Buena** anchorage, now functions as a giant community center offering theaters, workshops, the **Mexican Museum,** exhibition space, galleries, classes, and **Greens,** the best-known vegetarian restaurant in San Francisco.

## 1 ST. FRANCIS YACHT CLUB

This Spanish-style building overlooks the bay and the Marina yacht harbor. Badly damaged by a fire on Christmas day in 1976, the private club was completely remodeled by **Marquis Associates,** only to once again sustain heavy losses after the 1989 quake. ♦ Marina Blvd (at Baker St)

## 2 WAVE ORGAN

Located at the tip of the Marina jetty is this often described "very peculiar musical instrument" built by scientists from the **Exploratorium.** The "organ" is nothing more than a series of underwater tubes echoing the sounds of the changing tide which visitors can hear in a miniature amphitheater. Although chances are that what you hear will sound more like a gurgling toilet than organ music, the city and bay views here make this a worthwhile destination. ♦ Between Marina Green and Marina Blvd

## 3 MARINA GREEN

Area residents jog, bike, skate, fly kites, and sun-worship along this green swath of park that runs from the yacht harbor to **Fort Mason.** It's a glorious place to drink in the magnificent scenic beauty surrounding the bay. ♦ Marina Blvd (between Webster and Scott Sts)

## 4 PALACE OF FINE ARTS

Originally built in 1915 for the Panama-Pacific Exposition, the palace houses the **Exploratorium,** a science museum for kids and adults, and an auditorium used for lectures and film presentations. Architect **Bernard Maybeck**'s building was the pièce de résistance of his career as well as of the exposition. It has a great stage set consisting of a classical Roman rotunda with two curved colonnades, behind which is the curved exhibition shed. The setting is in the midst of a small park, complete with an artificial lake and waterfowl (including two swans). The palace became so popular that the buildings were retained and completely rebuilt after the Exposition ended. Restoration was completed in 1969, the year the **Exploratorium** opened as a science museum. The museum was conceived on the premise that one learns by doing, and the more than 650 exhibits require visitor participation. You can pull, push, and manipulate various objects to demonstrate principles of prisms, sound, electricity, lasers, plant behavior, and more. The special **Tactile Dome,** which some private groups have explored in the nude, has a separate admission charge and requires reservations (call 561.0362). ♦ Admission; children three and under free; free the first Wednesday of each month (excluding some special exhibitions). Daily Memorial Day to Labor Day; Tu-Su Labor Day to Memorial Day. 3601 Lyon St (between Bay and Jefferson Sts). Exploratorium events 563.7337. Palace of Fine Arts Theater 567.6642 &

## 5 THE BUCHANAN GRILL

★★$$ "Classic" describes this busy bar/restaurant, where every inch of wall is covered with pictures of sports personalities. Those who like their Buffalo chicken wings explosively hot will go for the ones here; they're doused in red-hot pepper sauce and accompanied by cooling celery sticks and blue cheese dipping sauce. Main courses include such comfort food as pot roast and mashed potatoes in a rich mushroom gravy, and a stellar steak sandwich with sautéed onions and mushrooms. ◆ Californian ◆ Daily lunch and dinner; Su brunch. Reservations recommended. 3653 Buchanan St (between Bay and North Point Sts). 346.8727 ♿

### 6 SAN FRANCISCO GAS LIGHT COMPANY BUILDING

This fine late-19th-century building, which originally held storage tanks for the San Francisco Gas Light Company, has been converted into offices. Notice the corner turret and consistent brick and stone detailing throughout. ◆ 3600 Buchanan St (at North Point St)

### 7 FORT MASON CENTER

Dating from the mid-1800s, when it served as a command post for the army that tamed the West, this proud reserve was added to by WPA workers in the 1930s. Today the area is part of the **Golden Gate National Recreational Area (GGNRA)** and houses theaters, classes, workshops, a restaurant, and art galleries, as well as trade shows and special exhibitions. ◆ Marina Blvd (entrance at Buchanan St). 441.5706 ♿

Within Fort Mason Center:

### SAN FRANCISCO MUSEUM OF MODERN ART RENTAL GALLERY

An arm of the **San Francisco Museum of Modern Art,** this gallery focuses on works of lesser-known, emerging northern California artists. It has frequently changing exhibitions. Artwork is offered for sale and/or rent. ◆ Free. Tu-Sa. Bldg A. 441.4777

### SAN FRANCISCO CRAFT & FOLK ART MUSEUM

Exhibitions of contemporary crafts, American folk art, and traditional ethnic art from home and abroad are on display. ◆ Nominal admission; free Saturday 10AM-noon and the first Wednesday of each month. Tu-Su. Bldg A. 775.0990 ♿

### YOUNG PERFORMERS THEATRE

This theater produces children's classics, adaptations, and new works, with children working alongside professional adult actors. The theater school offers classes for children preschool age and up. Parties are held after weekend shows (it's a perfect place for birthday celebrations). ◆ Bldg C, third floor. 346.5550 ♿

### J. PORTER SHAW LIBRARY

Part of the **San Francisco Maritime National Historic Park System,** this is a treasure trove of marine-related books. ◆ Tu-Sa. Bldg E, third floor. 556.9870 ♿

### THE MAGIC THEATRE

This experimental playhouse (founded in 1967) has achieved international recognition for its contribution to American theater. New plays by such writers as Pulitzer Prize winner Sam Shepard and poet/playwright Michael McClure have been produced here, as well as innovative works by emerging playwrights. ◆ Bldg D. 441.3687 ♿

### BAYFRONT THEATER

This theater hosts the best works of local and national theater groups, and it's the site of a variety of music and dance concerts. ◆ Bldg B. 441.5706 ♿

### COWELL THEATER

One of the Bay Area's most exciting performance spaces, its elegant design takes advantage of the architectural character of the more-than-75-year-old pier. Held here Saturday mornings is "West Coast Live," San Francisco's radio show to the world. For tickets, call 664.9500. ◆ Pier 2. 441.5706 ♿

### AFRICAN-AMERICAN HISTORICAL AND CULTURAL SOCIETY

This resource center provides accurate accounts of the culture and history of African-Americans. The society has art exhibitions, a museum, and a gift shop. ◆ Admission. Tu-Su. Bldg C. 441.0640 ♿

### MUSEO ITALO-AMERICANO

Dedicated to researching, preserving, and displaying the works of Italian and Italian-American artists, this museum also strives to foster the appreciation of Italian art and culture. ◆ Admission. W-Su. Bldg C. 673.2200 ♿

### MEXICAN MUSEUM

This museum collects, exhibits, and translates works of Mexicano (Mexican, Mexican-American, and Chicano) as well as Latino artists in an attempt to generate new perspectives on American culture. Plans for a new building on Mission Street (across from the

---

Restaurants/Clubs: Red | Hotels: Purple | Shops: Orange | Outdoors/Parks: Green | Sights/Culture: Blue

San Francisco Museum of Modern Art) are in progress with a scheduled date for completion in 1998. The new museum will have an increased exhibition space, and will be the largest facility devoted to Mexican art in the US. ♦ Nominal admission. W-Su noon-5PM. Bldg D. 441.0445 ♿

## Greens

★★★$$$ San Francisco's finest vegetarian restaurant is run by dedicated disciples of Zen Buddhism. Its opening in 1979 made vegetarianism stylish, and it's easy to see why. You won't find any ordinary vegetables-stirred-in-a-wok here; only tasty culinary creations so interesting you'll forget you're not eating meat. The soups, homemade breads, and salads can't be matched. The black-bean chili, herb-flavored potatoes baked in parchment, and Green Gulch salad with lettuces, Sonoma goat cheese, pecans, and oranges are all excellent. As an added bonus, you'll have a beautiful view of the bay and the Golden Gate Bridge. Check out the bathrooms—they belong in an architectural guidebook. Also visit the take-out counter if the weather puts in you in the mood for an impromptu picnic. ♦ Californian/Vegetarian ♦ M dinner; Tu-Sa lunch and dinner; Su brunch. Reservations recommended. Bldg A. 771.6222 ♿

## 8 Liverpool Lil's

★$ The cozy, publike atmosphere and reasonably priced food bring locals and enlisted folks from the Presidio back again and again. A hearty specialty for the hungry is the Manchester Wellington—ground round wrapped in ham and a flaky crust. This is a great place for a late supper. ♦ English ♦ Daily lunch and dinner. Reservations recommended. 2942 Lyon St (at Lombard St). 921.6664 ♿

## 9 Zinzino

★$ Marked by a blue Vespa over the door, this casual neighborhood restaurant strives to be the sort of place you might happen upon in Italy. Although the pastas sometimes miss the mark, the wood-fired pizzas are always right on. Validated parking for $2 at Wong's Auto Garage. ♦ Italian ♦ Daily dinner. Reservations recommended. 2355 Chestnut St (between Scott and Divisadero Sts). 346.6623 ♿

## 9 Cucina Paradiso

★★$$ Crisp white tablecloths, an open kitchen, a plant-filled patio, and friendly servers add to the welcoming atmosphere of this Italian restaurant. A typical meal might consist of arugula salad topped with grated parmesan followed by the saltimbocca—veal sautéed with white wine, sage, and prosciutto. ♦ Italian ♦ Daily dinner. 2373 Chestnut St

(between Scott and Divisadero Sts). 563.0217 ♿

## 10 Bechelli's Coffee Shop

★★$ Homemade desserts and more than 25 varieties of omelettes, along with traditional coffeehouse chow, are the draw at this charming little restaurant. The hamburger and thick french fries are a delight, and the all-American, housemade apple pie, cherry pie, and chocolate cake are classic. ♦ American ♦ Daily breakfast and lunch. 2346 Chestnut St (between Scott and Divisadero Sts). 346.1801 ♿

## 11 Cafe Marimba

★★$$ Open a trendy restaurant in a trendy neighborhood and sure enough, they will come. Which partly explains why this place has been a hit with the locals since the day it opened (reservations aren't taken, so expect to wait an hour or more for a table). The specialty of the house—*mole negro* of Oaxaca—is great, as is the taco bar (try the spiced octopus, shrimp, or snapper tacos). Mexican standards, such as enchiladas and quesadillas, round out the menu. ♦ Mexican ♦ M dinner; Tu-F lunch and dinner; Sa-Su brunch. 2317 Chestnut St (between Scott and Divisadero Sts). 776.1506 ♿

## 12 Judy's Cafe

★★$ This country-cute cafe features a dozen omelettes with a twist: taco style, with ground chuck and salsa; Italian, with sausage, mushrooms, and marinara sauce; Russian, with black caviar and cream cheese; and Nordic, with smoked salmon. The Texas version is filled with chili, and the farm-style omelette comes with ham, onions, and home fries. ♦ American ♦ Daily breakfast and lunch. 2268 Chestnut St (between Pierce and Scott Sts). 922.4588 ♿

## 13 Johnny Rockets

★$ A nostalgic re-creation of a 1950s diner with countertop jukeboxes (they're cheap to play, too), this fountain makes the best milk shake in town and is a good place for a late bite. ♦ American ♦ Daily lunch and dinner. 2201 Chestnut St (at Pierce St). 931.6258. Also at: Fisherman's Wharf, 81 Jefferson St (at Mason St). 693.9120; 1946 Fillmore St (at Pine St). 776.9878 ♿

## 14 E'Angelo

★★$$ Ignore the meat dishes and try the really fine pasta in this bustling, family-run place. The fettuccine carbonara, *tortellini papalina* (stuffed with veal in a cream sauce with prosciutto and peas), and lasagna draw raves. ♦ Italian ♦ Tu-Su dinner. No credit cards accepted. 2234 Chestnut St (between Pierce and Scott Sts). 567.6164 ♿

# Andalé TAQUERÍA

## 15 ANDALÉ TAQUERIA

★★$ Only in the Marina District would a taco place be as nattily put together as this architectural gem. A profusion of tables clutters an outdoor patio in front, all warmed by a corner fireplace. Inside, a copper pot of lacy palms, stippled walls, and wrought-iron fixtures gussy up what is really a fast-food restaurant. Traditional dinners feature *chiles rellenos* (stuffed chili pepper), tacos, and tamales, although the best choices here are the tacos and burritos filled with rotisserie-roasted chicken or mesquite-grilled beef. The *agua fresca* (freshly made fruit juices) and sangria are excellent. ♦ Mexican ♦ M-F lunch and dinner; Sa-Su breakfast, lunch, and dinner. 2150 Chestnut St (between Steiner and Pierce Sts). 749.0506 &

## 16 THE BODY SHOP

Satin-smooth celebrities, as well as regular folk, are rumored to stock up on body and bath products from this London-based firm. Try the peppermint foot lotion—it's heavenly on tired feet. ♦ Daily. 2106 Chestnut St (between Steiner and Pierce Sts). 202.0112 &

## 16 LUCCA DELICATESSEN

One of the city's many fabulous Italian delis, this place sells fresh cheese, cold cuts, pasta, salads, and frittatas, plus imported canned goods. The staff also makes savory sandwiches on delicious bread. ♦ Daily. 2120 Chestnut St (between Steiner and Pierce Sts). 921.7873 &

## 17 IZZY'S STEAKS & CHOPS

★★$$$ The memorabilia-covered walls and the dark wainscoting—topped with a shelf that's lined with every steak sauce and condiment ever made—add considerable charm to this first-rate steak house. Entrée accompaniments—potatoes, roasted carrots and onions, steamed broccoli, and especially creamed spinach—are excellent, too. ♦ Steak/Seafood ♦ Daily dinner. Reservations recommended. 3349 Steiner St (between Lombard and Chestnut Sts). 563.0487 &

## 18 BARNEY'S GOURMET HAMBURGERS

★$ For a quick, cheap bite to eat, nothing beats this joint, which offers all kinds of burgers— from big and beefy to turkey to vegetarian, chicken sandwiches, and a variety of salads. ♦ American ♦ Daily lunch and dinner. 3344 Steiner St (between Lombard and Chestnut Sts). 563.0307. Also at 4138 24th St (between Castro and Diamond Sts). 282-7770 &

## 18 BISTRO AIX

★★$$ Reserve a table on the heated patio and enjoy the skilfully executed dishes of this popular Mediterranean dining spot. All the appetizers prepared by Jonathan Beard are superb. Try the grilled pear salad with endive, radicchio, arugula, gorgonzola, and walnuts; or the mussels steamed in white wine with shallots and parsley. Top choices among the entrees include seared black pepper-crusted ahi tuna, roasted half-chicken with tarragon butter, mashed potatoes and ratatouille, and curried eggplant risotto with caramelized carrots and balsamic vinegar reduction. Organic vegetables are used "whenever possible." ♦ Mediterranean ♦ Daily dinner. Reservations recommended. 3340 Steiner St (between Lombard and Chestnut Sts). 202.0100 &

## 18 HAHN'S HIBACHI

★$ You'll find good Korean-style barbecued pork, chicken, and beef to go at this small take-out place, which also has a delivery service and five small tables for those who want to eat on the spot. ♦ Korean/Takeout ♦ M-Sa lunch and dinner. 3318 Steiner St (between Lombard and Chestnut Sts). 931.6284. Also at: 1710 Polk St (at Clay St). 776.1095 and 1305 Castro (at 24th St). 642.8151

## 19 CHESTNUT STREET

Between Fillmore and Divisadero Streets, Chestnut becomes a main shopping artery for Marina residents. In marked contrast to trendy Union Street just a few blocks away, it is characterized by ordinary groceries, drugstores, small restaurants, and bars. However, several chichi shops and cafes have sneaked in recently, making this a street definitely worth a stroll. ♦ Between Fillmore and Divisadero Sts

## 19 HOUSE OF MAGIC

If hocus-pocus is your thing, you'll enjoy this old-fashioned magic and joke store. ♦ Daily. 2025 Chestnut St (between Fillmore and Steiner Sts). 346.2218 &

## 20 MARINA INN

$$ Ideally located for family sight-seeing, this attractive 40-room inn is decked out in

---

Restaurants/Clubs: **Red** | Hotels: **Purple** | Shops: **Orange** | Outdoors/Parks: **Green** | Sights/Culture: **Blue**

107

an Early American theme. **Fort Mason** and Fisherman's Wharf are both nearby. Continental breakfast is included, although there is no restaurant. ♦ 3110 Octavia St (at Lombard St). 928.1000, 800/274.1420; fax 928.5909 ♿

## 21 PLUMPJACK WINES

This wine store, owned by the **PlumpJack Cafe** gang, has quickly become one of the best in the city. There is a large selection of California vintages, including hard-to-find small-vineyard wines. The bottles are beautifully displayed and fairly priced. PlumpJack Wines has an interesting website with information on tasting notes, receipes, food and wine pairings. ♦ Daily. 3201 Fillmore St (at Greenwich St). 346.9870 ♿

## 22 BALBOA CAFE

★$$ What used to be a hamburger place in the back room of a bar has been turned into an adventure in American cooking. But the elongated, juicy hamburger, tucked into a baguette, is still around, and is the one memorable item on the frequently changing menu. Recently procured by the owners of **PlumpJack Cafe,** the place is usually filled with socialites by day and lovelorn singles in the evening. ♦ Californian ♦ Daily lunch and dinner; Sa-Su brunch. 3199 Fillmore St (at Greenwich St). 921.3944 ♿

## 23 PLUMPJACK CAFE

★★$$$ An overpriced but pleasant neighborhood restaurant and a good place to enjoy chef Maria Helm's appetizers, including bruschetta topped with roasted beets, baby lettuces, goat cheese, and roasted garlic; gravlax with blini on the side; and a salad made from lettuce, gorgonzola, beets, and walnuts. ♦ Californian ♦ M-F lunch and dinner; Sa dinner. 3127 Fillmore St (between Filbert and Greenwich Sts). 563.4755 ♿

## 24 ART CENTER BED & BREAKFAST

$$ One three-room suite, two large studios and two small studios are available in this smoke-free, New Orleans-style building; each has a color TV, radio, private bathroom, and heating pads. The three suites have microwave ovens and refrigerators stocked with breakfast food; two have fireplaces. Bagels are delivered to all guests in the morning. A deck garden is available for sunbathing. This is an excellent value in a prime location, with good bus service just one block away. ♦ 1902 Filbert St (at Laguna St). 567.1526

## 25 LA CANASTA

★★★$ The only seating is on a bench outside, but the food is so tasty that fans don't mind sitting there and trying to balance their *chalupas* (tortillas layered with beans, meat, cheese, and guacamole), burritos, and tamales—and inevitably splattering their clothes. The burritos are outstanding. ♦ Mexican/Takeout ♦ Daily lunch and dinner. 2219 Filbert St (at Fillmore St). 921.3003. Also at: 3006 Buchanan St (between Union and Filbert Sts). 474.2627 ♿

TRATTORIA

## 26 PANE E VINO

★★★$$ This spot is so popular that even those with reservations may have to wait to be seated, but the food is worth it. All the pastas are superb, and if it's on the menu, try the braised rabbit (or any other long-simmered meat) or the whole roasted fish. ♦ Italian ♦ M-Sa lunch and dinner; Su dinner. Reservations recommended. 3011 Steiner St (at Union St). 346.2111 ♿

## 27 ROSE'S CAFE

★★★$ With Venetian glass chandeliers and glazed-tile bread ovens, this bakery-cafe serves rustic Italian fare. For dinner try the vegetable pastas *en papillote* or pan-roasted mussels, and for lunch try the delicious stuffed *focaccie,* plump round rolls, and salads. Whenever the sun shines, tables spill out onto the sidewalk where people congregate and wile away the afternoon in neighborly conversation, like any other day in Venice. ♦ Italian ♦ Daily breakfast, lunch, and dinner. 2298 Union St (at Steiner St). 775-2200 ♿

### 28 EXPRESSIONS/ A STORE NAMED DESIRE

The lavish decor draws you into rooms set up by the store's talented interior designers. Even if you can't afford the furniture, you'll get ideas. And if you're after a little dazzle, the accessories—cast bronze, porcelain, art— are less pricey. ♦ Daily. 2230 Union St (near Steiner St). 440.9383 &

### 29 DOIDGE'S

★★$$ One of the most popular brunch spots in San Francisco offers perfectly cooked omelettes, eggs Benedict and other egg dishes, and marvelous French toast with fresh fruit. ♦ American ♦ Daily brunch. Reservations recommended. 2217 Union St (between Fillmore and Steiner Sts). 921.2149

### 29 BONTÀ

★★★$$ Intimate and friendly, this tiny, well-regarded trattoria serves rustic Italian fare and fine homemade pastas such as ravioli stuffed with sea bass and angel hair pasta with tomatoes and garlic. Also recommended are the grilled mozzarella with mushrooms and the grilled beef with radicchio served in a balsamic-vinegar sauce. ♦ Italian ♦ Tu-Su dinner. Reservations recommended. 2223 Union St (between Fillmore and Steiner Sts). 929.0407 &

### 29 UNION STREET INN

$$$ The elegance of a 19th-century Edwardian home is combined with personal attention typical of a fine European pension. This six-room inn has a small but exquisite garden where breakfast, tea, and coffee are served, plus a parlor well stocked with books and magazines. The carriage house on the far side of the garden has a suite with a Jacuzzi. Other rooms have private vanities, but share baths. ♦ 2229 Union St (between Fillmore and Steiner Sts). 346.0424

### 30 LA NOUVELLE PATISSERIE

Dieters beware! Elegant, divinely decadent French pastries are yours to eat here or to take home. ♦ Daily. 2184 Union St (between Webster and Fillmore Sts). 931.7655. Also at: San Francisco Centre, Fifth St (at Market St). 979.0553 &

### 31 SHERMAN HOUSE

$$$$ Built in 1876 by Leander Sherman, founder and owner of the Sherman Clay Music Company, this structure was reopened as a luxury hotel in 1984 after being thoroughly refurbished by interior designer Billy Gaylord.

Chiefly Italianate in style, although heavily influenced by the Second Empire style of French architecture, it is considered one of the most handsome and well-preserved examples of its period. The house was awarded historical landmark status in 1972. Each of the 14 rooms and suites is unique, individually furnished in French Second Empire, Biedermeier, or English Jacobean motifs. The carriage house, tucked away behind formal gardens and cobblestoned walkways, contains three suites, one of which opens onto its own private garden with a gazebo. Another suite has its own roof deck. You can see pictures on their website. All rooms have wood-burning fireplaces, views of the Golden Gate Bridge and the bay, and modern amenities such as wet bars, wall safes, TVs and stereo systems, and mini-TVs and whirlpool baths in the black-granite bathrooms.

The large west wing consists of a three-story music and reception room with a grand piano and a ceiling enlivened by an ornate lead-glass skylight. This room has hosted such greats as Caruso, Tetrazzini, Victor Herbert, and Lillian Russell. Now only a family of finches serenades you from their small château— a large cage created especially for them, inspired by Château Chenonceau in the Loire Valley, France. A double staircase from the music room leads up to a comfort-able parlor where cocktails are served in the evening. Downstairs, classic French and nouvelle-style food is served. The discreet service and attention to minute details make the hotel popular with such celebrities as Shirley MacLaine, Meg Ryan, Winona Ryder, and Marlon Brando. There is 24-hour room service, secretarial and translation services, internet, laptops in all the rooms, and valet parking. ♦ 2160 Green St (between Webster and Fillmore Sts). 563.3600; fax 563.1882; www.theshermanhouse.com

### 32 YOSHIDA-YA

★★$$ Yakitori is a whole different form of Japanese food, featuring all sorts of combina-tions of fish, meat, and vegetables put on skewers and charcoal-grilled at your table. Here you can get such dishes as mushrooms stuffed with ground chicken and asparagus wrapped in sliced pork. The atmosphere in this beautifully decorated restaurant is relaxed and pleasant. ♦ Japanese ♦ Daily dinner. 2909 Webster St (at Union St). 346.3431 &

### 33 WRITER'S BOOKSTORE

This is the only used and discounted bookstore located in Cow Hollow. ♦ Daily. 2848 Webster St (at Union St). 921.2620 &

---

**Restaurants/Clubs: Red | Hotels: Purple | Shops: Orange | Outdoors/Parks: Green | Sights/Culture: Blue**

# Lights, Camera, Action: SF on Screen

San Francisco has always been a director's dream. If you count the early silent days, when the city was a major filmmaking center, literally hundreds of movies have been filmed here. What follows is a selective roster of important films shot entirely (or partially) in this city by the bay.

**The Barbary Coast** (1935) Howard Hawks's brawling, period adventure film starred Edward G. Robinson and Miriam Hopkins.

**Basic Instinct** (1992) Michael Douglas and Sharon Stone tangle in a tense thriller. Obsessed with cracking the case, tough but vulnerable Douglas descends into San Francisco's forbidden underground, where he finds within himself an instinct more basic even than that for survival.

**Bullitt** (1968) Cars go flying in the definitive San Francisco chase sequence. Steve McQueen plays a police detective; Peter Yates directs.

**The Conversation** (1974) Gene Hackman stars in Francis Ford Coppola's masterpiece of paranoia, probably the director's best film.

**Dark Passage** (1947) Humphrey Bogart and Lauren Bacall court and spark in an atmospheric thriller set in the foggiest Frisco you ever saw.

**Days of Wine and Roses** (1962) Under Blake Edwards's direction, Jack Lemmon and Lee Remick give memorable performances as they battle with the bottle.

**Dirty Harry** (1971) This action masterpiece from director Don Siegel stars Clint Eastwood as mean Inspector Callahan. Siegel's brilliant visuals show San Francisco to fine advantage.

**Fearless** (1993) Jeff Bridges plays a San Francisco architect who is more wildly alive and taking more risks than ever since he stared death in the face and discovered he was unafraid.

**48 Hours** (1982) Cop Nick Nolte and prisoner Eddie Murphy team up to solve a crime, incidentally wreaking havoc with a **MUNI** bus and provoking much violence.

**Freebie and the Bean** (1973) This comic cops-and-robbers movie stars James Caan and Alan Arkin, plus flying cars—all directed by Richard Rush.

**Guess Who's Coming to Dinner** (1967) This socially conscious interracial comedy was directed by Stanley Kramer, with Spencer Tracy, Sidney Poitier, and Katharine Hepburn. Katharine won an Oscar.

**Golden Gate** (1994) Joan Chen and Matt Dillon star in this yarn about a 1950s FBI agent fighting the "Red Menace" in San Francisco's **Chinatown.**

**Harold and Maude** (1972) A swinging septuagenarian (Ruth Gordon) and suicidal young-ster (Bud Cort) fall in love in Hal Ashby's popular black comedy.

**Invasion of the Body Snatchers** (1978) Bay Area filmmaker Philip Kaufman concocted this stylish remake of Don Siegel's scary original.

**I Remember Mama** (1948) Irene Dunne gives a memorable performance in this sentimental favorite.

**The Joy Luck Club** (1993) This uplifting story is set in San Francisco where four remarkable lifelong friends paint a tapestry of startling events that have shaped their lives.

**The Lady from Shanghai** (1949) See Orson Welles and Rita Hayworth stroll through **Steinhart Aquarium!** This pyrotechnic thriller was mostly shot in studios, but sharp-eyed viewers will spot several fascinating location sequences.

**Magnum Force** (1973) This *Dirty Harry* sequel feels the loss of director Siegel, but has amusing moments.

**The Maltese Falcon** (1941) So popular is this P.I. classic that a Dashiell Hammett walking tour has been put together following Humphrey Bogart's foot-steps. For information, call 707/939.1214.

**Mrs. Doubtfire** (1993) Robin Williams is no ordinary father as he disguises himself, hires on as a nanny in his ex-wife's home so he can spend more time with his children, and creates a new life with his family.

**Murder in the First** (1994) Christian Slater, as a prisoner sentenced to life in the dungeons of **Alcatraz** for stealing $5 for his starving sister, launches an attack on San Francisco attorneys.

**Out of the Past** (1947) Arguably the greatest film noir ever made, this features Robert Mitchum as a cynical detective and Jane Greer as the lethally attractive woman who proves his cynicism inadequate.

**Pacific Heights** (1990) Melanie Griffith, Matthew Modine, and Michael Keaton star in this powerful psychological thriller about two young San Francisco homeowners battling a pathological tenant.

**Pal Joey** (1957) This cleaned-up screen version of Rodgers and Hart's great musical features Frank Sinatra and Kim Novak.

**Petulia** (1968) Julie Christie, George C. Scott, and Shirley Knight star in Richard Lester's sad, moving love story about life in the 1960s. It's highly regarded by critics.

**The Presidio** (1988) Sean Connery and Mark Harmon team up to solve a murder at **The Presidio** military compound.

**The Rock** (1996) Sean Connery stars in this thrilling rescue at Alcatraz. The penthouse at the Fairmont is also in the movie.

**San Francisco** (1936) Clark Gable, Jeanette MacDonald, and Spencer Tracy find plenty of adventure in turn-of-the-century San Francisco. The Great Quake provides a shattering climax and a terrific special-effects scene.

**Star Trek IV** (1986) William Shatner, Leonard Nimoy, and the *Enterprise* crew drop into **Golden**

**Gate Park** in the 1980s. There are fantastic shots of 23rd-century San Francisco.

**Vertigo** (1958) James Stewart stars as an obsessed lover trying to remake Kim Novak into the dead Madeleine in this Hitchcock classic. It was shot at some of the city's most popular locales.

**A View to a Kill** (1985) Roger Moore, in his last James Bond role, must save **Silicon Valley** from destruction by villain Christopher Walken.

## 34 PREGO

★$$ Trendy but informal contemporary Italian restaurants are the rage in San Francisco, and this spot was one of the pace-setters. It's beautifully decorated, airy, and lively, but many say the quality of the food has fallen off in recent years. Best bet is *mezzelune alle melanzane* (spinach half moons filled with ricotta and parmesan and served on eggplant and fresh tomato slices). ♦ Italian ♦ Daily lunch and dinner. 2000 Union St (at Buchanan St). 563.3305 &

## 34 BETELNUT

★★★$$ Named for a seed found only in Asia, this comfortable yet exotic restaurant is so popular it's nearly impossible to get a reservation! Chef Barney Brown's (he's half Korean) pan-Asian menu includes delicious Singapore chili crab, spicy coconut chicken from Thailand, and a wonderful appetizer of sun-dried anchovies, peanuts, and chili from Taipei. All the food goes well with the Asian and American brews on tap and by the bottle. ♦ Pan-Asian ♦ Daily lunch and dinner. Reservations recommended. 2030 Union St (at Buchanan St). 929.8855 &

## 34 ORIGINAL COW HOLLOW FARMHOUSE

Marked by a big palm tree in front, this Victorian former farmhouse contains a complex of shops. In the rear is what was once the barn (the hayloft is still obvious); it's now a gallery. ♦ 2040 Union St (between Buchanan and Webster Sts)

Adjacent to the Original Cow Hollow Farmhouse:

## CAFÉ DE PARIS L'ENTRECÔTE

★$$ This restaurant gives a fresh Californian twist to French fare; the house favorite is steak with *pommes frites* (french fries). Live piano music on Friday and Saturday evenings evokes a cabaret atmosphere. ♦ French/Californian ♦ Daily lunch and dinner. Reservations recommended. 2032 Union St (between Buchanan and Webster Sts). 931.5006 &

## 35 BLUE LIGHT CAFE

★★$$ This cafe offers Cajun cuisine in a modern interior gussied up with galvanized-metal walls and glass panels etched with bayou scenes. The place is invariably crowded with young singles. The kitchen turns out a hearty, spicy meat loaf with mashed potatoes, a commendable pot roast, and tasty barbecued ribs. ♦ Cajun ♦ Daily dinner. 1979 Union St (between Laguna and Buchanan Sts). 922.5510 &

## 35 BED AND BREAKFAST INN

$$ Located on a quiet mews in the Union Street area, this was the forerunner of the bed-and-breakfast epidemic in the city. The word must have spread about its romantic atmosphere and excellent service—you'll have to reserve one of the 11 rooms (four with shared bath) well in advance. There is even a library and a garden for guests. ♦ 4 Charlton Ct (off Union St, between Laguna and Buchanan Sts). 921.9784 &

## 36 PERRY'S

★$$ Perry Butler escaped from Manhattan back in 1969, bringing with him the idea for this typical Upper East Side New York saloon. Originally popular as a singles' place, it has retained a fiercely loyal clientele over the years, but now the old regulars bring their kids. A smattering of singles can still be found at the traditional bar, which is reminiscent of the 1970s. Offerings include veal chops, steaks, calves' liver, *ahi* tuna, and such bar favorites as chicken fajitas, quesadillas, and excellent burgers and fries. ♦ American ♦ M-F breakfast, lunch, and dinner; Sa-Su brunch

---

Restaurants/Clubs: Red | Hotels: Purple | Shops: Orange | Outdoors/Parks: Green | Sights/Culture: Blue

## Union Street Shopping

VAN NESS AVENUE

Lombardo's Barber Shop
Black Horse London Pub
First Nail Care
Sofa á la Carte
S.F. Fitness
The Great Frame Up
Pet Grooming Headquarters
Union Garage
Post Box
Sherman Market

UNION STREET

Pacific Heights Inn

FRANKLIN STREET

Pacific Framing Company
womenswear Maxmillian
The Fitting Room Alterations
Italian deli Corsagna Bakery
furniture Von Demme
childrenswear Mudpie

Sherman Elementary School

GOUGH STREET

holistic health Chiromedica
nautical gifts, clothing The Sporting Company
Canyon Beachwear
bridal accessories Forget-Me-Knots

furniture Mudpie Home Works
Hespe Gallery
Mömen Futon
Best Nails

Images of the North Gallery
A Touch of Asia Gallery
shoes/clothing Dantone

Via Vai Italian restaurant
Georgiou womenswear
Brownie's tanning and fitness

Michelle, Bed, Bath, Body
Cow Hollow Shoe Repair
Scan's menswear

Marina Dental Care
Wonders of Tibet gifts
Decor home furnishings
Sushi Chardonnay
Bayside sports bar/restaurant
Michelle Aleksandar housewares

OCTAVIA STREET

Wolf Camera Photo Lab
mens- and womenswear Croll Sport
womenswear Caramia
hair salon Salon di Moda
womenswear Girlfriends
housewares Asian City Joon's
Caffé Union
jewelry Bay Moon
Italian restaurant Antipasti
womenswear Bryan Lee

lingerie Carol Doda's
mens- and womenswear Union
clothing Anokhi
David Clay Jewelers
Serge Matt Antiques

greeting cards Papyrus
jewelry Stuart Moore

UNION STREET

Fenzi Uomo menswear
B & A Estate jewelry
Radicchio Italian restaurant
The Treat Shop gifts
Loft gifts
Discovery Shop used womenswear

Mac cosmetics
Pavillon de Paris crystal/glass
Hourian Galleries
Erin Paige womenswear
Luisa's Italian restaurant
Union Nails
C.P. Shades womenswear
Jest Jewels jewelry, gifts
Pasta Pomodoro Italian restaurant
Noah's Bagels
The Enchanted Crystal gifts
Starbucks Coffee

LAGUNA STREET

Wells Fargo Bank

American restaurant/bar Perry's

Bus Stop bar
Union St. Goldsmith
Torrefazione Italian coffee
Joji's Japanese/American restaurant

Map continues on next page

## Union Street Shopping, continued

| | |
|---|---|
| womenswear **PeLuche** | **Helen René** *hair salon* |
| | **Glamour** *jewelry* |
| **Artisans Picture Framing** | **John Wheatman Interior Design** |
| *designer clothing* **Sasch** | **Dreamy Angeles Boutique** *womenswear* |
| **Extreme Pizza** | **Puffins** *jewelry* |
| *coffee shop* **Coffee Cantata** | **Union Garden Cafe** |
| *hair salon* **St. Tropez** | **Patronik Designs** *jewelry* |
| *bar/restaurant* **Union Ale House** | **Kicks** *women's hosiery* |

*(UNION STREET)*

**CHARLTON COURT**

| | |
|---|---|
| *gifts* **Eartheart** | **Union Gent** *hair salon* |
| *childrenswear* **Thursday's Child** | **Kozo** *handmade paper* |
| **Phoenix Florist** | **Mezzanine** *womenswear* |
| *juice bar* **Jamba Juice** | **Culot** *womenswear* |
| | **Blue Light Cafe** *Cajun restaurant* |
| | **Ambassador Toys** |
| | **Bank of America** |

**BUCHANAN STREET**

| | |
|---|---|
| *Italian restaurant* **Prego** | **Fumiki Asian Arts** |
| *Asian restaurant* **Betelnut** | **Shaw Shoes** *women's shoes* |
| *jewelry* **The Jewel Box** | **Union Street Plaza** *shops* |
| *pottery studio* **Color Me Mine** | **Farnoosh** *womenswear* |
| **Cafe de Paris L'Entrecôte** | **Amici's Pizzeria** |
| *shops* **Victorian Court** | **The Ocularium** *optician* |
| **Fog City Leather** | |
| | **Metro Theatre** |
| **Solar Light Books** | **Dosa** *clothing* |
| *Japanese fashions* **UKO** | **Z Gallerie** *gifts/posters* |
| *cosmetics* **Body Time** | **The Wherehouse** *CDs/tapes* |
| *men's and women's shoes* **Kenneth Cole** | **Bebe** *womenswear* |
| *shoes* **Nine West** | |
| *clothing* **Armani Exchange** | |

**WEBSTER STREET**

| | |
|---|---|
| *athleticwear* **Body Options** | **Opticians** |
| **PCS Pacific Bell Store** | |
| *clothing* **Bisou-Bisou** | **Mimi's** *accessories* |
| **Eurasian Interiors** | **The Bombay Company** *furniture* |
| *womenswear* **Vivo** | **Bohemia Glass** |
| *alterations* **Reids** | **Atys** *gifts* |
| *restaurant* **La Cucina** | **Tampico** *womenswear* |
| | **Nail Today** |
| *Southwestern restaurant* **Left at Albuquerque** | |
| **Union Street Travel** | **Lorenzini** *menswear* |
| *accessories* **Excessories** | **Gazoontite.com** *allergy-free bedding* |
| *upholstery* **Van Galen** | **Nida** *womenswear* |
| *furnishings* **Z Gallerie** | **Crepes a go-go** |
| | **Artiques Gallery** *custom framing* |
| *stationery* **Union Street Papery** | **Old & New Estates Jewelry** |
| *American crafts* **Twig** | **Three Bags Full** *womenswear* |
| *bakery* **La Nouvelle Patisserie** | **Nice Cuts** *hair salon* |
| *grocery* **City Pantry** | **Eyes in Disguise** *optician* |
| *liquor* **Michaelis** | **Coffee Roastery** |

**FILLMORE STREET**

| | |
|---|---|
| *florist* **The Bud Stop** | **The Humidor** |
| *womenswear* **Capezio** | **Images For Hair** *hair salon* |
| *furniture* **Expressions** | **Le Bouquet** *florist* |
| *day spa* **Novella** | **Nails 2001** |
| *candy* **The Chocolate Bear** | **Doidge's** *American restaurant* |
| *clothing* **Workshop** | **Bontà** *Italian restaurant* |
| | **Union Street Inn** *hotel* |
| *florist* **Bed of Roses** | **Halcyon Antiques** |
| *womenswear* **NNeka** | **Yanagi** *clothing* |
| **Sun Days Tanning Salon** | **Robert Henri Travel** |
| *Italian restaurant* **Rose's Cafe** | **Kelly 1 Salon** *hair salon* |
| | **Marina Submarine** |

*(UNION STREET)*

**STEINER STREET**

and dinner. 1944 Union St (between Laguna and Buchanan Sts). 922.9022. Also at: 185 Sutter St (between Montgomery and Kearny Sts). 989.6895 &

## 37 UNION STREET

In the 19th century this district was known as Cow Hollow because it was used as grazing land for the city's dairy cows. Since the 1950s the six-block stretch from Gough to Steiner Streets has undergone a dramatic metamorphosis, from neighborhood stores to chic shops and swinging bars. Its streets are lined with cleverly remodeled Victorian houses transformed into boutiques, art galleries, and cafes. Not all nearby residents are happy with the change, however; crowds can make parking difficult. (There is a parking garage at Buchanan and Union Streets, and buses run frequently along here.) ♦ Between Gough and Steiner Sts

## 37 BUS STOP

In business since 1900, this plain neighborhood bar provides an inkling of what the street was like before it was gentrified. The place draws a lot of local sports fans who just want an honest drink without having to come up with clever, sociable conversation. ♦ Daily. 1901 Union St (at Laguna St). 567.6905

## 37 JOJI'S

★$ Established in 1972, this unpretentious 20-seat restaurant has a faithful following of local people who like the low prices, French toast, and tasty teriyaki dishes. It's probably the best food value in the area. ♦ Japanese/American ♦ Daily breakfast, lunch, and dinner. 1919 Union St (between Laguna and Buchanan Sts). 563.7808 &

## 38 OCTAGON HOUSE

Home of the National Society of Colonial Dames, this beautifully preserved 19th-century house is now a museum, built on the strength of the once popular belief that eight-sided houses were lucky. It has been moved

across the street from its original location and the lower-floor plan has been changed, but the upper floor displays the original layout, with square bedrooms on the major axes and bathrooms and service areas in the remaining triangular spaces. ♦ Admission. Second Su, second and fourth Th of every month; closed in January. 2645 Gough St (at Union St). 441.7512 &

## 39 MUDPIE

Shop here for casual upscale clothing for children and newborns, including lots of European designerwear for the budding fashion-conscious. ♦ Daily. 1694 Union St (at Gough St). 771.9262 &

## 40 TONGUE N' GROOVE

It's a crapshoot as to whether the band is worth listening to, but you can't go wrong with the pool table, dart boards, and hefty draft beers. It's a casual, unpretentious place, best suited for a beer with a friend. There's live music every night but Tuesday. ♦ Daily. 2513 Van Ness Ave (between Union and Filbert Sts). 928.0404 &

## 41 CASEBOLT HOUSE

Built in the mid-1860s, this noteworthy Italianate house is one of the oldest in Pacific Heights. It's also a private residence. ♦ 2727 Pierce St (between Vallejo and Green Sts)

## 42 PACIFIC HEIGHTS MANSIONS

Some of the finest Victorian mansions grace the tree-lined streets that run along the crest of the hill, offering spectacular views north across the bay and to Golden Gate Bridge. The 1700 to 2900 blocks of Broadway have houses in Italianate, Stick, Georgian, Queen Anne, and Dutch Colonial styles. Look for Queen Anne houses on the 1600 to 2900 blocks of Vallejo Street, and mansions on Divisadero and Jackson Streets and Clay Street at Steiner Street. At **2776 Broadway** is a very contemporary home dramatically different from its neighbors; it was the first custom-designed solar home in San Francisco. All are private residences. ♦ Bounded by Steiner and Pierce Sts, and Pacific Ave and Broadway

## 42 APARTMENT TOWERS

Pacific Heights has many splendid towers in many different styles. Most of the apartments, built in the 1920s, have elaborate marble-faced entrance lobbies complete with doormen. The penthouses create interesting silhouettes along the skyline. ♦ Broadway (between Fillmore and Steiner Sts). Also at: Washington and Steiner Sts

### 43 CONVENT OF THE SACRED HEART

The former **Flood Mansion,** built in the Spanish Renaissance style by **Bliss & Faville** in 1916, is now an exclusive private school for girls. The building may be rented for private functions. ♦ 2222 Broadway (between Webster and Fillmore Sts). 563.2900 &

### 44 2000 BROADWAY

**Backen, Arrigoni & Ross**'s 1973 design is a modern version of the great apartment towers built along Broadway during the 1920s. This is a private residence. ♦ At Buchanan St

### 45 GOLDEN TURTLE

★★$$ Every Vietnamese dish prepared by owner/chef Kim Quy Tran exudes freshness in this cousin of the well-established haute spot just off Clement Street. Try the cigar-shaped imperial rolls stuffed with ground pork, prawns, and crab; the platter of mint leaves, rice noodles, cilantro, marinated carrots, cucumbers, and spicy fish sauce that get rolled up together in lettuce leaves; or the rosy beef salad accompanied by black sesame seed-studded toasts. The kitchen is particularly adept with beef, whether minced and wrapped in edible leaves or skewered and grilled. ♦ Vietnamese ♦ Tu-Su lunch and dinner. 2211 Van Ness Ave (between Broadway and Vallejo Sts). 441.4419. Also at: 308 Fifth Ave (between Geary Blvd and Clement St). 221.5285 &

### 46 3778 WASHINGTON STREET

A mixture of Bay Area and International styles, this house was built in 1952 by **Eric Mendelsohn,** whose trademark details such as the rounded corner bay and the porthole windows characterize this private residence. ♦ At Maple St

### 47 ROOS HOUSE

This 1909 structure by **Bernard Maybeck** is a highly personalized example of English Tudor with typical **Maybeck** window and eaves detailing. It is a private residence. ♦ 3500 Jackson St (between Locust and Spruce Sts)

### 48 3200 BLOCK OF PACIFIC AVENUE

One of the most unusual groups of houses in the city, this complex is located on a wedge-shaped lot that steps downhill. The entire block is clad in brown shingles and contains some of the city's best turn-of-the-century domestic architecture. Each house retains its own special identity with distinct window or doorway detailing while maintaining the unity of the entire block. **Nos. 3203** and **3277** are by **Willis Polk; No. 3233** is by **Bernard Maybeck;** and **Nos. 3232** and **3234** are by **Ernest Coxhead. No. 3232** is of particular interest for its fine doorways and bizarre balcony. All of the homes are private residences. ♦ Between Presidio Ave and Walnut St

### 49 SWEDENBORGIAN CHURCH

**Arthur Page Brown** built this church in 1884, and **Bernard Maybeck** and **A.C. Sweinfurth,** who were in Brown's office, worked on the designs, as you can see by the beautiful Craftsman-style detailing. The church is adjacent to a fine walled garden that is raised up above the surrounding street and contains trees, flowers, and shrubs from every continent on earth. Inside the church, where services are still held, is a large fireplace, as well as stained-glass windows by Bruce Porter and furniture by Gustav Stickley. ♦ 2107 Lyon St (at Washington St)

### 50 EL DRISCO HOTEL

$$ This San Francisco landmark has hosted many distinguished guests—including Presidents Eisenhower, Truman, and Nixon—because of its discreet ambience and unique location (it was Pacific Heights's only hotel for decades). Some of the 48 elegant rooms have spectacular views, and the English Victorian interiors favor the light colors of the bay. There's no restaurant, but continental breakfast is included in the room rate. ♦ 2901 Pacific Ave (at Broderick St). 346.2880, 800/634.7277; fax 567.5537

### 51 ALTA PLAZA PARK

One of a series of urban parks laid out when Pacific Heights was first developed, this green space is set on the top of the hill with terraces stepping down to Clay Street. The park offers superb views south and east to **St. Mary's Cathedral** and the **Civic Center.** Around it is an interesting mixture of mansions, apartment towers, and false-front Italianate row houses. ♦ Bounded by Steiner and Scott Sts, and Clay and Jackson Sts

The variable weather of San Francisco is often more noticeable in Pacific Heights, with the fog funneling through the Golden Gate Bridge and flowing around the shoreline and hills. At almost any time of year, you can climb up a gray hillside to the sound of foghorns and stare down onto a sun-drenched view of the other side.

---

**Restaurants/Clubs: Red | Hotels: Purple | Shops: Orange | Outdoors/Parks: Green | Sights/Culture: Blue**

# Fillmore Street Shopping

JACKSON STREET

Tully's Coffee Company
newsstand/juice bar Juicy News
Mail Boxes Etc.
Pacific Heights Cleaners

L.P. Nail Care

California restaurant Pauli's Cafe

FILLMORE STREET

Mayflower Market grocery store
Hueston's Appliance Service
S.F. Boot and Shoe Repair

Repeat Performance thrift shop
Paint Effects home paint
Tom Bergen goldsmith
GJ Mureton's Antiques
Yountville-Clothes for Children
Twenty Four Twelve hair salon
Zoe womenswear

WASHINGTON STREET

Pets Unlimited

Pub The B Spot
American restaurant/bar Alta Plaza

Belmont Florist
Gimme mens- and womenswear

Cottage Industries exotic imports
Bank of America
Nest antiques

CLAY STREET

Clay Theatre
home furnishings International Market Gallery
hair salon Architects & Heroes
womenswear Jim-Elle
Japanese restaurant Ten-Ichi
clothing Cielo
Jamba Juice
Noah's Bagels
Pacific Heights Travel Service

The Coffee Bean & Tea Leaf

La Posada Mexican restaurant
Seconds To Go thrift shop
Via Veneto Italian restaurant
Aumakua handmade gifts and collectibles

Next-to-New Shop thrift shop
Starbucks Coffee
Body Options sportswear
La Mediterranée Lebanese restaurant
Bluestone Main Flowers
D&M Liquors

SACRAMENTO STREET

Pete's Coffee & Tea
Browser Books
furniture/housewares Fillamento
womenswear Bebe
Italian deli/restaurant VIVANDE Porta Via
bakery/cafe Sweet Inspiration

menswear L'Uomo
gifts Winterbranch Gallery
beauty products BeneFit
Gallery of Jewels
greeting cards Papyrus
Express 1 Hour Photo
Dino's Pizza

Mike Furniture

Metro 200 womenswear

Jet Mail mail service
The Beauty Store beauty products
Pascual's furniture

Mozzarella di Bufala Italian restaurant

Wells Fargo Bank

CALIFORNIA STREET

fast food restaurant La Salsa
Cajun/Creole restaurant Elite Cafe

natural foods, juice bar OrganiCity
womenswear Mio
thrift shop Victorian House
womenswear Betsey Johnson

ice cream Rory's
exotic birds Spectrum
Thai restaurant 2001 Thai Stick

FILLMORE STREET

Royal Ground coffee

GNC Vitamins
Mrs. Dewson's Hats
Nail Gallery & Hair Too
Smith & Hawken garden supplies
Departures from the Past
Harry's Bar American restaurant
Chestnut Cafe American restaurant
The Brown Bag office supplies

PINE STREET

Pacific Heights Market
Japanese restaurant Osaka
Cedonna Artful Living

Johnny Rockets American restaurant
Zonal home gifts
Body Time toiletries
Fillmore Glass and Hardware

Map continues on next page

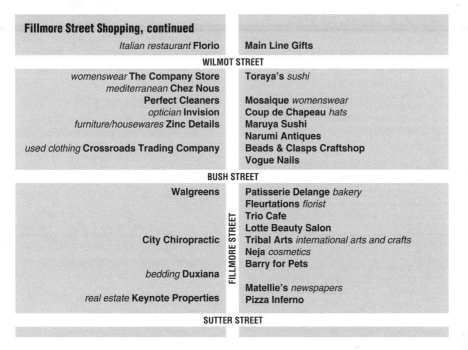

| | |
|---|---|
| *Italian restaurant* **Florio** | **Main Line Gifts** |

**WILMOT STREET**

| | |
|---|---|
| *womenswear* **The Company Store** | **Toraya's** *sushi* |
| *mediterranean* **Chez Nous** | |
| **Perfect Cleaners** | **Mosaique** *womenswear* |
| *optician* **Invision** | **Coup de Chapeau** *hats* |
| *furniture/housewares* **Zinc Details** | **Maruya Sushi** |
| | **Narumi Antiques** |
| *used clothing* **Crossroads Trading Company** | **Beads & Clasps Craftshop** |
| | **Vogue Nails** |

**BUSH STREET**

| | |
|---|---|
| **Walgreens** | **Patisserie Delange** *bakery* |
| | **Fleurtations** *florist* |
| | **Trio Cafe** |
| | **Lotte Beauty Salon** |
| **City Chiropractic** | **Tribal Arts** *international arts and crafts* |
| | **Neja** *cosmetics* |
| | **Barry for Pets** |
| *bedding* **Duxiana** | |
| | **Matellie's** *newspapers* |
| *real estate* **Keynote Properties** | **Pizza Inferno** |

*(FILLMORE STREET)*

**SUTTER STREET**

## 52 FILLMORE STREET

This street has developed from a nondescript, slightly seedy area into a smart thoroughfare of upscale boutiques, interesting thrift shops, and trendy restaurants, easily rivaling those on Union Street. ♦ Between Geary Blvd and Jackson St

## 52 JUICY NEWS

This newsstand and juice bar carries foreign food magazines, freshly blended fruit juices, and frozen yogurt. ♦ Daily. 2453 Fillmore St (at Jackson St). 441.3051 &

## 53 PAULI'S CAFE

★$$ Almost always crowded, this bright, cheerful space is the perfect setting for breakfast or lunch. Breakfasts feature standard American cuisine with a twist—such scrumptious dishes as Grand Marnier French toast, eggs Florentine, and blueberry pancakes with old-fashioned maple syrup. At lunch, try grilled lamb sausage on focaccia, lamb stew, or crab cakes. At dinner, there are 11 types of pasta, including fettuccine with smoked salmon, horseradish, capers, and sour cream, or sample the hearty center-cut pork chop in a red wine-lemon sauce with mashed potatoes. ♦ Californian ♦ M breakfast and lunch; Tu-F breakfast, lunch, and dinner; Sa-Su brunch and dinner. Reservations recommended for dinner. 2500 Washington St (at Fillmore St). 921.5159 &

## 54 REPEAT PERFORMANCE RESALE SHOP

This thrift shop is run by volunteers, with proceeds benefiting the **San Francisco Symphony.** There's often a good supply of evening wear. ♦ M-Sa. 2436 Fillmore St (between Jackson and Washington Sts). 563.3123 &

## 54 YOUNTVILLE— CLOTHES FOR CHILDREN

Look here for sophisticated sportswear for children. ♦ Daily. 2416 Fillmore St (at Washington St). 922.5050 &

## JACKSON FILLMORE

## 55 JACKSON FILLMORE TRATTORIA

★★★$$ There's almost always a wait, especially for tables; many customers choose to sit at the diner-style counter overlooking the antipasto selections. Few appetizers are better than the grilled portobello mushrooms: Roughly the size of a saucer, they are sliced, drizzled with olive oil, sprinkled with herbs and garlic, and arranged on a bed of arugula. The

---

gnocchi, if on the menu, are as light as a feather and worth the wait. Sure bets among the entrées are such braised dishes as woodsman-style chicken with sausage, mushrooms, and beans. ♦ Italian ♦ Daily dinner. Reservations required for three or more. 2506 Fillmore St (between Jackson St and Pacific Ave). 346.5288

## 56 WHITTIER MANSION

This red-brown sandstone mansion was completed in 1896 for William Whittier, a prosperous paint manufacturer. It's a private residence. ♦ 2090 Jackson St (at Laguna St)

## 57 SPRECKELS MANSION

Called the "Parthenon of the West," this is the grandest home in San Francisco. Architect **George Applegarth** built the limestone mansion in 1913 for German immigrant Claus Spreckels, a sugar czar in the Gold Rush era. Years later, movie-goers saw the mansion as the nightclub **Chez Joey** in the 1957 film *Pal Joey*, and again in the 1969 movie *The Eye of the Cat*. Writer Danielle Steel purchased the mansion in 1990, reportedly for $8 million. The garden was sold separately. ♦ 2080 Washington St (between Gough and Octavia Sts)

## 58 HAAS-LILIENTHAL HOUSE

One of the most grandiose Stick-style houses in the city, this 1886 confection is a great Romantic pile of forms with elaborate wooden gables and a splendid Queen Anne-style circular corner tower. Inside, it has a series of finely preserved Victorian rooms complete with authentic period furniture. Walking tours of surviving pre-World War I mansions in Pacific Heights take place every Sunday, sponsored by the **Foundation for San Francisco's Architectural Heritage.** The group departs from here at 12:30PM; call 441.3000 for details. Docent-led tours of the house are given on Wednesday and Sunday. It may also be rented for private functions (call 441.3011). ♦ Admission. W, Su. 2007 Franklin St (between Washington and Jackson Sts). 441.3004

## 59 LEM HOUSE

**Daniel Solomon & Associates** built this stucco-clad row house with an imposing Palladian window and rusticated base in 1986. It is a private residence. ♦ Cherry St (between Sacramento and Clay Sts)

## 60 SACRAMENTO STREET

A mixture of auto garages, movie theaters, ice-cream parlors, gift and antiques shops, boutiques, and a store that is open only two months each year to present an incredible selection of Christmas ornaments are located along this less overwhelming, less touristy version of Union Street. ♦ Between Baker and Spruce Sts

## 60 DOTTIE DOOLITTLE

If you've got plenty of money to spend on little clotheshounds, you'll like these fine kids' clothes, mainly European imports. ♦ Daily. 3680 Sacramento St (between Locust and Spruce Sts). 563.3244 ♿

## 61 ARAM'S MEDITERRANEAN RESTAURANT

★★$$ The brick patio at Aram's is one of the most delightful places for an alfresco dinner or brunch. The menu offers plenty of interesting entrees: wild striped bass, coq au vin, braised rabbit. Try the mixed meze platter which includes marinated mushrooms, grilled artichoke hearts, herb-roasted potatoes, goat cheese wrapped in grape leaves, hummus and roasted bell peppers. Owner Khajag Sarkissian started the Caravansary chain. ♦ Mediterranean ♦ Tu-Sa dinner; Su brunch. Reservations recommended. 3665 Sacramento St (between Locust and Spruce Sts). 474.8061

## 62 BEYOND EXPECTATIONS

★★★$ This is everything a cafe should be. The food, served cafeteria-style, is excellent, with most of it made on the premises (the morning cheese pie with blueberries is to die for). The coffee is terrific, as are the sandwiches, fluffy quiches, fresh salads, soups, and homemade baked goods. There are periodicals for reading, and a view of a pretty little garden from the back dining area. ♦ American ♦ M-Sa breakfast and lunch. 3613 Sacramento St (between Locust and Spruce Sts). 567.8640 ♿

## 63 BATH SENSE

This shop stocks all kinds of soothing, fragrant products for bath and body, including gift items created by local artists. ♦ M-Sa. 3610 Sacramento St (between Locust and Spruce Sts). 567.2638

## 63 TORTOLA

★$$ Healthful and tasty Southwestern and Mexican fare is the specialty of this casual place, which has spun off four quick-service shops in northern California. It offers burritos, tostadas, and tacos with various fillings, but is known for its "cup tamale," a fresh *masa* (corn dough tortilla) shell filled with chicken, moistened with a smoky chili sauce, and topped with black beans and salsa. Sausages from the Yucatán are mildly spiced with chilies and garlic and served with grilled polenta and black beans. ◆ Southwestern ◆ Tu-Sa lunch and dinner; Su dinner. Reservations recommended. 3640 Sacramento St (between Locust and Spruce Sts). 929.8181 ᕽ

### 64 JONATHAN-KAYE BY COUNTRY LIVING

Cluttered and dedicated to quality, this shop offers a charming selection of children's furnishings and toys. ◆ Daily. 3548 Sacramento St (between Laurel and Locust Sts). 563.0773 ᕽ

### 65 KEN GROOM'S PET SUPPLIES & GIFTS

Everything from basic collars to Burberry raincoats for the pampered dog, cat, or bird is on display at this well-stocked shop. ◆ M-Sa. 3429 Sacramento St (between Walnut and Laurel Sts). 673.7708 ᕽ

### 66 ELAINE MAGNIN NEEDLEPOINT

All the needlework accoutrements are sold here, including patterns for pillows that carry the words "Living Well Is the Best Revenge." Lessons are available, too. ◆ M-Sa. 3310 Sacramento St (between Presidio Ave and Walnut St). 931.3063 ᕽ

### 67 MARILYN BROOKS

You'll find amusing sportswear and unusual jewelry from Toronto. ◆ M-Sa. 3376 Sacramento St (between Presidio Ave and Walnut St). 931.3376 ᕽ

### 68 KOUCHAK'S

This shop carries imported handicraft and decorative items, and specializes in Persian tribal rugs. ◆ Daily. 3369 Sacramento St (between Presidio Ave and Walnut St). 928.7388 ᕽ

### 69 TOWN SCHOOL CLOTHES CLOSET

Clothing from some of San Francisco's wealthiest households can be found at this resale shop. ◆ M-Sa. 3325 Sacramento St (between Presidio Ave and Walnut St). 929.8019

### 69 RETURN TO TRADITION

These naturally dyed carpets are woven in a Turkish cooperative. ◆ M-Sa. 3319 Sacramento St (between Presidio Ave and Walnut St). 921.4180

### 70 FORREST JONES

Check out the culinary ware and piles of exotic-looking baskets here. ◆ Daily. 3274 Sacramento St (between Lyon St and Presidio Ave). 567.2483

### 71 OSTERIA

★★★$$ The kitchen at this popular neighborhood restaurant knows how to please its clientele. Green tagliatelle pasta with shrimp and garlic, and linguine with tomatoes and clams are two of the excellent pasta possibilities. Veal and fish are also featured among its extensive menu in grilled and simmered delightfully subtle flavorings. ◆ Italian ◆ M-Sa dinner. 3277 Sacramento St (at Presidio Ave). 771.5030 ᕽ

### 72 AMERICAN PIE

This place, which smells delightful, bills itself as "a contemporary general store," and so it is. Candy, toiletries, coffees, candles, and stationery are among the items sold. You'll find things here you can't live without. ◆ Daily. 3101 Sacramento St (at Baker St). 929.8025

### 73 V. BREIER

You'll find playful and charming contemporary and American decorative arts here. ◆ M-Sa. 3091 Sacramento St (between Broderick and Baker Sts). 929.7173 ᕽ

### 73 SUE FISHER KING

Chic tableware and home accessories that are aimed at upmarket households are sold at this elegant shop. ◆ M-Sa. 3067 Sacramento St (between Broderick and Baker Sts). 922.7276 ᕽ

### 74 WILLIAM SAWYER GALLERY

Contemporary paintings and sculpture by West Coast artists are featured at this gallery. Look for an off-white house with no sign. ◆ Tu-Sa. 3045 Clay St (between Broderick and Baker Sts). 921.1600

### 75 LA POSADA

★★$$ Good margaritas, tasty salsa, and large platters of flavorful Mexican food are offered in a curiously non-Mexican setting that's heavy on Victoriana. ◆ Mexican ◆ M-Sa lunch and dinner; Su brunch and dinner. 2298 Fillmore St (at Clay St). 922.1722 ᕽ

### 76 NEXT-TO-NEW SHOP

Mostly women's clothing, along with some household items and menswear, is sold at this resale shop run by the Junior League of San Francisco and stocked principally by its enthusiastic members. Proceeds benefit

---

**Restaurants/Clubs: Red | Hotels: Purple | Shops: Orange | Outdoors/Parks: Green | Sights/Culture: Blue**

community programs. ♦ M-Sa. 2226 Fillmore St (between Sacramento and Clay Sts). 567.1628 &

## 76 D&M LIQUORS

You'll find an incredible selection of California wines here. The specialties are champagne and sparkling wines—250 different varieties. ♦ Daily. 2200 Fillmore St (at Sacramento St). 346.1325 &

## 77 FILLAMENTO

Furniture and housewares, all on the cutting edge of design, are offered at this modern shop. ♦ Daily. 2185 Fillmore St (between California and Sacramento Sts). 931.2224 &

## 78 VIVANDE PORTA VIA

★★★$$ There is no doubt that owner/chef Carlo Middione makes the best pasta in the city, as well as some marvelous desserts. His bustling trattoria specializes in southern Italian fare; it also houses a deli that showcases prepared foods and high-quality specialty products to take out. All the dishes are simply prepared and rich in flavor from start to finish. ♦ Italian ♦ Restaurant: daily lunch and dinner. Deli: daily. 2125 Fillmore St (between California and Sacramento Sts). 346.4430 &

## 79 ELITE CAFE

★★$$ One of the few New Orleans-style restaurants in the city, it dishes up authentic Cajun and Creole fare. You'll find great-tasting raw oysters, seafood chowder, soft-shell crabs, baby back ribs, and pecan pie. The dark wood appointments, oyster bar in the window, and tall booths along the wall give the place a clubby ambience. Most of the time the service is professional and friendly, although occasionally, when they're jammed, it can be a bit curt. ♦ Cajun/Creole ♦ Daily dinner; Su brunch. 2049 Fillmore St (between California and Pine Sts). 346.8668 &

## 79 VICTORIAN HOUSE

Used clothing and bric-a-brac are sold by volunteers to benefit the nearby **California Pacific Medical Center.** ♦ M-Sa. 2033 Fillmore St (between Pine and California Sts). 567.3149 &

## 79 RORY'S

Try homemade ice cream in a turquoise-and-pink-neon parlor. This place specializes in "twist-ins"—swirls of nuts, chocolate, and other treats spun into the ice cream—and delicious homemade waffle cones. ♦ Daily. 2015 Fillmore St (between Pine and California Sts). 346.3692

## 79 SPECTRUM

It's fun to look at and talk to this choice collection of exotic birds, even if you aren't buying your own feathered friend. ♦ Daily. 2011 Fillmore St (between Pine and California Sts). 922.7113

## 80 HARRY'S BAR

★★$ Renowned for its social scene, this establishment features lots of dark mahogany and brass, a white-tile floor, a grand piano, and great hamburgers. The owner, genial Harry Denton, is one of San Francisco's most beloved characters. ♦ American ♦ Daily dinner. 2020 Fillmore St (between Pine and California Sts). 921.1000 &

## 80 CHESTNUT CAFE

★$ This pleasant place for a cheap feed, serves sandwiches, soups, and salads with an organic touch, as well as great energy drinks. ♦ American ♦ Daily breakfast and lunch. ♦ 2016 Fillmore St (between Pine and California Sts). 922.6510 &

## 80 THE BROWN BAG

This complete stationery store for desk fanatics has a good selection of cards, ribbons, and gold paper clips. ♦ M-Sa. 2000 Fillmore St (at Pine St). 922.0390 &

## 81 PACIFIC HEIGHTS CONFERENCE CENTER & CULINARY ARTS INSTITUTE

This landmark building is the only private residence built by the renowned architect **Arthur Page Brown** whose other projects include the **Ferry Building.** The 1895 structure's interior incorporates 17 different woods. It is now used for private functions. ♦ 2212 Sacramento St (at Laguna St)

## 82 HARD ROCK CAFE

★$$ Even if you didn't notice the life-size black-and-white cow outside you couldn't

# THE SKY'S THE LIMIT

The hilly Bay Area, especially San Francisco, is renowned for its sweeping views. Here are a few of the very best:

**Alamo Square** Victorian row houses on **Hayes** and **Steiner Streets** are backdropped by downtown skyscrapers.

**Gateway to Chinatown** Capture the sights and smells in this historic area at **Grant Avenue** and **Bush Street.**

**Golden Gate Bridge Vista Point** From the south end of the bridge at the toll plaza, you can see the islands in the bay, the bridge, and the north waterfront.

**Mount Tamalpais** On a very clear day, the summit views extend to the **Farallon Islands,** east to **Mount Diablo** and the east bay, and

sometimes as far as the Sierra Nevada, 200 miles away.

**Nob Hill** Easily reached by any of the three cable-car lines, this affords a spectacular view down **California Street** (at Powell St) straight to the bay.

**Ocean Beach** Sunset at this beach, on San Francisco's westernmost edge, affords beautiful views of the city.

**Strawberry Point** Catch a glimpse of San Francisco's skyline from the point just off **Highway 101** at the end of **Seminary Drive.** Look down on the bay, the bridge, and the north waterfront.

**Twin Peaks** From the top of **Market Street** you can scan the best of the Bay Area in every direction—the city, the bay and its islands, the bridges, and the mountains to the north and south.

miss this link in the popular chain because of the continuous line of people waiting to get in. This is where the younger set wants to hang out, scarf down burgers, and then take home a T-shirt bearing the famous logo. ♦ American ♦ Daily lunch and dinner. 1699 Van Ness Ave (at Sacramento St). 885.1699 ♿

## 83 IMAGINARIUM

This marvelous toy shop brings out the playful spirit in all its customers. ♦ Daily. 3535 California St (between Laurel and Spruce Sts). 387.9885 ♿

## 84 EPPLER'S BAKERY & CONFECTIONS

Throw your diet to the wind at this bakery with sensational Austrian specialties. ♦ Daily. 3465 California St (between Laurel and Locust Sts). 752.0825 ♿

## 85 LAUREL VILLAGE CAFE

★$ Stop here for a sandwich and a frozen yogurt. ♦ Cafe ♦ M-Sa breakfast and lunch. 3415 California St (at Laurel St). 751.4242 ♿

## 85 PEET'S COFFEE & TEA

One of the Bay Area's best-regarded coffee chains features beans and brews for coffee and tea connoisseurs. ♦ Daily. 3419 California St (at Laurel St). 221.8506 X. Also at: Numerous locations throughout the city

## 86 ELLA'S

★★★$ Line up here on weekends for one of the best brunches in San Francisco. It's a comfortable place with an open kitchen, a dining counter bedecked with fresh flowers, and simply set, closely placed tables. The housemade sticky buns alone are worth a visit. Other noteworthy items include chicken hash, buttermilk pancakes, and the fresh punch of ginger and orange juice. The lunch menu ranges from grilled fish and chicken potpie to a warm spinach salad with bacon, mushrooms, and a sherry vinaigrette. ♦ American ♦ Daily breakfast, lunch, and dinner. 500 Presidio Ave (at California St). 441.5669 (press 2 for the recorded daily menu)♿

## 87 RASSELAS

★★$ Named after the hero of a Samuel Johnson story, this place is both a good Ethiopian restaurant and a cushy jazz club (there's no cover charge) that's popular, crowded, and the scene of some great music. Classic Ethiopian fare includes *doro wat* (chicken simmered in a blend of red spices), *gomen* (greens cooked with onions and peppers), or *kik alecha* (yellow split peas flavored with herbs and peppers). ♦ Ethiopian ♦ Daily dinner. Reservations recommended. 2801 California St (at Divisadero St) 567.5010 ♿

---

**Restaurants/Clubs: Red | Hotels: Purple | Shops: Orange | Outdoors/Parks: Green | Sights/Culture: Blue**

# THE HAIGHT/ JAPANTOWN

The Haight is a district of extremes, an amalgam of subcultures that includes **Golden Gate Park**, **Buena Vista Hill**, **Ashbury Heights**, **Edgewood**, and the celebrated neighborhood of **Haight-Ashbury**. There are villas and ghetto flats, new developments and Baroque mansions, as well as what is probably the oldest house in San Francisco (at **329 Divisadero Street**), which was shipped around the Horn in sections as a gift for a homesick bride.

All this was once part of a 4,000-acre land grant to a man named José de Jesus Noe, the last alcalde (mayor) of San Francisco when the city was still known as Yerba Buena

and belonged to Mexico. The area was developed somewhat later than the one around Alamo Square just to the east (traditionally known as the Western Addition), so the houses have more of the ornate character of the 1890s. The Haight (as Haight-Ashbury is often known) was everything a proper 19th-century neighborhood should be, with more than a thousand Victorian houses (many still standing), the beginnings of an enormous park, and a landscaped strip for promenading called the **Panhandle**, which looked something like Boston's Commonwealth Avenue, except for the difference in the architecture of the homes.

The names of other nearby streets honor the men who worked to make **Golden Gate Park** possible: **Cole, Clayton, Shrader, Stanyan,** and **Ashbury.** The neighborhood's decline began in 1917, when the Twin Peaks tunnel encouraged people to move out toward the Sunset District, and it continued through the 1950s. The big houses were divided into flats and then divided again. Then there was "the Happening" and 1967's "Summer of Love"—the blossoming of the flower children and the hippie movement, which, depending on one's sociological viewpoint, either continued the decline or marked the neighborhood's rebirth. The flower children disseminated the values of their counterculture all around **Haight Street,** but idealism mixed with drugs and unemployment ultimately proved an ineffective formula for social improvement. The area fell into a state of marked decay and became a place where only the streetwise could walk comfortably. But with the rise in real-estate values around the city, a gentrification trend soon reached the Haight. While many drug-dazed drifters can still be seen asking for spare change and toting their bedrolls, the neighborhood has become home to middle-class and upper-middle-class professionals. The young execs and the New Wavers rub shoulders with washed-out, homeless remnants of the 1960s, resulting in an often tense bustle of eclectic eccentrics, tailor-made for brave people-watchers.

From **Masonic Avenue** to Stanyan Street, Haight Street is lined with some of the city's most interesting shops, bookstores, nightclubs, and cafes. It's a haven for vintage-clothing aficionados and those interested in the occult. And the rebellious spirit hasn't been silenced completely. In 1988 a chain drugstore was burned to the ground during the

construction stage, and a decision (probably a wise one) was made to avoid building in a part of town where such enterprises were so obviously unwelcome. Farther east, Hayes Street, popular with patrons of the performing arts, is also experiencing a renaissance with many unique boutiques and restaurants.

Japantown, *Nihonmachi* to its residents, is a surprising oasis—a pristine village located within the approximate boundaries of **Geary Boulevard** and **California Street,** and **Octavia** and **Fillmore Streets.** Ever since the end of World War II, when the city's Japanese-Americans returned from internment camps to find their former homes occupied, the greatest proportion have lived in other neighborhoods. Only about four percent of San Francisco's Japanese-Americans actually live in Japantown now, but most return here regularly for shopping and for social and religious activities. The construction of the **Japan Center** in 1968 inspired a community-renewal program, with residents and merchants of *Nihonmachi* working together to beautify the surrounding blocks. As you approach the center's main entrance from the north, the block-long **Buchanan Mall,** landscaped with flowering trees, resembles a meandering stream, with fountains by noted sculptor Ruth Asawa. On many weekends, especially during the spring Cherry Blossom Festival and the summer months, you can see a variety of Japanese cultural activities, from tea ceremonies and martial-arts presentations to flower arranging and musical performances. In the gardens along the neat rows of Victorians, you will see shrubs crafted into exotic shapes and a stone lantern here or there in well-tended grounds, planned with obvious respect for the tea-garden tradition.

## 1 NEPTUNE SOCIETY COLUMBARIUM

This domed mausoleum, which holds the ashes of 10,000 early San Franciscans, is one of the hidden secrets of the city. It was originally built for the **Oddfellows Cemetery** by **B.J. Cahill** in 1897, and has been restored to its original splendor, with stained glass, artwork, and silver and gold urns. Names of prominent families, many of whom have streets named after them, are everywhere. ♦ Daily mornings. 1 Loraine Ct (off Anza St, between Stanyan St and Arguello Blvd). 221.1838 ♿

## 2 STRAITS CAFE

★★$ This is one of the only restaurants in San Francisco to offer Singaporean cuisine, which is known for being spicy and subtly sweet. Specialties include the *kway pai ti* appetizer (pastry filled with vegetables and prawns), chicken and beef satay, chili crab, and basil chicken. ♦ Singaporean ♦ Daily lunch and dinner; Su brunch. Reservations recommended. 3300 Geary Blvd (at Parker Ave). 668.1783 ♿

## 3 SAN FRANCISCO FIRE DEPARTMENT MUSEUM

The colorful history of the early days of the fire department is recounted in displays of memorabilia and photos in this small museum. Horse-drawn fire wagons and the city's first fire bell are star attractions. ♦ Free. Th-Su afternoons. 655 Presidio Ave (between Bush and Pine Sts). 558.3546 ♿

## 4 MONTE CRISTO BED AND BREAKFAST

$ Located in a building that dates back to 1875, the inn's 14 rooms (3 with shared bath) are simply but tastefully furnished with authentic period pieces. Better yet, it's just two blocks from bustling Sacramento Street and near transportation to downtown. A buffet breakfast is served in the private dining room. ♦ 600 Presidio Ave (at Pine St). 931.1875

## 5 OSAKA

★★★$$ For years this place has maintained its reputation as one of the top sushi bars and Japanese restaurants in San Francisco. The impeccably prepared food is served in a comfortable, unpretentious setting of Formica-topped tables and blond-wood chairs with rush seats. *Yousenabe* (a seafood stew) and *ton katsu* (pork cutlet) are among the many highly recommended dishes served here. ♦ Japanese ♦ Daily dinner. 1923 Fillmore St (between Bush and Pine Sts). 346.2311 ♿

## 5 ORITALIA

★★★$$ The cooking in this restaurant represents an ingenious and original melding of Asian and Italian culinary styles. Try the wonderful portobello mushrooms, sliced and stacked like Lincoln Logs and doused in a fresh plum sauce, or the mixed shrimp, salmon, and calamari served *moo shu* style with whole wheat Mandarin pancakes. On the Western side of the menu, salmon may be wrapped in pancetta and served with white beans and broccoli rabe, or a chicken breast will be accompanied by mashed celery root with artichokes and tarragon. ♦ Asian/Italian ♦ Daily dinner. Reservations recommended. 1915 Fillmore St (between Bush and Pine Sts). 346.1333 ⅃

## 6 NARUMI ANTIQUES

This intriguing shop specializes in Japanese antiques, particularly 18th- and 19th-century dolls and stained glass. ♦ Daily. 1902B Fillmore St (between Bush and Pine Sts). 346.8629 ⅃

## 7 PATISSERIE DELANGE

You'll find fine French pastry at this friendly shop. Perfect for a light snack. ♦ Tu-Su. 1890 Fillmore St (at Bush St). 923.0711 ⅃

## 8 DUXIANA

Swedish bedding and linen are the specialties here, as well as the Dux bed, which has two sets of inner springs, and adapts to the contours of your body to help keep your spine straight while sleeping. ♦ Daily. 1803 Fillmore St (at Sutter St). 673.7134 ⅃

## 9 CAFE KATI

★★★$$$ The monthly-changing menu offers a host of intriguing combinations: steamed mussels and Thai salmon sausage with red curry; chicken breast stuffed with roquefort and walnuts and moistened with sage brown butter; crispy salmon fillet with Chinese five spices and a light oxtail broth; and filet mignon with house-dried tomatoes and a frothy herbed zabaglione. This is not the place to grab a bite and run; it's designed for an evening's entertainment, in cozy surroundings. ♦ Californian/Pacific Rim ♦ Tu-Su dinner. Reservations recommended. 1963 Sutter St (between Webster and Fillmore Sts). 775.7313 ⅃

## 10 RESTORED VICTORIAN ROW HOUSES

These painted ladies were moved from their former sites when the Western Addition was being destroyed in the name of urban renewal. They have been carefully restored and given front gardens, in contrast to their previous condition, when the houses were located on the street front. ♦ Bush St (between Gough and Fillmore Sts)

## 11 BEST WESTERN MIYAKO INN

$$ This eight-story, 125-room hotel is comfortable and reasonably priced. Sixty of the rooms are equipped with steam baths, and **Cafe Mums** offers Eastern and Western cuisine. ♦ 1800 Sutter St (at Buchanan St). 921.4000; fax 563.1278 ⅃

## 12 BENKYODO CONFECTIONERS

★$ The social hub of Japantown, this place specializes in Japanese confections and light lunches served at a counter. ♦ Japanese ♦ M-Sa breakfast and lunch. 1747 Buchanan St (at Sutter St). 922.1244

## 13 SANPPO

★★$$ Elegant Japanese food is served in a setting that's better than most. Offerings include *yakitori* (grilled skewered meat and vegetables), *nabemono* (clay-pot dishes), *udon* and *soba* noodles, *donburi* (rice with meat and vegetables), a particularly delicate and delicious tempura, and many other specialties, mostly seafood. ♦ Japanese ♦ Tu-Sa lunch and dinner, Su dinner. 1702 Post St (at Buchanan St). 346.3486 ⅃

## 14 JAPAN CENTER

This five acre shopping, dining, and entertainment complex is packed into three square blocks, the commercial and cultural center for northern California's more than 12,000 Japanese-American residents. Designed by **Minoru Yamasaki,** the center consists of three main commercial buildings: the **Miyako Hotel,** the **Kabuki 8 Cinema,** and the **Webster Street Bridge of Shops** (an Asian Ponte Vecchio), as well as several other smaller buildings. Designed as a miniature Ginza, the two-level shopping area encloses pedestrian malls, Japanese gardens, shops, restaurants, art galleries, and sushi bars. ♦ Bounded by Geary Blvd and Post St, and Laguna and Fillmore Sts ⅃

Within Japan Center:

### KABUKI SPRING & SPA

Japanese-style communal baths—including a giant hot tub, large cold tub, walk-in sauna, steam room, Japanese-style washing area, and Western-style showers—leave customers feeling relaxed and squeaky clean. Shiatsu (Japanese pressure-point massage) is the specialty. ♦ Daily. 1750 Geary Blvd (at Fillmore St). 922.6002 ⅃

### RADISSON MIYAKO HOTEL

$$$ Eastern and Western traditions merge in the 218 rooms and suites of this hotel. Most rooms are furnished in Western style with a

---

**Restaurants/Clubs: Red | Hotels: Purple | Shops: Orange | Outdoors/Parks: Green | Sights/Culture: Blue**

few Japanese touches, such as authentic shoji and hand-painted and lacquered *fusuma* screens, and niches for flowers and art objects. There is a variety of deluxe accommodations here. Ten luxury suites have private saunas. Two rooms and one suite combine American and Japanese accommodations and are ideal for families. One area has a king-size bed, while a second partitioned space is carpeted with heavy tatami mats and traditional down-filled futon bedding. The **Club Floor** has a private entryway and includes 14 deluxe rooms and suites, a whirlpool in every room, and a spacious lounge. Within the hotel are convention and meeting facilities, the **YoYo Tsumami Bistro,** and a cocktail lounge. Children 18 years old and under may stay free in their parents' room. ♦ 1625 Post St (at Laguna St). 922.3200, 800/533.4567; fax 921.0417 ♿

## THE PEACE PAGODA

The focal point of the center, the pagoda rises 100 feet in five tiers from the reflecting pool in the middle of the **Peace Plaza.** It was designed by **Yoshiro Taniguchi** of Tokyo, an authority on ancient Japanese structures.

## KINOKUNIYA BOOK STORE

Books about Japan in English and Japanese, as well as Japanese publications and recordings, are this store's focus. ♦ Daily. Kinokuniya Bldg, 1581 Webster St (at Post St). 567.7625 ♿

## MIFUNE

★★$ The Japanese version of fast food is served here, with every sort of noodle dish you could think of—and then some. ♦ Japanese ♦ Daily lunch and dinner. Restaurant Mall, Kintetsu Bldg, 1737 Post St (at Webster St). 922.0337 ♿

## MIKADO

Look here for an impressive collection of items that accessorize a kimono, from obis to tassels to footwear. There are also Japanese dolls, toys, and chinaware. ♦ Daily. Restaurant mall, Kintetsu Bldg, 1737 Post St (at Webster St). 922.9450 ♿

## ISOBUNE

★★$$ Sushi boats float past customers seated around an oblong bar as chefs launch their creations from the center. If you don't see what you want right away, wait until another boat sails by. ♦ Japanese ♦ Daily lunch and dinner. Restaurant mall, Kintetsu Bldg, 1737 Post St (at Webster St). 563.1030 ♿

## YOYO TSUMAMI BISTRO

★★★$$ The striking dining room of the **Radisson Miyako Hotel**—with mobilelike light fixtures that seem suspended in midair—is a good setting for chef Noel Pavia's first-rate fusion fare. Try the tempura salad, roasted cod with succotash, or braised lamb shank with adzuki-bean ragout. The upstairs bar-and-cocktail area is perfect for a *tsumami* (a small plate of appetizers). ♦ Californian Asian ♦ Daily lunch and dinner. 1611 Post St (at Laguna St). 922.7788 ♿

## KOJI OSAKAYA

★★$$ Japanese curry is among the specialties of this small eatery, which has a pleasant Asian ambience. ♦ Japanese ♦ Daily lunch and dinner. Kintetsu Bldg, 1737 Post St (at Webster St). 922.2728 ♿

## ASAKICHI

This shop offers a good selection of antique *tansu* chests and decorative objects. ♦ Daily. Kinokuniya Bldg, 1581 Webster St (at Post St). 921.2147 ♿

## ISUZU

★★★$$ Seafood, including sushi, is the specialty at this elegant Japanese restaurant, which was a favorite of the late actor Raymond Burr. ♦ Japanese ♦ M, Th-Sa lunch and dinner; W, Su dinner. Kinokuniya Bldg, 1581 Webster St (at Post St). 922.2290 ♿

## KIMONO SHIGE NISHI GUCHI

The excellent selection here makes this store great for browsing as well as for buying vintage kimonos. ♦ Daily. Kinokuniya Bldg, 1581 Webster St (at Post St). 346.5567 ♿

## KINOKUNIYA STATIONERY & GIFTS

This shop stocks lovely Japanese greeting cards and imported paper. ♦ Daily. Kinokuniya Bldg, 1581 Webster St (at Post St). 567.8901 ♿

## MURATA PEARLS

You'll find a huge selection of pearls at attractive prices. ♦ Daily. Kintetsu Bldg, 1737 Post St (at Webster St). 922.0666 ♿

## IKENOBO IKEBANA SOCIETY

This branch of Japan's largest flower-arranging school is its North American headquarters. On Saturday, from about 10AM to noon, you might be able to see the experts creating the weekly floral window displays. Call for a class schedule. ♦ Kintetsu Bldg, 1737 Post St (at Webster St). 567.1011 ♿

## MR. DANDY

Petite clotheshorses will find men's and some women's fashions in small sizes here. ♦ Daily. Kintetsu Bldg, 1737 Post St (at Webster St). 929.8633

## 15 SOKO HARDWARE

This is a great place to find rice cookers, Japanese garden tools, kitchen utensils, and even a state-of-the-art toilet. ♦ Daily. 1698 Post St (at Buchanan St). 931.5510 ♿

## 16 QUEEN ANNE HOTEL

$$ Although this is one of the largest bed-and-breakfasts in town, no two of the 49 rooms or suites are decorated alike. Each has a private bath, telephone, color TV, and king- or queen-size bed. Ten have fireplaces, and all are furnished with English and American antiques. Although there's no restaurant, a continental breakfast is served in the salon, and tea and sherry are offered every afternoon. Of architectural interest are the oak paneling in the hall, the carved Spanish-cedar staircase, and the fine inlaid floors. The structure was originally built by Senator James Fair, one of the Comstock silver kings, to house a girls' school. It served in turn as an elite gentlemen's club, a home for young working women, and finally a hotel. ♦ 1590 Sutter St (at Octavia St). 441.2828, 800/227.3970; fax 775.5212 ♿

## 17 HOTEL MAJESTIC

$$$ This hostelry has a long history, and, according to an 1888 document, it just might be the city's oldest surviving hotel. Today, its 58 rooms (including 9 luxurious suites) are replete with furniture from the French Empire and English manor houses, fine paintings, hand-painted four-poster beds, and many fireplaces. It runs a very high occupancy year-round and is often unavailable. ♦ 1500 Sutter St (at Gough St). 441.1100, 800/869.8966; fax 673.7331 ♿

## 18 AUDIUM

This theater was constructed specifically for audiophiles, in part with a grant from the National Endowment for the Arts. Listeners sit in concentric circles and are surrounded by speakers in sloping walls, the floating floor, and the suspended ceiling. A tape director feeds compositions through a console to any combination of 169 speakers. ♦ Admission. F-Sa. Children under 12 years of age not permitted. 1616 Bush St (at Franklin St). 771.1616

## 19 CATHEDRAL HILL HOTEL

$$$ This 400 room hotel is still known to many as the Jack Tar Hotel, a building reviled for its architectural tastelessness and vulgar multicolored façade. The name change accompanied the removal of the tacky colored panels and the complete refurbishing of all guest rooms with a contemporary décor. Indoor parking for guests is available at a fee, and a terrace features a small outdoor swimming pool. The restaurant serves breakfast, lunch, and dinner daily. ♦ 1101 Van Ness Ave (at Geary Blvd). 776.8200, 800/622.0855 in CA, 800/227.4730; fax 441.2841 ♿

## 20 ST. MARY'S CATHEDRAL

Built in 1971 by **Pietro Belluschi, Pier Luigi Nervi,** and **McSweeney, Ryan and Lee,** this modern cathedral consists of four hyperbolic paraboloids creating a 190-foot roof over a square plan on a podium. It seats 2,500 people around a central altar and is similar to other contemporary cathedrals in Liverpool and Brasília. ♦ Geary Blvd (at Gough St). 567.2020 ♿

## 21 1198 FULTON STREET

Stop here to ogle one of the grandest and most beautiful Victorian mansions in the city. It's a private residence. ♦ At Scott St

## 22 THE ARCHBISHOP'S MANSION INN

$$$ This has to be one of the most spectacular bed-and-breakfast inns in San Francisco. Built for an archbishop in 1904, the handsome building has been lovingly restored by its present owners. It features a three-story open staircase covered by a 16-foot-tall stained-glass dome, 18 fireplaces with magnificently carved mantelpieces, and Belle Epoque furnishings with Victorian and Louis XIV chandeliers. There are 15 guest rooms in all, each with a private bath; 10 rooms have fireplaces and several are suites. A continental breakfast is included, and there is a private dining room available for catered functions. ♦ 1000 Fulton St (at Steiner St). 563.7872, 800/543.5820

## 23 700 BLOCK OF STEINER STREET

The six almost identical houses by **Matthew Kavanaugh** have been carefully restored and painted. With the backdrop of the city's Financial District skyline, this late 19th-century row is often featured in tourist photographs. All

# SEVEN HILLS OF SAN FRANCISCO

As the Honorable James Bryce, onetime British ambassador to the US, once said, "The city itself is full of bold hills, rising steeply from the deep blue. . . one involuntarily looks up to the tops of those hills for the feudal castle, or the ruins of the Acropolis, that must crown them." San Francisco's topography boasts as many as 43 hills, but here are the famous 7, which, like the hills of Rome, have long been favorites of visitors to the city. Each hilltop offers its own breathtaking view.

**1. Telegraph Hill** Named for the signal station erected on its summit that informed the citizenry of the arrival of ships back in the early days, Telegraph Hill offers a wide panorama of northeast San Francisco and the bay. Because parking is all but impossible, public transportation is highly recommended. Board the *No. 39* bus at **Washington Square** for easiest access to the hill.

**2. Nob Hill** The home of palatial mansions built by the city's early mining and railroad tycoons (its name is derived from *nabob*, meaning Indian prince), this is the best known of San Francisco's hills. Robert Louis Stevenson described it as "the hill of palaces." In addition to its present-day luxury hotels, you'll find **Grace Cathedral** and many apartment houses and condos for those millionaires among us. The generally accepted boundaries of Nob Hill are **Bush, Larkin, Pacific,** and **Stockton Streets.** The hill is easily reached by any of the city's three cable-car lines.

**3. Rincon Hill** Located close to the southern portion of **The Embarcadero,** this hill (which literally means "corner" in Spanish) is only one and a half blocks long. Approach it from The Embarcadero on **Bryant Street** just south of **I-80.**

**4. Twin Peaks** From here, some 910 feet above sea level, you can partake of sweeping panoramic views of the city and Bay Area. Drive up the hill at the intersection of **Clarendon Avenue** and **Twin Peaks Boulevard;** then weave your way around the 12 curves to **Portola Drive.**

**5. Russian Hill** Named to honor the early Russians who settled here, today it is a mix of exclusive and bohemian cultures. It is within walking distance of **Downtown,** the **Financial District,** and **North Beach** and is noted for its colorful culs-de-sac and lovely bay views. This is the hill where you'll find **Lombard Street,** the crookedest street in the world. Russian Hill extends from **Pacific** to **Bay Streets** and from **Polk** to **Mason,** but its core is bounded by **Broadway, Chestnut, Larkin,** and **Taylor Streets.** The *Hyde Street* cable car takes you right to it.

**6. Lone Mountain** Once surrounded by graveyards, legend has it that **Richmond** district landscapers engaged in planting shrubbery dug up some unexpected remains. Lone Mountain is crowned by a tower that is part of the **University of San Francisco. The Presidio** and **Lincoln Park** are on its north side, **Golden Gate Park** on the south. From downtown, take **Geary Boulevard** west, turning left on **Parker Avenue.** Go two blocks to **Lone Mountain Terrace** at the edge of the campus.

**7. Mount Davidson** At 938 feet, this is the highest spot in San Francisco. At its summit is a concrete-and-steel cross, rising another 103 feet above the hill's summit. Easter sunrise services have been held here annually since 1923. From downtown, take **Market Street** southwest to where it becomes Portola Drive. Portola passes within one block of **Mount Davidson Park** and any exit to the left will get you to **Juanita Way,** which is the park's peripheral road.

are private residences. ♦ Between Hayes and Grove St

## 24 601 STEINER STREET

Constructed in 1891, this Queen Anne house, a private residence, boasts elaborate carving and a fine turret. ♦ At Fell St

## 25 SUPPENKÜCHE

★★$$ This German restaurant is popular for its venison with red cabbage and cranberry sauce, chicken stew, and pork schnitzel with spaetzle. ♦ German ♦ M, Sa-Su dinner; Tu-F lunch and dinner. Sa-Sun brunch. 601 Hayes St (at Laguna St). 252.9289 ♿

## 26 MAD MAGDA'S RUSSIAN TEA ROOM & MYSTIC CAFE

★★$ This eccentric little cafe offers great coffee, tea served in china pots from the 1940s, and tarot, palm, and tea leaf readings. There are also scones, bagels, croissants, sandwiches, and on weekends, blintzes. ♦ Tearoom/Cafe ♦ M-Tu, Su; W-Sa until midnight. 579 Hayes St (between Octavia and Laguna Sts). 864.7654 ♿

## 27 POWELL'S PLACE

★$ Owned by gospel singer Emmit Powell and run by his brother Mel, this soul food restaurant has great fried chicken, braised short ribs, and homemade pies. It's the real thing, with plastic tablecloths and an old jukebox. ♦ Soul food ♦ Daily breakfast, lunch, and dinner. 511 Hayes St (at Octavia St). 863.1404 ♿

## 28 PLACE PIGALLE

★$ This artsy cafe has a back room dedicated to monthly art exhibits, poetry readings, and live entertainment on the weekends. The copper-topped bar and sofas arranged in conversational groupings add warmth, as do the wines, beers, and coffee drinks. The small menu includes smoked salmon, quiche, and cheese plates. ♦ Cafe ♦ Daily lunch and dinner. No credit cards accepted. 520 Hayes Street (between Octavia and Laguna Sts). 552.2671 ♿

## 29 CAFE SINFONIA

★★★$ Chef/owner Tony Nika is Albanian, the food is Milanese, the prices are incredibly reasonable, and the result is a culinary treasure. *Pasta sinfonia* (linguine with Italian sausage, white wine, and mushrooms) is outstanding, as are the scallops sautéed in a delectable lemony sherry sauce. There's no wine list, but the house wine is decent. This tiny, gazebolike place is close to the Civic Center, and frequented by the performing-arts crowd. ♦ Italian ♦ M lunch; Tu-F lunch and dinner; Sa dinner. 465 Grove St (between Gough and Octavia Sts). 431.7899 ♿

## 30 294 PAGE STREET

Designed by architect **Henry Geilfuss,** this 1885 Victorian Stick-style house, a private residence, has been beautifully preserved. ♦ At Laguna St

## 31 TOOLS OF MAGICK

Uma, the proprietor, sells incense, oils, and other paraphernalia to magicians and soothsayers from all over the country. ♦ Tu-Su. 1915 Page St (between Shrader and Stanyan Sts). 668.3132 ♿

## 32 SKATES ON HAIGHT

This is one of the few places near **Golden Gate Park** to rent (or buy) in-line skates, roller skates, and all the pads you need to help cushion you against those inevitable tumbles. ♦ M, W-Su. 1818 Haight St (between Shrader and Stanyan Sts). SKATE.75 ♿

## 32 CLUB BOOMERANG

Another hip Haight Street hangout, this smoky, dark dancin' and drinkin' club replaced the once popular **Rockin' Robins** nightspot. Call for the latest lineup of live tunes. ♦ Cover. Tu-Sa. 1840 Haight St (between Shrader and Stanyan Sts). 387.2996 ♿

## 33 CHA CHA CHA

★★★$$ Most people come for tapas and the spicy grilled meats, washed down by excellent sangria. The food here reflects Spanish, Cajun, and Caribbean influences, including traditional dishes such as black-bean soup, Cajun shrimp, and fried calamari. Bright décor (including a collection of Santeria altars), friendly service, and reasonable prices make this restaurant one of Haight Street's best bets. Be prepared to wait for a table, although it has recently doubled its seating capacity. ♦ Latin ♦ Daily lunch and dinner. 1801 Haight St (at Shrader St). 386.5758 ♿

## 34 STANYAN PARK HOTEL

$ Another stylish establishment near **Golden Gate Park,** this building exhibits the designers' elegant style of transition from Queen Anne to Beaux Arts classicism. The hotel has 30 rooms and six suites; the suites have fireplaces and bay windows overlooking the park. A continental breakfast, and tea and cookies in the afternoon, are served in a private dining room. ♦ 750 Stanyan St (at Waller St). 751.1000; fax 668.5454 ♿

## 35 LA ROSA

Vintage tuxedos and dresses from the 1920s and 1930s are sold or rented to those who want to make a deliberate out-of-style statement. ♦ Daily. 1711 Haight St (at Cole St). 668.3744 ♿

## 35 RED VIC MOVIE HOUSE

A worker-owned-and-operated haven for art-film lovers. ♦ 1727 Haight St (between Cole and Shrader Sts). 668.3994 ♿

## 36 THE RED VICTORIAN BED & BREAKFAST INN

$$ The only surviving hotel on Haight Street was purchased in 1977 by artist Sami Sunchild, who strives to preserve the unique history and character of the building (circa 1904) in the form of an art gallery and bed-and-breakfast. The 18 guest rooms are quite nice—and each one is decorated in its own fanciful (sometimes eccentric) way. A continental breakfast is included, served in a private dining room. ♦ 1665 Haight St (between Belvedere and Cole Sts). 864.1978; www.redvic.com

## 37 WASTELAND

Vintage and contemporary clothing is dramatically displayed in what was once a theater. Notice the impressive facade graced with colorful gargoyles. ♦ Daily 1660 Haight St (at Belvedere St). 863.3150 ♿

**Restaurants/Clubs: Red | Hotels: Purple | Shops: Orange | Outdoors/Parks: Green | Sights/Culture: Blue**

### 38 Dharma

The fashion of the counterculture, essentially clothing from Third World countries, is sold here at reasonable, but definitely First World, prices. ♦ Daily. 1600 Haight St (at Clayton St). 621.5597 &

### 39 Mendel's Art Supplies and Stationery/ Far-Out Fabrics

An incongruous assortment of fascinating fabrics, feathers, buttons, and a vast variety of art supplies share retail space with office supplies. ♦ M-Sa. 1556 Haight St (between Ashbury and Clayton Sts). 621.1287 &

### 40 The Pork Store Cafe

★$ Once a butcher shop, with a porker immortalized in a stained-glass window to prove it, this place now draws locals to its counter for breakfast and burgers. ♦ American ♦ Daily breakfast and lunch. 1451 Haight St (between Masonic Ave and Ashbury St). 864.6981 &

### 41 Bound Together

The hours of business at this anarchist collective bookstore and meeting place tend to be irregular, befitting the political philosophy. ♦ Daily. 1369 Haight St (between Central and Masonic Aves). 431.8355

### 41 Recycled Records

Rare and hard-to-get tapes, CDs, and records are bought, sold, and traded here. ♦ Daily. 1377 Haight St (between Central and Masonic Aves). 626.4075 &

### 42 Pipe Dreams

*The* smoke shop of the 1960s, it offers an eclectic assortment of nontraditional smoking accoutrements such as water pipes, in addition to Egyptian jewelry, and T-shirts. ♦ Daily. 1376 Haight St (between Central and Masonic Aves). 431.3553 &

### 42 Magnolia Pub & Brewery

★★$$ This appealing brewery and restaurant is on the site of what was one of Haight-Ashbury's most notorious businesses in the 1960s. In those psychedelic times, it was a cafe called the **Drugstore,** and well-tended marijuana plants were on view in its window boxes. Dave McLean brews traditional British-style ales, and features five British hand pumps for cask-conditioned beers served at cellar temperature, a common practice in England. ♦ brewpub ♦ M-F lunch and dinner; Sa-Su brunch and dinner. 1398 Haight St (at Masonic Ave). 864.7468 &

### 43 Victorian Inn on the Park

$$ This Queen Anne-style mansion, once known as Clunie House, was built in 1897 (Queen Victoria's jubilee year) and is now a registered city and county landmark. All 12 rooms are furnished with antiques and large beds smothered in down comforters and pillows; several still have the original fireplaces, with turn-of-the-century handmade tiles. Fresh flowers are everywhere, and stunning old photographs provide a glimpse into the 19th century. Homemade baked goods are served for breakfast in the oak-paneled dining room, and wine is poured in the evening in the parlor. The top floor has a suite in the belvedere tower. ♦ 301 Lyon St (at Fell St). 931.1830, 800/435.1967

### 44 Country Cheese

You'll find excellent buys on dried fruit, cheeses, grains, and nuts—great for party givers. ♦ M-Sa. 415 Divisadero St (between Oak and Fell Sts). 621.8130 &

### 44 Ujama

Run by Nigerians, this shop specializes in well-priced African clothing and arts and crafts. ♦ M-Sa. 411 Divisadero St (at Oak St). 252.0119 &

### 45 1111 Oak Street

Completed in 1860, this is one of the oldest houses in San Francisco. It has been beautifully restored, and is now used for office space. Nearby buildings from the same era have also been converted for commercial use. ♦ Between Divisadero and Broderick Sts

### 45 San Francisco Stained Glass Works

Beautiful stained glass is made to order on the premises. The store also does repairs and provides classes for stained-glass hobbyists. ♦ M-Sa. 345 Divisadero St (between Page and Oak Sts). 626.3592 &

### 45 Cookin'

The recycled gourmet kitchen gear sold here has been a subculture secret. Cooks will be thrilled by the variety of wares, including oodles of cookie cutters, molds, vintage cherry pitters, grinders, and the like. ♦ Tu-Su. 339 Divisadero St (between Page and Oak Sts). 861.1854

### 45 Gamescape

The only serious game store in town carries everything from board games to fantasy games. You can find used games, too. ♦ Daily. 333 Divisadero St (between Page and Oak Sts). 621.4263 &

## 45 329 DIVISADERO STREET

The oldest house in San Francisco is well hidden in the middle of the block. Built in 1850, it has been moved twice, and a glimpse of it can be caught on Oak Street at Divisadero. It is a private residence.
♦ Between Page and Oak Sts

## 46 THE METRO HOTEL

$ This 23-room Victorian hotel is a well-kept secret, but known by some visiting Europeans. In the past, it was a residential hotel that was reputedly a home to shady ladies; in its current incarnation, the high-ceilinged rooms are full of innocent charm. There's a pleasant garden in the back that guests may use, a nice little adjoining coffee shop called **The Metro Cafe,** and off-street parking. ♦ 319 Divisadero St (between Page and Oak Sts). 861.5364; fax 864.5323

## 46 COMIX EXPERIENCE

Fans of the genre will enjoy perusing this collection of new and used comic books.
♦ Daily. 305 Divisadero St (at Page St). 863.9258 ♿

## 47 SPAGHETTI WESTERN

★$ The Wild West meets the even wilder Haight, and together they rustle up some decent grub. This place has been described as a "day" nightclub. ♦ Californian ♦ Daily breakfast and lunch. 576 Haight St (between Fillmore and Steiner Sts). 864.8461 ♿

## 48 THE MAD DOG IN THE FOG

★$ This brew pub is a comfortable place to knock back a few pints of bitter, throw some darts, and indulge in a genuine shepherd's pie. ♦ English/Irish ♦ Daily lunch and dinner. 530 Haight St (between Fillmore and Steiner Sts). 626.7279 ♿

## 49 TORONADO

Belly up to the bar and ask for your favorite brew—they're bound to have it at this friendly watering hole that proudly boasts 44 top-notch draft beers, one of the largest selections in the city. ♦ Daily until 2AM. 547 Haight St (between Fillmore and Steiner Sts). 863.2276 ♿

## 50 THEP-PHANOM

★★$ This intimate, attractively decorated restaurant serves a great combination of bright tastes and striking textures. Particularly good is the *tom kha ghi* (chicken soup with coconut milk and ginger). Other entrées include *kiew warm ghi* (green curry chicken) and *sam kasatr* (a fiery pork curry). Every dish is a wonderful bargain. ♦ Thai ♦ Daily dinner. 400 Waller St (at Fillmore St). 431.2526 ♿

## 51 GERMANIA STREET HOUSES

**Donald MacDonald** built these two minuscule dwellings in 1984. Each occupies a 20-by-20-foot footprint and proves that it is possible to build affordable housing in San Francisco. They have basic detailing and an almost cartoonlike form. ♦ At Steiner St

## 52 ZAZIE

★★$$ This tiny French bistro makes up for its size with impressive food. At breakfast, the Belgian waffles with caramelized pecans and the omelette specials win raves; lunch selections include a large variety of sandwiches. The dinner menu offers such hearty dishes as a bone-warming daube (a marinated beef stew), free-range chicken with garlic and herbs, and trout prepared a different way each day.
♦ French ♦ M-Sa breakfast, lunch, and dinner; Su breakfast and lunch. 941 Cole St (between Parnassus Ave and Carl St). 564.5332 ♿

## 53 ASHBURY MARKET

One of the best neighborhood markets in the city, this charming place offers a bounty of fruits and vegetables; fresh flowers; over two-dozen kinds of olive oil, hazelnut oil, and truffle oil; a wide selection of teas; dozens of mustards; and breads. The wine department has the best in French, Italian, and California labels, and the deli offers housemade scones, salads, and smoked trout. ♦ Daily. 205 Frederick St (at Ashbury St). 566.3134 ♿

## 54 SPRECKELS MANSION

Not to be confused with the other, grander **Spreckels Mansion** on Washington Street, this elegant edifice was built in 1887 and is situated on a hill next to **Buena Vista Park.** Formerly a bed-and-breakfast (Ambrose Bierce and Jack London were celebrated guests), it has been converted into a private residence. ♦ 737 Buena Vista Ave W (between Frederick St and Central Ave)

## 55 BUENA VISTA PARK

The park affords a wonderful view of the Coast Range Mountains as far as Mount Tamalpais to the north, Mount Hamilton to the south, and Mount Diablo to the east. Avoid this park after dark, however, as it can be a dangerous spot. ♦ Haight St (between Buena Vista Ave E and Buena Vista Ave W)

## 56 PARK HILL CONDOMINIUMS

Architects **Kaplan/McLaughlin/Diaz** converted the **St. Joseph's Hospital** building into residences in 1986. The former chapel is now a recreation center and the whole scheme has been repainted in warm, pastel shades.
♦ 355 Buena Vista Ave E (off Duboce Ave)

---

Restaurants/Clubs: Red | Hotels: Purple | Shops: Orange | Outdoors/Parks: Green | Sights/Culture: Blue

# THE MISSION/POTRERO HILL

**E**arly in the 1800s, the sunny, fog-free valley that is part of today's Mission District became a rural locale for San Francisco's resort activities. When a private franchise was granted permission to construct a 40-foot-wide planked toll road from present-day **Third Street** to **16th Street**, gambling houses, saloons, dance halls, pleasure parks, and racetracks sprang up among the farmhouses and country homes to take advantage of the increased traffic. Over the next 30 years, the number of people here grew from 23,000 to 36,000, and except for the adobe **Mission Dolores,** founded in 1776, not a trace of the area's previous Spanish influence remained. Instead, colorful Victorian row houses were built everywhere. Yankees, Germans, and Scandinavians moved in, and after the 1906 earthquake and fire ravaged the North Beach and South of Market areas, the homeless Italians and Irish followed. It was then that the residents began cultivating a kind of Spanish revival. Palm trees were planted along **Dolores Street,** turning it into a handsome boulevard; the mission's stucco was repaired; a pseudo-Spanish church was built alongside it; and red-tiled roofs appeared on buildings. Latinos began to pour into the area, and today the Hispanic population continues to expand, and restaurants and markets catering to their tastes thrive here.

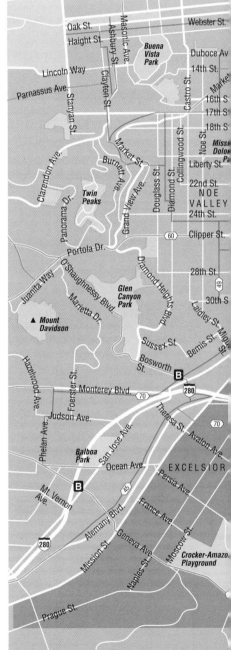

You'll find heavy traffic, palms, and a few parks in this area. (There are more children concentrated in this part of the city than anywhere else, so some streets serve as playgrounds.) Residential hotels are refuges for the impoverished elderly, and the district is a haven for followers of alternative lifestyles—**Valencia Street** caters to the new dot.com professionals. Many art groups have also made their homes in the area. There are many clubs in the district; most open in early afternoon and the beat goes on until 2AM. Blended into the Latino neighborhood are Filipinos, Samoans, Southeast Asians, most of the city's Native Americans, and remnants of the earlier Irish community.

The Spanish dubbed the land stretching south from the Mission *Potrero Nuevo* (new grazing ground). When industry expanded here from the Mission, marshlands were bridged to provide additional access and a five-mile streetcar line was added, making this area the city's first suburb. Today Potrero Hill is a community of small and colorful houses, with a few contemporary apartments basking in the sun while the rest of the city shivers—a place where some of the cottages have *banyas* (Russian steambaths) in the backyard. This is not tourist country. Instead of chic boutiques, you'll see utilitarian shops. At the foot of the hill are early-19th-century warehouses, including **Showplace Square,** which houses one of the largest wholesale furnishing centers in the West. The

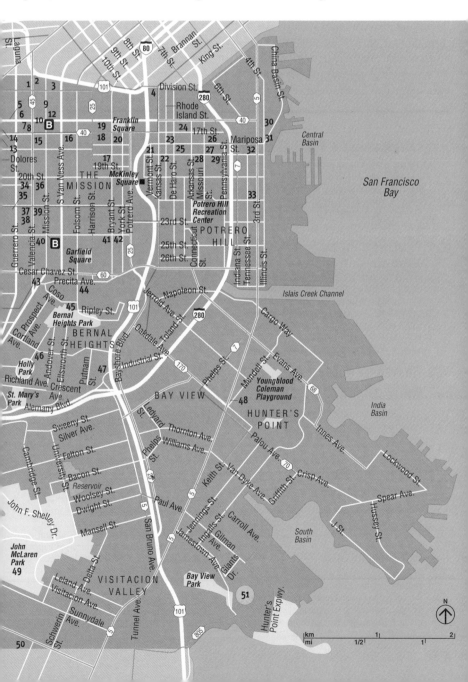

neighborhood remains working-class and heterogeneous, although there are signs of growing gentrification. The agreeable climate and sweeping views have attracted artists and professionals whose lifestyles range from bohemian to deluxe. The thriving community gardens adjoining **McKinley Square,** where neighbors work side by side, are proof of Potrero Hill's ability to assimilate many different ethnic groups.

The less congested **Outer Mission** is dotted with single-family homes. The land here was originally part of a Spanish land grant. In the Excelsior District, many of the original farmhouses rub shoulders with 1930s-style homes. **Bay View/Hunter's Point,** to the east of **Highway 101,** represents the largest concentration of African-Americans in the city, although in recent years lower housing prices have attracted Latino and Pacific Rim families as well. Hunter's Point is the most unsafe district in San Francisco—crime is rampant here, so if it's an area you want to survey, be very cautious. This district grew up around shabbily and hastily constructed temporary housing after World War II, when the largest shipyard on the West Coast stood at the water's edge. And nearby is **3Com Park** (formerly **Candlestick Park Stadium**) home to the **San Francisco 49ers.**

## 1 LEVI STRAUSS & CO.

The world's oldest blue-jeans manufacturing plant was built after the earthquake of 1906. The company conducts group tours of the plant by appointment. ♦ 250 Valencia St (at Clinton Park, between 14th St and Duboce Ave). 565.9160 ♿

## 1 PAULINE'S PIZZA

★★$$ Gourmet pizza is served in a variety of eclectic, eccentric expressions, from pesto pizza to a little number covered with chèvre. There's no atmosphere to speak of—just great pizza few Italians would recognize as their native food. Takeout is available. ♦ Pizza ♦ Tu-Sa dinner. 260 Valencia St (between 14th St and Duboce Ave). 552.2050 ♿

## 2 BUTTERFLY MISSION JAZZ

This club/restaurant features live jazz nightly in a 3,500-square-foot converted warehouse with a stage, full bar and Japanese koi pond. Pacific Rim cuisine by Erik Hopfinger. ♦ California/Asian ♦ 1710 Mission St (at Duboce St). 864-5575 ♿

## 3 SAN FRANCISCO HERB COMPANY

Spice up your life; buy herbs by the pound, wholesale. ♦ M-Sa. 250 14th St (between S Van Ness Ave and Mission St) 861.7174

## 4 SHOWPLACE SQUARE

In these restores brick warehouses are wholesale furniture and design showrooms, open to the trade. The Design Center consists of two warehouses linked by a modern, glass-faced atrium building used for exhibitions and conferences. A restaurant on the ground floor serves mediocre food in a very chic setting. ♦ M-F. 2 Henry Adams St (at Division St) 864.1500 ♿

## 5 16TH STREET

From Dolores Street east toward Mission Street and beyond, this thoroughfare is a microcosm of the Mission District's diverse flavors, including some Asian restaurants, Hispanic influences, and offbeat bookstores, cafes, and clubs. ♦ Between Folsom and Dolores Sts

## 5 BODY MANIPULATIONS

At this place (possibly the weirdest entrepreneurial effort in San Francisco), customers who like a primitive look may be pierced anywhere they want to be (yes, anywhere), ears being the tamest option. Scarring and branding are also offered for those who want to take bodily embellishments to their skin-deep limits, although you need to make an appointment for this service and are requested to bring your own design or at least have an idea of what you want. There's a tattoo studio upstairs, and the owners say that a professional medical consultant advises them. ♦ Daily. 3234 16th St (between Guerrero and Dolores Sts). 621.0408 ♿

## 6 ADOBE BOOKSTORE

You'll find used books, with an emphasis on antiquarian titles and first editions, at this shop. Poetry readings, mostly by local artists, are held frequently. ♦ M-Th, Su; F-Sa until 11PM. 3166 16th St (between Valencia and Guerrero Sts). 864.3936 ♿

## 7 TI COUZ

★★$ The focus in this cozy Breton creperie is the counter, where cooks make crepes with dozens of fillings: Savory choices include sausage, mushroom, and ratatouille, while sweet options might be apples, chocolate, or caramel. Sparkling hard cider, the traditional accompaniment to crepes, is served. ♦ French ♦ Daily lunch and dinner. 3108 16th St (at Valencia St). 252.7373 &

## 7 ALBION

There's live music—could be blues, acoustic rock, or whatever the person who's grabbed an open mike is offering—at this gaudy but intriguing bar. A young and artsy crowd, who scrutinize the rotating displays of art and wait their turn at the pool table, fills the place nightly. ♦ Daily to 2AM. 3139 16th St (at Albion St, between Valencia and Guerrero Sts). 552.8558 &

## 7 THE ROXIE

This vintage movie house (with seating for about 280) specializing in classic and esoteric movies is film-buff heaven. ♦ 3117 16th St (between Valencia and Guerrero Sts). 863.1087 &

## 8 BOMBAY BAZAAR

Just about every spice you could possibly need to flavor an Indian dish is sold here, in addition to dried peas, beans, ice cream, Indian groceries and videos. ♦ Tu-Su. 548 Valencia St (between 17th and 16th Sts). 621.1717 &

## 9 MISSION STREET

This is the Mission District's great commercial artery, with the heaviest concentration of activity that's of interest to strollers stretching from approximately 15th to Army Streets. The street buzzes with entrepreneurial energy, and the small businesses supply the neighborhood with produce (much of it geared toward Hispanic recipes). There are clothing shops for budget-minded buyers; furniture stores with some of the most garish, overwrought designs imaginable; small restaurants reflecting the area's diverse Hispanic populations. ♦ Between 15th and Army Sts

## 10 ESTA NOCHE

At San Francisco's first Latin drag-queen bar, some think the "ladies" are better looking than those who perform at the famous North Beach drag clubs. There's disco dancing to a salsa beat in the evenings. ♦ Cover. Daily. 3079 16th St (at Mission St). 861.5757 &

## 10 TAQUERÍA LA CUMBRE

★$ In its heyday, 20 years ago, this was the best *taquería* in town. But over the years, it grew into a large chain, and the style and food have become more impersonal. But there are still some good items on the menu: The *carne asada* (marinated beef) is a winner.

Made-to-order burritos weigh in at well over a pound each; the ones made with tongue or pork stomach have legions of fans. ♦ Mexican ♦ Daily lunch and dinner. No credit cards accepted. 515 Valencia St (at 16th St). 863.8205 &

## 11 MISSION DOLORES PARK

This green oasis on the fringes of the Mission District is where tennis players, dog walkers, and sun worshipers gather for neighborhood recreation. As with most big city parks this one is best enjoyed during daytime hours. ♦ Bounded by Dolores and Church Sts, and 20th and 18th Sts

## 12 THEATRE RHINOCEROS

Gay and lesbian issues are explored in the offbeat productions staged at this 112-seat theater. ♦ 2926 16th St (between S Van Ness Ave and Mission St). 861.5079

## 13 STAR WASH

One of the most glamorous laundromats in town, this clean and friendly spot shows video movie classics to relieve the washday blues. ♦ Daily. 392 Dolores St (at 17th St). 431.2443 &

## 14 MISSION DOLORES

Spanish settlers led by Captain José Moraga founded San Francisco's first mission in 1776, on the site of an Indian village, just five days before the signing of the Declaration of Independence. Formally called the **Mission San Francisco de Assisi,** this is the sixth of the 21 missions built by Franciscans along El Camino Real, the Spanish road linking the missions from Mexico to Sonoma, California. Though the mission was dedicated to St. Francis de Assisi, it became better known by its current name after a nearby lagoon called Lake of Our Lady of Sorrows (*dolores* is Spanish for "sorrow"). The city's oldest building, its structure has withstood four major earthquakes and is the only one of the original missions that has not been rebuilt. Its four-foot-thick adobe walls have survived the years without serious decay or extensive restoration. **Mission Dolores Basílica,** the larger church next door, was rebuilt in 1918 and was declared a basilica in 1952 by Pope Pius XII. In addition to several historical figures, more than 5,000 native Costanoan Indians are buried in the cemetery garden (most died from diseases transmitted by white settlers). ♦ Daily. Dolores St (at 16th St). 621.8203 &

## 15 ELBO ROOM

This is the Mission District's version of upper Market Street's popular **Cafe Du Nord,** filled

---

**Restaurants/Clubs: Red | Hotels: Purple | Shops: Orange | Outdoors/Parks: Green | Sights/Culture: Blue**

with an eclectic, alternative crowd and a suitably cool atmosphere. Wear lots of black or vintage clothing, order an imported beer, and you'll fit right in. ♦ Daily. 647 Valencia St (between 18th and 17th Sts). 552.7788 ♿

## 16 ODT THEATRE

Experimental music, theater, and dance are presented at this 187-seat theater. ♦ Daily. 3153 17th St (at Shotwell St, east of S Van Ness Ave). 863.9834 ♿

## 17 UNIVERSAL CAFE

★★★$$ Small, sunny, smartly designed, and a favorite with locals and serious foodies alike, this cafe is worth a visit just for its pan-seared filet mignon with whipped gorgonzola potatoes. Other specialties might include roast chicken with tomato *coulis* (thick puree) and braised greens, or roast salmon with avocado-leek salad. ♦ American ♦ M breakfast and lunch; Tu-F breakfast, lunch, and dinner; Sa-Su brunch and dinner. 2814 19th St (at Bryant St). 821.4608 ♿

## 18 THEATRE ARTAUD

This popular multidisciplinary theater showcases contemporary work by local, national, and international performers. The 300-seat space was formerly an American Can Company factory. ♦ Call for performance schedule. 450 Florida St (at 17th St). 621.7797 ♿

## 19 BYRON HOYT SHEET MUSIC SERVICE

This shop has the biggest selection of sheet music in the city. ♦ Tu-Sa. 2525 16th St (between Bryant and Harrison Sts). 431.8055 ♿

## 20 POTRERO HILL BREWING COMPANY

★★$$ The shiny steel tanks catch the sunlight in this dependably sunny neighborhood. Head for the outdoor patio for hearty sandwiches, soups, and salads. Good appetizer menu to accompany the handcrafted brew. ♦ American/Brewery ♦ Daily lunch and dinner. 435 Florida St (between 18th and Mariposa Sts) 552.1967 ♿

## 21 VERMONT STREET

The view is nice and the absence of mobs even nicer at southern San Francisco's answer to Lombard Street. ♦ South of 20th St to Mariposa St

## 22 610 RHODE ISLAND STREET

Designed for **Kronos Quartet** members Pat Gleeson and Joan Jeanrenaud, this contemporary home amid rows of traditional 19th-century houses became an object of controversy. Critics maintained that its industrial look was out of context in the neighborhood. The 24-foot-high living space covered in black asphalt shingles is visible to passersby. This private residence was built in 1989 by **Daniel Solomon.** ♦ At 18th St

## 23 BASIC BROWN BEARS

This small stuffed-animal factory has taken Elvis's advice and chosen the teddy bear as its official mascot. Don't miss the free 30-minute tour; at the end of the tour the staff will help you stuff your own teddy bear. Children love it. ♦ Daily. Tours: daily 1PM; also Sa 11AM 444 De Haro St (at Mariposa St). 626.0781 ♿

## 24 GARIBALDI CAFE

★★$$ Those who have an inside track on good places to dine are buzzing about this restaurant. The dining room is a fascinating conglomeration of white-and-gray high-tech furnishings set amid corrugated-metal walls. Lunchtime salads are excellent, and dinner always includes special seafood and pasta entrées. A take-out annex next door serves interesting dishes. ♦ Californian ♦ M-Sa lunch and dinner. Reservations recommended. 1600 17th St (at Wisconsin St). 552.3325 ♿

## 25 ANCHOR BREWING CO.

It's San Francisco's version of a Dickens tale: Fritz Maytag, a young, carefree college student who also happens to be heir to a washing-machine company, stops into his local beer hall, orders his first pint of Anchor Steam, and instantly becomes smitten with the rich amber brew, forgetting all about the family business. Meanwhile, Lawrence Steese is struggling to keep his old Anchor brewery out of bankruptcy and is desperately in need of a deep-pocketed partner. This is where our hero Fritz steps in and saves the day, much to the delight of beer aficionados around the world. For a tour of the delightfully anachronistic brewery and a tasting of what many consider one of the few *real* beers left, make reservations as far in advance as possible (at *least* two weeks in advance, although you might get lucky and fill in a no-show). ♦ Free. Daily. By reservation only. 1705 Mariposa St (at De Haro St). 863.8350 ♿

## 26 THE BOTTOM OF THE HILL

★$ This is the kind of neighborhood bar you always dreamed about: friendly bartenders, good bands playing every night, a well-maintained pool table, cushy bar stools, outdoor seating, a fireplace, good burgers, and a $4, all-you-can-eat barbecue on Sunday from 3:30 to 8PM. ♦ American ♦ M-F until 2AM; Sa 8PM-2AM; Su until 10PM. 1233 17th St (at Missouri St). 626.4455 ♿

## 27 SAN FRANCISCO BAR-B-QUE

★★$ Despite its limited menu and simple presentation, this restaurant always comes through with tasty, honest, addictive Thai-style barbecue dishes at modest prices. The chicken and pork ribs are the most popular, cooked to lean succulence and flavored with a medium-hot sweet-sour Thai sauce. ◆ Thai ◆ Tu-F lunch and dinner; Sa-Su dinner. 1328 18th St (between Pennsylvania and Missouri Sts). 431.8956

## 28 GOAT HILL PIZZA

★★$ The view of downtown is spectacular, and the food homey and filling. Family-style pastas and classic pizza such as pesto with feta and pepperoni are the favorites here. Monday is all-you-can-eat night. ◆ pizza ◆ M-F lunch and dinner; Sa dinner; Su brunch and dinner. 300 Connecticut St (at 18th St). 641.1440 ⑤

## 29 300 PENNSYLVANIA STREET

Situated on top of Potrero Hill, this was one of a series of mansions built as the city grew south of Market Street. A private residence, it was constructed in 1868. ◆ At 18th St

## 30 ESPRIT OUTLET

The popular San Francisco-based manufacturer has a huge clothing outlet here, frequented by the teen set and the young at heart. ◆ Daily. 499 Illinois St (at 16th St). 957.2500 ⑤

## 30 42 DEGREES

★★$$$ The chic decor and live jazz are not the only reasons people flock here. The Mediterranean cuisine caught the eye of *Gourmet* magazine. Try the chicken braised in white wine with mashed potatoes. (42 Degrees is the latitude that runs through the Mediterranean.) ◆ Mediterranean ◆ M-F lunch; We-Sa dinner. 235 16th at Illinois St. 777.5558 ⑤

## 31 THE RAMP

★★$$ Although hidden away in a boatyard, this place's reputation has spread by word of mouth, and an eclectic crowd of suits, gays, and boat workers gathers here for a good time. Hamburgers, salads, daily specials, and creative stews are the culinary attractions. There's also live music in the summer—jazz, salsa, rock—Thursday through Sunday, as well as an outdoor weekend barbecue. ◆ American ◆ Daily dinner; M-F lunch. 855 China Basin St (at the end of Mariposa St). 621.2378 ⑤

## 32 MOSHI MOSHI

★★$ Tucked into a wasteland of warehouses, this place serves good Japanese food at prices that are more than fair. The decor is simple—almost spare—with bleached-wood tables and chairs and pale-green walls. The menu offers all the classic favorites: chicken and steak teriyaki (served quite rare, as it should be), shrimp tempura and yakitori, as well as excellent sushi. The quality and value are hard to beat. ◆ Japanese ◆ Daily dinner; M-F lunch. Reservations required for six or more. 2092 Third St (at 18th St). 861.8285

## 33 MASSIMO CAFE

★★★$ This small lunch spot is a well-guarded San Francisco secret. Try some pasta with fresh crabmeat in a brandy-cream sauce or veal-stuffed tortellini in marinara sauce. The menu features daily specials and interesting cold plates, but Massimo himself will probably tell you what to order—even if you don't ask. Takeout and catering are available. ◆ Italian ◆ Tu-F lunch. 1099 Tennessee St (at 22nd St). 550.6670 ⑤

## 34 LIBERTY STREET

The blocks from Castro to Valencia Streets contain some of the best Italianate houses in San Francisco, unspoiled since the last century. **No. 159,** built in 1878, is where Susan B. Anthony—whose dollar coin we now seem to have forgotten—used to visit her fellow suffragists. **No. 109** was built in 1870. ◆ Between Valencia and Castro Sts

## 35 FLYING SAUCER

★★$$$ This ordinary-looking little storefront restaurant is short on ambience but big on culinary satisfaction. The menu, crafted by chef-owner Albert Trodjman, changes every six weeks and reflects what he calls "world-beat cuisine"—unusual cross-cultural combinations and dramatic presentations such as rack of lamb coated with pecans and served with wild rice and a tart mint-fig compote, or salmon blackened and served with spicy shrimp bread pudding. ◆ Californian/French ◆ Tu-Su dinner. Reservations recommended. 1000 Guerrero St (at 22nd St). 641.9955 ⑤

## 36 LA RONDALLA

★★$$ It's nothing to look at, but this is a hugely popular, extremely lively Mexican restaurant known for mariachi music, good margaritas, and year-round Christmas decor. The menu goes far beyond the usual tacos and enchiladas. You can get interesting grilled-pork creations and Mexican egg dishes for a fine late-night snack. And if you hanker

---

**Restaurants/Clubs: Red | Hotels: Purple | Shops: Orange | Outdoors/Parks: Green | Sights/Culture: Blue**

for goat meat, this place has it. ♦ Mexican ♦ Tu-Su lunch and dinner. 901 Valencia St (at 20th St). 647.7474 ♿

## 37 LUCCA RAVIOLI CO.

Great buys on imported cheeses are reason enough to patronize this deli, but there are also very good ravioli, tortellini, and other noodles, and tasty sauces to go with them. A tempting line of Italian cold cuts and other delicacies is available, too. ♦ M-Sa. 1100 Valencia St (at 22nd St). 647.5581 ♿

## 37 SAIGON SAIGON

★★$ Low prices and high quality make this upscale Vietnamese restaurant a neighborhood favorite. Begin with soft-shell crabs with a spicy dipping sauce, papaya-beef salad with nuances of fresh mint, or a gingery duck salad. Move on to black-peppered catfish or lamb kabobs with peanut sauce. If you insist on dessert, the crème caramel is simple, soothing, and satisfying. ♦ Vietnamese ♦ Daily lunch and dinner. 1132-34 Valencia St (between 23rd and 22nd Sts). 206.9635 ♿

## 38 GOOD VIBRATIONS

You can probably find out everything you've always wanted to know about sex—and then some—at this store. With an emphasis on health, education, quality, and fun, this one-of-a-kind retail and mail-order emporium valiantly tries to take the smut out of sex shops. ♦ Daily. 1210 Valencia St (at 23rd St). 974.8980, mail order 974.8990 ♿

## 39 THE ROOSTER

★★$$ This rustic restaurant, with rough wood floors and chandeliers made of rusted iron and shards of glass, specializes in peasant cooking from southern Europe and Asia. Entrées include such clay-pot dishes as lamb *tajine* (a Moroccan stew with olives and couscous) and beef stew in a red-wine sauce perfumed with orange, as well as paella. Dessert is not a strong point, except for the poached pear. ♦ Mediterranean/Asian ♦ M-F dinner; Sa-Su brunch and dinner. 1101 Valencia St (at 22nd St). 824.1222 ♿

## 40 LA TRAVIATA

★★★$$ You don't expect to find Italian restaurants in the Mission District, particularly one so good that it draws not only customers from neighborhoods across town but world-famous opera stars as well. Pictures of divas and great tenors line the walls, and opera plays constantly. The pastas are marvelous, and the chicken and veal dishes are first-rate. ♦ Italian ♦ Tu-Su dinner. Reservations recommended. 2854 Mission St (between 25th and 24th Sts). 282.0500 ♿

## 41 CHINA BOOKS AND PERIODICALS

This shop specializes in imported and American books on China's history and politics, with some of the works in Chinese and many in English. There is also a selection of Chinese peasant paintings and handicrafts. ♦ M-Sa. 2929 24th St (between Alabama and Florida Sts). 282.2994 ♿

## 41 LA VICTORIA MEXICAN BAKERY AND GROCERY

For more than 30 years, this place has been turning out Mexican specialties, including sugary wedding confections and custardy cones. ♦ Daily. 2937 24th St (at Alabama St). 642.7120

## 41 GALERIA DE LA RAZA/ STUDIO 24

Since its founding in 1970, this nonprofit gallery exhibiting works of Latino artists has gained worldwide renown. The adjoining studio supports the work of the gallery with sales of crafts representing contemporary and traditional arts of Latin American countries. ♦ We-Su. 2857 24th St (at Bryant St). 826.8009 ♿

## 42 ROOSEVELT TAMALE PARLOR

★★$ This place built its reputation around its crowd-pleasing tamales, which have drawn customers since 1922. Other traditional Mexican dishes are offered as well. Customers are an enthusiastic mix of gringos from north-of-Market neighborhoods and locals who share a common interest in a good, cheap feed. ♦ Mexican ♦ Tu-Su lunch and dinner. 2817 24th St (between York and Bryant Sts). 550.9213 ♿

## 42 ST. FRANCIS CANDY STORE

★★$ Not much has changed in this soda fountain since it opened its doors in 1918. It sells homemade ice cream and peanut brittle and has cases filled with candies that will take you back to your childhood. More substantial fare includes grilled cheese sandwiches and a daily blue-plate special. ♦ American ♦ Daily lunch and dinner. No credit cards accepted. 2801 24th St (at Bryant St). 826.4200 ♿

## 43 EL RÍO

Dance to the beat of Latin, Cuban, and Brazilian salsa and African world music. There are live shows on Thursday, Saturday, and Sunday. A wonderful courtyard awaits out back. ♦ Cover. Th, Sa-Su. 3158A Mission St (at Army St). 282.3325 ♿

## 44 MISSION DISTRICT MURALS

Painted by Mexican-American artists and other residents, these murals are a colorful example of community spirit. The artists have brightened and humanized their urban environment with vivid wall paintings dispersed throughout the neighborhood between Mission and York Streets and 14th and Army Streets, adorning banks, restaurants, schools, housing projects, and community centers. Some of the murals are inside buildings. Sightseers may take a self-guided walk or a two-hour, eight-block walking tour given by the **Precita Eyes Mural Arts Center** every Saturday at 1:30PM. Group tours can be arranged at other times with advance notice. Forty murals are covered on the tour. Maps are available from the center, in addition to a checklist of all Mission District murals. ◆ Nominal fee; discount for seniors, students, and children. Arts Center: 348 Precita Ave (at Folsom St). 285.2287

## 45 170-80 MANCHESTER STREET

Built on the slopes of Bernal Heights in 1986 by **William Stout,** these modern, stucco-clad houses capture the spirit of the white architecture of the modern movement. They are private residences. ◆ At Bernal Heights Park (south end of Folsom St)

## 46 THE LIBERTY CAFE

★★$$ The menu of this charming cafe features only four appetizers and four main courses, but each is perfectly prepared. The Caesar salad is excellent; the chicken potpie has a burnished puff-pastry crust and a lightly thickened filling of roasted pearl onions, carrots, and big chunks of potatoes and chicken; the trout is coated in cornmeal, pan-seared, and served with lemony spinach and sautéed baby artichokes; and the banana cream pie is rich and creamy. ◆ American ◆ Tu-F lunch and dinner; Sa brunch and dinner; Su brunch. 410 Cortland Ave (at Bennington St). 695.8777 &

## 47 FARMERS' MARKET

Saturday is the big shopping day at this open-air market where California farmers sell their seasonal produce at prices lower than those in most supermarkets. ◆ Sa-Su. 100 Alemany Blvd (between Crescent and Putnam Sts). 647.9423

## 48 THE BAYVIEW OPERA HOUSE

The city's oldest theater opened its doors in 1888. Seating 300, it has been renovated and provides the community with a variety of plays, dance concerts, and musical theater. ◆ Call for information on shows. 4705 Third St (at Oakdale Ave). 824.0386 &

## 49 JOHN MCLAREN PARK

The city's second-largest park was named for the man who created its biggest one, **Golden Gate Park.** Several residential districts make use of the rugged, wooded tract: Bayshore, Portola Valley, Bay View, and the Outer Mission. The steep slopes offer good views of Visitacion Valley and the San Bruno Mountains. ◆ Bounded by Moscow and Delta Sts, and Felton St and Geneva Ave

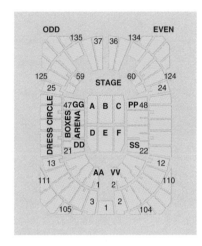

## 50 COW PALACE

Everything from livestock shows to the Beatles has been booked here (see the floor plan above). With a seating capacity of 10,300 to 14,300, it offers an ever-changing series of events. ◆ Geneva Ave (at Santos St), Daly City. 469.6000 &

## 51 3COM PARK

The former **Candlestick Park Stadium** is home to the **San Francisco 49ers** with seating for up to 60,000 people. Built in 1960 by **John S. Bolles and Associates,** it is situated on a rocky promontory overlooking the bay, the site suffers from exposure to bitter cold winds and occasional flooding, and is widely regarded as one of the most uncomfortable places in which to watch—or play—a game. It was the first major league baseball stadium to be constructed entirely of reinforced concrete, and there is movable seating for the switch between baseball and football. In 1995, in the ultimate commercialization, the park sold its name (for a sizable fee) to the technology company 3COM, although most fans have refused to adopt the new name. ◆ Take Candlestick Park Exit off Hwy 101 S, to Giants Dr at Gilman Ave. 49ers tickets 468.2249 &

---

Restaurants/Clubs: Red | Hotels: Purple | Shops: Orange | Outdoors/Parks: Green | Sights/Culture: Blue

# NOE VALLEY/CASTRO/ UPPER MARKET

The Noe and Eureka Valleys snuggle below the protective eastern slopes of Twin Peaks and share much of the same history, climate, and architecture. Both also underwent dramatic population shifts in the 1970s, as escalating real-estate prices in fashionable, white-collar neighborhoods north of Market Street drove hordes of young professionals to the more affordable southern reaches of San Francisco. For many, it was their first trip across the main Market Street artery that had for years bisected sociologically distinct

parts of the city. Both valleys are quaint neighborhoods of Victorian storefronts and homes, and were originally called Horners' Addition after Mormon Gold Rush pioneers Robert and John Horner, who made their fortune selling food to gold diggers. (A street named Horner was renamed **23rd Street** in 1861.)

Noe Valley, separated from Eureka Valley by the ridge of **22nd Street,** was historically part of the 4,000-plus-acre land grant given to the last Mexican mayor of San Francisco, José de Jesus Noe, by California governor Pio Pico in the 1840s. Noe's ranch house was one of the first buildings in the district and stood at the corner of 22nd and **Eureka Streets.** The area was once filled with blue-collar German and Irish families. Later, a sprinkling of gay residents moved in and the neighborhood gained a somewhat bohemian outlook. More recently, Noe Valley has been called San Francisco's Greenwich Village, although continued gentrification suggests movement in a more conservative direction. It still includes an eclectic mix of families and bohemians who moved from other parts of the city. While it's technically part of the greater Mission District, residents, who consider themselves a breed apart, have always insisted they live in Noe Valley. In this relaxed urban village, residents frequently spot raccoons in their backyards, gather for an annual picnic and a local history day at the library, and spend the weekends fixing up their old houses. Between **Dolores** and **Diamond Streets, 24th Street** is a lively shopping area dispensing the stuff of everyday life, with supermarkets, coffeehouses, and ethnic delis where you can buy a burrito, a knish, and a quiche, all within a two-block range. **Church Street,** named for the many houses of worship that once stood there, is fast developing as another commercial thoroughfare, with most of the shops concentrated between 24th and **30th Streets.** To preserve the small-town atmosphere, with people shopping and chatting together, one residential group has promoted a hard stance against establishments selling liquor. In **Upper Noe Valley,** steep streets and hills create truly spectacular housing sites.

At the same time that double-income heterosexual couples were flocking to Noe Valley, Eureka Valley was becoming a magnet for gays from everywhere in the country. **Castro Street** is the main thoroughfare, and so strong is its impact that the area is commonly known as the Castro District rather than Eureka Valley. This center of San Francisco's gay social life is a crowded collection of unique shops, bars that stay open until 2AM, and restaurants, mostly concentrated on Castro between Market and **20th Streets.** The gay influence extends to the Upper Market area, which was also part of Noe's land grant in the early 1800s. San Francisco's gay and lesbian population is well organized, and it has been said that no politician can win an election in the city without gay support. Legislation is always being put forth to test the limits and tolerance of the nongay community, making San Francisco a bellwether of social change. Although the scourge of AIDS has caused more than 18,000 deaths here, it also has united the gay community, focusing its political spokespeople on finding government funding for research, and banding it together in efforts to offer solace and assistance to the afflicted.

### 1 THE WILLOWS INN

$ Popular with the gay and lesbian community, this quiet, 12-room bed-and-breakfast inn in a 1904 Edwardian is central to the Castro, the Mission, and downtown and near easy connections to **BART** and **MUNI.** The graceful California Gypsy Willow furniture was designed specifically for each room, and the place has a restful, European-country look.

Restaurants/Clubs: Red | Hotels: Purple | Shops: Orange | Outdoors/Parks: Green | Sights/Culture: Blue

There is a telephone, washbasin (guests share the bathrooms), and kimono in each room, and a continental breakfast is served with a morning paper. Complimentary sherry and truffles are left in each room in the evening. ♦ 710 14th St (at Church St). 431.4770

## 2 MECCA

★★★$$$ Start off a meal here with chef Lynn Sheehan's herbed flatbread that's served with different toppings—the hummus and pickled spring onions variety is a particular favorite. Other wonderful appetizers include goat cheese wrapped in grape leaves with beets, and Caesar salad. Mediterranean flavors come through on grilled tuna accompanied by a ragout of artichokes and sun-dried tomatoes. Gourmet pizzas are a hit, topped with housemade venison sausage and goat cheese, or wild mushrooms and roquefort. The circular zinc bar is the restaurant's action hub, while velvet drapes lend a sensual style to the dining room. ♦ American/Mediterranean ♦ Daily dinner. Reservations required. 2029 Market St (between Dolores and 14th Sts) 621.7000

## 3 CAFE DU NORD

★★$$ For those in the know, this basement-level, windowless club/cafe is the place to see and be seen. Moody lighting, a gilt-edged ceiling, dark wood paneling, musty oil paintings, and a stylish crowd combine to give this place the decadent air of a speakeasy. Jazz is the main theme for entertainment here and it varies from night to night; straight jazz, bebop, acid jazz, big band, vintage blues, and salsa are all featured. The small American-style dinner menu with a Mediterranean twist offers soup and pasta of the day; arugula salad; filet mignon; and garlic roasted chicken breast four nights a week. ♦ Californian/Mediterranean ♦ Cover. W-Sa dinner; music nightly. Reservations recommended. 2170 Market St (at Sanchez St). Cafe 861.5016, entertainment information 979.6545

## 4 THE RANDALL MUSEUM

The emphasis at this nature and history museum is on participation, with live animals and a petting corral, a ceramics room, a woodworking shop, a seismograph, and biology classes. An environmental learning garden is currently under construction. Many special workshops and events are offered, especially during the summer. ♦ Free. Tu-Sa. 199 Museum Way (at Roosevelt Way between 14th and 17th Sts). 554.9600 ♿

## 5 LA MÉDITERRANÉE

★★★$ This Middle Eastern-inspired restaurant offers good food in intimate surroundings at excellent prices. The lemony hummus with fresh herbs is a good starter. Among the popular main courses are the "Levant" sandwiches, pinwheels of cream cheese and other ingredients, which change daily; ground lamb kabob served with rice; and chicken drumsticks marinated in pomegranate sauce and baked. Main courses come with salad or a cup of soup. They provide sidewalk tables for smoking patrons. ♦ Middle Eastern ♦ Tu-F lunch and dinner; Sa-Su brunch and dinner. 288 Noe St (at Market St). 431.7210. Also at: 2210 Fillmore St (between Sacramento and Clay Sts). 921.2956; 2936 College Ave (between Ashby Ave and Russell St), Berkeley. 510/540.7773 ♿

## 6 JOSEPH SCHMIDT CONFECTIONS

This small shop is where chocoholics go to worship. Joseph Schmidt, who has mastered chocolate sculpture, creates bowls, flowers, sports equipment, animals, bottles, and automobiles in his edible medium. He also makes the best chocolate truffles in town—

# PLUM PATHS FOR PEDAL PUSHERS IN THE CITY BY THE BAY

There's no better way to get a feel for San Francisco than to ride through it on a bicycle. Don't be put off by the city's famous hills—just rent a bike with many gears, and follow the numbered bicycle-route signs erected by the Department of Parking and Traffic. These placards help cyclists find the most direct and least hilly routes to a variety of places. They also have the advantage of letting drivers know that they are sharing the road with two-wheelers. Not all the routes are on city streets; some veer off on to bike paths and lanes, as in **Golden Gate Park.** Sunday morning is a good time to hit the road—car traffic is minimal and the bike paths have fewer cyclists. Be sure to carry a map of the routes within the city as well as those in the park, water, and extra clothing. The weather can change dramatically: foggy and cold one minute on the **Golden Gate Bridge,** blistering hot the next in **Sausalito.** Whatever your destination, you're sure to have a fun time seeing the sights of San Francisco by bike. For information on rentals, see "Bicycles" in the Orientation chapter.

maybe anywhere. ♦ M-Sa. 3489 16th St (between Church and Sanchez Sts). 861.8682 ⟨

## 7 INN ON CASTRO

$$ One of the smaller guest houses in the city (eight rooms, each with private bath), this inn's intimate surroundings make it truly a home away from home. Although located in an Edwardian town house, its interiors are contemporary: white walls, track lighting, classic Modern furniture, brilliant flowers, and the original art of one of the owners. Upstairs, breakfast is served every morning on an extensive and ever-changing collection of imported china and stoneware dishes. ♦ 321 Castro St (at Market St). 861.0321 ⟨

## 8 IXIA

When daisies just won't do, this unusual florist specializes in exotic, esoteric plants and flowers. ♦ M-Sa. 2331 Market St (between Noe and Castro Sts). 431.3134

## 9 THE NAMES PROJECT

This is the visitor's center for those who create the panels of remembrance that form the AIDS quilt. The quilt has been exhibited around the world to commemorate those who have died of AIDS and to draw attention to the toll the epidemic has taken. ♦ Daily. 2362A Market St (between Noe and Castro Sts). 863.1966. ⟨

## 10 TWIN PEAKS

Always lively, always friendly, this was the first gay drinking establishment in San Francisco to come out of the closet by having large picture windows where clients could see and be seen. ♦ Daily. 401 Castro St (off Market St). 864.9470 ⟨

## 10 THE BEAD STORE

All kinds of nifty beads and unique pieces of jewelry are displayed for those who want to do things themselves, or have their adornment done by someone else with lots of talent. ♦ Daily. 417 Castro St (off Market St). 861.7332 ⟨

## 11 MARCELLO'S PIZZA

★★$ In San Francisco, this is as close as you're likely to come to a New York-style pizza. There's a smattering of small, crowded tables, but most customers grab a slice to go. It's one of the few places nearby where you can find sustenance late at night. ♦ Pizza/Takeout ♦ Daily lunch and dinner; M-Th, Su until 1AM, F-Sa until 2AM. 420 Castro St (off Market St). 863.3900 ⟨

## 12 CASTRO THEATRE

San Francisco officialdom dubbed this structure the finest example of a 1930s movie palace in the city. Designed by **Timothy Pflueger** in 1922, the 1,600-seat theater has earned its reputation because of its remarkable Spanish colonial architecture. The auditorium ceiling is probably the most noteworthy feature, an extraordinary affair cast in plaster to resemble a giant cloth canopy tent, complete with swags, ropes, and tassels. And in what better setting could you enjoy an ever-changing series of movies from Hollywood's heyday? Anybody who swoons over *Camille* or drools over the exquisite timing in *Bringing Up Baby* will want to take in a flick at this classic theater. ♦ 429 Castro St (off Market St). 621.6120 ⟨

Once a year a fire hydrant at 20th and Church Streets is painted gold. It's believed to be the only hydrant in the city that continued to function during the 1906 earthquake and fire, and is credited with saving the area. A memorial plaque in the sidewalk next to the hydrant reads: "Though the water mains were broken and dry on April 18, 1906, yet from this Greenberg hydrant on the following night there came a stream of water allowing the firemen to save the Mission District."

---

Restaurants/Clubs: Red | Hotels: Purple | Shops: Orange | Outdoors/Parks: Green | Sights/Culture: Blue

**17th STREET**

| | CASTRO STREET | |
|---|---|---|
| | Bank of America | Twin Peaks *bar* |
| | | Hot Cookie |
| | | Castro Smoke House *cigarettes/magazines* |
| | | Faerie Queen Chocolates |
| | Noah's Bagels | The Bead Store |
| | Marcello's Pizza | The Castro Cheesery *cheese/coffee/chocolate* |
| | Louie's Barber Shop | Castro Theatre |
| | Rossi's Deli | Travel Trends *travel agency* |
| | *casualwear* In-Jean-Ious | Bayview Bank |
| | Cove Cafe | Take One Video |
| | Thailand Restaurant | Sliders Diner |
| | *bar* Daddy's | Ben & Jerry's *ice cream* |
| | California Federal Bank | All American Boy *menswear* |
| | *menswear/men's shoes* Rolo | Fuzio *restaurant* |
| | The Bar on Castro | Cliff's Variety *hardware/fabrics* |
| | Osaka Sushi | A Different Light *bookstore* |
| | *American restaurant* Welcome Home | La Salsa *fast food restaurant* |
| | *take-out* A. G. Ferrari Foods | Presto Prints 1-Hour Film Processing |
| | Valley Pride Market | |
| | | |
| | Walgreens | |

**18th STREET**

| | CASTRO STREET | |
|---|---|---|
| | *bar* Harvey's | Bank of America |
| | Tully's Coffee Co. | The Sunglass Hut |
| | *toiletries* The Body Shop | The Sausage Factory *Italian restaurant* |
| | *pizza* Escape from New York | Castro Video |
| | *gifts* Mainline | |
| | *gifts* Planet Weavers | The Patio Café *American restaurant* |
| | *Chinese* Canton Restaurant | |
| | Browser's Nook Antiques | Don't Panic *music/T-shirts* |
| | *menswear* Citizen | Under Cover *undergarments* |
| | *gifts* Home | |
| | *Japanese restaurant* Nirvana | Benefiting the AIDS Community *gifts* |
| | Always Tan and Trim | Herth *real estate* |
| | | |
| | | Headlines *cards/clothing* |
| | Great Earth Vitamins | Notorious for Hair *salon* |
| | *Italian restaurant* Caffè Luna Plena | |
| | *bakery/cafe* Luna Dolce | |
| | *florist/nursery* Hortica | |
| | Brand X Antiques | |
| | *liquor* Friendly Spirits | Skin Zone *skin care/cosmetics* |
| | *menswear* Worn Out West | Anchor Oyster Bar & Seafood Market |
| | *mailbox services* PO Plus | |
| | *optician* Eye Gotcha | |
| | | Clobba *clothing* |
| | Buffalo Whole Food & Grain Company | Bruno Hair Design |
| | *health food* | China Court *restaurant* |

**19th STREET**

| | |
|---|---|
| *menswear* High Gear | |

### 13 ROLO

Definitely not for the introverted, this shop offers fashions for men who like to push the outer limits of style. ♦ Daily. 450 Castro St (between 18th and Market Sts). 626.7171. Also at: 2351 Market St (between Noe and Castro Sts). 431.4545; 1301 Howard St (at Ninth St). 861.1999

### 14 CLIFF'S VARIETY

This Castro Street institution is actually two shops side by side. One carries all manner of fabrics, spangles, and feathers for making costumes or embellishing a smashing drag getup; the other sells straightforward household needs, such as hardware and paint. It's beloved for its folksy merchandising approach and cordial staff. ♦ M-Sa. 471-479 Castro St (between 18th and Market Sts). 431.5365 ♿

### 15 FIREWOOD CAFE

★★$ At peak hours the line extends to the sidewalk but it moves fast. Specialties are the rotisserie chicken, gourmet pizza, and grilled marinated vegetables. Skip dessert. ♦ Cal/Ital

Daily lunch and dinner. 4248 18th St (at Diamond St). 252.0999

### 16 A DIFFERENT LIGHT

The only store in San Francisco devoted to both gay and lesbian literature. ♦ Daily until midnight. 489 Castro St (at 18th St). 431.0891 &

### 17 THE MIDNIGHT SUN

Boy meets boy at this popular gay video bar, sleekly designed with a galvanized-metal exterior. ♦ Daily to 2AM. 4067 18th St (between Noe and Castro Sts). 861.4186 &

### 17 BODY

Rather revealing men's sportswear for the let-it-all-hang-out crowd is in this shop. ♦ Daily. 4071 18th St (between Noe and Castro Sts). 861.6111

### 17 DOES YOUR MOTHER KNOW?

We won't tell her if you shop here for unusual, outrageous, and funny greeting cards. ♦ Daily. 4079 18th St (between Noe and Castro Sts). 864.3160 &

### 17 PATIO CAFE

★$$ Located at the back of a small shopping mall is a brick-walled room that opens onto a charming garden, where patrons usually prefer to dine. It's particularly busy during the day for brunch, when 15 omelettes and a half-dozen kinds of pancakes are featured. There's something for everyone on the laundry-list menu, which leans toward sandwiches, burgers, and such generic American food as meat loaf, spaghetti, grilled chicken, and fried calamari. ♦ American ♦ Daily breakfast, lunch, and dinner. Reservations required for parties of six or more. 531 Castro St (between between 19th and 18th Sts). 621.4640

### 18 HOT 'N' HUNKY

★★$ Yet another chrome-and-tile burger joint, this one capitalizes on the gay clientele in both its name and its interior appointments, such as pictures of Marilyn Monroe. Fans contend that this eatery has the best burger in the city. ♦ American ♦ Daily lunch and dinner. 4039 18th St (between Noe and Castro Sts). 621.6365. Also at: 1946 Market St (at Duboce Ave). 621.3622 &

### 19 ROSIE'S CANTINA

★★$ This pleasant and open corner restaurant features a straightforward menu of Mexican fare. After ordering at the counter, you can sit at one of the few tables or have your food wrapped to go. ♦ Mexican ♦ Daily

lunch and dinner. 4001 18th St (at Noe St). 864.5643

### 20 NOBBY CLARKE'S FOLLY

This attractive, eclectic construction was built in 1892 by Alfred Clarke, who worked as a clerk in the police department. It was alleged to have cost $100,000—a fortune then—and originally included a 17-acre estate. Today it is an apartment house. ♦ 250 Douglass St (at Caselli Ave)

### 21 HORTICA

When your rooms look empty but you don't have the money for furniture, try plants instead. The horticultural accomplishments here are quite artful. ♦ Daily. 566 Castro St (between 19th and 18th Sts). 863.4697 &

### 21 BRAND X ANTIQUES

A lovely selection of antique and estate jewelry and collectibles is on display. It's not cheap, but it's awfully nice. ♦ Tu-Su. 570 Castro St (between 19th and 18th Sts). 626.8908 &

### 22 BUFFALO WHOLE FOODS & GRAIN COMPANY

Smaller than the Nob Hill branch, this health-food store is packed with select organic produce, plentiful breads, packaged convenience foods, and lots of vitamins. ♦ Daily. 598 Castro St (at 19th St). 626.7038 & Also at: 1058 Hyde St (between Pine and California Sts). 474.3053 &

### 23 SKIN ZONE

All kinds of toiletries and soaps are sold here to enhance the body beautiful. ♦ Daily. 575 Castro St (between 19th and 18th Sts). 626.7933 &

### 23 ANCHOR OYSTER BAR & SEAFOOD MARKET

★★$$ When you have a yen for chowder and shellfish, this neat little place, with a counter and a few tables, satisfies it nicely.

---

Restaurants/Clubs: Red | Hotels: Purple | Shops: Orange | Outdoors/Parks: Green | Sights/Culture: Blue

And if you get a hankering for an "oyster shooter" (an oyster in a shot glass with Bloody Mary mix, Worcestershire sauce, a touch of Tabasco, and a squeeze of lemon), you'll find that here too. ♦ Seafood ♦ M-Sa lunch and dinner; Su dinner. 579 Castro St (between 19th and 18th Sts). 431.3990 ₺

## 24 SPIKE'S COFFEES AND TEAS

They carry about 30 varieties of well-displayed coffees here, plus chocolates for those who want to indulge all their minor vices at once. ♦ Daily. 4117 19th St (between Castro and Collingwood Sts). 626.5573

## 24 CASTRO VILLAGE WINE COMPANY

More than 400 California wines are stocked here. The shop offers wine tastings, and shipping is available. ♦ Daily. 4121 19th St (between Castro and Collingwood Sts). 864.4411 ₺

## 25 3733-3777 AND 3817-3871 22ND STREET

The panels framing the plaster floral arrangements and the banded laurel (which looks like the letter X) are trademarks of builder **John Anderson**. These private residences were built in 1905 and 1906. ♦ Between Sanchez and Castro Sts

## 26 3780 23RD STREET

Constructed in 1865, this white Italianate Victorian is believed to be the oldest house in Noe Valley. It's a private residence. ♦ At Church St

## 27 NOE'S NEST

$$ There are six rooms to let at this private residence: a self-contained unit with a kitchenette; a garden room with a private deck and a fireplace; a room with a Jacuzzi; a room with a 1920s brass bed; and a penthouse with a dynamite view and a steam room. Each unit has a TV, a VCR, and a phone. The owner, Sheila Rubinson, offers a buffet breakfast. Her quarters represent excellent value for those who want a homey place away from home. ♦ 3973 23rd St (between Sanchez and Noe Sts). 821.0751

## 28 FIREFLY

★★★$$ You might miss this small place were it not for the bright yellow door and the glowing firefly above the entrance. The ambience here is comfortable and eclectic with mismatched flea market furniture and food that owners Brad Levy and Veva Edelson characterize as home cooking from around the world. That might include appetizers of pot stickers with shrimp and scallops, chopped chicken livers, or potato latkes with apple sauce. Main course choices may be barbecued chicken with mashed potatoes, grilled tuna with buckwheat noodles, or beef brisket. For dessert, try the chocolate chip cake. ♦ Californian. ♦ Daily dinner. 4288 24th St (at Douglass St). 821.7652 ₺

## 29 BACCO RISTORANTE ITALIANO

★★$$ At first glance the menu might seem ordinary, but the preparations are anything but. Try the gnocchi, tender and light, or the simply sauced pastas, cooked exactly as they should be with just a little bite. The main courses are equally outstanding, especially the lamb chops and any veal dish. For dessert the warm chocolate cake, with a slightly runny center, is a real winner. To top it all off, the consummate Italian waiters are efficient yet friendly, with a good sense of humor. ♦ Italian ♦ Daily dinner. Reservations recommended. 737 Diamond St (between 24th and Elizabeth Sts). 282.4969 ₺

## 30 LITTLE ITALY RISTORANTE

★★$$ A bustling, happy place to eat dinner, it looks lately as if some remodeling and general freshening up are in order. The portions are huge, the vegetable platters should be shared, and the garlic is applied with a generous hand. The chicken, steak, and sausage contadino is a wonderful, rustic dish, but you'll reek of garlic for days. Early birds who dine between 5:30PM and 6:30PM get to have a "friend dine free." ♦ Italian ♦ Daily dinner. Reservations recommended for three or more. 4109 24th St (between Castro and Diamond Sts). 821.1515 ₺

## 30 PEEK-A-BOOTIQUE

New and lots of used clothing and toys for infants and children line the shelves of this pleasant shop. ♦ Daily. 1306 Castro St (at 24th St). 641.6192 ₺

## 31 OCEAN FRONT WALKER

Whimsical 100-percent-cotton clothing for adults is this store's specialty. ♦ Daily. 4069 24th St (between Noe and Castro Sts). 550.1980. Also at: 1458 Grant Ave (between Union and Green Sts). 291.9727 ₺

## 32 RAT & RAVEN

This friendly neighborhood bar carries just about every brand of beer imaginable. There's a pool table and a dart board. ♦ Daily. 4054 24th St (between Noe and Castro Sts). 285.0674 ₺

## 33 ELISA'S HEALTH SPA

Here's a legitimate place to get the knots worked out of your body. Massage, an outdoor hot tub, a sauna, and a steam room are offered. Prices are discounted from noon to 4PM. ♦ Daily. 4026-1/2 24th St (between Noe and Castro Sts). 821.6727

# TEA TIME

After exploring this exciting city, what could be more soothing to the spirit than a relaxing afternoon tea? Coffee-crazed San Franciscans can find their favorite brew on nearly every corner, but finding a good cup of tea and a pleasant place at which to enjoy it may prove more of a challenge.

In recent years, afternoon tea has replaced cocktails as a nonalcoholic alternative to Happy Hour with friends or as an informal setting for business meetings. But a bit of linguistic confusion prevails. Perhaps because the experience can be so uplifting, it often is called "high tea." But any English person knows that high tea is a light supper of cold meats, fish, salads, and tea, usually served Sunday night.

Afternoon tea, by contrast, is a snack served late in the day that consists of tea, finger sandwiches, scones, and pastries. The Duchess of Bedford is said to have originated the tradition (partly to show off her beautiful tea services) in 1830. Since dinner was served quite late in those days, she decreed that tea be served at 5PM, and the late-afternoon restorative became all the rage.

Here are some of the many spots in San Francisco where you can indulge in afternoon tea. They afford a pleasant alternative to the city's ubiquitous coffeehouses—even the duchess would approve.

**King George Hotel** (334 Mason St, between O'Farrell and Geary Sts, 781.5050) is steeped in all the charm of a small European hotel. Afternoon tea is served on the mezzanine, along with assorted finger sandwiches, biscuits, and trifle. Tea is served Monday through Saturday from 3 to 6PM.

**Mad Magda's Russian Tea Room and Mystic Cafe** (579 Hayes St, between Octavia and Laguna Sts, 864.7654) offers a wide variety of English and Russian teas with biscuits, blintzes, or borscht, as well as sandwiches and salads. Tea is served in 1940s china pots and flowered cups. In warm weather, sit on the patio with its greenery and flowers. Before leaving, have a psychic reading. Tea is served daily.

**Mark Hopkins Inter-Continental San Francisco** (1 Nob Hill, California and Mason Sts, 392.3434) With its contemporary-looking glass ceiling and airy garden atmosphere, the lobby-level **Nob Hill Terrace** makes a fine setting for afternoon tea, which is served daily from 2:30 to 5:30PM. The tea consists of assorted sandwiches (perhaps Scottish smoked salmon, or a combination of English cheddar, cucumber, and York ham), scones and fancy pastries, and a choice of darjeeling, Earl Grey, English breakfast, jasmine, or orange pekoe tea.

**Ritz-Carlton San Francisco Lobby Lounge** (600 Stockton St, at Pine St, 296.7465) serves a traditional English tea in formal surroundings—marble, French decor, and towering floral arrangements. Fourteen varieties of tea, plus sandwiches, cookies, scones, and all the trimmings are available. Special events include fashion-show teas, etiquette teas, and even Teddy Bear teas for children at Yuletide. Tea is served daily from 2:30 to 4:30PM.

**Teahouse at the Japanese Tea Garden** (Golden Gate Park, 752.1171) offers a truly unique setting to enjoy Japanese tea and a plate of simple cookies served by a staff wearing traditional costume. A reflective stroll along the manicured paths winding past flowers, shrines, and pools adds to the experience. The teahouse is located next to the **Asian Art Museum** on the northwest side of the **Music Concourse.** Tea is served daily from 10AM to 5:30PM.

**Teaz** (Ghirardelli Square, 900 North Point St, at Larkin St, Plaza level, 346.3488) is modeled after a European tea salon. The 16-seat "tea bar" sells 75 to 100 teas from all over the world. Also offered are such typical accompaniments as cookies, scones, and flavored sugars. The interior is decked out in ivory and gold, and graced by painted Louis XIV-style furniture. Tea-leaf readings are offered several times a week. Tea is served daily, with extended hours in the summer.

**VIVANDE Ristorante** (670 Golden Gate Ave, between Van Ness Ave and Franklin St, 673.9245) A medieval Italian ambience pervades here—despite its anachronous location in a skyscraper. At lunchtime the place is taken over by **City Hall**'s movers and shakers; dinner draws people en route to the **Performing Arts Center.** But between 2:30 and 5PM daily it serves as a delightful refuge, with an afternoon tea that includes a savory and a sweet tray with such tempting treats as chocolate cake with raspberry puree, gelato, and semolina pudding.

**Westin St. Francis Compass Rose** (335 Powell St, between Geary and Post Sts, 397.7000) boasts dramatic lighting, rich Oriental rugs, comfortable wing chairs, soaring wooden columns, and sprays of orchids. The tea service is just as lovely. It includes warm scones, preserves, finger sandwiches, strawberries, and petit fours. Choose from eight varieties of tea. Tea is served daily from 3 to 5PM.

---

Restaurants/Clubs: Red | Hotels: Purple | Shops: Orange | Outdoors/Parks: Green | Sights/Culture: Blue

### 34 1051 NOE STREET

Constructed in 1891, this home is one of the 387 tower houses built in San Francisco. The tower was generally unconstructed within and is there just for show, although it's in dire need of a paint job. This is a private residence. ◆ At Elizabeth St (between 24th and 23rd Sts)

### 35 SPINELLI COFFEE CO.

Serious coffee for caffeine addicts is poured daily. The store does its own roasting too. ◆ Daily. 3966 24th St (between Sanchez and Noe Sts) 550.7416. Also at: 919 Cole St (between Carl St and Parnassus Ave). 753.2287; 2455 Fillmore St (at Jackson St). 929.8808; 504 Castro St (at 18th St). 241.9447; 2255 Polk St (at Green St). 928.7793 ⅃

### 36 STREETLIGHT

One of the largest selections of used CDs in the Bay Area can be found here. The store also carries a wide array of mainstream and unconventional music from classical to Cajun, used videos, and out-of-print and collectible 45s and LPs. The staff is notably helpful. ◆ Daily. 3979 24th St (between Sanchez and Noe Sts). 282.3550 ⅃

### 36 COLORCRANE

A marvelous hand-painted floor depicting a bird's-eye view of downtown is a main attraction at this office- and art-supply shop that also provides photocopying services. ◆ Daily. 3957 24th St (between Sanchez and Noe Sts). 285.1387

### 37 NOE VALLEY TIEN FU

★★$ This Chinese restaurant is particularly noted for its green-onion pancakes, though the vegetable dishes and spicy garlic shrimp are also excellent. ◆ Hunan/Chinese ◆ Daily lunch and dinner. 3945 24th St (between Sanchez and Noe Sts). 282.9502. Also at: 3011 Fillmore St (at Filbert St). 567.0706 ⅃

Stretching 7.29 miles, Mission Street is San Francisco's longest thoroughfare.

### 37 THE REAL FOOD COMPANY

Get real with the groceries and very high-quality organic produce sold here. ◆ Daily. 3939 24th St (between Sanchez and Noe Sts). 282.9500. Also at: 1023 Stanyan St (between Carl St and Parnassus Ave). 564.2800; 2140 Polk St (between Vallejo St and Broadway). 673.7420 ⅃

### 38 PANETTI'S GIFTS

An eclectic, oftentimes amusing selection of gift items and handmade jewelry is for sale here. ◆ Daily. 3927 24th St (between Sanchez and Noe Sts). 648.2414 ⅃

### 39 24TH ST. CHEESE CO.

Three hundred different cheeses are offered along with excellent pâtés, fine wines, and specialty food items. ◆ Daily. 3893 24th St (at Sanchez St). 821.6658

### 39 TUGGEY'S

Noe Valley's beloved hardware store offers personal service to do-it-yourselfers. It's been in the neighborhood since the early 1900s and hasn't changed much since. ◆ Daily. 3885 24th St (between Church and Sanchez Sts). 282.5081 ⅃

### 40 HOLEY BAGEL

Ex-New Yorkers rejoiced when this business opened in San Francisco. Here's the place to find those foods dear to a Jewish-food lover's heart: bagels made daily, smoked fish, pickled tomatoes, and knishes. ◆ Daily breakfast and lunch. 3872 24th St (between Church and Sanchez Sts). 647.3334. Also at: 3218 Fillmore St (between Lombard and Greenwich Sts). 922.1955; 1206 Masonic Ave (at Haight St). 626.9111; 308 Strawberry Village (at Redwood Hwy), Mill Valley, Marin County. 381.2600 ⅃

### 40 MATSUYA

★★★$$ San Francisco's first sushi bar, this little hole-in-the-wall establishment has been serving many of the same people for over 30 years. The chef prepares some of his own secret concoctions. Trusting customers simply ask him to do something special and he takes it from there. ◆ Japanese ◆ M-Sa dinner. 3856 24th St (between Church and Sanchez Sts). 282.7989

### 41 COVER TO COVER BOOKSELLERS

This neighborhood bookstore is known for its excellent children's section and knowledgeable staff. Your kids will love it. ◆ Daily. 3812 24th St (at Church St). 282.8080 ⅃

### 42 NOE'S

A neighborhood tavern with a vaguely publike appearance, this place specializes in Irish coffee. It opens pretty early for those who hanker for a drink along with their sunshine. ♦ Daily at 7AM. 1199 Church St (at 24th St). 282.4007 ⟁

### 43 HOMES OF CHARM

Reasonably priced Victorian furniture, lighting, hardware, and bric-a-brac are carried in this shop, which has been around since 1964. It also stocks a variety of items for creating a country kitchen. ♦ Wed-Su. 1544 Church St (at Duncan St). 285.8297 ⟁

### 44 SPECKMANN'S

★$$ This out-of-the-way *bierstube* (pub) which serves up traditional, though unremark-able German fare. The sauerbraten is more sweet than sour, and so is the cabbage, but the crunchy potato pancakes are a welcome accompaniment. Wiener schnitzel, another specialty, is served with roasted potatoes and peas and carrots. Wash it down with an excel-lent German beer. The deli in the front of the restaurant is the place to buy sausages, cold cuts, cheeses, and specialty items. ♦ German ♦ Daily lunch and dinner. 1550 Church St (at Duncan St). 282.6850 ⟁

### 45 LEHR'S GERMAN SPECIALTIES

German imports of all kinds, including cosmetics, magazines, records, gourmet foods, and beer steins, make it fun to browse here. ♦ Daily. 1581 Church St (at 28th St). 282.6803 ⟁

### 46 ONE STOP PARTY SHOP

Stock up on cards, glitter, gift bags, banners, balloons, and all the other stuff that makes a party fun. It's the only store of its kind in Noe Valley. ♦ Tu-Su. 1600 Church St (at 28th St). 824.0414 ⟁

### 47 DREWES MEATS

This friendly meat-and-fish market was estab-lished as the **Fairmount Market** in 1888 by German immigrant Frederick Drewes and his partner, Otto Dierks. It has had only two names and three owners since it opened. ♦ Daily. 1706 Church St (at 29th St). 821.0515 ⟁

### 48 CAFE J

★★$$ Chef Eliscio Soto has created a Latin, Basque and French dinner menu that Noe Valley residents are raving about. His signature dish is *pariatta*, an Argentinean seafood mixture over risotto. The garden at Cafe J blooms year-round and the brick patio is the best in the valley for alfresco dining. ♦ Latin/Mediterranean ♦ Daily break-fast, lunch, and Tu-Sa dinner. 1708 Church St (between Day and Church Sts), 970.2208.

**T**he heart of San Francisco's fog belt encompasses a large expanse lined with row after row of single-family, pastel-colored, look-alike houses, and is thought by some to be the best place in the city to raise children.

During the 1920s and 1930s, the Sunset emerged as a residential neighborhood, with most of the houses financed by the Federal Housing Administration (FHA). Developer Henry Doelger paved over the sand dunes and built two houses a day throughout the Depression, selling them for $5,000 each. Many of the San Franciscans who first settled

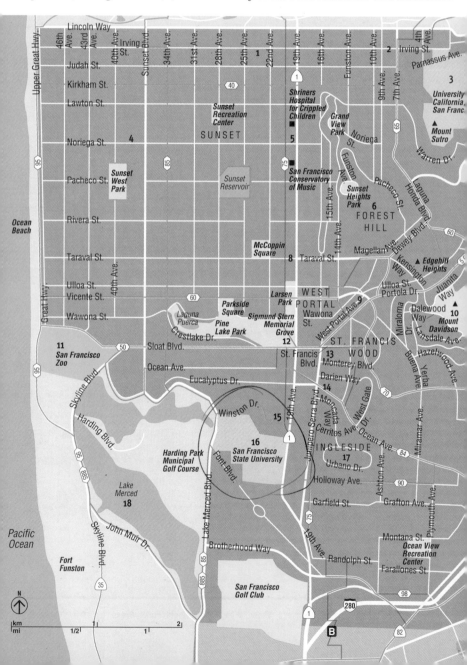

here are now retired. The general image of the district is of conservative, white, middle-class families, although international stirrings are gradually being felt with the advent of a number of Asians around Noriega Street and a young Irish colony. The **Ingleside** area, the site of one of San Francisco's early racetracks, is predominantly African-American and Latino. And on **Irving Street** in the so-called **Inner Sunset,** cafes and clubs offer different kinds of ethnic dancing and entertainment, as well as restaurants and shops with an international flavor. This area is home to the **San Francisco Conservatory of Music, Stonestown Galleria** and <u>**San Francisco State University.**</u> Also here is **Lake Merced,** originally named **Lake of Our Lady of Mercy** and part of a surrounding ranchero granted by José Castro to José Antonio Galino in 1835. Today it is a standby reservoir for the city, as well as its "backyard fishin' hole."

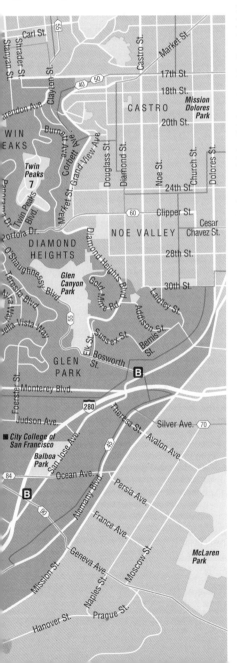

**Stern Grove** comes alive on Sunday during the summer, when thousands settle in for picnics and free jazz and classical-music concerts. Beautiful **St. Francis Wood** is an expensive development of large homes with gates and fountains designed by Beaux Arts architect **John Galen Howard.** Nearby is sedate, middle-class **West Portal,** whose diagonal and curving streets make it look somewhat like a Swiss village. It lies at the foot of three hills: **Mount Davidson, Forest Hill,** and **Edgehill Heights.** Land here was originally part of a Spanish land grant.

Twin Peaks, an area containing the second- and third-highest hills in the city, offers wonderful 360° panoramas of the Bay Area. Even view-crazy San Franciscans left the area alone until World War II, but today it is a very popular neighborhood, with spectacular houses the size of great villas and many apartment complexes. On the south side, single-family homes face the **San Bruno Mountains** and the ocean. The upscale neighborhood known as **Forest Hill,** which was planned in 1913 and had racially restrictive covenants until the 1950s, remains a generally conservative and stable family bastion, full of handsome houses and lush landscaping. Tucked away in **Glen Park,** a neighborhood with the feeling of a small village, lies **Glen Canyon,** where, according to old-timers, Russian smugglers once hid their contraband.

## 1 MARNEE THAI

★★$ Although it's one of the most popular in the city, the food has lost a bit of its edge recently. The signature dish is a fresh, thin corn-and-ginger cake that is deep-fried to a honey brown. Other top choices are raw spinach leaves filled with dried shrimp and ginger, and spicy green papaya salad with wedges of tomatoes and whole green beans. ♦ Thai ♦ M, W-Su lunch and dinner. Reservations recommended. 2225 Irving St (at 23rd Ave). 665.9500 &

## 2 IRVING STREET

This is a main shopping thoroughfare for residents of the Sunset District. Stores, cafes, and small restaurants (with a heavy emphasis on Asian cuisines) are concentrated between 5th and 26th Avenues. The area is not chic, but serves the day-to-day needs of the locals.

## 3 UNIVERSITY OF CALIFORNIA, SAN FRANCISCO

Adolph Sutro contributed the land that became the 107-acre **Parnassus Campus** of one of the world's great centers for biomedical research. Professional schools of medicine, pharmacy, nursing, and dentistry, as well as a separate graduate studies division, are here. The campus also includes the **Langley Porter Psychiatric Institute and Hospital,** which was the city's first psychiatric hospital and training center, and the **Medical Center,** composed of **Moffitt/Long Hospitals** and the **Ambulatory**

**Care Center.** In addition, the campus contains two of the country's major social- and public-policy institutes, and at least 600 community outreach programs, some of which operate on a statewide level. The medical center pioneered the study and treatment of infant respiratory distress syndrome. On campus, the **Cole Hall Cinema** presents weekly movies and stages lectures and entertainment for the general public (call 476.2542 for details). ♦ Entrance at 513 Parnassus Ave (bounded by Parnassus Ave, Fourth Ave, Crestmont Dr, Clarendon Ave, and Stanyan St). Weekly campus tours 476.4394 &

Within the Parnassus Campus:

## SUTRO TV TOWER

In 1968 this tower was built on top of Mount Sutro; it supports TV antennae for several of San Francisco's stations. Once a controversial design because of its tripod form and size, it is now an accepted part of the landscape. ♦ Off Warren Dr

## 4 POLLY ANN ICE CREAM

This parlor dishes up 400 flavors (50 on any given day), including passion fruit, litchi, guava, jackfruit, and taro. For less exotic tastes, owner Charles Wu offers Bumpy Road (his answer to Rocky Road) and coffee rum fudge. If it's too hard to decide what to order, spin the flavor wheel and hope you like what it lands on. Oh, and bring your pooch—they'll give the lucky pup a free Doggie Cone. ♦ Daily. No credit cards accepted. 3142 Noriega St (between 38th and 39th Aves). 664.2472 &

# THE YEAST ALSO RISES

San Franciscans lay such possessive claim to sourdough bread that many visitors assume it originated here. But the truth is the ancient Egyptians actually whipped up the first batch of sourdough more than 4,000 years ago. Columbus supposedly carried a sour starter on his voyage to America, and the Pilgrims routinely used sour starters in bread making.

When commercially available yeasts and baking powders began to be produced in the 19th century, sour starter fell out of favor. (The starter, a combination of fermented flour, water, and sugar that makes the dough rise, had to be sustained from batch to batch, with the baker replenishing the ingredients weekly.) Once cooks could readily purchase yeast and baking powder, the use of sour starters was largely limited to folks who lived far from settlements. During the Alaskan Gold Rush in the 1890s, for instance, prospectors used sour starters so extensively they earned the nickname "sourdoughs." And since many set sail for the Yukon goldfields from San Francisco, the bread became inexorably linked with the city.

Although it is, of course, possible to bake sourdough bread anywhere, San Franciscans maintain that the flavor of their loaves cannot be duplicated. Chef and cookbook author Bernard Clayton, determined to test this chauvinistic assertion, imported samples of San Francisco sourdough starter to his home in Bloomington, Indiana. Each time, however, no matter how carefully he tried to preserve the integrity of the starter, the batch metamorphosed into what he called "Bloomington sourdough bread," which had a distinctly different flavor. "I came to appreciate," he finally lamented, "that to bake San Francisco sourdough bread consistently I would probably have to live there."

Clayton and other aficionados claim that the unique flavor of the local bread can be attributed to the spores, fungi, and bacteria that waft through the San Francisco air. So popular is this theory, in fact, that one of the chefs at a top **Nob Hill** hostelry is rumored to have maintained the same batch of sourdough starter for years in a box on the hotel's roof so it may absorb all those atmospheric San Francisco treats.

## 5 CASA AGUILAR

★★★$$ Considered by many to be the finest Mexican restaurant in the city, this place has won a loyal following with its inventive, well-prepared food, large portions, and festive atmosphere. Giant paper fruits and colorful icons are scattered about the small dining room. The chicken mole and *puerco de Morelos* (pork, salsa, potatoes, tomatoes, onions, and jalapeño peppers) are especially recommended. The no-reservations policy ensures a long wait, but the food really is incredible. ◆ Mexican ◆ Daily breakfast, lunch, and dinner. 1240 Noriega St (at 20th Ave). 661.5593 ♿

## 6 FOREST HILL

This upscale community, planned in 1913 by **Mark Daniels,** who also designed Sea Cliff (a well-to-do neighborhood near The Presidio), follows the contours of a hill and is favored by those who like big homes and don't mind a lot of fog. A triangular piece of manicured lawn and a huge urn, located before Magellan Avenue, suggest a sense of formality for the area. ◆ Main entrance is on Pacheco St (off Dewey Blvd)

Within Forest Hill:

### FOREST HILL ASSOCIATION CLUBHOUSE

Rented out for weddings and other events, this Tudor-inspired building was built, along with the gardens, by neighborhood volunteers in 1919. **Bernard Maybeck** was the architect. ◆ 381 Magellan Ave (at Montalvo Ave). 664.0542 ♿

## 7 TWIN PEAKS

The Costanoan Indians believed that these peaks were created when the Great Spirit separated a quarreling couple with a clap of thunder in order to have peace. Spanish explorers named them "Breasts of the Indian Girl." Then unimaginative Americans changed the name to Twin Peaks. The steep, grassy slopes are a wonderful, if windy, lookout point, providing a 360° view of the entire bay—the best vista in San Francisco. At night, the crest is surrounded by a sea of twinkling lights spreading in every direction. It was from this spot that **Daniel Burnham** conceived his city plan in 1905. Today the view provides cause for reflection on civilization and the effects of "progress"; too often the panorama is marred by smog from polluted air, and you can see how the hills have been carved up and nearly obliterated by stacks of housing developments. Take a sweater; the winds here are chilly even in the summer. ◆ Off Twin Peaks Blvd

## 8 TARAVAL STREET

Another of the Sunset's main shopping streets, this one is less lively than Irving Street. Most of the activity is concentrated between 14th and 23rd Avenues.

## 9 WEST PORTAL AVENUE

In this shopping area that serves neighborhood residents, most of the small businesses are concentrated between Ulloa Street and 15th Avenue.

On West Portal Avenue:

### CAFE FOR ALL SEASONS

★★$$ Donna Katzl's food at this trendy, attractive Forest Hill establishment is tasty and fresh with creative pastas always on the menu. She was included in *Great Women Chefs.* It's worth a visit if you're in the area. ◆ Californian ◆ M-F lunch and dinner; Sa-Su brunch and dinner. 150 West Portal Ave (at 14th Ave). 665.0900 ♿

## 10 MOUNT DAVIDSON

Part of Adolph Sutro's 12,000-acre estate, this is the highest spot in San Francisco, rising 938 feet. A great white concrete-and-steel cross looms 103 feet above the summit. George Davidson, surveyor for the US Coast and Geodetic Survey, originally surveyed the mountain in 1852 and dubbed it Blue Mountain. It was later renamed in his honor. Easter sunrise services have been held at the base of the cross since 1923. ◆ Off Portola Dr

## 11 SAN FRANCISCO ZOO

In recent years, the zoo (see the map on p. 154) has had its share of woes, including the 1989 earthquake, which damaged a few exhibits; scandals regarding some zookeepers' treatment of the elephants; and design flaws in the much-heralded primate center. Still, millions of dollars have been spent on innovative exhibitions, and management is dedicated to transforming this 66-year-old institution into a world-class zoo; it already attracts more than a million visitors annually. Natural habitats are gradually taking the place of cramped, fenced enclosures, with nearly a thousand exotic animals hanging from treetops, roaming through fields, and

---

Restaurants/Clubs: **Red** | Hotels: **Purple** | Shops: **Orange** | Outdoors/Parks: **Green** | Sights/Culture: **Blue**

153

SAN FRANCISCO ZOO

lounging on foggy islands. These settings enable visitors to see the animals behaving more naturally. The **Thelma and Henry Doelger Primate Discovery Center** highlights this philosophy. Here, from multilevel walkways, you can watch many species of monkeys and apes leap from tree to tree. **Gorilla World** is one of the planet's largest naturalistic gorilla exhibits, with two young and five adult gorillas.

This is also one of only a handful of zoos in the country that have koalas. The cuddly, eucalyptus-eating marsupials, native to Brisbane, Australia, live on a grassy knoll in **Koala Crossing.** When the weather is bad, they move to an indoor thicket of eucalyptus boughs. Black tie is always required on **Penguin Island,** where a colony of more than 54 Magellanic penguins with names such as Anne Arctica, Popsicle, and Oreo nestle in specially landscaped burrows. The **Lion House** is home to African lions and Siberian, Sumatran, and Bengal tigers. A crowd always shows up at 2PM (except on Monday) to watch the feeding of the big cats. The **Children's Zoo** features a **Barnyard** where you may pet and feed the assorted menagerie of domestic animals, as well as an **Insect Zoo,** featuring everything from a working beehive to the hissing cockroach. The *Zebra Zephyr Train* takes you on an informa-

tive 20-minute safari tour, daily during the spring, summer, and fall, and on weekends in the winter.

The zoo opened in 1929, and now takes up 65 of its allocated 125 acres of land. New attractions include the **Feline Conservation Center,** where rare and endangered small cats such as snow leopards and pumas are bred and researched, and the **Australian WalkAbout,** featuring wallabies and kangaroos. ♦ Admission. Free the first Wednesday of every month. Daily. Tours weekends. Sloat Blvd (at 45th Ave). 753.7080 &

## 12 Sigmund Stern Memorial Grove

A 63-acre grove of eucalyptus, redwood, and fir trees shelters a sunken natural amphitheater. This is a favorite spot among city dwellers for its free, Sunday-afternoon summer concerts, which showcase a variety of programs from opera to jazz to dance. Reserve a picnic table in advance (call 666.7027 the Monday morning preceding the concert) to make the most of the day. Most of the park's benches are reserved for senior citizens and people with disabilities, on a first-come, first-served basis. The gingerbread **Trocadero Clubhouse** in the grove was once a gambling house and hideout for Abe

## THE BEST

**Barbara Stauffacher Solomon**
Artist/Writer

In San Francisco, the edge of the city is the center of the city. That line—where the land meets the water—is the domain of seagulls, fishermen, and frail strongmen, athletes and aesthetes, dreamers, dolphins, drunks, and me. I was born here.

**The Embarcadero:** Walk the piers stretched straight out onto the bay; scan the streets and skyscrapers shooting straight up **Telegraph Hill.** Parade with the palm trees down San Francisco's new **Embarcadero Promenade.** Delight in pelicans, tugboats, triathletes, and kids flying along the *Ribbon of Light* (urban art-cum-skateboarding "utopia" designed by me, Vito Acconci, and Stanley Saitowitz).

Rueff, a political shyster. It was renovated by **Bernard Maybeck,** who left the two bullet holes in the door as souvenirs of the shootout that led to Rueff's capture, and was spruced up again in the 1980s. ♦ Sloat Blvd (at 19th Ave). ♿

## 13 ST. FRANCIS WOOD

Beautifully landscaped, this development of large, expensive homes has gates and a fountain designed by **John Galen Howard,** noted Beaux Arts architect. It is rich in Spanish Revival structures. Although a well-established, affluent neighborhood, it is bourgeois and located in the less-than-fashionable southern fog belt (the cream of San Francisco's society lives on the north side of the city). The entry gate—marked by gardens and a central fountain—is an impressive site. ♦ Portola Dr (at St. Francis Blvd)

## 14 COMMODORE SLOAT SCHOOL

This renovation of an existing public grammar school, together with a new extension by **Marquis Associates,** has been designed as a series of courtyards. It is faced in stucco and sports a nautical look, with large portholes that have become a feature of the school's design. ♦ Ocean Ave (at Junipero Serra Blvd)

## 15 STONESTOWN GALLERIA

California's first regional shopping center, and the third in the entire US, was built and owned by the Stoneson family in 1951, then sold to a Chicago realty firm in 1990. Shops are located beneath skylit vaulted ceilings in a Neo-Classical setting with bubbling fountains. It was originally conceived as a city-within-the-city, and although much of the merchandising has gone upscale, the original concept still remains. There is a medical building, a supermarket, a movie theater, a drugstore, two main department stores **(Nordstrom** and **Macy's),** and 120 other shops selling everything from specialty foods to music boxes. The free parking gives this mall an edge over downtown stores. ♦ Daily. 19th Ave (at Winston Dr). 564.8848 ♿

## 16 SAN FRANCISCO STATE UNIVERSITY

This 100-acre campus, part of the California state university system, provides undergraduate and graduate programs for approximately 26,000 students. Celebrated graduates have included actor Danny Glover, singer Johnny Mathis, authors Anne Rice and Ernest Gaines, Congressman Ron Dellum, and San Francisco's mayor, Willie Brown. The university's **McKenna Theatre** often has programs that are open to the public including a monthly chamber music series. ♦ 1600 Holloway Ave (at 19th Ave). 338.1111 ♿

## 17 INGLESIDE

One of the city's first racetracks opened here to a crowd of 8,000 people on Thanksgiving Day in 1885. Twenty years later the track was closed, and Ingleside Terrace was built in its place. Development was slow until the Twin Peaks Tunnel was completed in 1917 and large-scale residential construction began. The loop of the racetrack is now Urbano Drive. ♦ Bounded by Junipero Serra Blvd, Holloway Ave, Ashton Ave, Ocean Ave, and Cerritos Ave

## 18 LAKE MERCED

Once part of a ranchero, this large, tree-lined freshwater lake is one of San Francisco's standby reservoirs. It is also a popular trout-fishing hole, with good catches available year-round. Small craft for trips around the lake can be rented at a boathouse run by the **Recreation and Parks Department.** Rowboats, canoes, and paddleboats are available every day (weather permitting). **The Boathouse** bar and restaurant (1 Harding Blvd, off Skyline Blvd., 681.2727) is nearby, and a barbecue area is located across the road from the restaurant. ♦ Boat rentals: daily from an hour before sunrise to an hour after sunset. Off Harding Blvd (adjacent to the zoo). 681.3310

Restaurants/Clubs: Red | Hotels: Purple | Shops: Orange | Outdoors/Parks: Green | Sights/Culture: Blue

# GOLDEN GATE PARK

**B**y the middle of the 1800s, the relatively new city of San Francisco was determined to shape itself along the grandiose lines of the well-established East Coast and European metropolises. Civic pride, fueled by a desire to have a public park comparable to New York City's Central Park, was behind the development of **Golden Gate Park,** a 1,017-acre oasis of greenery, museums, and recreational facilities stretching from the Haight to the Pacific Ocean. The project's beginnings were tempestuous and mired in difficulties. Squatters, who claimed ownership by right of possession, slowed progress for years after the city originally petitioned the board of land commissioners for the property in 1852.

Renowned landscape architect Frederick Law Olmsted, who had designed New York City's Central Park, paid a visit to the proposed park site, laughingly called ``the great sand bank,'' at the invitation of the board of supervisors. He took one look at the seemingly inhospitable tract of land, declared the project impossible, and advised that another location be chosen. But William Hammond Hall took up the gauntlet, and designed a layout for a park that respected the land's natural contours. By 1866 plans were under way to transform the barren, windswept, shifting sand dunes into a verdant oasis that would function as the lungs of the city.

Work began in 1871 with reclamation and development of the **Panhandle,** the block-wide strip of land between **Fell** and **Oak Streets** that leads into the park from **Baker** to **Stanyan Streets.** Public-spirited citizens donated funds for most of the buildings and statues in the park.

A dour and determined young Scot named John McLaren was the gardening wizard whose expertise and vision shaped the park that many naysayers had regarded as a white elephant. When he took on the formidable task in 1890 as superintendent of gardening, his formula was to plant grass to "tack down the sand," and then plant trees. Though many of his initial efforts were buried underneath mounds of sand, his crews persistently coaxed and coddled the struggling plants with manure and humus. Through perseverance that continued for more than half a century, until his death at age 96, McLaren lovingly tended his "white elephant"; trees grew and thrived, and the park evolved into a forest enhanced by lakes and meadows.

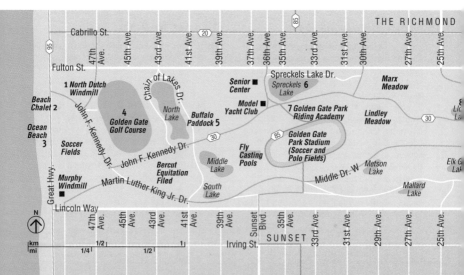

Affectionately known as "Uncle John," McLaren developed a correspondence with horticulturists all over the world that paid off with a rich bounty of plants and trees. He planted about a million trees and introduced 700 new species of trees and shrubs to California in 1931 alone. His germinated seeds grew into gigantic trees up to 80 feet tall.

The feisty Scotsman battled regularly with City Hall to prevent the encroachment of non-park-related enterprises into *his* empire. One time, he thwarted construction of a streetcar line through the park by arguing that some of his precious trees would have to be uprooted to accommodate it. In turn, the engineers explained that they had planned the route through unplanted areas, but McLaren insisted they were wrong. When the supervisors arrived at the site the following morning to mediate the argument, they were greeted by shrubbery, small trees, and rhododendrons, which resulted in their veto of the streetcar proposal. What they didn't know was that 300 of Uncle John's employees had been busy planting all those shrubs only the night before. McLaren continued to shape the park until the end of his life, firmly rooted in his conviction that it was a place to be used and enjoyed, rather than a look-but-don't-touch showplace. He forbade "keep off the grass" signs, and tucked pompous-looking statues into corners where they would soon be hidden by rapidly growing shrubs. After the city's 1906 earthquake and fire McLaren had to rebuild many of the landscaped areas because thousands of displaced residents had set up camp in the park. At age 90, still superintendent of the park, he was asked what he wanted for a birthday gift; his response was "10,000 yards of good manure." When he died, Uncle John took one last ride through his beloved park on 14 January 1943 with 400 grieving gardeners and foremen standing at attention. His statue stands at the entrance of the **Rhododendron Dell.**

In the 1970s it was discovered that much of the park was dying, as trees planted when the park was first born had reached maturity. A reforestation program was instituted, and thousands of new trees were planted.

**Golden Gate Park** today is a countryside of flower beds, meadows, lakes, gardens, waterfalls, rolling hills, and forests. You could spend days in it and be unaware of the surrounding metropolis. The park offers something for everyone: recreational facilities for baseball, soccer, horseshoe pitching, fly casting, golf, horseback riding, tennis, and picnicking. And it has a huge network of walking paths and bicycle tracks, more than

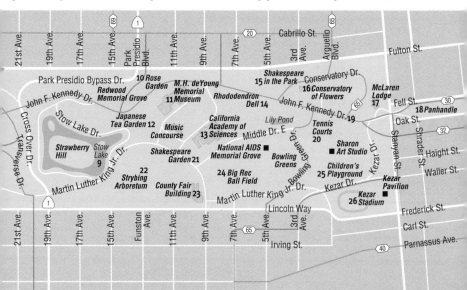

6,000 varieties of flowers, dozens of species of trees, bowling greens, boccie courts, a football field, stables, and checker pavilions.

Over the years, the park has been the site of many special events, including the famous annual Bay to Breakers race, which features more than 100,000 runners, joggers, and walkers (many of them dressed in costumes—or wearing nothing at all) panting their way to the finish line at **Ocean Beach;** the summer *Shakespeare in the Park* festival; the free *Opera in the Park* concert in September; and *Comedy Celebration Day* in July.

Some park structures were damaged in the earthquake that struck on 17 October 1989. Although the bandshell in the **Music Concourse** sustained extensive damage, it has reopened, and is as splendid as ever.

The park is well used by residents and visitors by day (especially on Sunday, when a large section of **JFK Drive,** which traverses the park, is closed), but city-sense is advised: Lone strollers and joggers should stick to populated areas. Neither parking (unless authorized for special events) nor sleeping is permitted in the park after dusk. Rain or shine, several free guided walking tours take place on the weekends from May through October. Lasting an hour and a half to two hours, these tours operate under the auspices of the **Friends of Recreation and Parks.** For information on meeting places and itineraries, call 221.1311. The **Panhandle** and **Golden Gate Park** also have beautiful—albeit unmarked and obscure—bicycle trails, including the seven-and-a-half-mile route from the Panhandle through the park out to **Lake Merced.** To find out more about bike, bus, or special-interest tours, call 263.0991.

## 1 NORTH DUTCH WINDMILL

Built in 1902, this windmill was rededicated in 1981 after its restoration. Surrounding it is the **Queen Wilhelmina Tulip Garden,** a rainbow of color in the spring. ♦ Near 47th Ave and JFK Dr

## 2 BEACH CHALET

Built in 1925, and restored in 1996, this visitor center has exhibits on park history while the surrounding 1930s murals depict scenes of the era. The **Beach Chalet Brewery and Restaurant** upstairs (1000 Great Highway, 386.8439) offers microbrew on tap, good food, and panoramic views of Ocean Beach. ♦ Near John F. Kennedy Dr, off Great Highway.

## 3 OCEAN BEACH

When San Franciscans say "the beach," they are referring to this one, which stretches the length of the Great Highway. The undertow is extremely dangerous, swimming is prohibited, and wading is inadvisable, but it's fun for sunning, strolling, and beach games. ♦ Off the Great Highway

## 4 GOLDEN GATE GOLF COURSE

This nine-hole course is open to the public. ♦ Daily. Off 47th Ave (between JFK Dr and Fulton St). 751.8987

## 5 BUFFALO PADDOCK

Strictly speaking, the shaggy creatures that roam this 35-acre enclosure are American bison. The park is home to 14 of them (1 male and 13 females), many brought here in 1984 to replace descendants of the original herd, which was genetically weakened from years of inbreeding. ♦ West end of JFK Dr (east of Chain of Lakes Dr)

## 6 SPRECKELS LAKE

This small lake is the setting for operating and watching model motorboats and sailboats. It is also a way station for a variety of migratory birds. ♦ 36th Ave (off Fulton St)

## 7 GOLDEN GATE PARK RIDING ACADEMY

A great way to see the park is on one of the guided trail rides offered here. The jaunts last about an hour (they're all walking, no cantering or trotting) and must be scheduled two or three days in advance. Riders must be at least eight years old. ♦ 36th Ave (at JFK Dr). 668.7360

## 8 PORTALS OF THE PAST

These two columns once graced the porch of a Nob Hill home, and were all that remained after the 1906 earthquake. They suffered some damage in the quake of October 1989. ♦ North side of Lloyd Lake (off JFK Dr)

## 9 STOW LAKE

This is the largest lake in the park and the only place to rent bicycles, rowboats, paddle-boats, and motorboats. Bring your own food to picnic by the shore, or pick up something at the small concession stand. ◆ Boathouse and snack bar: Tu-Su. Stow Lake Dr (between Martin Luther King Jr. and JFK Drs). 752.0347

Within Stow Lake:

### STRAWBERRY HILL

Located in the middle of **Stow Lake** is this artificial island, which once stored water for

the park. The cascading **Huntington Falls** add to the picturesque setting. On its shores is the elaborate **Chinese Pavilion,** a gift from the government of Taiwan in 1984 and a popular spot for weddings, relaxation, and reflection. Footbridges connect from the shore, and a winding road leads to the island's 428-foot-high peak, from which there are good views of the city.

## 10 ROSE GARDEN

Fifty-three beds of award-winning roses bloom here in great variety. ◆ South end of Park Presidio Blvd (between JFK Dr and Fulton St)

# CHILD'S PLAY

A trip with your children in tow doesn't usually provide much in the way of rest and relaxation . . . but if you come to San Francisco, your vacation doesn't have to be as comically disastrous as *National Lampoon's Vacation* implies (remember Chevy Chase and his pack on their way to Wally World?). This city bends over backward to please everyone, even the most inquisitive toddlers and easily bored teenagers, so here's a guide to San Francisco's most amusing (and even educational) family-oriented sights, shops, and restaurants.

**1 Alcatraz** Both the ferry ride and the spooky atmosphere at the "Rock" make this excursion a favorite with youngsters. Rent the excellent audio-tour headset on the island; it will help your kids imagine what this former federal prison was like back in the days when Al Capone and the Birdman roamed its halls. The steep walk up to the prison and the somber nature of the tour make this an activity best suited to older children.

**2 Cable Cars** These quaint conveyances never fail to delight the kiddies, especially if you sit in the open-air section of the car on a hilly route. The wait to climb aboard can be long (see the cable-car routes on the inside back cover of this guide), but street performers are usually around to keep children and their parents amused.

**3 California Academy of Sciences** This well-appointed facility in **Golden Gate Park** includes the **Steinhart Aquarium,** the **Morrison Planetarium,** and the **Natural History Museum.**

**4 The Cannery, Ghirardelli Square, and Pier 39** All three of these lively tourist meccas at Fisherman's Wharf are replete with interesting shops, informal restaurants, and free performances by jugglers, mimes, musicians, and dancers. Kids will especially enjoy the **Ghirardelli Chocolate Manufactory;** nobody can resist indulging in a luscious sundae, float, or a steaming cup of chocolate with whipped cream at this ice-cream parlor-cum-chocolate factory.

**5 Exploratorium** Located within the **Palace of Fine Arts,** this dynamic, hands-on science museum will keep school-age kids (and their parents) busy for

hours. The museum store has a great selection of educational and science-related toys and the grounds include a lovely duck pond.

**6 Golden Gate Park** The **Children's Playground,** with its carousel, is great fun for toddlers on up. There are all kinds of boats for rent on **Stow Lake,** and remote-control craft to watch at **Spreckels Lake.** Bicycles, in-line skates, and roller skates are available to rent, too. Other kid-pleasing attractions include the **Buffalo Paddock,** the **Japanese Tea Garden,** and the **Strybing Arboretum.**

**7 National Maritime Museum** Give little landlub-bers a taste of life at sea. This museum employs photographs, memorabilia, and models to evoke the nautical history of the region, while the nearby **Hyde Street Pier** boasts three wonderful old sailing ships open to the public.

**8 The Randall Museum** Young nature fanciers will enjoy the animals at the **Petting Corral,** the gigantic whale skull, and other exhibits at this wildlife and California-history museum.

**9 Restaurants J & J Restaurant** is always crowded with families and carts filled with Chinese appetizers; **Hard Rock Cafe** appeals to all ages who come to enjoy a hamburger and gawk at the rock memorabilia.

**10 San Francisco Zoo** There's a lot more to this zoo than lions and tigers and bears, oh my! Highlights include the **Primate Discovery Center** (with a family of seven gorillas), the **Children's Zoo,** a gorgeous old carousel, **Koala Crossing,** the **Zebra Zephyr Train** tour, an energy-expending playground, and feeding time at the **Lion House.**

Restaurants/Clubs: Red | Hotels: Purple | Shops: Orange | Outdoors/Parks: Green | Sights/Culture: Blue

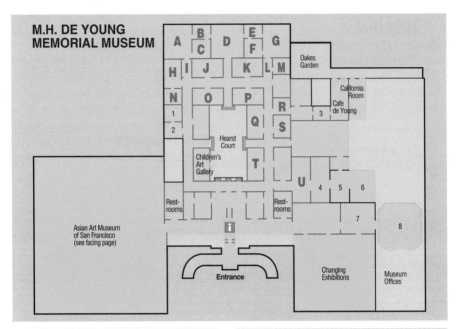

M.H. DE YOUNG MEMORIAL MUSEUM

## AMERICAN ART

A Early 19th Century. Landscapes and portraiture
B 19th Century. Shaker furniture and folk art
C 19th Century. Sculpture
D Mid-19th Century. Paintings; Belter furniture
E 19th Century. Genre paintings
F Late 19th and Early 20th Centuries. Sculpture
G Impressionists and Expatriates. Paintings
H Late 18th and Early 19th Centuries. Paintings; Federal-period furniture
I Dufour wallpaper; Samuel Gragg chairs
J Late 18th and Early 19th Centuries. Decorative arts; paintings
K Mid-19th Century. Paintings
L Late 19th Century. Paintings
M Trompe l'oeil and Still-Life Paintings
N Federal parlor from 1805 Massachusetts house
O 17th and 18th Centuries. Colonial period arts
P Late 19th Century. Paintings
Q Late 19th Century. California paintings; furniture
R 20th-Century Regionalism. Paintings
S Arts and Crafts Movement. Stickley furniture; ceramics; paintings
T Early 20th Century. Paintings
U Contemporary Bay Area. Paintings; sculpture

## BRITISH ART

1 George III dining room in the Adam style
2 Regency Anteroom. Furniture; silver

## GLASS GALLERY

3 Drinking vessels dating from the 16th century

## TEXTILES

4-6 Changing exhibitions

## AFRICAN ART

7 Works from sub-Saharan Africa

## ART OF THE AMERICAS

8 Works from Mesoamerica, Central and South America, and the West Coast of North America

The fortune cookie was invented in San Francisco during the turn of the century by Makoto Hagiwara, chief gardener of the Japanese Tea Garden in Golden Gate Park.

The first buffalo born in San Francisco was delivered in Golden Gate Park on 21 April 1892.

## 11 M.H. DE YOUNG MEMORIAL MUSEUM

The museum evolved from the California Midwinter International Exposition of 1894, held in the park, when civic leader and *San Francisco Chronicle* publisher Michael de Young initiated a building program to establish a permanent museum and expand its size and collections. The museum will be closed for reconstruction and reopen 2005.

## ASIAN ART MUSEUM

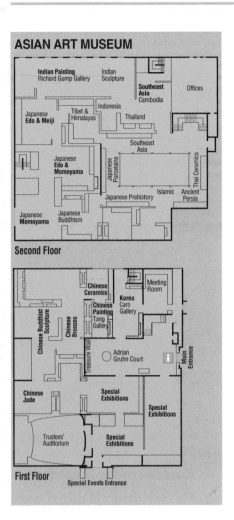

**Second Floor**

Indian Painting
Richard Gump Gallery

Indian Sculpture

Southeast Asia Cambodia

Offices

Japanese Edo & Meiji

Tibet & Himalayas

Indonesia

Thailand

Japanese Edo & Momoyama

Japanese Porcelains

Southeast Asia

Thai Ceramics

Japanese Prehistory

Islamic

Ancient Persia

Japanese Momoyama

Japanese Buddhism

**First Floor**

Chinese Ceramics

Meeting Room

Chinese Painting

Korea Caro Gallery

Chinese Buddhist Sculpture

Chinese Bronzes

Tang Gallery

Treasure Wall

Adrian Gruhn Court

Main Entrance

Chinese Jade

Special Exhibitions

Special Exhibitions

Trustees' Auditorium

Special Exhibitions

Special Events Entrance

## ASIAN ART MUSEUM OF SAN FRANCISCO

This museum opened in 1966 after Avery Brundage donated his world-famous collection of Asian art to San Francisco. It is being relocated to the **Civic Center** in the former main library in October 2001.

## 12 JAPANESE TEA GARDEN

This and the **Music Concourse**—both built for the California Midwinter International Exposition

of 1894—are the only structures gardener McLaren did not have torn down after the fair ended. In 1895 the tea garden became the charge of the Hagiwara family, who tended it with loving devotion. Makoto Hagiwara is credited with inventing the fortune cookie here. Ironically, the cookies have come to be called Chinese fortune cookies and are a favorite item of the tourist trade in Chinatown. The Hagiwara family maintained the garden until World War II, when they, along with 110,000 other Japanese-Americans, were sent to internment camps. This jewel of **Golden Gate Park** is so artfully designed that even the hordes of visitors cannot mar the tranquil experience.

Architecture, landscape, and humans blend subtly and beautifully in a harmonious pattern of bridges, footpaths, pools, flowers, trees, statuary, shrines, and gates. It is especially breathtaking in April when the cherry trees are in bloom. The *Bronze Buddha,* donated by the Gump brothers in 1949, was cast in Japan in 1790. The **Shinto Pagoda** is a five-tiered wooden shrine. The **Moon Bridge,** also called the **Wishing Bridge,** casts its semicircular reflection in the pool below, making a full circle.

The piles of old stones in a clearing behind the tea garden are the disassembled remains of a medieval Cistercian monastery from Spain. In 1932 William Randolph Hearst bought the monastery, had it dismantled and shipped over here, and later donated it to the **M.H. de Young Memorial Museum.** Except for the reconstruction of the chapel portal, which still stands in the **de Young**'s central court, and the unobtrusive incorporation of some of the ruins in retaining walls and rockeries around the park, the majority of the stones have never been reassembled, largely due to lack of funds. There is also a gift shop and a **Tea House,** serving tea, soft drinks, juices, and cookies. ♦ Admission; reduced admission for seniors and children (6-12); free children 5 and under; free daily 9AM-9:30AM Mar-Oct; 8:30AM-9AM, 5PM-6PM (or until sunset) Nov-Feb. Daily. Near the Asian Art Museum (between JFK and Martin Luther King Jr. Drs). 752.4227, gift shop 752.1171

## 13 CALIFORNIA ACADEMY OF SCIENCES

A special favorite of families, this nonprofit scientific institution (see the plan on p. 162) is located on the south side of the Music Concourse, facing the **M.H. de Young Museum.** The academy was founded in 1853 just following the Gold Rush, and is the West's oldest scientific institution. The facility incorporates museums, exhibit halls, a planetarium, and an aquarium. The various exhibition halls are often rented out for elegant private

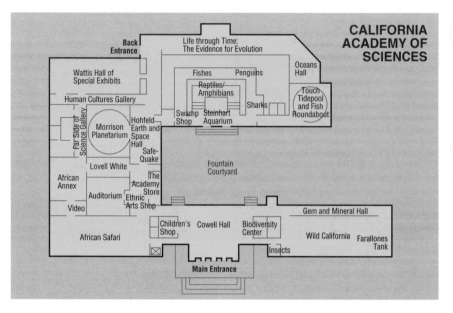

CALIFORNIA ACADEMY OF SCIENCES

functions (guests don't seem to mind being watched by the immobile menagerie as they wine and dine). ♦ Admission includes entry to all attractions; additional fee for Laserium. Free the first Wednesday of every month; reduced admission for seniors and children (6-17); free children 5 and under. Daily. South side of the Music Concourse (between Middle Dr E and JFK Dr). 750.7145

Within the California Academy of Sciences:

## Steinhart Aquarium

This classic European-style aquarium is a must-see—especially for children. It holds the most diverse collection of sea life in the world, with more than 14,000 species of fish, plus an array of reptiles, amphibians, marine mammals, and penguins. When you enter, there's invariably a crowd gathered around the rails overlooking the **Swamp,** a simulated native habitat for alligators, lizards, tortoises, and other reptiles. Check out the bird-eating spider, too. You can watch the beloved seals, dolphins, and penguins being fed. A particular favorite, though it makes some viewers dizzy, is the **Fish Roundabout,** where visitors find themselves surrounded by a doughnut-shaped 100,000-gallon tank in which an assortment of sea life, including sharks and bat rays, glides past. Don't miss the **Touch Tidepool,** where you may pick up and inspect live sea urchins, sea cucumbers, hermit crabs, and sea stars. The aquarium is also home to the largest living tropical-coral-reef exhibit in the US.

## Morrison Planetarium

Entertaining and educational sky shows are presented in northern California's largest indoor universe, beneath a 65-foot-high dome.

Also part of the planetarium is the **Laserium,** where, for an additional charge, viewers may gaze at intricate, multicolored light patterns drawn onto the planetarium dome by a one-watt krypton gas laser as a five-watt argon laser slices the air with searing blue beams. All this is done to the accompaniment of stereo music that holds particular appeal for young rockers—and for older folk, who may find it all very reminiscent of the light shows of the psychedelic 1960s and 1970s. The hour-long light-and-music show is choreographed in advance, but no two performances are exactly alike. Tickets are available in advance through **BASS** outlets or at the academy a half-hour before showtime. ♦ Planetarium 750.7141

## Wild California

Dazzling dioramas display California's grandeur—from a southern desert to wave-hammered islands—in this handsome hall, which allows viewers the thrill of exploration without the perils. One highlight is the exhibition of battling, life-size elephant seals set against a 14,000-gallon aquarium and seabird rookery display.

## Wattis Hall of Special Exhibits

Formerly the site of an anthropological display, this hall now features special exhibits that change about every four months. They range in theme from monarch butterflies to endangered species to the science behind the TV show "Star Trek."

## African Safari

African animals are portrayed in their natural habitat in a series of dioramas. The **African**

**Waterhole** exhibition includes on-location animal recordings and a lighting cycle from dawn to dusk.

## FAR SIDE OF SCIENCE GALLERY

Get a hilarious perspective on science with 159 original *Far Side* cartoons by well-known zany cartoonist Gary Larson.

## HOHFELD EARTH AND SPACE HALL

You'll get all shook up on the popular **Safe-Quake,** which simulates two of San Francisco's famous tremors. Also, under a neon solar system, you may learn about forces that shape the earth and the planets. Another favorite exhibit is the **Foucault Pendulum,** which swings continually as the earth rotates, knocking over a set of pins about every 20 minutes to demonstrate the progress of our revolving planet.

## GEM AND MINERAL HALL

More than 1,000 specimens, from gold to granite, may be found here, including a 1,350-pound quartz crystal from Arkansas. Bauble lovers leave wide-eyed.

## DISCOVERY ROOM FOR CHILDREN

These hands-on nature exhibits are of interest to adults as well as children. They are also ideal for people with disabilities—there is a lot to touch and all exhibits are easy to reach. ♦ Tu-Su

## THE ACADEMY STORE

Located near the entrance hall, this is a fine place to find books, posters, toys, and gifts for naturalists of all ages. ♦ Daily. 750.7330

## THE ACADEMY CAFE

$ On the lower level of **Cowell Hall,** this cafeteria serves family fare—essentially hot dogs, sandwiches, and salads. ♦ American ♦ Daily lunch.

## LIFE THROUGH TIME: THE EVIDENCE FOR EVOLUTION

This permanent exhibition housed in the **Peterson-McBean Hall** journeys through 3.5 billion years of evolution, using living specimens, fossils, and models. The trip begins with early life in the sea, where visitors encounter the radiation of single-celled organisms, and continues on through the millennia, with dinosaur exhibitions and displays chronicling the development of mammals.

## 14 RHODODENDRON DELL

The memorial to John McLaren honors him with his favorite flower. There are more than 3,000 plants and 500 species here. ♦ Between Middle Dr E, JFK Dr, and the California Academy of Sciences

## 15 SHAKESPEARE IN THE PARK

A temporary outdoor theater is erected annually in **Liberty Tree Meadow** for professional performances of the Bard's work. ♦ Free. Sa-Su Labor Day through 30 Sept. Off JFK Dr (west of The Conservatory). 831.5500 &

## 16 THE CONSERVATORY OF FLOWERS

The oldest existing building in the park, **The Conservatory** was modeled after the Palm House at Kew Gardens in London and erected by **Lord and Burnham** in 1878 for eccentric millionaire James Lick. The structure was shipped from Ireland around Cape Horn and survived both the 1906 earthquake and a major fire. The building sustained extensive damage during a wind and rain storm and is closed to the public indefinitely. A campaign is underway to restore the conservatory. ♦ Off JFK Dr. General information 750.5105 &

## 17 MCLAREN LODGE

The home of John McLaren throughout his long term as superintendent of the park now serves as the headquarters of San Francisco's Recreation and Parks Department. Park information and maps are available in this Richardsonian Romanesque pile of sandstone. ♦ M-F. Fell St (at Stanyan St). 831.2700 &

## 18 PANHANDLE

The trees here are the oldest in the park. Beginning with barley, then sand grass, then blue gum and live oak trees, park engineer William Hammond Hall gradually worked up the botanical chain as the hardier plants took root and more diversified shrubs could be planted. ♦ Bounded by Baker and Stanyan Sts, and Oak and Fell Sts

## 19 JFK DRIVE

On Sunday, this street is closed to auto traffic from Kezar to Transverse Drives, and open to roller skaters, in-line skaters, skateboarders, and joggers, many of them locomoting to private rhythms emanating from their headphones. Skate-rental facilities are located nearby on both Fulton and Haight Streets. ♦ Between Kezar and Transverse Drs

Restaurants/Clubs: Red | Hotels: Purple | Shops: Orange | Outdoors/Parks: Green | Sights/Culture: Blue

## 20 TENNIS COURTS

Some 21 courts, just north of the **Children's Playground,** draw players of all levels of expertise. ♦ Nominal fee. Reservations required. Off Bowling Green Dr (at Middle Dr E). Advance reservations 753.7101, same-day reservations 753.7001

## 21 SHAKESPEARE GARDEN

Flowers and plants mentioned in Shakespeare's sonnets and plays are featured in this garden. ♦ Martin Luther King Jr. Dr (at Middle Dr E)

## 22 STRYBING ARBORETUM

This arboretum is a quiet sylvan retreat, with many paths among the 6,000 or so species of trees, plants, and shrubs, both native and exotic. Be sure to visit the **Garden of Fragrance** for visually impaired nature lovers, watched over by a statue of St. Francis of Assisi. Labels are in Braille and plants are selected especially for their taste, touch, and smell. Maps are available at the **Strybing Bookstore** at Ninth Avenue and Lincoln Way, and tours are given daily. ♦ Free. Daily. Ninth Ave (off Lincoln Way). 661.1316

## 23 SAN FRANCISCO COUNTY FAIR BUILDING

Known as the **Hall of Flowers** to locals, this building is used for special events ranging from cat shows to floral exhibitions. ♦ Ninth Ave (off Lincoln Way)

## 24 BASEBALL DIAMONDS

You may play on the two baseball diamonds in the **Big Rec Ball Field** with advance reservations, or, if you prefer softball, there's a first-come, first-served softball diamond near the **Children's Playground.** ♦ Off Martin Luther King Jr. Dr (at Seventh Ave). 753.7024

## 25 CHILDREN'S PLAYGROUND

One of the first public playgrounds to be built in an American park, this includes a gloriously restored carousel housed in a turn-of-the-century Greek temple. The animals and turning platform were made in New York by the Herschell-Spillman Company around 1912, and came to San Francisco sometime after the 1939 World's Fair on Treasure Island. The brilliantly colored menagerie consists of 62 animals, 2 chariots, 1 turning tub, and 1 rocker, all revolving to various show tunes, polkas, and mazurkas coming from the 55-year-old organ. Children under 39 inches ride free if accompanied by a paying adult. ♦ Carousel: nominal fee. Daily June-Sept; Th-Su Oct-May. Off Martin Luther King Jr. Dr (near Kezar Dr)

## 26 KEZAR STADIUM

This 10,000-seat facility is used for community activities, high school sports, soccer, and track. ♦ Kezar Dr (at Martin Luther King Jr. Dr)

## THE BEST

### The late Pat Steger
Beloved Society Editor, *San Francisco Chronicle*

One of the best things about San Francisco is its compactness: It's so easy to get around, on foot or on cable car, and like Paris (a nice place to visit but I certainly wouldn't want to live there) there is a surprise at almost every corner: Maybe it's the view, a cable car rolling by, a beautiful Victorian home, a garden full of blossoming flowers.

The city's main shopping street, **Post,** has gone through a renaissance with all sorts of new boutiques and shops including **Giorgio Armani, Bulgari, Escada,** a remodeled **Cartier, Gump's,** and **Eddie Bauer.** It's very definitely a Madison Avenue-type area, but shop doors aren't locked, and browsers are welcomed.

Walking south from **Union Square** on **Stockton Street,** you will cross **Market,** walk to **Mission** and then turn right and discover a new part of San Francisco: the **Yerba Buena Gardens and Center for the Arts.** A wonderful new park in the heart of what was once no man's land and full of drifters. There are still some street people around—after all, this is San Francisco, and they love it, too.

Just across the street from the gardens is the fantastic **San Francisco Museum of Modern Art,** in a dramatic brick building. Both the center and **SFMoMA** have restaurants and shops, which are well worth shopping.

This is the part of San Francisco that makes walking a pleasure: It's flat, no hills. The very popular **Lulu's** (huge platters of food, meant to be passed around and shared) with its quieter annex, **Lulu Bis.** And a couple blocks more there's the intimate and delicious **Fringale Restaurant** on Fourth Street.

Following Mission Street down to **The Embarcadero** and the bay, there's **Boulevard,** the showplace restaurant owned by chef Nancy Oakes (crab cakes and desserts are fabulous).

# SAN FRANCISCO IN FACT...

To learn more about the history, residents, architecture, and life in general in this popular West Coast city, here are a few pages worth flipping through before you tour the town.

## Fiction

**The San Francisco Comic Strip Book of Big-Ass Mocha** by Don Asmussen, (Russian Hill Press, 1997). In this first compilation of San Francisco Comic Strip by this leading cartoonist, Asmussen shares the zany side of city life. To prepare for your visit, read "A Reader's Guide to Muni," "San Francisco's Coffee Houses," and "Don Johnson & Other Myths."

**Dead Languages** by David Shields (Knopf, 1989). Growing up in the 1960s in San Francisco, a stutterer struggles in a family of articulates. Some of his cures are amusing, some sad. A latter-day **Catcher in the Rye.**

**Dead Man** (Warner Books, 1994) and **Menaced Assassin** (Warner Books, 1993), by Joe Gores. The author was actually a private detective in San Francisco before he became an award-winning screenwriter and author.

**Dreaming** by Herbert Gold (Fine, 1988). Hutch Montberg loves the California lifestyle he has so carefully constructed for himself, but now he's in trouble with the mob. This is the life and death of a salesman, West Coast edition. Gold tunes into the customs, speech, and settings of the hip bourgeoisie of San Francisco.

**Face Value** by Lia Matera (Pocket Star Books, 1995). In this Laura DiPalma mystery, multiple murders and delightfully complex characters help carry a plot that moves from a striptease bar in the city to a guru's mysterious island retreat.

**The Maltese Falcon** by Dashiell Hammett (Knopf, 1930). In this famous detective story, private eye Sam Spade roams the city looking for a bird statue said to be worth a fortune.

**The Mistress and Other Stories** by Gina Berriault (Dutton and Company, 1965). In each of these 15 short stories, an intellectual San Francisco man or woman experiences a moment of truth during the course of mundane home or social activity.

**Second Chances** by Alice Adams (Knopf, 1979). A group of long-term friends suddenly, with amazement, see themselves growing old, and look back to try to understand their pasts. The story is set primarily in sharply recalled San Francisco and North Carolina scenes.

**Strangers at the Gate** by Leonard Gross (Random House, 1995). The sights and sounds of San Francisco pervade this tale of a murder investigation involving tens of thousands of illegal immigrants fleeing Hong Kong in anticipation of Communist China's takeover in 1997.

**Tales of the City/Further Tales of the City/More Tales of the City** by Armisted Maupin (HarperCollins Publishers, 1994/1989/1989). The Oscar Wilde inscription in **Tales of the City** says it all: "It's an odd thing, but anyone who disappears is said to be seen in San Francisco."

## Nonfiction

**The Best of Herb Caen: 1960-1975** (Chronicle Books, 1991) and **Herb Caen's San Franicsco: 1976-1991** (1992, Chronicle Books) by Herb Caen. From the time he began writing for the San Francisco Chronicle more than 50 years ago, Caen has been the undisputed voice of the city and one of the country's best-known columnists. His best and most enduring columns are collected in this book.

**Captain Richardson** by Robert Ryal Miller (LaLoma Press, 1995). This biography of William A. Richardson, an English maritime officer who "jumped ship" in San Francisco Bay in 1822 to begin a new life in California, illuminates much of the history of California during the Mexican and Gold Rush eras.

**Hometown San Francisco** by Jerry Flamm (Scottwell Associates, 1994). History, biography reminiscence, and anecdote are woven together to form a tapestry of San Francisco from 1906 to the mid-century when it was a wide-open town.

**Internet San Francisco** (Hayden Books, 1994). This slim volume provides addresses, descriptions, and reviews of San Francisco's best Internet sites as well as information about on-line communicating.

**San Francisco Almanac** by Gladys Hansen (Chronicle Books, 1995). Name your subject—movies, sports, maritime history, Victorian houses—and you're sure to find it in this gold mine of information.

**San Francisco, the City's Sights and Secrets** by Leah Garchik (Chronicle Books, 1995). Garchik provides a philosophic tour of both the well-known and little-known delights of "everybody's favorite city." More than 150 glorious photographs of the city as it is today are included, as well as historical black-and-white photos and lively text.

**San Francisco, the Painted City** by Harry L. Jones (Gibbs-Smith, 1992). This book contains a collection of unique views of such famous sites as **Colt Tower** and **Telegraph Hill**, the **Golden Gate Bridge, Chinatown, Fisherman's Wharf, Golden Gate Park,** the **Financial District,** and the **Transamerica Pyramid.** One hundred and fifty years of history are seen through artists' eyes.

**This is San Francisco** by Robert O'Brien (Chronicle Books, 1994). Here is an affectionate, lively, carefully researched chronicle of the city from its inception to the end of World War II; an unabashedly romantic portrait of San Francisco's streets, neighborhoods, and people in the "present day" 1940s.

---

Restaurants/Clubs: Red | Hotels: Purple | Shops: Orange | Outdoors/Parks: Green | Sights/Culture: Blue

Endless rows of stucco dwellings line the avenues of the staunchly middle-class and family-oriented Richmond District. The area contains more residential land than any other in San Francisco, and that's how the residents want it to stay. In fact, political donnybrooks have been aimed at developers who wanted to knock down single-family homes and replace them with multiple units.

In another era the Richmond was known as "the dunes," and it took all day to reach **Seal Rocks** by railroad and horse-drawn carriage from downtown. Before 1900 most of the San Franciscans in the windy, foggy Richmond were the deceased inhabitants of the **Municipal Cemetery** or the **Chinese Cemetery**. After a street was cut through the area in 1863, however, a few roadhouses opened, and the first of what would turn into a series of **Cliff Houses** was built by Sam Brannan, though it soon burned to the ground.

Then along came Adolph Sutro, an engineer who made his fortune in the Comstock Lode. As mayor of the city, he set about to open the Richmond for development and created a Victorian fantasy castle on the bluff to replace the **Cliff House** that had been destroyed. Then he erected a fabulous group of glass-enclosed, oceanside swimming pools called the **Sutro Baths**; planted **Sutro Forest**; and built his own house and elaborate gardens, which he opened to the public. After providing such incentive for people to visit the area, the "Father of the Richmond" built a steam railroad on **California Street** to ease their way. Now only ruins mark the place where the once spectacular baths were situated, and a few marble statues are all that remain of the mansion. But Sutro's project served its purpose—to attract potential residents to the district. Thousands of houses were built here between 1910 and 1930. While many are bland stucco homes of no distinction, one neighborhood offers exceptions: **Sea Cliff.** This long-established enclave of the well-to-do, tucked between **Lincoln Park** and the **Presidio**, contains many grand mansions, a number of them built on sheer rock cliffs overlooking the **Pacific Ocean.**

After World War I, hundreds of Russians and East European Jews moved into the Richmond District. Their religious centers

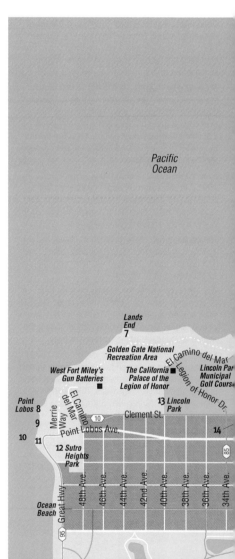

still form the major landmarks: **Temple Emanu-El,** on **Arguello Avenue** at **Lake Street,** and the gold-domed **Cathedral of the Holy Virgin,** on **Geary Boulevard** at **26th Avenue.** Russian restaurants and Jewish businesses continue to thrive alongside the enterprises of the Japanese who moved in after World War II. More Japanese live here than in any other neighborhood. And so many Chinese have bought houses along **Clement Street** that the stretch between **First** and **11th Avenues** is called "New Chinatown."

Clement Street mingles the traditions of Asia and Europe in a profusion of Chinese restaurants, Italian pizzerias, Irish bars and bookstores, Russian bakeries, Asian markets, and Middle Eastern and German delis. Austrians, Armenians, Hungarians, Ukrainians, Czechs, and Caucasian refugees from Shanghai and Singapore are all united into Clement's warmhearted community. The concentration of inexpensive restaurants is staggering, and given the keen competition, there's a lot of turnover.

**The Presidio,** on the other hand, is a district apart. This former military outpost is more than 200 years old and encompasses 68 square miles of land and water. A large portion of the area became part of the **Golden Gate National Recreation Area (GGNRA).**

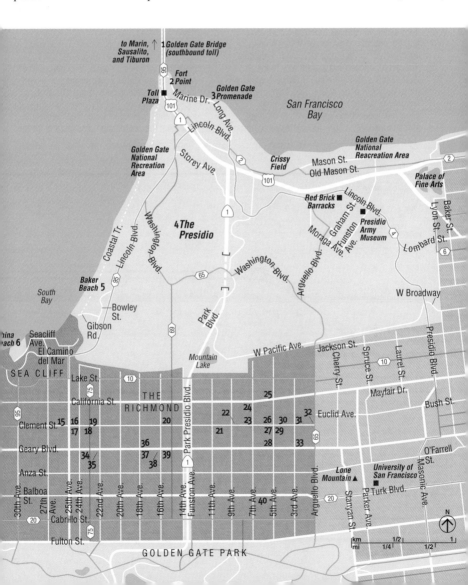

In addition to verdant scenery and a variety of views, it has two great beaches (**Ocean Beach** and **Baker Beach),** old-time fortifications, a golf course, a lake, and picnic sites everywhere. The promenade at **Crissy Field** passes the restored tidal marsh, recently reclaimed from an asphalt-covered industrial area.

## 1 GOLDEN GATE BRIDGE

San Francisco's pride and joy (see plan p. 167) is undoubtedly one of the most beautiful bridges in the world, on account of its spectacular location, graceful lines, Moderne detailing, and emblematic color. The clear span of more than 4,200 feet was the longest in the world until 1959, when New York City's Verrazano-Narrows Bridge was built. Although there is some controversy about who actually designed the bridge—some scholars say an engineer named Charles Ellis should get the credit—Joseph Strauss was chief engineer of the project, which took four and a half years and $35 million to complete. It was finally inaugurated on 28 May 1937, when President Roosevelt punched a telegraph key in the White House, giving the cue 3,000 miles away for a clamor of bells, sirens, and foghorns, squadrons of Navy planes, and the most enormous peacetime concentration of naval strength ever. Over 200,000 pedestrians had swarmed across the structure the day before, and an endless parade of politicos' vehicles traversed the bridge the day after its opening.

At mid-span, the roadway is 260 feet above the water, a height requested by the Navy to allow its battleships to pass beneath. One of the piers is located in the water and the other is on the Marin shore. The main cables are 36.5 inches in diameter. The bridge was designed to withstand winds of more than 100 miles per hour and to be able to swing at mid-span as much as 27 feet. The best views are from Vista Point on the Marin side and from **Fort Point** below on the San Francisco side.

On 24 May 1987, more than 200,000 pedestrians took over again to celebrate the bridge's 50th anniversary. Winners in a hard-fought battle with local bureaucracies, they took advantage of the closure of the bridge for a few hours and walked across, their weight flattening the center span, causing the bridge

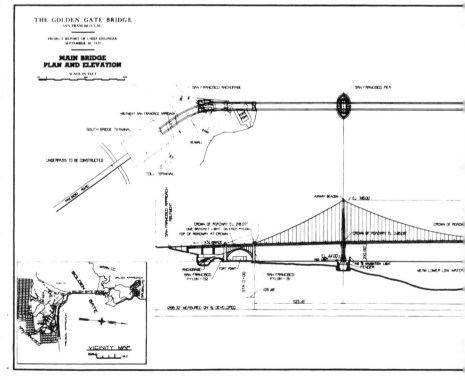

to drop 10 feet. The celebration included marching bands, poster contests, steelworkers from where the bridge steel was made, fireworks displays, more politicos, and the lighting of the 746-foot-tall towers.

Although the bridge was built for the automobile age, its designers wisely included sidewalks, recognizing the fact that it must be crossed on foot to be properly appreciated. The bridge is 1.2 miles across, and the walk, round-trip, takes about an hour. Pedestrians use the walk on the east side daily from 5AM to 9PM. Bicyclists share the path Monday through Friday, but must use the west side on the weekend. Don't forget to take a sweater—it's awfully windy up there. There's a convenient parking area east of the **Toll Plaza,** and nearby, a glass roundhouse containing a **Visitor's Center.** One of the two surrounding gardens is a memorial to the bridge workers; the other is a friendship garden that pays tribute to Pacific Rim nations.

Since its opening, the bridge has become as symbolic of San Francisco as the Eiffel Tower is of Paris. On the darker side, both structures have an unenviable record for suicides.

But the bridge itself is in good health and has aged well. With the additional girders installed in 1987 and new suspender ropes, it is stronger than ever and just as beautiful—the most photographed man-made structure built in the world. ♦ Hwy 101

## 2 FORT POINT

The fort lies under the southern end of the Golden Gate Bridge and was built between 1853 and 1861 to guard San Francisco from sea attack. It houses a museum filled with old swords, guns, cannons, uniforms, and historic photographs of earlier days. There are guided tours (advance reservations required); Civil War cannon-loading and -firing demonstrations are held at noon when the museum is open. ♦ Free. W-Su. Off Lincoln Blvd (at Long Ave; take Long Ave to Marine Dr). 556.0505 ♿

At Fort Point:

## COASTAL TRAIL

 On a sunny day, this trail, stretching from the Golden Gate Bridge to the **Cliff House,** is a must for bikers, joggers, and heavy-duty walkers. It's not the easiest trail to follow, with several splits, dead ends, and a detour through actor/comedian Robin Williams's neighborhood in the China Beach area, but the tranquillity and the spectacular scenery make it another of the many reasons for San Franciscans' ongoing love affair with their city. ♦ Starts at Fort Point and ends at Point Lobos

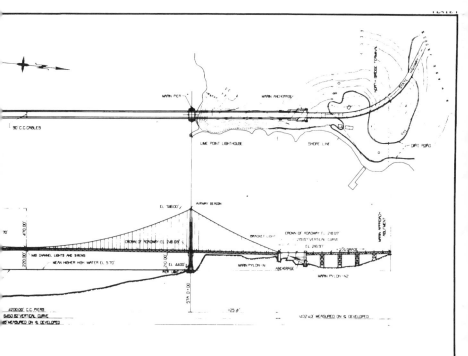

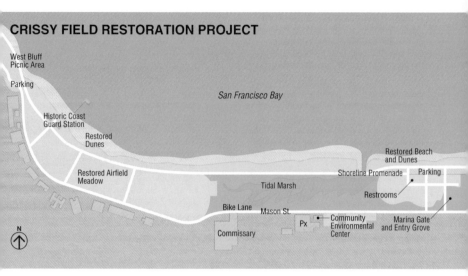

CRISSY FIELD RESTORATION PROJECT

West Bluff Picnic Area

Parking

San Francisco Bay

Historic Coast Guard Station

Restored Dunes

Restored Airfield Meadow

Restored Beach and Dunes

Shoreline Promenade    Parking

Tidal Marsh

Restrooms

Bike Lane    Mason St.

Px    Community Environmental Center

Marina Gate and Entry Grove

Commissary

N

## 3 GOLDEN GATE PROMENADE

The promenade extends from **Fort Point** underneath the Golden Gate Bridge past **Crissy Field** tidal marsh, along the **Marina Green** to **Aquatic Park** and provides three and a half miles of spectacular bay views. It's also popular for biking, fishing, sailboarding, and sunbathing. ♦ Between Fort Point and Aquatic Park

## 4 THE PRESIDIO

Located at the entrance to the Golden Gate on the northernmost point of the San Francisco peninsula, **The Presidio** was a military outpost for more than 200 years. In the 1770s, while American colonists were writing the Declaration of Independence, the Spanish rulers of Mexico established a series of missions and military posts on the West Coast. The farthest north of these posts was this spot. The original installation was a walled camp 100 yards square surrounded by a palisade-type wall.

When the Mexicans gained their independence in 1822, they took over the site until it was forcibly possessed in 1846 by the United States. Originally, the 1,400-acre area consisted of bare hills and rocks. In the 1880s it was planted with pine and eucalyptus trees that today form one of the most beautiful wooded areas in the city. Union regiments trained here during the Civil War. After the 1906 earthquake and fire, it became a refugee camp for the homeless and injured. During World War II it was the headquarters of the Fourth Army and Western Defense Command.

The site is no longer a military outpost, and most of it recently became part of the **Golden Gate National Recreation Area (GGNRA).** Despite the change, the historic buildings will be retained, but 301 newer structures will be torn down to allow for the creation of open space or forest.

Established in 1972, the **GGNRA** encompasses 34,000 acres and is one and a half times larger in area than San Francisco. The park covers more than 68 square miles of land and water, including 28 miles of the Pacific Ocean, Tomales Bay in Marin, and the San Francisco coastline. Its diverse natural environment offers sandy beaches, rugged headlands, grasslands, forests, lakes, marshes, and streams. While the area around **Fort Mason** in San Francisco has been developed, the rest of the expansive preserve is maintained as closely as possible in its natural state by the National Park Service. Places to visit include Baker Beach off Lincoln Boulevard and the gun emplacements **Battery Chamberlain, Battery Crosby,** and **Batteries Cranston, Marcus Miller,** and **Boutelle** near the Golden Gate Bridge. A Historical Trail Guide produced by the National Park Service features the many historic and scenic points; additional information is available by calling the **Visitor's Information Center** at 561.4323. ♦ Main entrances: Lombard St (at Lyon St), Presidio Blvd (at Broadway), Arguello Blvd (at Jackson St), Lincoln Blvd (at 25th Ave), and Golden Gate Bridge Toll Plaza.

Within The Presidio:

## PRESIDIO ARMY MUSEUM

Formerly the **Old Station Hospital** and built in 1857, this is the oldest surviving building in **The Presidio.** On view are numerous uniforms, weapons, photographs, and other memorabilia pertaining to the Army's history in San Francisco. Closed at press time, the museum will reopen spring 2001. ♦ Free. W-Su. Lincoln Blvd (at Funston Ave). 561.4323 &

## FUNSTON AVENUE OFFICERS' HOUSING

This group of houses along Funston Avenue constitutes some of the oldest and—depending on whom you ask—finest Victorian structures in San Francisco. Built in 1862, these elegant wood-frame structures housed Army officers for over a century. ♦ Off Lincoln Blvd

## RED BRICK BARRACKS

Built in the Georgian style between 1895 and 1897, the stately brick barracks flanking the **Parade Ground** off Montgomery Avenue served as the enlisted men's first permanent barracks at **The Presidio.** ♦ Off Funston Ave (at Lincoln Blvd)

## 5 BAKER BEACH

Although swimming is dangerous at this mile-long stretch of sandy shore, the fishing is fine, especially for striped bass. There are picnic and barbecue facilities, as well as drinking water and rest rooms, but no camping. Dogs on leashes are allowed. ♦ Daily sunrise to 7PM. Main entrance at SW corner of Gibson Rd (off Lincoln Blvd)

At Baker Beach:

## BAKER BEACH BUNKERS

These concrete bunkers were built to defend the Golden Gate Bridge from aerial attack during World War II. ♦ Battery Chamberlain (next to Baker Beach)

## 6 CHINA BEACH

Nuzzled into a cove is one of the few San Francisco beaches where swimming is permitted. Popular with locals, this small stretch of sand was named after the Chinese fishers who used to camp here. No dogs are allowed. There are public rest rooms and limited parking. ♦ Daily sunrise to 7PM. At the end of Seacliff Ave (off El Camino del Mar)

## 7 LANDS END

The wonderful views from this promontory should be appreciated by the skilled hiker only. ♦ Park at Point Lobos Ave and Merrie Way and follow the marked trails, or go to the lot at El Camino del Mar and Point Lobos Ave adjacent to the USS San Francisco Memorial and follow the trail to Lands End

## 8 POINT LOBOS

The beautiful westernmost tip of San Francisco was named by the Spanish after the sea lions, whom they called lobos marinos (sea wolves). ♦ Follow the trails from the parking lot at El Camino del Mar and Point Lobos Ave

## 9 SUTRO BATHS

Opened in 1896 by Adolph Sutro, this three-acre spa resembled the baths of imperial Rome in scale and splendor. Six saltwater swimming pools heated to different temperatures sparkled beneath a colored glass roof. The building was destroyed in a spectacular fire in 1966. Today the remains look like classical ruins. An algae-covered puddle is all that is left of the baths, but the National Park Service is considering a laser-image reconstruction of the once majestic structure. ♦ Follow the trails from the parking lot at El Camino del Mar and Point Lobos Ave

## 10 SEAL ROCKS

Four hundred feet offshore and below the **Cliff House,** the rocks swarm with sea lions and various seabirds. Watching them loll about is a favorite Sunday pastime for San Franciscans. ♦ Offshore from the Cliff House (off the Great Hwy)

## 11 CLIFF HOUSE

San Francisco families used to make day trips from the big city to sun at this resort spot, originally built in 1863. Later the house became associated with local powerbrokers, crime bosses, and their molls. When the schooner Parallel, loaded with dynamite, crashed on the rocks below, one whole wing of the building was lost in the explosion. Seven years later, on Christmas Day, the original building burned to the ground.

Adolph Sutro rebuilt it in 1895, and this one also burned within the year. Little remains of the fifth and last building on the site, which opened in 1909. Architecturally insensitive remodeling and repair work have obliterated the building's original character. It now houses the **Cliff House Restaurant,** a disappointing tourist lure (386.3330) and a small National Park Service visitors' center (556.8371). Soon the area may get a whole new look, for The **National Park Service** is considering a $19.6-million renovation. If everything goes as planned, the existing structure will get a much-needed face-lift and a **Museum of Urban Amusements** will be built, along with a visitors' center and an elaborate stairway to the **Sutro Baths.** ♦ 1090 Point Lobos Ave (at the Great Hwy)

Within the Cliff House:

## MUSÉE MÉCANIQUE

This large collection of antique mechanical amusement machines, a tawdry tribute to the days of the penny arcade, claims to be the world's largest collection of coin-operated automatic musical instruments. ♦ Free. Daily. 386.1170 ♿

## CAMERA OBSCURA

Children love this replica of Leonardo da Vinci's invention. The camera is trained on **Seal Rocks** and Ocean Beach and the image magnified on a giant parabolic screen. ◆ Nominal charge. Daily, weather permitting. 750.0415 ♿

## 12 SUTRO HEIGHTS PARK

Its bluff-top site overlooking the **Cliff House** and ocean beyond makes this park an ideal spot for sunsets and beach views. This was formerly the home and grounds of Adolph Sutro, a mining engineer, mayor, and one of the city's great benefactors. He bought much of the seafront property in the city and planted a forest of eucalyptus on Mount Sutro. The park has a haunting charm, with fragments of statuary lying half-hidden among the groves of fir, Monterey cypress, and Norfolk Island pine. Take a close look at the rock cliffs. Because of slides, the slope has been reinforced with concrete and finished to look just like the real rock. ◆ Point Lobos Ave (at 48th Ave)

## 13 LINCOLN PARK

Some 270 verdant acres on the Point Lobos Headlands provide striking views of the bay and Golden Gate Bridge. ◆ Main entrance Clement St (at 34th Ave)

Within Lincoln Park:

### LINCOLN PARK MUNICIPAL GOLF COURSE

Tee off at this 18-hole public course that offers sweeping views of the Golden Gate Bridge. ◆ Daily, sunrise to sundown. 34th Ave (at Clement St). 221.9911

### WEST FORT MILEY'S GUN BATTERIES

This former military site is fun to explore. Picnic and barbecue facilities, drinking water, and rest rooms are available. ◆ Lincoln Park (next to the VA Hospital). Ranger station 556.8371

"It's an odd thing, but anyone who disappears is said to be seen in San Francisco. It must be a delightful city and possess all the attractions of the next world."

Oscar Wilde

San Francisco has about 3,200 restaurants and bars, or one for every 230 residents.

The San Francisco Ballet Company, founded in 1933 by Adolphe Bolm, is the oldest resident classical ballet company in America.

## THE CALIFORNIA PALACE OF THE LEGION OF HONOR

Having undergone a $36-million seismic retrofitting and modernization in 1995, this museum commands a broad view of the city and the bay from its hilltop site in the park. Originally built in 1916 by **George Applegarth,** the building's design is based on the Palais de la Légion d'Honneur in Paris, and was given to the city in 1924 by Mr. and Mrs. Adolph Spreckels in memory of California's dead in World War I. The museum features paintings, sculpture, and decorative arts presented in a chronological sequence, illustrating the development of European art from the medieval period through the beginning of the 20th century. In addition, there are six subterranean galleries as well as a garden cafe. ◆ Lincoln Park (off Legion of Honor Dr). 750.3600 ♿

## 14 TSING TAO

★★$ This plain Chinese restaurant is distinguished by good food at remarkably low prices. The chili-pepper prawns are a favorite. Consider also the braised chicken legs, the hot-and-sour soup, and the shredded pork with garlic and eggplant in Szechuan sauce. The waiters are as helpful as can be, so don't hesitate to question them about dishes that sound good. ◆ Mandarin/Szechuan ◆ Daily lunch and dinner. 3107 Clement St (at 34th Ave). 387.2344 ♿

## 15 GRECO-ROMANA

★★$ If you can deal with the poor service, this informal restaurant is worth a visit for pasta with meat sauce and pasta shells with tuna. On the Greek side, just about any lamb dish is a winner; try the moussaka with ground lamb and eggplant, or the flaky spanakopita. Good pizzas and fresh salads are also offered. ◆ Greek/ Italian ◆ Tu-Su lunch and dinner. 2448 Clement St (at 25th Ave). 387.0626 ♿

## 16 FAMILY SAUNA SHOP

Treat yourself to a dry-heat, Finnish-style sauna, whirlpool hydrotherapy, therapeutic massage, or herbal facial at this clean, well-run place. It's a far cry from luxurious, but they do a fine job. ◆ Daily. 2308 Clement St (at 24th Ave). 221.2208 ♿

## 17 SHIMO

★★$$ Chef Shimo-san expertly carves fish and seafood that is so fresh, it nearly jumps off your plate. Start lunch or dinner off with the *ama ebi* (raw prawns), *saba* (mackerel), or *mirugai* (briny clams). The tempura treats have the lightest touch of sesame oil. ◆ Japanese ◆ Tu-Su dinner. 2339 Clement St (at 24th Ave). 752.4422

## 17 BILL'S PLACE

★$ One of the most popular hamburger joints in the neighborhood also makes old-fashioned milk shakes—a far cry from what's offered by fast-food chains. Eat on the back patio in good weather. ◆ American ◆ Daily lunch and dinner. 2315 Clement St (at 24th Ave). 221.5262 &

## 18 NARAI

★★$$ This is one of the few places in San Francisco to offer Chou Chow cooking, a Cantonese offshoot that makes use of chili peppers, duck, goose, and citrus fruit. As the owners are Thai (but of Chou Chow extraction), the menu also includes Thai food. Among the offerings are chicken and coconut-milk soup and *larb ped,* chicken infused with lime and chilies. One of the Chinese delights is pompano, lightly breaded with rice flour, deep-fried, and sprinkled with garlic. ◆ Chinese/Thai Tu-Su lunch and dinner. 2229 Clement St (between 23rd and 24th Aves). 751.6363 &

## 18 MESCOLANZA

★★$$ Decorated in an understated way with blue-gray walls and blue-and-white tablecloths, this always-packed place attracts a loyal and enthusiastic clientele who come for the first-rate fare. The pizza's cracker-crisp crust doesn't need fancy toppings, and the gnocchi rival any Italian grandmother's. ◆ Italian ◆ Daily dinner. Reservations recommended. 2221 Clement St (between 23rd and 24th Aves). 668.2221 &

## 19 YET WAH

★$$ Several branches of this restaurant chain are scattered around the Bay Area, but they are all under different ownership and offer very different dining experiences. This outpost has larger quarters and a more civilized ambience than the popular Chinatown branch. Specialties include glazed walnut prawns, scallops with ginger and garlic, chicken chow mein, and lemon chicken. ◆ Mandarin ◆ Daily lunch and dinner. 2140 Clement St (at 23rd Ave). 387.8040. Also at: Pier 39 (The Embarcadero, at Grant Ave). 434.4430; 5238 Diamond Heights Blvd (at Gold Mine Dr). 282.0788 &

## 20 ABBE'S

Very gently used clothing from the closets of the city's gentlewomen is this shop's stock in trade. It's a real designers' graveyard for those who want to resurrect high fashion on a budget. ◆ Tu-Sa. 1420 Clement St (at 15th Ave). 751.4567 &

## 21 ROYAL THAI

★★$$ All the standard dishes are here, including chicken and coconut-milk soup; chicken with basil; and Thai crepe, an airy pancake filled with shrimp, pork, peanuts, and tofu. Regulars also like the pad thai and the green papaya salad with green beans, carrots, and peanuts. The ingredients are fresh and the service is friendly. ◆ Thai ◆ M-F lunch and dinner; Sa-Su dinner. Reservations recommended. 951 Clement St (at 11th Ave). 386.1795 &

## 22 CLEMENT STREET BAR AND GRILL

★★$$ The kitchen specializes in creative pastas, grilled meats, and fowl, all at reasonable prices. The dark wood paneling, plants, and linen tablecloths contribute to the pleasant, relaxed ambience. ◆ American ◆ Tu-F lunch and dinner; Sa-Su brunch and dinner. Reservations recommended. 708 Clement St (at Ninth Ave). 386.2200 &

## 23 HAIG'S DELICACIES

In addition to coffees and teas, this long-established specialty shop carries a marvelous collection of olives, Middle Eastern baked goods, and other pantry foods from India, Europe, and the Middle East. ◆ M-Sa. 642 Clement St (at Eighth Ave). 752.6283 &

## 24 THE VILLAGE MARKET

A popular destination for the Pacific Heights-Presidio folks, this chic natural-foods market boasts a giant fountain at the entrance. It offers organic fresh and frozen fruits and vegetables, coffees, specialty mustards, canned truffles, and some organic wines. ◆ Daily. 4555 California St (at Eighth Ave). 221.0445 &

## 25 MANDALAY

★$$ The city's first Burmese restaurant is best suited to the gastronomically curious. Green-tea salad and satay dishes are among the interesting menu choices. ◆ Burmese ◆ Daily lunch and dinner. 4348 California St (at Sixth Ave). 386.3895 &

## 26 LAST DAY SALOON

Extremely popular with the post-college crowd, this bawdy but friendly bar books a variety of dance bands—from reggae to rock—Wednesday through Sunday. The bottom floor has pool tables and dart boards, while the top floor is for dancing. ◆ Cover. Daily until 2AM. 406 Clement St (at Fifth Ave). 387.6343 &

---

**Restaurants/Clubs: Red | Hotels: Purple | Shops: Orange | Outdoors/Parks: Green | Sights/Culture: Blue**

## 27 TAIWAN RESTAURANT

★★$ This airy, contemporary Deco restaurant serves Taiwanese food, not often seen in San Francisco. Taiwanese cuisine rejects the fire of Hunan and Szechuan in favor of subtle sweet/salty and garlicky flavors. Not to be missed are the pork-filled boiled dumplings or roasted chicken. ♦ Taiwanese ♦ Daily lunch and dinner; F-Sa until midnight. Reservations recommended. 445 Clement St (at Sixth Ave). 387.1789 &

## 27 TOY BOAT DESSERT CAFE

★$ In addition to selling windup toys, this delightful little ice-cream parlor makes delicious coffees, Italian sodas, and desserts. Especially good are the peanut-butter-and-chocolate-cookie sandwich and the mildly tart Key lime pie. ♦ Coffeehouse/Ice-cream parlor ♦ Daily. 401 Clement St (at Fifth Ave). 751.7505 &

## 28 CAFÉ RIGGIO

★$$ Redolent of garlic, this popular trattoria uses local California products and fresh ingredients. Spinach salad topped with marinated squid is a nice starter. Follow with pasta or one of the half-dozen veal dishes, including scallopini topped with a mound of mushrooms and sun-dried tomatoes. ♦ Italian ♦ Daily dinner. 4112 Geary Blvd (at Fifth Ave). 221.2114 &

## 29 NEW GOLDEN TURTLE

★★$$ Once, this and its sister restaurant (the **Golden Turtle** on Van Ness Avenue, in Pacific Heights) were *the* outposts for the city's best Vietnamese food. But the owners sold this location about a year ago, and although the menu has remained the same, the food no longer rates as highly as that found on Van Ness Avenue. The best dishes are crisp imperial rolls and five-spice chicken. ♦ Vietnamese ♦ M dinner; Tu-Su lunch and dinner. 308 Fifth Ave (at Clement St). 221.5285. Also at: 2211 Van Ness Ave (between Broadway and Vallejo St). 441.4419

## 30 MAI'S

★★$$ There are things on the menu here not to be missed by any Asian-food gourmet. The *la lot* beef (exotically seasoned charcoal-grilled ground beef wrapped in a leaf resembling that of a grape) is spectacular. Also try the imperial rolls and the chicken salad. ♦ Vietnamese ♦ Daily lunch and dinner. 316 Clement St (between Third and Fourth Aves). 221.3046 &

## 30 BLUE DANUBE

This popular 1960s-style coffeehouse usually plays classical music. When the weather is sunny, a wall of glass doors overlooking Clement Street is opened wide. ♦ Coffeehouse Daily. 306 Clement St (between Third and Fourth Aves). 221.9041 &

# SAN FRANCISCO SUN 'N' SURF

Expect anything! San Francisco's beaches can be sun drenched one day and enshrouded in fog the next. Always scenic and beautiful, some of the city's beaches are ideal for swimming, while others are limited to sunbathing and picnicking due to treacherous conditions along the rocky coastline. A chancy proposition on those beaches with treacherous conditions, yes, but you can always count on some warm and sunny days when the surf is calm. Here are some of San Francisco's favorites:

**Baker Beach** This mile-long beach, off 25th Avenue, is part of the Golden Gate National Recreation Area. Although it is a good weather sandy beach, dangerous waves make swimming off-limits. Its views of the Bay Area entice hikers, fisherfolk, and picnickers.

**China Beach** Located at 29th Avenue between **Lincoln Park** and **The Presidio,** this 600-foot sandy beach cove was once a campsite for Chinese fishermen. Part of the **Golden Gate National Recreation Area,** the beach is popular for sunbathing and picnicking, and is one of the few swimming beaches in the city. Lifeguards are on duty during the summer.

**Land's End Beach** You'll find this secluded spot at **End Trail** off **Merrie Way** in the **Richmond District.** The no-swimming beach is difficult to reach, but the views are rewarding. Clothing is considered optional by the beach's mainly gay sunbathers.

**Ocean Beach** Located between **Lincoln Way** and **Fulton Street** on the westernmost edge of Golden Gate Park, is the prime destination for locals and visitors alike. **Cliff House** provides a popular vantage point; just offshore is the outline of **Seal Rocks,** those stony offshore islands that are usually inhabited by shore birds and a colony of sea lions. Bring binoculars for a closer look. On a clear day the **Farallon Islands** some 30 miles distant are also visible. Swimming is not allowed here because of dangerous tides and the undertow, but its wide sandy beach is fine for walking, jogging, and sunbathing.

**Phelan Beach** This cove-tucked small beach is used primarily for swimming and sunning and sports, with a lifeguard on duty April through October. You'll find it at **El Camino del Mar** in the **Richmond District.**

## 31 PLOUGH & STARS

A real Irish bar with live Irish music every night, it's at its wildest, of course, on St. Patrick's Day. ♦ Daily until 2AM. 116 Clement St (at Third Ave). 751.1122 ♿

## 32 SATIN MOON FABRICS

This shop provides a wide selection of designer fabrics for those who know how to sew a fine seam. ♦ Tu-Sa. 32 Clement St (at Arguello Blvd). 668.1623 ♿

## 33 PAT O'SHEA'S MAD HATTER

★★$$ As well as being a friendly neighborhood sports bar, this place boasts a fine kitchen, which produces delicious and unusual specials such as roast salmon on a bed of mushrooms infused with a tarragon vinaigrette; leg of lamb with pearl onions, fennel, and potatoes au gratin; and homey chicken potpie and pot roast with mashed potatoes. And the crème brûlée is much better than average. ♦ American ♦ Daily lunch. Reservations required for large parties. 3848 Geary Blvd (at Third Ave). 752.3148 ♿

## 34 KHAN TOKE THAI HOUSE

★★★$$ Diners leave their shoes at the entrance and are seated at low, intricately carved tables positioned over pits that accommodate their legs. Among the specialties are coconut-chicken soup with succulent pieces of chicken and mushrooms; prawn salad with touches of lime and lemongrass; and duck salad with its earthy flavor and texture, thanks to the powdered rice sprinkled on top. With a good wine list and food prices only slightly higher than at more modest Thai places, this makes a fine setting for special occasions. ♦ Thai ♦ Daily dinner. 5937 Geary Blvd (at 24th Ave). 668.6654

## 35 TON KIANG

★★$$ The long menu specializes in the food of China's Hakka region, but is rounded out with Cantonese and northern Chinese selections; helpful servers will guide you through it all. Best bets are the clay-pot dishes: braised pork in a rich sauce lightened with tofu and vegetables, or delicious squares of pork-stuffed tofu stewed with carrots, celery, and pieces of pork. ♦ Hakka/Cantonese ♦ Daily lunch and dinner. 5821 Geary Blvd (at 22nd Ave). 387.8273. Also at: 3148 Geary Blvd (at Spruce St). 752.4440 ♿

## 36 HONG KONG FLOWER LOUNGE

★★★$$ This San Francisco branch of a well-patronized restaurant operation (also in Hong Kong and suburban Millbrae, California) was a hit the moment the doors opened. Fish tanks in back display the daily seafood selection, but don't expect much help from the harried staff. Top menu choices are Peking duck; crab bathed in wine sauce; minced squab in lettuce cups; wok-charred calamari topped with fried peppers; roast chicken; dry-braised green beans; and roast baby pig with pickled vegetables (a frequent special). ♦ Cantonese ♦ Daily lunch and dinner. Reservations recommended. 5322 Geary Blvd (between 17th and 18th Aves). 668.8998 ♿

## 37 JOE'S

Here's where you'll find the best ice cream out on the avenues, particularly the "Its"— Joe's version of the famous "Its It" (vanilla ice cream sandwiched between two oatmeal cookies and dipped in chocolate). ♦ Daily. 5351 Geary Blvd (at 18th Ave). 751.1950 ♿

## 38 RUSSIAN RENAISSANCE

★$$$ The walls and ceiling here are something of a landmark—and even worth a visit in themselves. They're covered with murals depicting scenes from Russian folklore and history, a 14-year labor of love by artist Serge Smernoff. Among the specialties are chicken Kiev and veal scallopini with eggplant and mushrooms. All entrées include soup, salad, dessert, and coffee. ♦ Russian ♦ Wed-Su dinner. 5241 Geary Blvd (at 17th Ave). 752.8558

## 39 MIKE'S CHINESE CUISINE

★★$$ A favorite Cantonese restaurant, this place is known for its steamed fish and excellent egg rolls. It also crosses into a few other provinces and does a commendable Peking duck and Mongolian beef. ♦ Cantonese ♦ M, W-Su dinner. 5145 Geary Blvd (between 15th and 16th Aves). 752.0120 ♿

## 40 CHINA HOUSE SEAFOOD

★★$$ Classic fare with some subtle twists is the hallmark of the China House menu. For vegetarian pot stickers, delicate wrappers enclose a crunchy mix of greens and herbs; for Snow Mountain chicken soup, a mound of egg whites floats on the rich, vegetable-laden broth—a sensory delight. Lion's head consists of two huge, delicately textured pork balls resting on a mound of creamy cabbage cooked in an intense broth. ♦ Chinese ♦ Daily dinner. Reservations recommended. 501 Balboa St (at 6th Ave). 387.6038 ♿

The first public school in the United States opened in San Francisco on 3 April 1848.

---

Restaurants/Clubs: Red | Hotels: Purple | Shops: Orange | Outdoors/Parks: Green | Sights/Culture: Blue

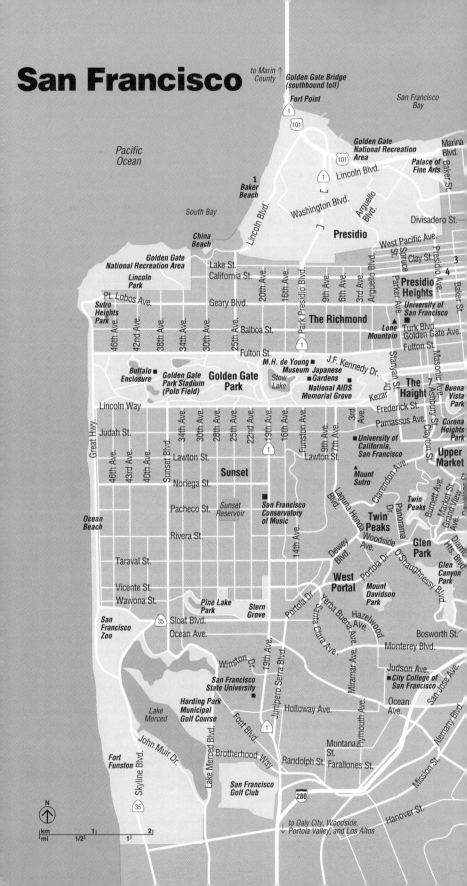

# GAY SAN FRANCISCO

## Symbols

While all of the establishments in this section are gay-friendly and popular with gay visitors and locals, those that are specifically gay-oriented are identified with the following symbols

♂    predominantly/exclusively gay-male–oriented

♀    predominantly/exclusively lesbian-oriented

♂
♀    predominantly/exclusively gay-oriented with a male and female clientele

The "world's gay and lesbian capital" in the minds of many, San Francisco is also one of the US's most striking and beautiful cities. The setting is dramatic enough, with the hills, the bay, and the famous fog. Throw in the uniquely charming architecture, world-class restaurants and cultural institutions (including one of the best Asian art museums in the country), and a vibrant multicultural mix, and it's clear why this city of just 725,000 has become a favorite destination for all manner of travelers, both novice and seasoned—but perhaps none more than gays and lesbians.

When the famous gold rush began at Sutter's Mill in 1848. San Francisco became known as a place to get rich quick—and to spend it all, as the miners and other high rollers flooded to the pleasure palaces of the Barbary Coast. Such was its reputation as "Sodom by the Sea," that when the famous 1906 earthquake leveled the city, the moral guardians of the time saw the righteous hand of God at work.

But the city rebuilt and continued to cultivate a freewheeling reputation through the years, becoming a magnet for the counterculture, including the flower children and their "Summer of Love" in the late 1960s, and the thousands of gays and lesbians who flocked here to escape intolerance and find a vibrant subculture that promised freedom, acceptance, and belonging. Queer San Francisco grew from a half-hidden demimonde to a militant community demanding its rights to something approaching a pillar of the establishment today. With homosexuals estimated at some 27 percent of the city's population, current mayor Willie Brown is just the latest in a long line of progressive local officials who embrace gay and lesbian San Franciscans as a powerful and positive force in the city's political, cultural, and economic life. There are three openly gay and lesbian members of the powerful Board of Supervisors, and many more throughout the municipal government. San Francisco has long been at the forefront of instituting antidiscrimination legislation for homosexuals and transgendered people. In 1997, the city even took on such powerful entities as **United Airlines** and the Catholic Church over equal treatment of their employees.

The queer community of San Francisco is predominantly young (the average age is 31), and pervasive. Unlike other cities that have only one or two gay-popular neighborhoods, gays and lesbians live in every part of this metropolis. There are, however, a few hotspots, like lesbian-popular **Noe Valley** and the **Mission;** guppie-laden **Pacific Heights;** the anything-goes **SoMa (South of Market);** and such areas outside the city proper as **Berkeley.** But homo central is definitely the **Castro.** First settled by gay men in the early 1970s, along with New York City's Christopher Street, this roughly 14-square-block area became a defining symbol of gay America. Today the Castro is less male and more diverse, but still a lively center of the city's queer culture.

Visitors to the Bay Area will find that in many parts of the city's gay and lesbian community a small-town intimacy reigns, with people placing more value on personal growth, spiritual exploration, and human rights than in most other urban areas. But like New Englanders, the locals can have a certain surface reserve that is easily cracked if you make the first move. Many folks still tend to be politicized but are less "in your face" about it these days. Lesbians play a larger and more visible role here than ever, and there are plenty of suitable venues for visiting lesbians to enjoy.

Through all its travails—earthquakes and epidemics, gold rushes and market crashes, strikes and sit-ins—San Francisco has preserved a sense that it is in America's progressive cultural and social vanguard. It's easy for visitors to get swept up in that feeling, too, as they explore the ins and outs of the gayest city in the US.

## 1 NORTH BAKER BEACH

The easiest to find of San Francisco's gay/lesbian nude beaches, this bit of sandy shore is located between the **Presidio** and **Lincoln Park.** Walk north along the ridge toward the Golden Gate Bridge (the trail can be tricky, so watch your step); you'll see the beach below. The sand is especially fine and the water is great for in-the-buff bodysurfing, but the surf can be dangerous at times. ♦ Daily sunrise to 7PM. Main entrance at end of Gibson Rd (off Bowley St)

## 2 MEXICAN MUSEUM

In **Building D** of the **Fort Mason Center,** a US Army command post dating from the mid-19th century, this contemporary museum has featured among its exhibitions Chicana lesbian artist Ester Hernandez and such well-known gay Mexican artists as Rodolfo Morales and Nahum Zenil, who deal with the realities of being gay in a conservative Latin society. ♦ Admission; free first Wednesday of the month. W-Su noon–5PM. Marina Blvd and Laguna St. 441.0404 ♿

## 3 THE LION PUB

Dark wood, lots of plants, and a roaring fire (not to mention great martinis) make this friendly, low-key Pacific Heights bar and lounge a true fave with queer professionals between 20 and 50. Wednesday's "Macho Night" is quite popular, and on weekends the crowd is almost all male. ♦ Daily 3PM–2AM. 2062 Divisadero St (at Sacramento St). 567.6565

## 4 ELLA'S

★★★ $ The exceptional fare and reasonable prices have folks lining up just about every day for just about every meal at this comfy, gay-owned neighborhood eatery with simple tables, an open kitchen, and a counter bedecked with flowers. The menu offers a fresh take on old faves—an open-faced turkey sandwich livened with sage dressing, or chicken salad with carrots, cucumbers, and curry vinaigrette. The very popular brunch features spiced oatmeal-apple pancakes, fried cheese grits with eggs and toast, and a ham and mushroom omelette with cider-roasted onions and Swiss cheese. ♦ American ♦ M-F breakfast, lunch, and dinner; Sa-Su brunch and dinner. 500 Presidio Ave (at California St). 441.5669 ♿

## 5 ALTA PLAZA

★★★$$$ Excellent updated American fare, friendly service, and live jazz five nights a week mark this elegant, gay-owned bar and restaurant in Pacific Heights. In the upstairs dining room, executive chef Amey Shaw puts freshness first in such dishes as salmon cakes served with a green-peppercorn aioli, and teriyaki lamb riblets with a sweet mustard sauce. For entrées try the gnocchi with spinach in a splendid cream-and-mascarpone sauce, or the steak *bavette,* grilled to perfection and served with a mouthwatering salsa verde. Downstairs in the bar and cocktail lounge is a good-looking guppy crowd—especially around Happy Hour—and a DJ on weekends. ♦ New American ♦ Restaurant: M-Sa dinner; Su brunch and dinner. Bar: daily 4PM–2AM. 2301 Fillmore St (at Clay St). 922.1444

## 6 PACIFIC HEIGHTS HEALTH CLUB

With separate-but-equal facilities for men and women (both gay/lesbian and straight), this first-rate gym is more for a serious workout than for cruising—not that it doesn't happen.

---

**Restaurants/Clubs: Red | Hotels: Purple | Shops: Orange | Outdoors/Parks: Green | Sights/Culture: Blue**

The free weights, machines, and personal trainers are just about all you could ask for in a health club. Besides sauna, steam, Jacuzzi, and tanning beds, there's also a retractable roof to let the sunshine in. ♦ M-Sa 6AM-10PM; Su 7AM-10PM. 2356 Pine St (between Fillmore and Steiner Sts). 563.6694

## 7 Haight-Ashbury

Haight-Ashbury is actually an intersection but it's also the general name for the Upper Haight, or Haight Street west of Divisadero. This strip of Haight Street, between beautiful **Buena Vista Park** and **Golden Gate Park,** is where the hippie movement was born in the late 1960s and still keeps its counter-culture feel. It's a great place to shop for cutting-edge street fashion, grab a bite to eat, or just stroll and see the sights. Buy crystals and tie-dye clothes from the boutiques but be careful of what you buy off the street kids; for fifty bucks you'll probably get a bag of oregano.

## 7 Trax

♂ This is the only gay bar in the neighborhood, although the whole area is very mixed. Dark and calm compared to the chaos outside, **Trax** offers a friendly place to have a drink after shopping or dinner. Wednesday and Friday nights it becomes the **Love/Haight Lounge,** Trax and the small bar becomes a crowded club with cute young boys, go go dancers, and friendly conversation. Daily noon–2AM. ♦ 1437 Haight St (between Ashbury and Masonic). 864.4213

## 8 Theater Rhinoceros

♂♀ The oldest gay and lesbian theater company in America (founded by Alan Estes in 1977) is known for its innovative stagings of performance art, comedy, musicals, and drama. The main theater, which has premiered works by Charles Ludlum, Jane Chambers, and the Five Lesbian Brothers, seats about 150 people and puts on a five-work season September through June; there's a smaller studio theater in the basement. The name comes from the "lavender rhino" (gentle and peaceful until provoked), a symbol of the early gay rights movement in Boston. ♦ Box office: Tu.-Su. 2926 16th St (between S Van Ness Ave and Mission St). 861.5079

In March 1996, Mayor Willie Brown presided over the first mass gay and lesbian wedding—some 200 couples—ever sponsored by a US city.

The city's official song, "I Left My Heart In San Francisco," was penned by a homesick gay couple, Douglass Cross and George Cory, in 1954.

## 9 Blondie's Bar and No Grill

♀ Specializing in jazz, swing, and martinis, most days the dim, purple neon-lit club attracts a cosmopolitan mix of genders and orientations (though some nights up to half the crowd might be lesbians). ♦ Daily 2PM-2AM. 540 Valencia St (between 17th and 16th Sts). 864.2419

## 10 Esta Noche

♂ Young Hispanic guys and those in search of *amor latino* dance to a salsa beat in this Mission District spot, mixing with the transvestites who put on awesome Wednesday night drag shows that define camp. Weekend nights are also popular here. ♦ Cover F-Su 9PM-3AM. M-Th 1PM-2AM; F-Su 1PM-3AM. 3079 16th St (between Mission and Valencia Sts). 861.5757 ♿

## 11 San Francisco Women's Center— Women's Building

The strength and history of women united is depicted in a beautiful mural covering part of the building. The center is a particularly important resource for women of color and lesbians, with regular meetings, readings, workshops, and events. ♦ M-F. 3543 18th St (between Valencia and Guerrero Sts). 431.1180

## 12 Club Lexington

♀ One of San Francisco dykedom's more recent additions—and its only seven-day-a-week nightspot—is a cozy space with a few artsy touches (wriggly bars on the windows, light fixtures suggestive of mammaries, and wavy toilet paper dispensers in the rest room) tarting up the green-and-red-painted premises of what's essentially a neighborhood barroom. The lively mix of girls, ranging in age from 21 to 61, tend to be a bit of an artsy bunch—the neighborhood being what it is—and the jukebox is eclectic, throwing out tunes from 1960s Motown to the Butthole Surfers. ♦ Daily 3PM-2AM. 3464 19th St (at Lexington St). 863.2052

## 13 Osento

A sanctuary for unwinding and/or socializing, all to a sound track of soft, relaxing music, this women's day spa offers patrons a large Japanese-style hot tub, a sauna, a steam hut, massage service, and a meditation room; there's a bracing outdoor cold-plunge, and a deck for nude sunbathing. ♦ Admission. Daily 1PM-1AM. 955 Valencia St (between 21st and 20th Sts). 282.6333

## 14 Good Vibrations

You can probably find out everything you've always wanted to know about sex—and then some—at this women-owned and -operated co-op, which they describe as a "clean, well-lighted place" for sex books, toys, and videos. The emphasis here is on health, education, quality, and hot sex; the staff is helpful and informative and the selection is huge. ♦ Daily. 1210 Valencia St (between 24th and 23rd Sts). 974.8980, mail order 800/289.8423

### 15 VALENTINE'S

★★★$$ This bright, yet intimate, neighborhood cafe created by Kunal Mukherjee and his lover Daniel Morrison is considered to be the most innovative and exciting vegetarian restaurant in the city, with a wonderful array of Indian, Italian, Middle Eastern, and Thai dishes. Start with the cold Vietnamese spring rolls or the delectable pot stickers, then move on to the likes of the North Indian Plate (vegetable curry with Basmati rice, vegetable dal, and sweet Bengal tomato chutney). Such outstanding desserts as chocolate turtle torte and fresh fruit crumble (served with Tahitian vanilla gelato) are made fresh daily. ♦ International/Vegetarian ♦ M-F dinner; Sa-Su brunch and dinner. 1793 Church St (between 30th and Day Sts). 285.2257

### 16 EROS

♂ A goodly range of guys between 20 and 50 prowl around this two-story safe-sex club, a sort of bathhouse without the private rooms. Downstairs is a lounge with skin flicks, sauna, steam room, and showers, while the upstairs offers various cushioned alcoves—albeit little real privacy—for doing what comes naturally. Don't forget to bring an ID. ♦ Admission. M-Th, Su 4PM-midnight; F-Sa 4PM-4AM. 2051 Market St (between Dolores and 14th Sts). 864.3767

### 17 SPARKY'S

★$ One of the few in the city to remain open around the clock, this friendly neighborhood diner is a great place for late-night munchies or an afternoon burger. There's usually a line after the bars close, when the food and the crowd look their best. It's conveniently located across the street from **The Pilsner,** so that if you don't find beefcake you can always get a pancake. ♦ Diner ♦ Daily 24 hours. 242 Church Street (between 15th and Market Sts). 626.8666

### 18 THE PILSNER

♂ Since the ban on smoking in bars took effect, this neighborhood hangout has become very popular. The large backyard patio is great on a sunny day and ideal to grab a cigarette. The pool table, jukebox, and friendly local crowd keep this bar busy every night; and the variety of draft beers keep the crowd happy. Very busy on weekends, **The Pilsner** offers both cruising and conversation. Daily 9AM-2AM. ♦ 225 Church St (between 15th and Market Sts). 621.7058

### 18 CHOW

★★$ The prices in this comfortable yet trendy diner-style room are so reasonable that you can almost afford to buy the local art right off the walls, but the food, mostly Italian but ranging all over the map, can be excellent, from standard quick pastas and wood-fired pizzas and daily sandwich and vegetarian specials to Asian-inspired starters like a Thai-style noodle salad or wontons. Or go all out beginning with rock-salt-roasted mussels and ending with Rose's warm ginger cake with pumpkin ice cream and caramel sauce. A wide range of microbrews and wines by the glass help wash it down. No reservations are taken, so there's always a fashionable crowd waiting to eat, but you don't have to wait on the premises; if you ask the hostess, she will come get you next door at **The Pilsner** or bookstore when your table is ready. ♦ Italian ♦ Sun-Th 11AM-11PM; F-Sa 11AM-midnight. 215 Church St (between 15th and Market Sts). 552.2469

### 19 2223 MARKET

★★★$$ One of the few upscale restaurants in the Castro, this place draws a friendly, eclectic, and heavily gay clientele. Dinner crowds line up for chef Melinda Randolph's culinary delights on the order of wild-mushroom fettuccine and roasted chicken with garlic mashed potatoes, or a sophisticated grilled salmon with mustard-braised lentils and broccoli rabe with roasted-red pepper rouille. The ever-changing pizza menu is a winner, too, as are the huge colorful murals that bring a Mardi Gras atmosphere to mind. ♦ Californian/ Continental ♦ M-F dinner; Sa-Su brunch and dinner. Reservations recommended on weekends. 2223 Market St (between Sanchez and 16th Sts). 431.0692 ♿

### 20 UNCLE MAME

You can't miss the funky window display, with vintage monitors playing reruns of the "Howdy Doody Show," "I Love Lucy," and "Sonny and Cher." Everything camp and kitsch is here: Pee Wee Herman lunch boxes, Barbie dolls that speak French, Pope John Paul II fans, snow globes, and Spam banks. There's even an old-fashioned photo booth in the back. ♦ Mon-Th noon-7PM; Fr-Sa noon-11PM; Sun noon-5PM. 2241 Market St (between Noe and Sanchez Sts). 626.1953

### 21 METRO BAR AND RESTAURANT

★★$$ Apart from creditable Hunan fare (and some of the best pot stickers in town), this

---

Restaurants/Clubs: **Red** | Hotels: **Purple** | Shops: Orange | Outdoors/Parks: **Green** | Sights/Culture: Blue place is known for its wonderful balcony on the second floor just perfect for people watching, a fun Sunday-afternoon beer bust, and Tuesday evening karaoke that's a mix of straight and gay folks. ♦ Chinese ♦ Restaurant: daily dinner. Bar: daily 1PM–2AM. 3600 16th St (at Noe St). 703.9750

## 22 CAFE FLORE

★★$ Possibly the closest thing to a sidewalk cafe this side of Paris, this highly popular hangout (sometimes dubbed "Cafe Hairdo") is a great place to meet people or just sit over a coffee, beer, or white wine with a bored existential look on your face. Writers, artists, and other creative types abound here. Tasty, inexpensive salads, burgers, and daily specials are served, and the only thing missing is a good gas heater on the outside patio for cold days. ♦ Cafe ♦ Daily. 2298 Market St (at Noe St). 621.8579 &

## 23 THE MUSCLE SYSTEM

♂ Cruisy, high energy, and boys-only, both branches of this gym offer a good selection of free weights, Universal equipment, and personal training, as well as a sauna and cardio machines. The clientele at the Hayes Street location (which has a Jacuzzi) is a bit older. ♦ M-F 6AM–10PM; Sa-Su. 2275 Market St (between Sanchez and 16th Sts). 863.4700. Also at: 364 Hayes St (between Franklin and Gough Sts). 863.4701

## 24 BAGDAD CAFÉ

★$ One of the few in the city to remain open around-the-clock, this friendly neighborhood diner is a great place to grab a quick bite any time. There are lots of streetside windows for people watching, and art and photography exhibits from local talent on the walls. On the downside, the food (on the order of salads, burgers, and a breakfast menu served all day) can be hit or miss. ♦ Diner ♦ Daily 24 hours. 2295 Market St (at Noe St). 621.4434 &

## 24 JOSIE'S CABARET AND JUICE JOINT

♂♀ One of the only venues in town that presents a daily roster of talented, outrageous, and inspired queer performance artists, stand-up comics, and drag stars, this place also offers great vegetarian fare, baked goods, and (of course) juice. Among the headliners that have played the 100-seat performance space are Lea DeLaria, Lypsinka, Charles Busch, and Marga Gomez. ♦ M-Th 10AM–4PM; F 10AM–8PM; Sa 9AM–8PM; Su 9AM–4PM. 3583 16th St (at Market St). 861.7933 &

## 25 INN ON CASTRO

♂ $$ With just five rooms (each with private bath), this is one of the smaller guest houses in the city (and almost exclusively gay male); its intimacy, though, is a big part of its charm. The Edwardian exterior contrasts with the contemporary look inside, featuring classic modern furniture, track lighting, and the original art of one of the owners. Upstairs, breakfast is served on an extensive and ever-changing collection of imported china and stoneware. ♦ 321 Castro St (between Market and 16th Sts). 861.0321 &

## 26 UNDER ONE ROOF

♂♀ Staffed entirely by volunteers, this gift shop donates 100 percent of its proceeds to AIDS charities. It offers a lovely array of clothes, greeting cards, candle holders, hand-crafted collectibles, and one-of-a-kind items. During the Christmas season it becomes a winter wonderland, featuring some of the most unique and festive decorations in the city. ♦ M-Sa 11AM–7PM; Su 11AM–6PM. 2362B Market St (between Noe and Castro Sts). 252.9430, 800/525.2125

## 26 THE NAMES PROJECT

This is the visitors' center for the AIDS quilt that has been exhibited around the world to commemorate those who have died and to draw attention to the epidemic's toll. Although the actual quilt is at 310 Townsend Street (between Fourth and Fifth Sts), some panels are always on display here, and you can locate the panel of a friend or loved one, find out how to contribute a new panel, or make one on the spot with materials provided. ♦ Daily noon–7PM. 2362A Market St (between Noe and Castro Sts). 863.1966 &

## 26 LEATHER ZONE

♂♀ An impressive selection of new and used leather items—both naughty and nice—at this shop includes jackets, harnesses, studded jockstraps, hoods, and beyond. An inspiration to the novice, this store is a necessity to the leather dudes and dudettes of the Castro. ♦ M-Sa 11AM–7PM; Su noon–6PM. 2352 Market St (between Noe and Castro Sts). 255.8585

## 26 DETOUR

♂ Locals either love or hate this black hole with earsplitting music and a heavy cruise scene. A decor heavy on chain-link fencing is one reason why the Falcon porn video, *In Hot Pursuit*, was filmed here atop the pool table. The funky mix of tattooed skinheads, "urban primitives," and young guppies taking a walk on the wild side also makes this a prime place to come if you want some action. Sunday nights are especially hot, and the tunes are always on the cutting edge. ♦ Daily 2PM–2AM. 2348 Market St (between Noe and Castro Sts). 861.6053 &

## 27 MARKET STREET GYM

♂ This popular co-ed facility not only has the usual panoply of weights, machines, aerobics,

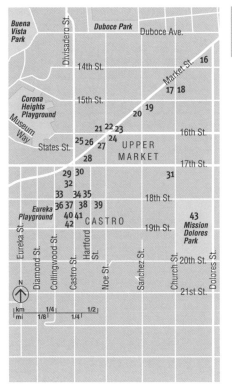

# A RIVER RUNS THROUGH IT

Near **Sonoma** wine country about 1.5 hours north of San Francisco is the town of **Guerneville** (pop. 3,500) and the resort area of **Russian River,** which takes its name from the eponymous river running through it. With its shops, restaurants, bars, and inns, Guerneville has been the area's main gay and lesbian gathering place since the 1970s, and its attractions—redwood forests, wineries, and coastal beaches—keep San Franciscans coming back, especially in summer. The most popular "resorts" are basic, but socially oriented. Small cabins, campsites, and motel rooms are the most common lodging.

Premier among the local homo resorts is the casual and cruisy **Fifes** ($$; 16467 River Rd, 707/869.0656, 800/734.3371; fax 707/869.0658) in Guerneville. At the edge of the river, this rustic 15-acre compound for men and women offers simple accommodations in 50 cabins and cottages, as well as 100 campsites. On-site facilities include a pool, sundeck, private beach, small gym, a restaurant, the **Bunkhouse** country-western bar, and the **Signs** disco. Day-trippers are also welcome.

Also on **River Road,** though less elaborate, the friendly, mixed male and female, and laid-back **Willows** ($$; 5905 River Rd, 707/869.2824, 800/953.2828; fax 707/869.2764) sits at the river's edge, and offers 60 tent sites, 13 bedrooms with television and VCRs, a living room with fireplace, and a library with a grand piano. Breakfast is provided, and guests enjoy a private beach, sun deck, hot tub, sauna, nude sunbathing, and canoes.

Slightly smaller, and nestled on three lush wooded acres within walking distance of town, **Highlands** ($$; 14000 Woodland Dr, between Morningside Dr and Woodland Rd, 707/869.0333; fax 707/869.0370) is a popular spot for men and women, offering privacy and a swimsuit-optional pool and hot tub. There are 16 cabins and rooms (some with kitchens and fireplaces), as well as tent sites.

For a friskier, party atmosphere, try the mostly male **Russian River Resort** ($$; Fourth and Mill Sts, 707/869.0691, 800/417.3736; fax 707/869.0698). The 24 rooms here are small and plain, but the guys come to party and play to a loud dance beat by the pool, in the hot tub, at the poolside bar, or in the indoor video bar. There's also a great restaurant that serves lunch and dinner daily, and has nightly piano music. The premises are open to nonguests as well. The "Triple R" is also the proud sponsor of Leather Weekend each August.

and personal training, but is also one of the gayest and cruisiest gyms for men in the city. The guys are buff, friendly, and frisky; check out the Jacuzzi. ♦ M-F 6AM–10PM; Sa-Su 8AM–8PM. 2301 Market St (at Noe St). 626.4488

## 28 THE CAFE

♂♀ Excellent is the music and hot are the friendly young guys and gals in attendance at this fun dance bar up a flight of stairs. When not cruising, shooting pool, or writhing on the small dance floor, the patrons cheer and whistle from the balcony overlooking the intersection of Market and Castro at every muscle, drag, or leather queen that walks by. Lines can be a block long on Friday and Saturday night, so come early; the 4PM Sunday tea dance is also copacetic. ♦ Daily 12:30PM–2AM. 2367 Market St (between Noe and Castro Sts). 861.3846

Restaurants/Clubs: **Red** | Hotels: **Purple** | Shops: **Orange** | Outdoors/Parks: **Green** | Sights/Culture: **Blue**

## 29 Marcello's Pizza

★★$ Practically an institution, this small but very popular joint makes some of the tastiest pizza around. Choose from such innovative toppings as clams, pesto chicken, pineapple and ham, roasted rosemary potato and onion, or more traditional variations. Calzones, hot grilled subs, and salads are also on the menu. ♦ Pizza/Takeout ♦ M-Th, Su 11AM-1AM; F-Sa 11AM-2AM. 420 Castro St (between 18th and Market Sts). 863.3900 &

## 30 Castro Theater

The city declared this remarkable Spanish Colonial structure a landmark in 1977, calling it San Francisco's finest example of a 1920s movie palace. Inside the 1,600-seat theater sports an awesome plaster ceiling resembling a giant cloth canopy. The loyal, enthusiastic audience revels in the theater's opulence and the thrill of seeing favorite classics as they were originally presented. If you're lucky, you'll be at a performance where the theater's multi-pipe organ rises from the orchestra pit and the organist regales moviegoers before the show. Special events are also staged here, such as concerts of the **Gay Men's Chorus,** and numerous film festivals, including the International Gay and Lesbian Film Festival. ♦ 429 Castro St (between 18th and 17th Sts). 621.6120 &

## 30 Twin Peaks

Also known as "the Glass Coffin," this landmark gay bar founded in 1972 is one of the oldest in the Castro, and the first to put in huge picture windows so folks could see and be seen. These days, the crowd around the beautiful antique wooden bar is a friendly, relaxed mix of guys and gals mostly in the age 40-60 range. ♦ Daily noon-2AM. 401 Castro St (at 17th St). 864.9470 &

## 30 Orphan Andy's

★$ Filling breakfast fare, sandwiches, and burgers rule at this around-the-clock coffee shop where Day-Glo hair, piercings, and tattoos are de rigueur. It's a lifesaver during or after a night of partying, though at 4AM the staff and patrons can get a bit edgy. Check out the jukebox with its one-of-a-kind recordings scattered within a diverse selection of pop and rock. ♦ Diner ♦ Daily 24 hours. 3991 17th St (between Hartford and Castro Sts). 864.9795

## 30 Harvey Milk Plaza

A small brick plaza in front of the **Castro** and **Market MUNI** station was dedicated in 1985 to the slain civil rights leader and former member of the San Francisco Board of Supervisors. At the railway's entrance is a plaque giving a thumbnail history of Milk's career in the city—from 1973 when he opened a camera store at 575 Castro (now occupied by a shop called **Skin Zone**) up to his assassination at **City Hall** in November 1978. The memorial concludes movingly with a quote from Milk: "I am all of us." ♦ Market and Castro Sts

## 31 The Parker House

$$ One of the Castro's newer all-homo properties is run by Bob O'Halloran, an alumnus of the local Joie de Vivre hotel chain, and his lover Bill Boeddiker, in a three-story, yellow manse of brick, stone, and wood dating from 1909. The combination of a loving renovation and can-do hospitality makes for a winning stay with guests (an even mix of men and women) who are free to relax in the library—complete with fireplace and piano—or outside on the large sundeck, the landscaped lawn, gardens, or brick patio. The five rooms are a mix of contemporary and antiques—depending on the floor—but all share floral themes, earth tones, and pine wood. Four of the guest rooms have private baths and all offer voice mail and modem ports. Breakfast is included. ♦ 520 Church St (between 18th and 17th Sts). 621.3222, 888/520.7275; fax 621.4139

## 32 Bar on Castro

This is the latest addition to the scene at the former home of **Castro Station** and it's getting quite a crowd. Newly redecorated with plenty of space to lounge, this is a friendly bar for cruising or conversation. Pull up an ottoman and watch the DJ spin or shoot some pool with friends. Tables in the front and a smoking patio in the back (closed at 11PM) help keep the boy traffic circulating.♦ M-F 3PM-2AM; Sa-Su noon-2AM. 456B Castro St (between 18th and Market Sts). 626.7220

## 32 Daddy's

The smell of leather can be as intoxicating as the drinks in this friendly neighborhood joint where basic black doubles as decor and dress code. Porn films grace the video screens while a chronologically diverse mix of guys cruise, chat, or work the pool tables or pinball machines. Hang out with the less hard-core boys up front or join the serious leathermen in the back bar. ♦ M-F 9AM-2AM; Sa-Su 6AM-2AM. 440 Castro St (between 18th and Market Sts). 621.8732

## 32 All American Boy

The local outpost of this gay-oriented men's clothing shop specializes in fun, California-casual clothes and accessories for men. For that super-macho look, try on the butchy-kitschy line of going-out gear inspired by Tom of Finland. ♦ M-Sa 10AM-9PM; Su 11AM-7PM. 436 Castro St (between 18th and Market Sts). 861.0444

## 32 IN-JEAN-IOUS

♂
♀ It's not just jeans at this friendly gay-owned shop, but all manner of activewear, club wear, shoes, hats, and accessories. The T-shirt collection is funnier than most, and a major best-seller is a local artist's campy takes on the popular Barbie doll: imagine Big Dyke Barbie, Drag Queen Barbie, and Trailer Trash Barbie. ♦ M-Sa 10AM–9PM; Su 11AM–7PM. 432 Castro St (between 18th and Market Sts). 864.1863

## 33 THE PENDULUM

♂ This longstanding Castro watering hole caters mostly, but not exclusively, to an African-American clientele. There's a friendly and very cruisy mix of chaps of all ages milling about the big horseshoe-shaped bar or the busy pool table. It's no wonder people keep coming back, as the bartenders and staff here truly make everyone feel at home. ♦ Daily 7AM–2AM. 4146 18th St (between Castro and Collingwood Sts). 863.4441 &

## 34 FUZIO

★★$$ The first of a new chain to take pastas from around the globe and put them in one yummy restaurant. Casual and friendly, the crowd is as cute as the food is good. The firecracker pork fusilli is spicy hot and the Chinese chicken salad is cool and fresh. The full bar and very affordable prices keep the boys and girls waiting in line, so have a drink and enjoy the sights. ♦ M-Th, Su 11AM–10PM; F-Sa 11AM–11PM. 469 Castro St (at 18th St). 863.1400 &

## 34 A DIFFERENT LIGHT

♂
♀ The warm and welcoming local branch of America's largest gay and lesbian bookseller is a must-visit. The latest in fiction, nonfiction, poetry, self-help, magazines, cards, videos, music, and (of course) erotica are stocked here. Gay, lesbian, and transgender authors give regular readings as well. Karen Bornstein, Quentin Crisp, Eileen Myles, and Robert Tiard are just a few such and scribblers. ♦ Daily 10AM–midnight. 489 Castro St (at 18th St). 431.0891, 800/343.4002 &

## 35 CASTRO COUNTRY CLUB

♂ A popular alternative to the bar scene (especially for nondrinkers), this mostly male place charges a nominal cover for a whole day's access to a friendly, relaxed space reminiscent of a family room. You'll find screened movies, comfy lounging areas, occasional art openings, and even a sundeck. The crowd on the front steps on weekends is deliciously cruisy. ♦ Cover. M-Th, Su 11AM–11PM; F-Sa 11AM–midnight. 4058 18th St (between Hartford and Castro Sts). 552.6102

## 36 THE EDGE

♂ A kind of disco lounge in the Twilight Zone, this dance palace seems stuck in the 1970s with its black walls, chrome, and mustachioed clones heavy on denim and leather. Mostly the guys boogie and cruise (each other, or the passing flesh on 18th Street through the window). ♦ Daily noon–2AM. 4149 18th St (between Castro and Collingwood Sts). 863.4027 &

## 37 HARVEY'S

♂
♀ ★$ Local cops trashed this longtime gay gathering spot, known back in 1979 as the **Elephant Walk,** in response to the "White Nights" riots at **City Hall** (provoked by the light sentence meted out to Harvey Milk's assassin). Today the place has turned into a sort of homo Hard Rock Cafe, what with an eclectic and growing collection of homosexual memorabilia that includes items having to do with Liberace, Sylvester, Greg Louganis, the Lady Bunny, José Sarria, Agnes Moorehead, Barbara Stanwyck, Harvey Milk, and many, many others. The fare is simple, running toward burgers, pasta, and salads, but the real star at brunch is "Eggs Harvey," poached and served with spinach and herb gravy on a sun-dried–tomato focaccia. The bar attracts a nice mix of locals and tourists, and the martinis are some of the best (and biggest) in town. ♦ American ♦ Restaurant: daily brunch and dinner. Bar: daily 11AM–2AM. 500 Castro St (at 18th St). 431.4278 &

## 37 BADLANDS

♂ One of the most popular bars in the Castro attracts a motley bunch of twenty- to fortysomething guys, most of whom just stand around and stare. Truth to tell, it's quantity and not quality that you'll find here, though a 60-foot bar, hundreds of license plates on the walls, and the mean drinks poured by the butch, friendly bartenders do give the place a special edge. The hi-energy tunes (spun periodically by live DJs) are some of the best around, though oldies (and rock-bottom beer specials) on Sunday draw a major crowd. ♦ M-F 11:30AM–2AM; Sa-Su 11AM–2AM. 4121 18th St (between Castro and Collingwood Sts). 626.9320

## 38 JAGUAR

♂
♀ The staff at this erotic emporium is so eager to please that they've been known to demonstrate the use of cockrings and nipple clamps. Whether or not you opt for such personal attention, it's fun (and sometimes educational) to browse for sex supplies, gift items, cards, magazines, and novelties. ♦ M-Th; F-Sa 10AM–midnight; Su 10AM–11PM. 4057 18th St (between Hartford and Castro Sts). 863.4777

---

**Restaurants/Clubs: Red | Hotels: Purple | Shops: Orange | Outdoors/Parks: Green | Sights/Culture: Blue**

## 38 THE MIDNIGHT SUN

♂ What's billed as the oldest gay video bar in the country (it was started in 1969) still packs in upwardly mobile queers in their twenties and thirties. With a galvanized metal exterior, high ceilings, huge projection screens, and a L-O-U-D sound system, the place can be cruisy enough; sometimes, though, the *Absolutely Fabulous*, *Barbarella*, and *Sound of Music* clips prove too distracting. Saturday comedy night is the most popular, and movie musical Tuesday doesn't do too badly, either. ♦ Daily noon–2AM. 4067 18th St (between Hartford and Castro Sts). 861.4186 ዼ

## 39 HOT 'N' HUNKY

★★$ Yet another chrome-and-tile burger joint, this one capitalizes on the gay clientele in both its name and interior appointments (pictures of Marilyn Monroe and such). Fans contend that it has the best burgers and shakes in town, and the jukebox is pretty good, too. ♦ American ♦ Daily lunch and dinner. 4039 18th St (between Noe and Hartford Sts). 621.6365. Also at: 1946 Market St (at Duboce Ave). 621.3622 ዼ

## 40 CAFFÈ LUNA PIENA

★★★$$ The garden at the casual, romantic "Full Moon Cafe" is a lovely place to dine

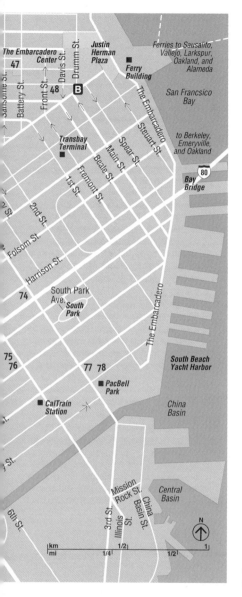

## 40 DOES YOUR FATHER KNOW?

♂ Hallmark could learn a thing or two from
♀ this shop, which mixes stuffed animals, calendars, greeting cards, and reasonably priced jewelry with erotic videos and anatomically correct dolls. ♦ M-Th 9:30AM–10PM; F-Sa 9:30AM–11PM; Su 10AM–9PM. 548 Castro St (between 19th and 18th Sts). 241.9865

## 41 DON'T PANIC!

♂ Like elsewhere, the local branch of the
♀ national gay chain specializes in clever and witty T-shirts. ♦ M-Th 10AM–10PM; F-Sa 10AM–11PM; Su 11AM–9PM. 541 Castro St (between 19th and 18th Sts). 553.8989

## 41 UNDERCOVER

♂ Of late this is *the* place to shop for clubbing
♀ rags in the Castro, with a totally cool lineup of shorts, shirts, and slacks, as well as dainty underthings. The shop also carries a selection of fabulous fake furs, along with such designer accessories as belts, bracelets, earrings, and sunglasses. ♦ M-Sa 11AM–8PM; Su 11AM–7PM. 531 Castro St (between 19th and 18th Sts). 864.0505

## 41 PATIO CAFÉ

★$$ Located at the rear of a small shopping mall, this eatery features a brick-walled room that spills into a charming garden where patrons dine outdoors in fine weather. It's especially busy at brunchtime, when 15 omelettes and a half-dozen kinds of pancakes are featured. The "scene" and the cute waiters help make up for the uninspiring sandwiches, burgers, and generic American offerings (à la meat loaf and spaghetti) on the laundry-list menu. ♦ American ♦ Daily brunch and dinner. Reservations required for six or more. 531 Castro St (between 19th and 18th Sts). 621.4640

## 42 HARVEY MILK INSTITUTE

♂ This continuing ed program for the gay and
♀ lesbian community offers dozens of one- and two-day workshops focusing on a variety of relevant subjects. You might learn more about local gay lore from historian Trevor Hailey, study Drag 101 with the Sisters of Perpetual Indulgence, meet a funny guy in "Queer Stand-up Comedy," or even hook up with the outdoorsy dyke of your dreams in "Intro to Rock Climbing." Fees vary, but most are within the $45-$95 range. Locations of workshops are listed in the course catalog; call for a free copy or more info. ♦ 584 Castro St (between 19th and 18th Sts), Suite 451. 552.7200

alfresco, and is especially popular with brunchers. Apart from such morning favorites as the delicious oatmeal-almond French toast, there's a great selection of salads, sandwiches, and pastas, as well as imaginative entrées like sesame-encrusted catfish with lentil bean cake in a tomato coulis. The beer and wine list is superb. ♦ New American ♦ M brunch; Tu-Su brunch and dinner. Reservations recommended on weekends. 558 Castro St (between 19th and 18th Sts). 621.2566

## 43 MISSION DOLORES PARK

Just a short stroll from the Castro, this patch of green is the perfect place to sunbathe with the boys on a warm day while taking in a stunning view of the city skyline. Just watch out for the dope-pushing kids at the park entrance, and don't linger after dark. ♦ Bounded by Dolores and Church Sts, and 20th and 18th Sts

## 44 THE CINCH SALOON

A kitschy, pseudo-Southwestern decor combines with pool tables, computer games, a jukebox, and a large-screen TV to make this a comfortable neighborhood hangout. The staff and patrons (mostly in their thirties and forties) are very friendly, and the owners sponsor numerous benefits throughout the year in addition to the regular roster of events—beer busts, buffet nights, 49ers Sundays, pool tournaments, and holiday drag shows. ♦ Daily 6AM–2AM. 1723 Polk St (between Clay and Washington Sts). 776.4162 &

## 45 THE SWALLOW

One of San Francisco's few remaining piano bars is still a classy, popular pick for a friendly cast ranging from Gen-X to late Baby Boomer guys (and a few gals), who love to sit around the piano and along the long bar belting out Broadway and pop classics. They're accompanied by ivory ticklers who seem to know just about every song ever written. ♦ Daily 9PM–1AM. 1750 Polk St (between Clay and Washington Sts). 775.4152

## 46 CLUB FUGAZI

OK, so it's touristy and lowbrow, but Steve Silver's *Beach Blanket Babylon* is still lots o' campy fun and one production every visitor (especially every queer visitor) should see. Featuring the biggest hats, biggest hair, and most outlandish costumes you're likely to ever see on stage, this show has been wowing audiences for more than two decades and still going strong. No one under 21 is admitted except for the Sunday matinee. ♦ Admission. Daily. Reservations required three to four weeks in advance. 678 Green St (between Stockton and Powell Sts). 421.4222 &

## 47 PARK HYATT HOTEL

$$$$ This 360-room hotel in the downtown financial district is way up on the list of best (and gay-friendliest) places to stay in the city, especially if you're in town on business and need such standard extras as two phones and 24-hour room service. Two Mercedes are also available to shuttle you through the downtown area, and the hotel offers a full business center and 14 meeting rooms. Afternoon tea and caviar are served in the lobby lounge; the lobby bar features a pianist nightly from 6:30–10PM, and the elegant, woody Park Grill restaurant is open for breakfast, lunch, and dinner. ♦ 333 Battery St (between Sacramento and Commercial Sts). 392.1234, 800/233.1234; fax 421.4233 &

## 48 101 CALIFORNIA STREET

With the Bank of America building and the Transamerica Pyramid, this cylindrical structure co-designed by gay architect Philip Johnson is the third major landmark in the Financial District. Completed in 1983, its silvery reflective glass looks especially beautiful when seen from the bay at dusk. Although the lobby is rather ungainly, a sloping glass wall slicing across the 90-foot-tall columns makes a dramatic sight. The north-facing plaza on California Street is flanked by two mid-rise blocks cut on the diagonal. Inside, the sleek Atrium restaurant makes a sophisticated dining experience for lunch or dinner. ♦ At Davis St

## 49 N' TOUCH

Disco-era mirrors and flashing lights are big at this long, narrow dance bar popular with San Francisco's many young gay Asians and their admirers. Strippers are on hand several nights a week, and Tuesday's karaoke night is quite the thing. ♦ Daily 3PM–2AM. 1548 Polk St (between California and Sacramento Sts). 441.8413

## 50 KIMO'S

The perfect place to people watch on Polk (thanks to lots of windows), this place serves cocktails priced to sell—for breakfast, even. The upstairs bar is complemented by a dance floor and stage where strippers and dragsters do their thing. ♦ Daily 8AM–2AM. 1351 Polk St (at Pine St). 885.4535

## 51 QT II

*Saturday Night Fever* is stayin' alive in the disco lighting and mirrored wall tiles around the stage here, and there's always some kind of event to lure in the mature crowd, be it live weekend music acts, an amateur take-it-off contest, or the bevy of pro strippers that packs the place on Sunday evening. Or maybe it's just the hustlers plying their trade. ♦ Daily noon–2AM. 1312 Polk St (between Bush and Pine Sts). 885.1114 &

## 52 NOB HILL LAMBOURNE

$$$ Just three blocks from Union Square, this small, elegant, and gay-popular hotel combines graciousness with business-oriented extras in its 20 rooms—two-line phones, fax machines, even a personal computer. Decorated in contemporary or period styles, each room also has kitchen facilities, and the rate includes continental

breakfast and an afternoon wine reception. ♦ 725 Pine St (between Stockton and Powell Sts). 433.2287; 800/274.8466; fax 433.0975

## 53 HOTEL TRITON

$$$ Within striking distance of Union Square and Chinatown, the 140 smallish rooms here are stocked with playful and sophisticated modern furniture decorated in a pink-and-gold color scheme. This wacky hotel has a gay-friendly staff and hosts numerous gay and lesbian events throughout the year, including Wigstock West. It also works hard to make nice with the fashion and entertainment industry, so expect to see some glitzoids loitering about. There's no restaurant. ♦ 342 Grant Ave (between Sutter and Bush Sts). 394.0500, 800/433.6611; fax 394.0555 &

## 54 QUEEN ANNE HOTEL

$$ One of the city's most comfortable and unique hostelries had already had numerous lives when it was converted to a hotel in 1981—first as **Miss Mary Lake's School for Girls** in 1890, then as the **Cosmos** men's club, and finally as the Episcopal **Girls Friendly Society Lodge.** Today, each of the 49 rooms and suites are individually designed and furnished with antiques; eight have wood-burning fireplaces, and one has two. Complimentary continental breakfast is included, as are afternoon tea, sherry, and cookies. ♦ 1590 Sutter St (at Octavia St). 441.2828, 800/227.3970; fax 775.5212

## 55 POLK STREET

The stretch between Geary and California Streets known as "Polk Gulch" was the focus of the city's gay population until most of the action moved to the Castro district. Currently, that portion of Polk is in transition, populated by drifters and young male hustlers, and much of the glitz of the 1970s has been lost to shops whose wares are in questionable taste. North of California Street it gets better, with a mix of old neighborhood food stores, antiques shops, bookstores, restaurants, and charming specialty shops. ♦ Between Geary and Lombard Sts

## 55 GIRAFFE VIDEO LOUNGE

♂ This video and dance bar is the biggest gay nightspot in the Polk, drawing a mixed bag of boys (scruffies, guppies, and a few heteros) from 20 to 50. Music vids are everywhere (along with some giraffe-themed odds and ends), and there's plenty of seating for hanging out over cocktails while drag

DJ Charlene Dubois plays current dance hits. ♦ Daily 8AM–2AM. 1131 Polk St (between Post and Sutter Sts). 474.1702

## 56 MOTHERLODE

♂ At this transvestite and transgender bar in the roughish Tenderloin district, the thirtysomething-and-up gents don't seem to mind the high-priced drinks, pounding house music, or snotty staff attitude, just so long as they can vie for the attention of the "ladies" who make their living here. The new faux-classy space is small, but a nice contrast to the seedy neighborhood. ♦ Daily 6AM–2AM. 1002 Post St (at Larkin St). 928.6006

## 57 DOTTIE'S TRUE BLUE CAFÉ

★★★$ Breakfast just doesn't get much better than the freshly baked breads, scones, and muffins at this beloved spot— and the fresh poached eggs with corned beef is the best in town at this place that looks like a 1940s diner. The gay owners who recently took it over have increased the vegetarian offerings, especially at lunch; try the black-bean chili, the vegetable tarts, or the scrumptious roasted eggplant sandwich with goat cheese and tomatoes. ♦ American ♦ M, W-F breakfast and lunch; Sa-Su brunch. 522 Jones St (between O'Farrell and Geary Sts). 885.2767 &

## 58 THE PRESCOTT HOTEL

♂
♀ $$$ Close to Union Square, this 166-room hotel boasts an Edwardian decor in deep jewel tones and a first-rate, friendly staff. The guest rooms, however, are smallish, but offer such amenities as mini-bars, hair dryers, and terry-cloth robes, and complimentary wine, hors d'oeuvres, coffee, and tea are served. Best of all, guests will have better luck than ordinary mortals getting a table at **Postrio,** Wolfgang Puck's exciting on-premises restaurant (which also does room service). ♦ 545 Post St (between Mason and Taylor Sts). 563.0303, 800/283.7322; fax 563.6831 &

## 59 NEIMAN MARCUS

Give in to those base shopping urges while taking in the work of gay architect **Philip Johnson,** who designed this controversial structure built on the corner of Union Square in 1982. The only remnant of the turn-of-the-century **City of Paris** store that occupied the site is an enormous glass dome, incorporated as part of the **Rotunda** restaurant. At Yuletide, the store erects the most dramatic Christmas tree in the city. ♦ M-Sa; Su noon–6PM. 150 Stockton St (at Geary St). 362.3900 &

---

Restaurants/Clubs: Red | Hotels: Purple | Shops: Orange | Outdoors/Parks: Green | Sights/Culture: Blue

## 60 CENTER FOR THE ARTS

The gay and lesbian communities are well represented at this 55,000-square-foot contemporary arts center, part of the beautiful **Yerba Buena Gardens** complex. To date, the exciting array of exhibitions, screenings, and performances has featured a variety of artists, from **Pomo Afro Homos** to the **Stephen Petronio** dance company and the **San Francisco Gay Men's Chorus.** ♦ 701 Mission St (at Third St). Program information 978.2787

## 61 SAN FRANCISCO MUSEUM OF MODERN ART (SFMOMA)

In January 1995, in celebration of its 60th year, the museum relocated its collection from the **Veteran's Building** in the **Civic Center** to new, larger quarters across from **Yerba Buena Gardens.** Its handsome brick box home was designed by the internationally acclaimed Swiss architect **Mario Botta** and features a 125-foot cylindrical skylight that channels light down to the first-floor atrium court. More than 17,000 works are housed on the museum's four floors; such queer and bisexual artists as Georgia O'Keeffe, Larry Rivers, Frida Kahlo, Jasper Johns, Robert Mapplethorpe, Andy Warhol, and Duane Michaels are represented in the permanent collection, along with the likes of Picasso, Matisse, Kandinsky, Calder, and Noguchi. And don't miss Jeff Koons's exquisitely campy statue *Michael Jackson and Bubbles.* ♦ Admission; free first Tuesday of the month; half-price Thursday evening. M-Tu, F-Su 11AM–6PM; Th 11AM–9PM. Tours daily. 151 Third St (at Minna St). 357.4000

## 62 THE PHOENIX HOTEL

$$ A one-acre oasis of respectability in a downscale neighborhood, this gay-owned 44-room inn feels much like a resort. It has a pool, garden, and outdoor cafe; massage and other spa services are also available on site. Popular with artsy and celebrity types, the place has hosted the likes of Linda Ronstadt, Faye Dunaway, Ziggy Marley, and the late JFK Jr. The rooms feature the works of Bay Area artists, and there's a hot new lounge for afternoon and evening cocktails. On-site parking and continental breakfast are included. ♦ 601 Eddy St (at Larkin St). 776.1380, 800/248.9466; fax 885.3109 ও

## 63 ABIGAIL HOTEL

$$ Built in 1926 to house members of visiting theater groups, this gay-owned six-story hotel was remodeled in 1990 in an arty European style. Gone are the grinning moose head and the family of stuffed elk; now there's a cozy, British feeling, complete with antiques, down comforters, and turn-of-the-century English art. While still not quite luxurious, the 61-room hotel is a good value and conveniently located to many cultural attractions and performance venues, including **Louise M. Davies Symphony Hall** and the **War Memorial Opera House.** Included is daily continental breakfast in the hotel's **Millennium** restaurant, which also happens to boast one of the finer organic vegetarian menus in the city. ♦ 246 McAllister St (between Hyde and Larkin Sts). 861.9728, 800/243.6510; fax 861.5848

## 64 MAD MAGDA'S ♂♀ RUSSIAN TEA ROOM

★★$ This comfy, eccentric gay-owned cafe in Hayes Valley features a variety of soups, salads, and specialty treats such as a fresh mint lemonade. It's great for meeting a friend for lunch or just dropping in for coffee or a glass of Cabernet. Homo photo exhibitions and regular performances are also on the menu, along with tarot card and tea readings indoors or on the warm-weather patio. ♦ Tearoom ♦ M-Tu 8AM–9PM; W-F 8AM–midnight; Sa 9AM–midnight; Su 9AM–7PM. 579 Hayes St (between Octavia and Laguna Sts). 864.7654 ও

## 65 SAN FRANCISCO PERFORMING ARTS LIBRARY & MUSEUM (PALM)

With a gallery and collection focusing on the Bay Area, this nonprofit institution naturally has works by a bushel of theater queens, including Leonard Bernstein, Jerry Herman, Cole Porter, and Lorenz Hart. Make an appointment to view videos or listen to recordings. ♦ Free. W 1–7PM; Th-F 11AM–5PM; Sa noon–5PM. 401 Van Ness Ave., Fourth floor (by the Opera House). 255.4800; fax 225.1913 ও

## 66 JAMES C. HORMEL ♂♀ GAY AND LESBIAN CENTER

Located in a wood-paneled circular room in the seven-story **San Francisco Public Library** (known to locals as "New Main"), this center is a landmark in homosexual history: It is the first facility of its kind in the world to be housed in a public institution. Named for its single largest benefactor, a member of the Hormel meatpacking dynasty (and controversial ambassadorial nominee—still waiting, at press time, for confirmation after two years), the center is dedicated to research on gay and lesbian culture. Highlights of the collection include material from filmmakers Rob Epstein and Peter Adair, journalist Randy Shilts, pioneering lesbian publishers Barbara Grier and Donna McBride of Naiad Press, and of course the personal papers and memorabilia of martyred San Francisco supervisor Harvey Milk. A dramatic 22-foot trompe-l'oeil ceiling mural by Charley Brown and Mark Evans, *Into the Light,* depicts gays and lesbians and the names of famous homos throughout history. ♦ M, F-Sa; Tu-Th 9AM–8PM; Su noon–5PM. 100 Larkin St (at Grove St), Third floor. 557.4400

## 67 THE NEW CONSERVATORY THEATRE CENTER

This theater school and performing arts complex offers professional classes and productions. In addition to classrooms and rehearsal spaces, the center has three theaters and an art gallery featuring paintings, sculptures, and photographs in exhibitions that change quarterly. It's also home to the "Pride Season," a subscriber-based gay and lesbian performance program that has included the world premiere of the all-gay version of Jack Heifner's *Vanities,* a revival of John Herbert's 1967 classic *Fortune and Men's Eyes,* and Helen Eisenbach's *Lesbianism Made Easy.* ♦ Exhibits: Tu-Sa noon–7PM. 25 Van Ness Ave (between Oak and Fell Sts). 861.8972

## 68 CoCo CLUB

♀ This intimate basement space with redbrick walls, black ceilings, and a small stage puts on a variety of popular lesbo-soirees; be sure to come early if you want to get a seat. The "Speakeasy" CoCo Club (formerly "Comme Nous") on Saturday brings on performers from 9PM to midnight, and on the last Friday of the month the ever-intriguing "In Bed With Fairy Butch" features entertainment ranging from erotic readings and performance art to a side-splitting dyke dating game. Afterwards, there's great dancing to some of the best music around. ♦ Cover. F-Sa 8PM–2AM. Closed first Friday of the month. 139 Eighth St (at Minna St). 626.2337

## 69 STORMY LEATHER

♀ Women into the bondage or the fetish look will groove on the well-made and elegant leather, rubber, and plastic goodies at this woman-owned boutique. Other accessories include handcuffs, whips, and such items from the toy chest, and there's a good selection of books, magazines, and greeting cards as well. ♦ M-Sa noon–7PM; Su 2–6PM. 1158 Howard St (between Seventh and Eighth Sts). 626.1672

## 70 HOLE IN THE WALL

♂ Billing itself as a "nasty little biker bar," this place certainly acts the part, with chains and barbed-wire sculptures hanging from the ceiling, and spontaneous sexual combustion in dark corners. Hippies, bikers, drag queens, and leathermen meet here to play pool, pinball, or talk to their demons in private. The music ranges from industrial trance to punk to acid rock. Avoid the weekend lines; you can get just as good a taste of the place during the week. ♦ M, F-Su 6AM–2AM; Tu-Th noon–2AM. 289 Eighth St (between Folsom St and Clementina Alley). 431.4695

## 71 RAWHIDE II

♂
♀ The huge dance floor at this popular country and western spot is usually packed with two-steppers and a fiercely loyal following of dudes mostly in their thirties and forties. The animal heads staring out from the walls are supposed to create a "down-home" kind of feel, but they're actually rather creepy. Two-stepping and line dance lessons are offered Tuesday through Friday. ♦ Cover F-Su. M-Th 4PM–2AM; F-Sa noon–2AM; Su 1PM–2AM. 280 Seventh St (at Folsom St). 621.1197

## 72 ENDUP

♂
♀ Make your disco nap a good one, because weekends are wild at this club, what with great music and high energy. "Fag Fridays" feature deep house and tribal tunes, and the all-day Sunday tea dance really packs them in both indoors and out on the relaxing patio. In between, Saturday's "Girl Spot" is the dyke dance event of the week. ♦ Cover. F 10:30PM–5:30AM; Sa 8PM–2AM; Su 6AM–9PM. 401 Sixth St (at Harrison St). 487.6277, 263.4850; Girl Spot 337.4962

## 73 BLOW BUDDIES

♂ Until San Francisco rescinds its ban on bathhouses, this safe-sex club for the orally fixated is one of the few such venues in town. To the beat of trancelike music, the premises offer plenty of dark corners, a lounge, open-air backyard, and a range of men in all ages, shapes, and sizes. The best turnout is on Friday, Saturday, and Sunday. Bring an ID for admission. ♦ Cover. Th 8PM–4AM; F-Sa 9PM–6AM; Su 6PM–2:30AM. 933 Harrison St (between Fifth and Sixth Sts). 863.4323

## 74 THE BOX

DJ Page Hodel spins the hottest funk, soul, and hi-energy dance grooves for a Gen-X crowd every Thursday at one of the city's top dance venues. Going strong since 1989, the secret to its success is an exceptional mix of people of every sexual persuasion, race, color, and hairdo who come here to do one thing: shake their boo-tays. Upstairs there's a bar and lounge area with balconies for scoping out the main dance floor, while downstairs,

---

Restaurants/Clubs: **Red** | Hotels: **Purple** | Shops: **Orange** | Outdoors/Parks: **Green** | Sights/Culture: **Blue**

a smaller (and often packed) dance floor plays funk, soul, and hip-hop. ◆ Cover. Th 9PM–2AM. 715 Harrison St (between Third and Fourth Sts).

## 75 BRINCA AT THE TROCADERO

♂ *Brinca* means "jump" in Spanish, and the *machos* at this lively Saturday-night Latin dance club for guys 18 and older *brincan mucho,* to an upbeat mix of Latin and house music. All the while, hot go-go *muchachos* shake it in huge cages above the large dance floor. ◆ Cover. Sa 10PM–3AM. 520 Fourth St (between Brannan and Bryant Sts). 227.4622

## 76 BIZOU

★★★$$ In a romantic, old-fashioned, and gay-popular SoMa bistro with glazed walls the color of mustard, Loretta Keller prepares such favorites as tempura-fried green beans, Catalan shrimp, and fresh grilled sardines. The slow-simmered and gently baked dishes are just the thing on a foggy day. Desserts are memorable, especially the summer berry pudding, with its dense, moist cakey texture and plenty of fruit. ◆ French ◆ M-F lunch and dinner. Reservations recommended. 598 Fourth St (at Brannan St). 543.2222

## 77 CLUB TOWNSEND

♂♀ Some of the hottest gay and lesbian dance happenings in town take place at this massive but user-friendly venue. Saturday night's "Club Universe" is still the ne plus ultra of the San Francisco gay dance experience, with hundreds of young bare-chested dudes, hot chicks, and go-go dancers writhing until dawn to hi-energy house decibels on one of the top sound and light systems in the world. On special occasions big-name recording artists work the crowd into a major frenzy. "Club Q," held the first Friday of each month, is widely considered to be the best and biggest dance party for women in San Francisco, drawing a sea of sapphic sisters of all ages, colors, and backgrounds. On Sunday, the "Pleasuredome" is popular for its tea dance that rocks until dawn's early light; the music is a mix of hi-energy dance, techno, and house—sometimes throwing in some old Donna Summer and Gloria Gaynor on "Disco Inferno" nights. After all that, the expansive lounge apart from the dance floor is a welcome sight indeed to catch your breath. ◆ Cover. Club Q: F 9PM–3AM. Club Universe: Sa 9PM–7AM. Pleasuredome: Su 8PM–6AM. 177 Townsend St (at Third St). 985.5241; Pleasuredome 985.5256

## 78 ASIA

♂ This twice-monthly dance blowout for young Asian guys and those who dig them, at the otherwise mixed dance club **King Street Garage,** can be mind-blowing for its intense energy. Go-go boys and giant Chinese dragons projected onto the walls add atmosphere, but of course it's really all about the multitude of hot twentysomethings who come here to party their butts off. ◆ Cover. Second and fourth F of the month 10PM–5AM. 174 King St (between Second and Third Sts). 974.6020, 285.2742

## 79 PIAF'S RESTAURANT & CABARET

★★★$$$ Edith would be proud to have her name on this popular cabaret dinner spot. The French food is delicious, the atmosphere is charming, and the crowd is cute. Live cabaret every night includes a diverse group of performers from drag queens to singing divas, all sure to make your roast quail over frisée followed by almond-crusted halibut fillet with sautéed spinach and fennel mashed potatoes taste better. Musicians tickle the ivories every night as happy eaters and drinkers at the full bar enjoy partaking of Paris and Piaf. ◆ French ◆ Tu-Sa dinner; Su brunch and dinner. 1686 Market St (at Gough St). 864.3700 &

## 79 ZUNI RESTAURANT & BAR

★★$$$ Although the original menu of this dining spot featured Southwestern fare (hence the name), this multilevel contemporary restaurant with floor-to-ceiling windows now offers a Mediterranean style of cooking. Chef and co-owner Judy Rogers offers Malaspina oysters from British Columbia that can be washed down with a frosty espresso granita, followed by roast chicken with bread salad (bread and greens in a Champagne vinaigrette). Or try one of the pizzas baked in the brick oven. The place usually attracts hordes of great-looking men and women of every sexual orientation. ◆ Californian/Mediterranean ◆ Tu-Su lunch and dinner. Reservations recommended. 1658 Market St (between Franklin and Haight Sts). 552.2522 &

## 80 ALFRED SCHILLING

★★★★$$$ This restaurant's great food is also a work of art that draws a loyal queer following. Chef Schilling prepares dishes using only organic produce and the freshest fish, chicken, and pasta from his open kitchen which, surrounded by high ceilings, gives the restaurant a feeling of a culinary performance space. Start off with prawn soup flavored with Cognac or tuna carpaccio with balsamic vinegar syrup and Indian salad. The salmon burger, served on a lemon brioche with a slice of fresh pineapple and paprika aioli, is heaven sent, as is the rabbit with mustard sauce, sautéed spinach, and new potatoes. For the sweet of tooth, don't miss the wonderful array of pastries made right on the premises (Schilling is also one of the city's premier chocolate makers). Oenophiles will be delighted with the wine selection specializing in California wine boutiques. The tastefully off-the-wall decor has been described as "Egyptian brothel." ♦ New American ♦ M lunch; Tu-Sa lunch and dinner. 1695 Market St (at Gough St). 431.8447 &

## 81 Carta

★★★$$ The look of the French countryside enhances this newly renovated bar and dining room that's famed for its innovative cuisine. The menu focuses on a different country every other month—Brittany, Tuscany, Turkey, India, the Caribbean, and Brazil, among others—and dinner always includes twelve small dishes and four large dishes. January and August feature "best of the year" for the complete month. The desserts are exceptional, and the wines are specially chosen to complement the courses. A couple of outside tables make for a truly delightful experience in fair weather. ♦ International ♦ Tu-Sa lunch and dinner; Su brunch and dinner. 1772 Market St (at Octavia St). 863.3516 &

## 82 Martuni's

Show-tune maniacs will get a kick out of this friendly, charming spot which draws a cast of characters who make the rounds of piano bars, getting progressively drunk and braying along to their pop Broadway favorites. The lighting's soft, the staff friendly, and the crowd in the front bar a nice mix of pretty guppies, lipstick lezzes, and older gents. At times, though, the music from the cabaret room in back can be just a tad intrusive. ♦ Daily 2PM–2AM. 4 Valencia St (at Market St). 241.0205 &

## 83 The Stud

♂♀ Rock, funk, oldies, new wave, and world-beat music draw a big crowd to this funky hangout. The owner and sexy bartender Michael has turned the space into a fun party place for the cute, mixed clientele of men and women. Tuesday night's "Tranny Shack." Stud is an over-the-top drag show hosted by the hilarious Heklina. Many consider it the "trashiest" club night in town, with a mix of disco, drag, and dance tunes. Saturday night's "Sugar" Stud turns the small space into a hot, positive-energy dance club that stays pounding until four in the morning. The 20- to 30ish hip crowd is a great mix of gays and lesbians, and the music is cutting-edge fun. Life is sweet. ♦ Cover some nights. M-F, Su 5PM–2AM; Sa 5PM–4AM. 399 Ninth Street (at Harrison St). 252.7833

## 84 Red Dora's Bearded Lady Cafe and Truck Stop

♀ ★$ Part gallery, part performance space, part eatery, and all lesbian, the smoke- and booze-free atmosphere here is fun and laid back. Entertainment runs the gamut from open-mike nights to underground cabaret mix of musicians to readings by such writers as Jewelle Gomez and Kris Kovick. The gallery features monthly exhibits of paintings, photos, and other works by local lesbians and gays. The cafe serves delicious vegetarian treats from tofu burgers to pastries, along with coffee, tea, and soft drinks. The free movie nights are always fun, but space is limited, so get here early. ♦ Vegetarian/Cafe ♦ M-F 7AM–7PM; Sa-Su. No credit cards accepted. 485 14th St (at Guerrero St). 626.2805

## 85 San Francisco Eagle

♂ One of the best, and best-known, leather bars in the country, this grizzled old bird's been roping in a butch but friendly herd since 1972. The thirty- and fortysomethings can get frisky in this large, comfortable space complemented by a huge covered patio and a leather shop, but they generally do their acting out elsewhere. The Sunday afternoon beer bust is a major crowd-pleaser. ♦ M-F 4PM–2AM; Sa-Su noon–2AM. 398 12th St (at Harrison St). 626.0880 &

## 86 Gold's Gym

♂♀ This is the largest and most popular gym in San Francisco for gays and lesbians, and their straight friends. The huge space has any equipment you could possibly hope for and classes throughout the day. It's cruisy all the time, but the large facility allows you to escape predators easily if you're looking for a serious workout. Changing rooms are complete with showers, steam rooms, and dry saunas but lockers fill up fast after work hours, when it gets very crowded. A small cafe in the front has light, healthy meals and power drinks for gym boys on the run. ♦ Admission. M-Th 5AM–12PM; F 5AM–11PM; Sa 7AM–9PM; Su 8AM–8PM. 1001 Brannan (at 9th St). 552.4653

---

**Restaurants/Clubs: Red | Hotels: Purple | Shops: Orange | Outdoors/Parks: Green | Sights/Culture: Blue**

# ARCHITECTURE TOURS

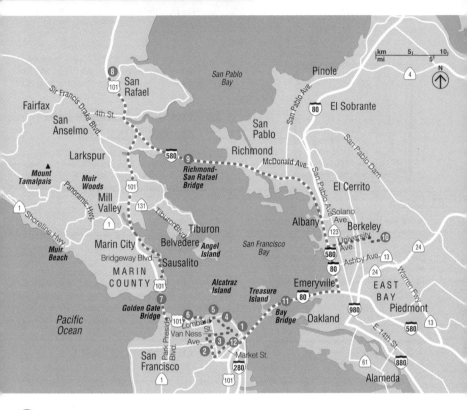

**S**an Francisco is a haven for both Victorian architecture (including the "Painted Ladies"–Queen Anne houses with elaborate ornament highlighted in bright colors) and pioneering Modern and Post-Modern structures, built after the 1906 earthquake and fire devastated the city.

## Bay Area Architectural Blitz

Before embarking on this driving tour of the Bay Area's architectural highlights, review a commercial road map of the area and familiarize yourself with the following directions. Plan on parking the car at some points so you can really admire the buildings.

This tour begins at the (1) **Ferry Building,** at the foot of **Market Street,** designed by architect **Arthur Page Brown** in 1894. Modeled after the Cathedral Tower in Seville, Spain, this building was for many years the tallest in San Francisco. Drive down Market past the (1) **Hyatt Regency Hotel,** a distinct component of the San Francisco skyline designed by **John Portman and Associates** in 1973, and the (1) **Crown Zellerbach Building,** a 1959 design by **Hertzka and Knowles** and **Skidmore, Owings & Merrill** set back from the street at **Battery.** Make a "soft" right onto **Sutter Street** to see the **Citicorp**

**Building,** a 1984 **William Pereira and Associates** design, with its lovely atrium. At **1 Sutter** (on your left) is the **Crocker Galleria,** a three-level, glass-barrel-vaulted shopping arcade modeled after Milan's vast Galleria Vittorio Emanuele, and on your right is the **Hallidie Building,** designed by **Willis Polk and Company** in 1917, which purports to have the world's first curtain-wall glass facade. Take a left at **Stockton Street,** and turn right on Market. Continue to **McAllister Street** and bear right to the (2) **Civic Center,** acclaimed as the most magnificent assortment of Beaux Arts buildings in the US. There you will see **City Hall,** the main part of the complex, designed in 1915 by **Bakewell and Brown; Louise M. Davies Symphony Hall,** designed by **Skidmore, Owings & Merrill,** which first opened in September 1980 and was remodeled in 1992; the glorious and opulent **Opera House,** which opened on 15 October 1932; and the **Veteran's Building,** former home of the **San Francisco Museum of Modern Art,** also by **Bakewell and Brown.** Turn right on **Franklin Street** and left on **Geary** until you reach **(2) St. Mary's Cathedral at Gough Street.** Continue to **Laguna Street,** make a right, then right again on **California Street.** Continue across **Van Ness** and up **Nob Hill** to Jones Street, where Lewis P. Hobart's **(3) Grace Cathedral** is located. This lovely Neo-Gothic church was modeled after Notre Dame in Paris. Head on to **Mason Street** to see the city's most illustrious hotels: the **(3) Mark Hopkins Inter-Continental** (familiarly known as "The Mark"), best known for **Timothy Pflueger**'s **Top of the Mark** cocktail lounge with its panoramic vista of the bay and the city's hills, and the **Fairmont,** which opened in 1907 in celebration of the city's renaissance one year after the earthquake. Continue downhill on California to the **Financial District.** At **Kearny Street** view the **(3) Bank of America World Headquarters,** a 1969 structure by **Wurster, Bernardi & Emmons Inc.** and **Skidmore, Owings & Merrill,** with **Pietro Belluschi** as design consultant, with its dark-red marble facade that changes colors with the time of day. Turn left on **Sansome Street** and left on **Washington** past the **(3) Transamerica Pyramid,** designed in 1972 by **William Pereira and Associates,** which has become a landmark because of its singular form and position at the end of **Columbus Avenue.** Take Columbus Avenue toward North Beach—en route notice the Art Deco-ish **(4) Coit Tower** on top of **Telegraph Hill,** and turn left on **North Point Street** until you reach **(5) Ghirardelli Square,** the converted chocolate factory that is now a shopping complex. The transformation was done by **Wurster, Bernardi & Emmons Inc.** and **Lawrence Halprin & Associates** from 1962 to 1967. Turn left on Van Ness, right on Bay, and head westward through the **Marina District to Marina Boulevard.** At **Lyon** and **Baker Streets** is **Bernard Maybeck**'s **(6) Palace of Fine Arts,** with its characteristic Roman rotunda with two curvilinear columns. Next, head north on **Highway 101,** across the **(7) Golden Gate Bridge** into Marin County. Take the **Alexander Avenue** exit, veer right, and drive through downtown **Sausalito** (note the private homes clinging to the

steep hillside). At the end of town, get back on Highway 101 north. You may want to make a side trip to **Tiburon** and **Belvedere,** where you'll see some of the most expensive housing in the country. Continue north on Highway 101 for 15 miles, past **San Rafael,** to the **North San Pedro** Road exit, to take a look at the **(8) Marin County Civic Center** by Frank Lloyd Wright, begun in 1957 (Wright died in 1959). Built atop the crests of three low hills, this was one of the American master's last efforts. Note the prevalence of the circle motif in the building's design, including the decorative grilles, pavements, and custom-designed furniture; be sure to walk up to the viewing deck next to the library. Then return south on Highway 101 through San Rafael and take the **I-580** exit. Drive across the **(9) Richmond-San Rafael Bridge;** look to the right and see **San Quentin** prison. Follow signs for **Oakland** through the industrial area along **Cutting** and **Hoffman** Boulevards, and join **I-80** at Albany. Exit at **University Avenue** and travel 11.5 miles east until you reach the **(10) University of California, Berkeley,** at **Oxford Street.** Turn right on Oxford and left on **Durant.** Park at the garage on Durant and **Telegraph Avenue** or on the street. On campus see the **(10) Campanile** (there's a great view of the Bay Area from the top) and the handsome granite-clad **(10) Mining and Metallurgy Building** of 1907 by **John G. Howard,** who designed many buildings and other structures on campus. Afterward, drive up Durant to **Piedmont** and take a look at the **(10) Sigma Phi** frat house, designed by famed Arts and Crafts architects, the brothers **Greene & Greene.** Most of the old mansions on this strip are fraternity or sorority houses. Turn left on Piedmont, left on Bancroft Way, and continue down University Avenue. Follow University to I-80/I-580 southbound for San Francisco. Return to the city via I-80 across the **(11) Bay Bridge** (toll). Then exit on **Fremont Street,** take a left onto **Howard Street,** and go past **(12) Yerba Buena Gardens,** which include the mostly underground **Moscone Convention Center** by **Hellmuth, Obata & Kassabaum,** and the **Center for the Arts Galleries and Forum** by **Fumihiko Maki** and **Center for the Arts Theater** by **James Stewart Polshek,** which opened in 1993.

## House Calls: San Francisco's Premier Estates

For a tour of some of the city's most notable residences, start at the top of **(1) Telegraph Hill,** and walk down the **Filbert Steps** on the east side. Some of the oldest houses in San Francisco are perched precariously on these steep slopes—notice the Carpenter Gothic style of many. Access to these homes is only by footpath and steps. Turn right on **(2) Powell Street,** where you will see a particularly fine row of Post-Modern houses on the west side of **(3) Vandewater Street,** a short alley between Powell and **Mason Streets,** half a block south of **Bay Street.** Note the condominiums by **Esherick, Homsey, Dodge & Davis,** at **No. 22; Donald MacDonald, No. 33;** and **Daniel Solomon, No. 55.** All three structures were built in 1981. Turn left onto

Mason Street, right onto **Francisco Street,** and continue across **Columbus Avenue** up **Russian Hill** to **Leavenworth Street.** Turn left here and cross **Union Street** to the corner of **(4) Green Street,** where you can see one of the best examples of 1930s-style apartment towers.

Continue on Leavenworth Street until **California Street,** turn right, and follow the cable-car tracks to **Van Ness Avenue;** cross Van Ness and continue to **Franklin Street.** Turn right and look for the superb Queen Anne-style **(5) Haas-Lilienthal House** at **2007** Franklin Street (tours are available) in affluent Pacific Heights, with many substantial dwellings on its slopes. From Franklin Street, turn left on

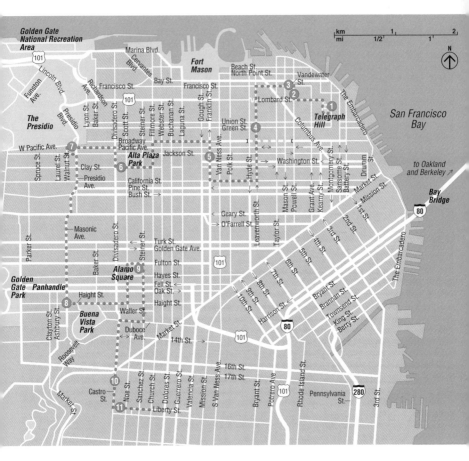

**Broadway.** You will pass a series of apartment towers and mansions as you approach **The Presidio,** and many fine Victorian houses on the surrounding streets. Take a left on **Fillmore Street,** then a right on (6) **Clay Street** to see the row of false-fronted Italianate houses between **Fillmore** and **Divisadero Streets** opposite **Alta Plaza Park.**

Now turn right on Divisadero Street, continue to the summit of the hill, and take a left at **Pacific Avenue.** The famous (7) **3200 Pacific** block between **Presidio Avenue** and **Walnut Street** boasts houses by **Bernard Maybeck, Ernest Coxhead, Willis Polk,** and others. Turn left on Walnut Street, left on **Jackson Street,** and right on Presidio Avenue, which zigzags and becomes **Masonic Avenue** (veer right when the road divides, or, if you miss the split, turn right onto **Geary Boulevard** and left onto Masonic Avenue). Cross the **Panhandle**

of Golden Gate Park to **Haight Street,** which runs through the (8) **Haight-Ashbury District,** with its many ornate late-Victorian houses, some painted in bright colors that emphasize their elaborate facades. Turn left onto **Haight Street** to **Scott Street,** turn left, and then right onto **Fulton Street** six blocks away, where you can see the group of identical 19th-century houses on the east side of (9) **Alamo Square.** Turn right onto **Steiner Street.** Head south to **Duboce Avenue** and take a right. Proceed to **Castro Street,** turn left, and then continue to **Market Street.** At Market and Castro is (10) **Castro Commons,** a condominium complex completed in 1982, designed by **Daniel Solomon & Associates.** A gridded wall separates the triangular courtyard from busy Market Street. Four blocks farther south along Castro Street at (11) **Liberty Street** is a good cross section of older San Francisco dwellings of various styles.

## THE BEST

### Kimberly Fishman
Group Coordinator/The Phoenix Hotel

It's hard not to have a good time in San Francisco. The architecture, landscape, weather, food, people, etc. are just great! Stop by **The Phoenix**

**Hotel** for their complimentary City Guide devised by their staff—full of great suggestions on all kinds of sights, sounds, and tastes of the city.

If you have a car, the best view of the city and the entire Bay Area is from **Mount Tamalpais** in **Marin County.** Only a 30-minute drive from downtown.

# DAY TRIPS

**B**eyond San Francisco's immediate boundaries are the thriving, vital cities of the **East Bay,** where the weather is often warmer and sunnier than in fog-covered San Francisco. **Berkeley,** across the **Bay Bridge** is home to the state's prestigious branch of the **University of California.** Oftentimes derisively called "Berserkley" by nonresidents and residents alike, it is a city with a political matrix that's frequently radical and either totally out of sync with the rest of the nation or on the cutting edge of political change. Also across the Bay Bridge is **Oakland,** a metropolis locked in a struggle to combat drugs and poverty--not to mention overcoming the ravages of 1991's devastating fire in the hills--and working hard to enlarge its position as a strong commercial and convention center.

In contrast, on the northern side of the **Golden Gate Bridge** are the softly undulating hills of mellow **Marin County.** Cross the bridge, and the first town you'll reach is **Sausalito,** a little gem of a place frequently compared to the hill towns on the Riviera. Once a fishing village, Sausalito is now an upscale community of suburbanites who enjoy their pretty hillside homes, abundant greenery, and quaint village atmosphere.

The prosperous **Peninsula** area to the south of San Francisco is home to **Stanford University,** one of California's finest private institutions of learning, and **Silicon Valley,** the center of the worldwide internet and computer industry. It is also home to many Bay Area millionaires, who have settled in such posh communities as **Hillsborough, Los Altos, Woodside,** and **Portola Valley.** One of the most magnificent mansions in the area, **Filoli,** with its superb gardens, is now a landmark open to the public.

About two and a half hours south of the city lies the magnificent **Monterey Peninsula,** home of the popular **Monterey Bay Aquarium,** the charming seaside village of **Carmel** (where Clint Eastwood was once mayor), and some of the most stunning coastal scenery in the world.

Finally, if you're a wine connoisseur, no trip to the Bay Area would be complete without a visit to **Napa** and **Sonoma** wine country. In addition to possessing some of the world's finest vineyards, the Napa and Sonoma areas are home to lovely inns, marvelous massage centers, idyllic scenery, and enough good restaurants to warrant a special trip. For a complete guide to this beautiful region, consult *ACCESS Wine Country California,* also from ACCESS Press.

AREA CODE 415 UNLESS OTHERWISE INDICATED.

## Marin County

Blessed with a sense of whimsy and an affluent, educated, and creative populace, Sausalito doesn't march in lockstep with most suburban communities. In the 1970s the town's mayor was Sally Stanford, who had retired to the bayside community after years of running San Francisco's premier bordellos, lending new meaning to the term "Madam Mayor." Stanford died in 1982.

To really savor the day, take a ferry ride to Sausalito, starting at San Francisco's **Ferry Building** (located at the foot of Market St and The Embarcadero call 923.2000) or at **Fisherman's Wharf** (for scheduling information, call 705.5555). You can also get there in a half-hour via **Golden Gate Transit** buses (923.2000) or by automobile across the Golden Gate Bridge. If you decide to drive, be aware that parking in Sausalito is usually difficult and the city's traffic cops are uncannily vigilant. Parking is likely to be easiest on the hilly streets.

When you've debarked from the ferry in Sausalito, walk left along the shoreline (called **Bridgeway Boulevard**), and drink in the bay views and glorious vistas of San Francisco. Right by the ferry pier, which is in the heart of downtown Sausalito, you'll see the

MARIN COUNTY

If you're feeling flush, have breakfast, or dinner at the

Burch's **Gallerié** at No. 539 (332.7764). The gallery, once a firehouse, is filled with Burch's work. (She's a local artist who is nationally known for her bright-colored jewelry and other accessories.)

Nearby is the convivial **Bar with No Name,** more popularly known as the **No-Name,** for the obvious reason; no sign identifies the place (757 Bridgeway Blvd, 332.1392). Sometimes there's live jazz, and invariably there's a local clientele swapping conversation around communal tables.

If you're feeling flush, have breakfast, or dinner at the **Casa Madrona** (801 Bridgeway Blvd, 331.5888), a delightful little hotel that meanders up the hillside where **Mikayla** offers a terrace for alfresco dining. The food is Californian/Asian.

Continue walking along Bridgeway Boulevard or hop aboard one of the buses that frequently makes its way along the street, checking first to see if it stops at the **Bay Model** (Marinship Way, off the east side of Bridgeway Blvd, 332.3871). Be sure to have plenty of change in your pocket—the buses require exact fare.

The **Bay Model** is a working model of the whole San Francisco Bay and the Delta region. It features interactive exhibits, self-guided tours, and a permanent exhibit of the World War II shipyard, "Marinship." It is open Tuesday through Sunday from Memorial Day to Labor Day; the rest of the year it's open Tuesday through Saturday. Arrangements for tours may be made for groups of 10 or more by calling in advance. Admission is free.

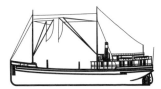

Docked near the **Bay Model** is the *Wapama* (pictured above), a steam-powered 1915 schooner that once hauled lumber and passengers. *Wapama* tours take place Saturday at 11AM; on Saturday at 12:30PM there's also a tour of the *Hercules,* a venerable old steam tub (free admission; children under 12 years of age are not permitted on the vessel tours).

Farther north along Bridgeway Boulevard is a community of floating homes (Sausalito doesn't like to call them houseboats). Turn onto **Gate 6 Road.** (If you end up on the freeway, you've gone too far.) The

small **Viña de Mar Park,** named for Sausalito's sister city in Chile. The park delights the eye with statues of elephants and a fountain that came from the Panama-Pacific Exposition of 1915. You may take a photo in front of the park, but you may not walk in. (It's been closed to the public for many years because it drew drug addicts and other unsavory characters.) For visitors with an extended agenda, stay at the **Hotel Sausalito** (16 El Portal at Bridgeway, 332.0700, 888/442.0700, www.hotel-sausalito.com.) a romantic French Riviera syle inn with 16 rooms and suites overlooking Vina del Mar Park. Or try the nearby **Inn Above Tide** (30 El Portal, 332.9535) which features sweeping views of the bay. Bridgeway Boulevard is still called **Old Town,** reflecting its status as a historic district where the first Portuguese fishers settled in the late 18th and early 19th centuries. Walk past **Scoma's** (588 Bridgeway Blvd, 332.9551), a popular seafood restaurant with a branch in San Francisco, and **Horizons,** right next door (331.3232), one of the best places in town to enjoy a drink on the deck. Stop if you're ravenous, but be forewarned that the view is often more satisfying than the meal. Upstairs from Horizons is a fine dining experience that can't be duplicated anywhere in the Bay Area. **Ondine** (558 Bridgeway, 331.1133), housed in a 1898 yacht club, is the new home of Chef Seiji Wakabayashi. He blends French, Californian and Asian cuisines for a healthy innovative dining experience. Enjoy the jewel-box view of the city. Just beyond the waterside restaurants, look out onto the bay and see if the seal sculpture by Bay Area artist Benny Bufano is visible (it pops out at low tide). Walk back along the side of the street with all the shops, some of them charming, some just selling touristy whatnots and junk. Take a short detour to explore the shops along **Princess Street.** If you feel energetic, keep on walking—Princess leads to the back streets, which are lined with lovely homes. If you get lost, just keep walking downhill and you'll eventually be back on Bridgeway, where you should pop in at Laurel

greatest concentration of homes can be seen at **Gates 5, 6,** and **6½.** Some are spacious, some are funky, some are exquisite little waterborne jewels. One even has a helipad (you'll find it on **Issaquah Dock,** at the very end). Issaquah Dock, at Gate 6, also has more serious gardeners than any of the other piers. Arguments continue to rage between those charged with protecting the bay and the "anchor-outs." those who live freely anchored out in the water on what in some cases appear to be floating junkyards. (Anchor-outs prefer to drop anchor in the bay rather than tie their boats to the docks.) Those who anchor out are generally a breed apart from those who tie their homes up at piers and pay to have their waste pumped. For years, city leaders have tried to roust the bohemian anchor-outs, and for years, the rebellious anchor-outs have successfully blocked those moves.

## Muir Woods, Mount Tamalpais, and Point Reyes

Muir Woods, on Shoreline Drive in **Mill Valley,** is a national monument located in the middle of **Mount Tamalpais State Park.** Both are open daily until sunset (Park Ranger Station, Pan-Toll, is at 801 Panoramic Hwy, Mill Valley; Muir Woods information 388.2595, Mount Tamalpais and ranger station 388.2070). Within the approximately 559 acres of redwoods are many trails, some paved and wheelchair-accessible.

Those who can stay for only a short time can see many of the highlights in one to two hours. Within Muir Woods are some of the tallest and oldest coast redwood trees in the state, and a stand of virgin redwoods. The oldest tree has been around for 1,100 years; the tallest is 257 feet high. This tranquil wonderland of proud, giant trees also includes **Redwood Creek,** where steelhead and salmon come to spawn and then die (there's no fishing). A **Visitors' Center,** built in the rustic 1930s style of cedar and stone, was deliberately designed to look inconspicuous. It's located at the park's main entrance, and includes a snack bar and gift shop.

Hardy types can hike from Muir Woods to the surrounding **Mount Tamalpais State Park.** "Mount Tam," as it's popularly known, rises majestically 2,221 feet above sea level. The park includes a variety of terrain, and is renowned for its sensational panoramic views on clear days and its abundance of colorful wildflowers during the springtime. There are many trails, suitable for hikers of all levels. The park is home to a variety of wildlife: herds of deer, many types of birds, some snakes (including the seldom-encountered rattlers), and the rarely seen bobcats and mountain lions.

There is no public transportation going into the woods or park, but among the companies that offer private tours to the redwoods are **A Day in Nature** (673.0548) and **Great Pacific** (626.4499), **Ocean View Hiking Tours** (383.4252). If you are driving from San Francisco, take **Highway 101** north across the Golden Gate Bridge and turn off at the **Stinson**

**Beach-Highway 1** exit. Follow the signs to the area's parking lots.

If hiking Mount Tam doesn't do you in, you might want to tackle some of the scenic trails a little farther north at the **Point Reyes National Seashore.**

There's backcountry camping, stables, a lighthouse on a spit of land that affords great whale watching in season (approximately January through May), and miles and miles of stunning unspoiled seashore.

If all this touring has given you an appetite, Marin boasts at least two outstanding restaurants: **The Lark Creek Inn** (234 Magnolia Ave, Larkspur, 924.7766), where owner/chef Bradley Ogden turns out magnificent American regional cuisine in a sublime country setting; and the informal, exuberant **Buckeye Roadhouse** (15 Shoreline Hwy, near Hwys 101 and 1, Mill Valley, 331.2600), run by the same team that owns the very popular **Fog City Diner** in San Francisco and **Mustards Grill** in Yountville.

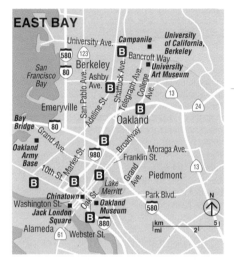

## University of California, Berkeley

Across the Bay Bridge in the bustling East Bay lies Berkeley, which manages to combine an East Coast intellectual energy with a Californian New Age consciousness. A city of ideas, both worthy and wacky, Berkeley rates a visit because of its outstanding university, restaurants, and cultural programs, as well as its quirky lifestyle. This is also the site of some of the Bay Area's best bookstores, including **Cody's** (2454 Telegraph Ave, at Haste St, 510/845.7852) and **Black Oak Books** (1491 Shattuck Ave, at Vine St, 510/486.0698).

The easiest way to reach Berkeley from San Francisco is by **BART** (510.465.BART) a half-hour ride from downtown. Get off at the **Berkeley** station and walk east for three blocks on Bancroft Way to reach the southern end of the campus. The **Visitor Information Center** is located in **University Hall, Room 101,** at University Avenue and Oxford Street. Free student-led campus tours, lasting approximately one and three-quarters hours, include the interior of the main library, a typical classroom, the interiors of most of the sports facilities, the exterior of the **University Art Museum,** and a typical 500-seat lecture hall. The tours are on Monday, Wednesday, and Friday at 10AM and 1PM, and occasionally on Saturdays (510/642.5215). Reservations are not necessary, but it's a good idea to confirm scheduled tours, as the campus closes between semesters and on holidays. There is a modest charge for the ride to the top of the Campanile (pictured), the campus tower that provides an aerial view of the Bay Area. To fully appreciate the intellectual energy that swirls around this campus, visit when classes are in session.

After the tour, go on to explore some of the campus offerings in greater depth. **The University Art Museum,** just off campus in a 1970 building designed by **Mario Ciampi,** has a good collection emphasizing 20th-century painting and sculpture. The museum is open Wednesday through Sunday; admission, free on Thursday 11AM to noon and 5 to 9PM (2626 Bancroft Way, 510/642.0808). Within the museum you'll find the **Pacific Film Archive,** a large movie library, and the **George Gund Theater,** which schedules a wide range of international films during the week (510/642.1124).

The university's **Phoebe Hearst Museum of Anthropology** is in **Kroeber Hall** (Bancroft Way and College Ave, 510/643.7648). Named after its principal benefactor, the museum focuses on cultural anthropology. A gift store sells ornaments, books, and ethnic arts and crafts. It is open daily; nominal admission; free Thursday.

The **Lawrence Hall of Science** (Centennial Dr, near Grizzly Peak Blvd, 510/642.5132) is a memorial to Ernest O. Lawrence, the first **University of California** professor to win a Nobel Prize (he won for physics in 1939). A favorite destination for visitors, the hall contains an interactive science museum, traveling science exhibitions, and a planetarium. Opened in 1968, it was designed by the San Francisco firm **Anshen and Allen** in an octagonal shape to represent the eight branches of physical science. Two levels of the building offer splendid views. If you have time, there's a 50-minute show in the planetarium. (Children under six are not admitted.) The hall is open daily; nominal admission. The planetarium's shows are on Saturday and Sunday at 1PM, 2:15PM, and 3:30PM; additional nominal admission.

The **University of California's Botanical Garden** is located in **Strawberry Canyon,** just above the stadium (510/642.3343). There are wonderful views of the bay from this site. Free tours take place Saturday and Sunday at 1:30PM and last about an hour. The garden is arranged according to the plants' geographical origins, and includes a redwood grove,

a large native-plants section, South African plants, Asian plants, and economic plants (those used for food, fiber, and medicine). Another area is dedicated to plants that eat insects, a desert and rain-forest house filled with orchids, cacti, and succulents, and a garden of rosebushes. There's a nice lawn for sun worshiping and tables for picnicking.

Just outside the university campus, on ever-popular **Telegraph Avenue,** the street scene is alive with street musicians, small shops, and food, jewelry, and clothing vendors (you can still buy top-quality tie-dyed T-shirts, pants, and undergarments here).

Seven blocks north of the campus is **Chez Panisse** (1517 Shattuck Ave, 510/548.5525), generally regarded as the birthplace of Californian cuisine and the training ground for many famous Bay Area chefs. Although some critics sniff that her place isn't what it used to be, celebrity owner/chef Alice Waters is determined to maintain her high standards and keep her menus fresh and original. Even if you don't care to splurge for the expensive prix-fixe meals downstairs, be sure to try the lighter meals—which include inventive pizzas and calzones—upstairs at the **Chez Panisse Cafe.** A few miles away is **Cafe Fanny** (Cedar and San Pablo Sts, 510/524.5447), another Alice Waters venture (it's named after her daughter), which offers breakfast at a stand-up counter or at benches outside.

## Oakland

Even though Gertrude Stein scathingly said of her hometown that "there is no there there," in fact, there is quite a bit here to see and enjoy. Oakland has a thriving port (it has taken substantial business away from the port of San Francisco), wonderful historic buildings, a restored **Old Town,** and charming residential neighborhoods.

The easiest way to get to Oakland is by **BART.** The ride is a mere 12 minutes from San Francisco's **Powell Street** station to the city center, where you'll get off at **12th Street and Broadway.** The restored **Old Oakland** area is on the right of Broadway, and Oakland's **Chinatown** (still unspoiled by tourism) sits on the left. Chinatown is dotted with restaurants, herbalists, and shops catering to the needs of daily life. In addition to the Chinese, the neighborhood is home to many other Asian immigrants, including Old Oakland, bounded by **8th and 10th Streets,** and **Broadway** and **Washington Streets,** is a historic Victorian neighborhood of structures dating from 1868 to 1881. The buildings have been restored and developed by architects **Storek & Storek** as a retail and office complex. The **Pro Arts Gallery** (461 Ninth St, 510/763.4361) features the work of Bay Area artists, and mounts exhibitions and major art events, including the famous Open Studios in June.

If you're thirsty, head for the **Pacific Coast Brewing Co.** (906 Washington St, between 9th and 10th Sts, 510/836.2739). The brewmasters will draw one of the specialty brews or any of the 19 other beers in stock while you relax, possibly over some pub grub or a game of darts. Another tempting possibility is the long-established **Gulf Coast Oyster Bar and Restaurant** (Eighth and Washington Sts, 510/836.3663), where you'll enjoy some of the tastiest Cajun meals to be found outside of Louisiana.

HEINOLD'S
FIRST & LAST CHANCE SALOON
*Since 1883*

On Oakland's waterfront is **Jack London Square,** a rather contrived but pleasant waterfront development, and, nearby, the **Jack London Village,** another touristy oasis, featuring several shops and a museum. Between the village and the square is Jack London's transplanted sod-roofed log cabin, where he once passed a Yukon winter, another attraction open to the public. One of the most authentic watering holes in the area is **Heinold's First and Last Chance Saloon** (56 Jack London Sq, 510/839.6761), a favorite hangout of the celebrated writer. At the dock is **Scott's Seafood Grill & Bar** (73 Jack London Sq, 510/444.3456), one of the outstanding seafood restaurants in the area. For earthier waterfront ambience, try the produce warehouse district, covering about 24 blocks east of the square and south of Broadway. The **FDR Pier** (Clay St and The Embarcadero) gives good views of working port operations, as do **Port View Park,** next to the **Seventh**

**Street Terminal,** and **Middle Harbor Park** (at Middle Harbor Rd).

Also worth a visit is the historic **Paramount Theater** (21st St and Broadway), a spectacular example of Art Deco architecture by **Timothy Pflueger.** Inside the movie palace, which has been converted to general entertainment use (conventions, symphonies, theater, ballet, classic movies, and such), there's a mind-blowing assemblage of gilt, silver railings, columns, and marble. Two-hour tours are offered the first and third Saturday of each month at 10AM, but not on holidays or when an activity is planned within the theater. No reservations are required. There is a small charge, and no children under age 10 are allowed. For more information, call 510/465.6400.

Definitely try to make room for a trip to **The Oakland Museum** (10th and Oak Sts, 510/238.2200), about a 15-minute walk from the **Paramount Theater.** Covering a four-block site, the multilevel building (see the plan below) with terraced gardens was designed by **Kevin Roche.** The structure incorporates galleries of ecology, history, and art, all of which emphasize California's diversity. The museum is open Wednesday through Sunday; donation.

Science buffs and stargazers are flocking to the new **Chabot Space & Science Center** (10000 Skyline Blvd, 510/530.3480, www.chabotspace.org) in the

## OAKLAND MUSEUM

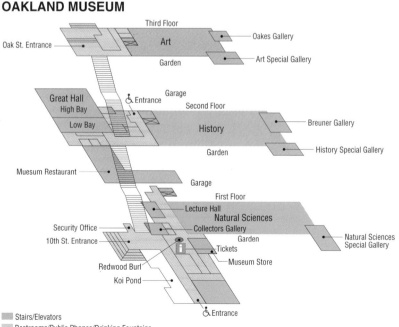

Oakland Hills near Joaquin Miller Park. You can explore the center, experience the Tien MegaDome Theater and watch the night sky in the Ask Jeeves Planetarium.

Another point of interest is **Lake Merritt** (bordered by Lakeside Dr, Lakeshore Ave, and Grand Ave; information 510/562.7275, sailboat house 510/444.3807), which offers boat rentals, sailing lessons, gondola rides (510/663.6603) a strolling/jogging path, a garden center, and a bird sanctuary. If you're ready to sit back and relax for a while, catch a movie at the grandiose **Grand Lake Theatre** (Grand Ave and Lake Park, 510/452.3556)- they don't make 'em like this anymore. And, finally, top off your day with a meal at the **Bay Wolf Cafe** (3853 Piedmont Ave, 510/655.6004), a lively, upscale restaurant serving Californian cuisine with French and Italian influences.

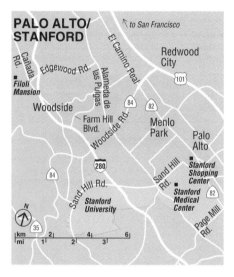

## Palo Alto/Stanford University

Fueled by the intellectual fires at **Stanford University,** Palo Alto is an oasis of energy and culture in the suburban desert. (OK, it's a mixed metaphor and a trifle hyperbolic, but you get the idea.) Movie houses play foreign and art films, restaurants serve a variety of international cuisines to a casual-chic crowd, a bookstore and a cappuccino place mark every corner, and everything from child-care centers to exercise facilities reflects cutting-edge thinking. Furthermore, there's excellent shopping, from a lively downtown with trendy boutiques to the **Stanford Shopping Center,** a mall so magnificent that more than one local has asked that her ashes be scattered here.

Rail service on **Caltrain** will get you to the peninsula. (Get off at **Palo Alto** and then walk downtown through the pocket park to the shopping center.) For rail schedule information, call or 800/660.4287 (in the Bay Area). If you plan on doing a lot of local

exploration, the best way to approach this area is by automobile. Take **Highway 280,** heading south, exiting at **Sand Hill Road.** It's the turnoff right after **Woodside Road.** Take Sand Hill Road east for 10 traffic lights, and you'll find yourself at the **Stanford Shopping Center** (between Sand Hill and Quarry Rds, west of El Camino Real). The shopping center is also served by **SamTrans** bus 7F. The ride takes about an hour from San Francisco. For scheduling information, call 800/660.4287 (in the Bay Area).

The **Stanford Shopping Center** is a retailing paradise and one of the most attractive mercantile complexes to be found, incorporating 150 stores in an open mall. It is anchored by several of the leading department and specialty stores in the Bay Area, including **Bloomingdales** (650/463.2000), **Macy's** (650/326.3333), **Nordstrom** (650/323.5111), and **Neiman-Marcus** (650/329.3300). Travel services include **Thomas Cook Foreign Exchange** (800/287.7362) and **American Express** (800/528.4800). In addition, you can choose from a variety of restaurants at various price levels. After you've shopped yourself into a state of hunger, there's **Bravo Fono** (650/322.4664), a lovely spot for lunch and memorable homemade ice cream. **Max's Opera Cafe** (650/771.7300) serves overstuffed deli sandwiches, and **Ristorante Piatti** (650/324.9733) offers Italian fare.

Although dedicated shoppers can easily spend the entire day at this mall-to-end-all-malls, Palo Alto's thriving downtown shouldn't be neglected. In addition to a host of interesting boutiques (mostly along **University Avenue** and its cross streets), Palo Alto is home to a number of fine restaurants, including the ever-popular **Il Fornaio** (Italian; 520 Cowper St, 650/853.3888), **Maddalena's** (French; 544 Emerson St, 650/326.6082), **MacArthur Park** (American; 27 University Ave, 650/321.9990), and **Cafe Pro Bono** (Italian; 2437 Birch St, 650/326.1626). And if you're an old-movie buff, be sure to take in a classic flick at the wonderfully restored **Stanford Theater** (221 University Ave, 650/324.3700), which warms up audiences with lively organ music on weekend nights.

One-hour tours of Stanford University, one of California's most prestigious private educational institutions, are given free of charge daily, at 11AM and 3:15PM. It's best to call ahead (650/723.2560) to be sure that tours are being offered, as the university closes to the public for holidays, semester breaks, and final exams. The tour begins at the information booth in front of the **Main Quad** (at the end of **Palm Dr**). Tours cover the central campus area, including administration buildings, classrooms, student union, bookstore, art gallery, chapel, **Hoover Tower,** and the main quadrangle area. The tower's observation platform (open daily from 10AM to 11AM and from 1PM to 4:30PM; nominal admission) offers panoramic views of the area. The **Stanford Memorial Chapel** and the **Leland Stanford Jr. Museum** both suffered structural damage during the 1989 earthquake. The museum is still closed, but the church reopened in 1992. Tasty, inexpensive food is offered at the **Tresidder Student Union** on campus, which includes a coffeehouse, cafeteria, and bakery counter.

Visitors can also tour the **Stanford Linear Accelerator Center (SLAC),** a world-class physics laboratory with a mind-blowing two-mile-long linear electron accelerator. Tours are available by appointment only (call 650/926.2204); not recommended for children under 11. You might also want to visit the **Stanford Medical Center** (advance reservations required; call 650/723.7167) or take the hospital's "Art in the Atrium" audio tour. For more information, call 650/723.4000.

## Filoli Mansion

Located in the exclusive community of **Woodside,** this mansion was built between 1916 and 1919 by architect **Willis Polk** for prominent San Franciscans Mr. and Mrs. William B. Bourn II. The 16 acres of gardens were laid out by Bruce Porter, with the subsequent help of Isabella Worn. The homesite was chosen partly because it was near the Spring Valley Water Company, headed by Bourn, and partly because it reminded him of Ireland's Lakes of Killarney. The Bourns lived at the mansion until their deaths in 1936, whereupon the estate was acquired by Mr. and Mrs. William P. Roth, who kept it until 1975. Mrs. Roth then deeded it to the National Trust for Historic Preservation. The mansion is an important example of American country-house architecture, and is one of the few in the state intact in its original setting. The house and gardens are within the **Crystal Springs Watershed,** south of San Francisco. The now-mature gardens reflect the meticulous care during the nearly 40 years the Roths occupied the estate. The garden is a successful blend of the formal and the natural. A focal point is the Italian Renaissance **Tea House,** designed by **Arthur Brown Jr.,** who also designed the nearby Carriage House, dominated by a bell tower. The structure houses a collection of antique carriages.

**Filoli** is best reached by taking Highway 280 to the **Edgewood Road** exit, then turning right on Cañada Road. Follow Cañada Road and keep an eye peeled for the small, unobtrusive sign on the right side of the road. The gate on the left side is where you enter. The house and gardens are open for guided tours Tuesday through Saturday from mid-February to mid-November; advance reservations are required, and there is an admission charge. You may also take the self-guided tours every Friday and the first Saturday and second Sunday of every month from March through November; reservations are not required and there is an admission fee. Limited wheelchair access is available, but prior notification is requested to

ensure that special entrance arrangements can be made. Guided hikes through the property are available by reservation from September through June. Children accompanied by an adult are welcome.

One hour south of San Francisco on scenic Highway 1 is **Costanoa Coastal Lodge and Camp,** an upscale camp connected to four state parks, 30,000 acres of foot trails and a spectacular wildlife preserve. Includes spa facilities. 2001 Rossi Rd at Hwy 1, Pescadero, 650/879.1100. 877/262.7848, 800/738.7477. *www.costanoa.com*

## Santa Cruz

Ninety minutes south of San Francisco on the coast, the laid-back, college-town feel of Santa Cruz has a lot to do with the University of California, Santa Cruz (831/459.0111). Its eight colleges form an impressive campus nestled among the redwoods. For more Californiana, check out the history of one of the area's central attractions at the **Surfing Museum** (Lighthouse Pt, off Westcliff Dr, 831//429.3429). But the real reason you should stop here is to ride on the Giant Dipper at the **Santa Cruz Beach Boardwalk** (831/426.7433), considered by most wooden-roller-coaster aficionados to be the best in the world.

The best food in this town is not found at fancy French restaurants. **India Joze** (1001 Center St, between Union St and Chestnut St Extension, 831/427.3554) serves excellent Indian/Indonesian/Middle Eastern fare, and the calamari is widely acclaimed. For a casual meal on a rose-garden patio, stop in at **The Crêpe Place** (1134 Soquel Dr, at Seabright Dr, 831/429.6994), where you can choose from a variety of crepes or create your own combination. The ultimate in Santa Cruz hippie-vegetarian fast food can be found at **Dharma's** (4250 Capitola Rd, between 42nd and 43rd Aves, 831/462.1717)—known as McDharma's until the litigious burger company sued over the "Mc."

## Monterey Peninsula

The peninsula is two and a half to three hours from San Francisco, but the scenic drive makes getting there half the fun. **Interstate 280** is rightfully known as America's most beautiful interstate, and it provides the quicker route south. Exit Interstate 280 at **Highway 17** to **Santa Cruz,** then pick up **Highway 1** south to **Monterey** and **Carmel.** It takes longer to follow Highway 1 all the way down the coast, but the quaint towns make the drive worthwhile.

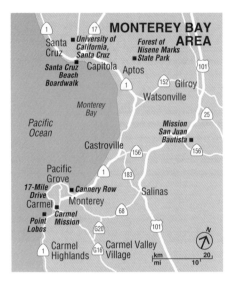

**MONTEREY BAY AREA**

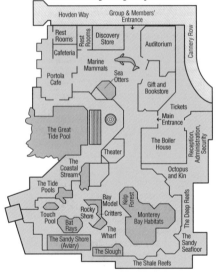

**Monterey Bay Aquarium**

The capital of Hispanic California, Monterey has preserved its heritage. Discover downtown's Spanish architecture on the **Path of History,** a three-mile walking tour. Maps are available from the Visitor **Information Center** (401 Camino el Estero, at Del Monte Ave). Monterey's sardine canneries inspired John Steinbeck's description, "a poem, a stink, a grating noise, a quality of light, a tone, a habit, a nostalgia, a dream." His **Cannery Row** (on the bay between David Ave and the Coastguard Pier, south to Lighthouse Ave), shut down by the depletion of the local sardine schools, has been renovated into a collection of shops, galleries, and restaurants, with much of the area's old character (but not the stench) preserved. A modern but must-see attraction is the **Monterey Bay Aquarium** (886 Cannery Row

on the bay, 408/648.4888), a renowned collection highlighting the local underwater ecology, including Monterey's giant kelp forests (see the floor plan).

Carmel, just south of Monterey, is the home of the **Carmel Mission** (3080 Río Rd, 408/624.3600), one of the most beautiful and well preserved of the California missions. It was founded in 1770 by Friar Junipero Serra and is his final resting place. Poets and painters later discovered the spectacular coast around Carmel that had attracted the Spanish settlers, and formed an artists' community that thrives to this day. Although undeniably touristy, Carmel has been preserved as a small Mediterranean-type village, with no street addresses on downtown buildings and no traffic signals (but *lots* of traffic, especially on weekends). Former mayor Clint Eastwood was an integral part of the fight to prevent development. Stop in at Clint's **Hog's Breath Inn** (San Carlos St between Fifth and Sixth Aves, 408/625.1044), though he probably won't be around. For a romantic and scenic stay-over, try the **Highlands Inn** (Highland Dr, off Hwy 101, 408/624.3801), where Sean Penn and Madonna honeymooned. The lounge at the stately old hotel is a wonderful place to enjoy a cocktail as the sun sets.

The Monterey Peninsula you've seen on TV, and really shouldn't miss in person, can be found on the **17-Mile Drive.** The circular tour takes you past grand and pricey homes, past some of the world's most famous championship golf courses, and along California's stunning central coastline. If you can't bear to leave this area or pass up the great golfing, check in at the expensive **Lodge at Pebble Beach** along the 17-Mile Drive (408/624.3811).

If you're feeling a mite peckish, try one of the following stellar peninsula restaurants: **Fresh Cream** (Heritage Harbor complex at Pacific and Scott Sts, Monterey, 408/375.9798), **The Old Bath House** (620 Ocean View Blvd, Pacific Grove, 408/375.5195), or **Casanova** (Fifth Ave between Mission and San Carlos Sts, Carmel, 408/625.0501).

## Wine Country

Any visit to the Bay Area should include a few relaxing days of wine tasting, bike riding, and even hot-air ballooning in the wine country. The valleys of this primarily northern California region stretch from the Pacific coast to the Sierra Nevada, carpeting the area with more than 400,000 acres of vineyards. Fabled **Napa** and **Sonoma** counties, just one and a half to two hours north of San Francisco, are dotted with nearly 300 wineries producing such premium wines as Chardonnay, Cabernet Sauvignon, Zinfandel, Syrah, and Pinot Noir, as well as charming bed-and-breakfast inns and some of the best restaurants in the country. September and October are the height of the grape harvest, and the aroma of fermenting wine is everywhere.

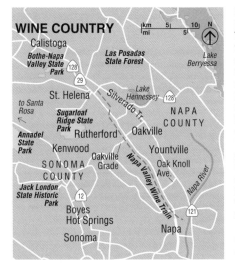

WINE COUNTRY

Calistoga
Bothe-Napa Valley State Park (128)
Las Posadas State Forest
Lake Berryessa
29
Lake Hennessey (128)
St. Helena
to Santa Rosa
Sugarloaf Ridge State Park
Silverado Tr.
NAPA COUNTY
Annadel State Park
Rutherford
Oakville
Kenwood
Oakville Grade
Yountville
SONOMA COUNTY
Oak Knoll Ave.
Jack London State Historic Park
12
Napa Valley Wine Train
Napa River
Boyes Hot Springs
121
Sonoma
Napa
km 5 10 N
mi 5

If you don't mind rousing the ire of the locals, you might want to go for a ride on the **Napa Valley Wine Train.** This controversial enterprise, which involves three-hour dining, drinking, and sight-seeing excursions in Pullman lounge cars, was fought by many valley folk who feared it might change the serious nature of the wine industry. You won't see much of Napa while on the train—passengers don't disembark en route—but the food is delicious and the surroundings are quite luxurious. For more information, contact the train company (1275 McKinstry St, 707/253.2111, 800/427.4124). If you opt for a great meal without the choo-choo ride, **Bistro Don Giovanni** (4110 St. Helena Hwy, 707/224.3300) is a popular spot for gourmet dining in the city of Napa. Napa wineries include the family-run **Trefethen Vineyards** (1160 Oak Knoll Ave, 707/255.7700), **Stag's Leap Wine Cellars** (5766 Silverado Trail, 707/944.2020), and **The Hess Collection Winery** (4411 Redwood Rd, 707/255.1144), which offers a high-powered art collection as well as a number of popular wines.

Almost halfway into the valley as you drive from San Francisco, **Yountville** is where the wine country begins to stir the emotions. George Yount, who came here in search of new frontiers, was the first US citizen to be ceded a Mexican land grant—the 12,000 acres making up the heart of Napa Valley called **Rancho Caymus.**

While in Yountville, try an old-fashioned American breakfast at **The Diner** (6476 Washington St, 707/944.2626), Italian fare at popular **Piatti** (6480 Washington St, 707/944.2070), the exuberant Californian cuisine at **Mustards Grill** (7399 St. Helena Hwy, 707/944.2424). The **Vintage Inn** (6541 Washington St, 800/351.1133 in CA, 800/982.5539) and the bed-and-breakfast-style **Maison Fleurie** (6529 Yount St, 707/944.2056) are two good bets for lodging. Nearby wineries include **Domaine Chandon** (1 California Dr, 707/944.2280), which produces sparkling wine by the traditional *méthode champenoise* and also has a very highly regarded (and expensive) restaurant; the venerable **Robert Mondavi Winery** (7801 St. Helena Hwy, Oakville, 707/963.9611); and the **Beaulieu Vineyard** (1960 St. Helena Hwy, Rutherford, 707/963.2411).

Another option is a hot-air balloon. This art of riding above the ground was discovered by the French aristocracy in 1783. (The first balloon flight was made by a sheep, a duck, and a rooster!) Today, the wine country's stunning scenery has turned ballooning in northern California into big business. It's a costly experience, but one you won't soon forget. **The Wine Country Balloon Safaris** (707/829.9850, 888/238.6359) can provide this bird's-eye view of the vineyards. In Vallejo, at **Six Flags Marine World** (2001 Marine World Pkwy, 707/644-4000) you can ride the 150-foot tall Medusa roller coaster. Constructed at a cost of $15 million, this serpentine super-coaster reaches speeds of 65 mph.

Most wineries offer tastings and tours around the storage casks. Some take you through limestone caves carved out long ago by Chinese laborers. Though some of the wines can probably be purchased more cheaply at discount shops, one advantage to buying at the source is that you might discover one you like that's not easily found elsewhere. Production of these special wines, often called "reserves," is usually limited by the wineries. Most now charge a small fee for tastings, but tours are usually free.

The town of Napa, the largest in the wine country, was laid out in 1848 by Nathan Coombs, who got the property from Nicholas Higuerra, holder of the original Spanish land grant. It was the activity surrounding the Gold Rush that spurred the city's growth. After the first harsh winter in the gold fields, miners sought refuge in town and found work in the cattle and lumber industries. The first settlers planted vineyards from cuttings given to them by padres of the Sonoma and San Rafael Missions, and from those modest beginnings, the surrounding valley's reputation as the center of the American wine industry evolved. For free maps and brochures on valley attractions, contact the **Napa Valley Conference & Visitors Bureau** (707/226.7459).

**St. Helena,** a friendly small town in the heart of the vineyards, has come alive in the past few years with some exceptional restaurants and inns. And yet, walking down Main Street is like taking a step back in time—it's easy to imagine long white dresses and parasols emerging from the arched doorways of the stone buildings. Main Street is a portion of the valley's main highway, and has been a significant thoroughfare all the way back to the days of the horse and buggy. The stone bridges and buildings in the area were constructed by European stonemasons and Chinese laborers in the late 19th century. Outlaw Black Bart, who led a dual life as a schoolteacher and wrote poetry when he wasn't busy robbing stagecoaches, was one of the notorious characters who made his way through Main Street before his capture in 1883. Author Robert Louis Stevenson and his new bride also passed through the town. The newlyweds spent most of the summer of 1880 in nearby **Calistoga.**

St. Helena is heaven on earth for serious foodies. Some good—no, make that great—dining choices: **Terra** (1345 Railroad Ave, 707/963.8931), **Ristorante Tra Vigne** (1050 Charter Oak Ave, 707/963.4444), and **Trilogy** (1234 Main St, 707/963.5507). The Rhineland-inspired **Beringer Vineyards** (2000 Main St, 707/963.7115) and, by appointment only, **Frog's Leap** (3358 St. Helena Hwy, 707/963.4704) are among the wineries worth a visit.

With its geysers, hot springs, and lava deposits, Calistoga is a clear-cut reminder of the valley's tempestuous geological beginnings. Some of the eruptions formed the gray stone with which the Italian and Chinese workers built bridges and wineries. The first spa at Calistoga was built by Sam Brannan, California's first millionaire. He designed a spectacular hotel, now known as **Indian Springs,** to attract wealthy San Franciscans. Brannan also brought the first railroad to the valley and donated a costly engine to the first fire department. He coined the name Calistoga by combining the names California and Saratoga (the famous New York resort). Set in the middle of the wine country, this small town, with its Western-style main street still intact, is known for its mineral water and mud baths. Almost every motel or inn is equipped with at least a Jacuzzi. Contact the **Calistoga Chamber of Commerce** (1458 Lincoln Ave, 707/942.6333) for a list of spas.

Quaint Calistoga hotels include the **Larkmead Country Inn** (1103 Larkmead La, 707/942.5360) and the **Mount View Hotel** (1457 Lincoln Ave, 707/942.6877). There are also some very good restaurants here, including **All Seasons Café** (1400 Lincoln Ave, 707/942.9111) and the **Catahoula Restaurant & Saloon** (1457 Lincoln Ave, 707/942.BARK). Be sure to tour **Sterling Vineyards,** which is entered via a scenic tramway (1111 Dunaweal La, 707/942.3300); the **Clos Pegase** winery (1060 Dunaweal La, 707/942.4981;) and its

art gallery, designed by **Michael Graves;** and the gracious **Château Montelena** (1429 Tubbs La, 707/942.5105).

In the nearby and less congested **Sonoma Valley** lies the historic town of **Sonoma** with its eight-acre plaza, the largest in California. The plaza, laid out by General Mariano Vallejo in 1835, is ringed by boutiques, restaurants, and galleries. The stone structure dominating the area is **City Hall,** built to look the same on all sides. Wonderful adobe structures from the Mexican era, Western-type edifices, and stone buildings surround the plaza. Vallejo's soldiers trained here, and this was the site of the 25-day Bear Flag Party revolution in 1846 (still celebrated each 14 June). Contact the **Sonoma Valley Visitors Bureau** (453 First St E, 707/996.1090), for maps and information about the valley.

When you get hungry from all this touring, try **The General's Daughter** (400 West Spain St, between 4th W and 5th St W, 707/938-4004), housed in a Victorian built in 1864 for General Vallejo's daughter. Sonoma's **Ristorante Piatti** (405 First St W, 707/996.2351) serves regional Italian cuisine, and the **Feed Store Cafe & Bakery** (529 First St W, 707/938.2122). A little farther afield in Sonoma County is **John Ash & Co.** (4330 Barnes Rd, Santa Rosa, 707/527.7687), where both the food and the prices are breathtaking. This area is also rich in pleasant accommodations, including the **Thistle Dew Inn** (171 W Spain St on the Plaza, 707/938-2909), the **Victorian Garden Inn** (316 E Napa St, Sonoma, 707/996.5339, 800/543-5339), and the luxurious **Sonoma Mission Inn & Spa** (18140 Sonoma Hwy, Boyes Hot Springs, 707/938.9000, 800/862-4945. This luxurious spa, available for day use. The spa is a true spa, created in the European tradition and based on the benefits of the property's thermal mineral springs. The Inn's historic golf course provides the most beautiful golf experience in the wine country. **MacArthur Place** is a renovated estate offering 33 guestrooms (29 E MacArthur St, 707/938-2929, 800/722-1866, info@macarthur-place.com).

The town of Healdsburg (north of the town of Sonoma off Hwy 101) sustains the charm of smalltown life. **Honor Mansion** (14891 Grove St, Healdsburg, 707/433.4277, 800/554.4667) offers Victorian splendor and a gourmet breakfast in the mansion's formal dining room. While in Healdsburg, visit the villa and gardens of Ferrari-Carrano Vineyard & Winery (8761 Dry Creek Rd, Healdsburg, 707/433.7266.)

Among the valley's noteworthy vintners are **Benziger Family Winery** (1883 London Ranch Rd, Glen Ellen, 707/935.4046) which offers a free vineyard tram tour, **Gundlach-Bundschau** (2000 Denmark St, Sonoma, 707/938.5277), a historic and lovely winery, the **Buena Vista Winery** (1800 Old Winery Rd, Sonoma, 707/938.1266), the **Matanzas Creek Winery** (6097 Bennett Valley Rd, Santa Rosa, 707/528.6464), and **Kenwood Vineyards** (9592 Sonoma Hwy, Kenwood, 707/833.5891).

# HISTORY

**1579**
Sir Francis Drake anchors on the northern California coast.

**1595**
Captain Sebastian Cermeno claims the land for Spain and names it *Puerto de San Francisco.*

**1769**
Spanish explorers, led by Don Gaspar de Portola, discover **San Francisco Bay.**

**1775**
Explorers Ayala and Canizares enter San Francisco Bay.

**1776**
Padre Junipero Serra founds the **Mission of St. Francis** on the shore of **Lake Dolores,** already home to the Costanoan Indians. Captain Juan Bautista begins building **The Presidio.**

**1792**
George Vancouver anchors off **Yerba Buena Cove,** the spot from which San Francisco grew.

**1794**
The protective **Castillo de San Joaquin** is established on the site of **Fort Point,** now overshadowed by the approach to the **Golden Gate Bridge.**

**1806**
California is declared a province of the Republic of Mexico.

**1835**
Homes are built at Yerba Buena Cove on the site of the present downtown **Financial District.** The rest of the city, with its 43 hills, is occupied largely by *ranchos.*

**1846**
The American flag is raised in **Portsmouth Square,** and **Yerba Buena** becomes San Francisco. Captain John C. Fremont coins the term "Golden Gate."

**1848**
The Gold Rush begins. The first commercial bank is established in San Francisco, and the first American public school opens in the city.

**1850**
Legislature creates Bay region counties: San Francisco, **Contra Costa, Marin, Santa Clara, Sonoma, Solano,** and **Napa.** The city of San Francisco is incorporated. California is admitted to the Union.

**1854**
The first lighthouse is built on **Alcatraz Island.** Principal streets in San Francisco are lighted with coal gas for the first time.

**1855**
**St. Ignatius College** (later the **University of San Francisco**) is founded.

**1860**
The first Pony Express rider arrives in San Francisco from St. Joseph, Missouri. A telegraph line opens between San Francisco and Los Angeles.

**1862**
Direct telegraph between San Francisco and New York is established. San Francisco supports the Union Army; a company of cavalry, known as the "California Hundred," sails east. *The San Francisco and San Jose Railroad* formally opens.

**1864**
Young reporter Mark Twain begins writing about life in San Francisco for *Morning Call.*

**1867**
The first steamer sails from San Francisco to Alaska.

**1869**
The transcontinental railroad is completed, providing new trade and travel routes to the West.

**1870**
**Golden Gate Park** is established by Order 800, an act to provide for the improvement of public parks in the City of San Francisco.

**1872**
The first Japanese ship arrives in San Francisco loaded with tea.

**1873**
Ground is broken for the world's first cable street railroad on **Clay Street.**

**1875**
The *Northern Pacific Coast Railroad* is inaugurated, running from San Francisco to Tomales, via **Sausalito.**

**1876**
Electricity lights up San Francisco just in time for author Jack London's birth.

**1898**
The **Ferry Building** opens.

**1904**
The Bank of Italy, later to become Bank of America, is created by Italian merchant A.P. Giannini.

**1906**
Earthquake and fire destroy much of the city.

**1915**
The Panama-Pacific International Exhibition, commemorating the opening of the Panama Canal, opens in San Francisco. More than 18 million people attend.

**1927**
**San Francisco International Airport** opens.

**1933**
**Coit Tower** is erected.

**1934**
5 July is "Bloody Thursday," when a head-on confrontation between the Industrial Association scabs, the International Longshoremen's Union, and the police takes place.

**1936**
**The San Francisco–Oakland Bay Bridge** opens.

**1937**
The **Golden Gate Bridge** opens.

**1939**
**Treasure Island** is created for the Golden Gate International Exposition; the **Maritime Museum** opens.

**1945**
The United Nations Charter is founded in San Francisco.

**1960**
**Candlestick Park** opens.

**1963**
After nearly one hundred years, **Alcatraz** is closed because of old age.

**1967**
The "Summer of Love" comes to San Francisco: hippies, the Free Speech Movement, drugs, and the sexual revolution.

**1972**
The **Golden Gate National Recreational Area** is established; the **Bay Area Rapid Transit (BART)** System opens.

**1974**
**BART** makes its first run through the Transbay tube.

**1978**
Mayor George Moscone and Supervisor Harvey Milk are shot to death in their offices.

**1982**
The **San Francisco 49ers** win **Superbowl XVI** against Cincinnati. They repeat their victory 2, 7, 8, and 13 years later.

**1986**
The Downtown Plan limits building in San Francisco.

**1989**
A 7.1 earthquake at Loma Prieta, east of **Santa Cruz,** rocks San Francisco and Oakland.

**1993**
**Yerba Buena Gardens,** the multimillion-dollar arts and cultural center, officially opens.

**1994**
Most of the 200-year-old **Presidio,** the nation's oldest continuously used military post, is transferred from the Army's jurisdiction to become part of the **Golden Gate National Recreation Area.**

**1995**
**Candlestick Park** is renamed **3COM Park.**

**1998**
**E-line,** a Muni light-rail system, opens along The Embarcadero.

**2000**
**PacBell Park,** the city's new baseball stadium, opens. The **International Terminal** opens at San Francisco Airport. F-line, a Muni streetcar line featuring restored street cars. runs along the northern Embarcadero, connecting Union Square to Fisherman's Wharf. Harry Bridges Plaza opens at the foot of Market Street.

# INDEX

# T

# U

## RESTAURANTS

Only restaurants with star ratings are listed below. All restaurants are listed alphabetically in the main (preceding) index. Always call in advance to ensure a restaurant has not closed, changed its hours, or booked its tables for a private party. The restaurant price ratings are based on the average cost of an entrée for one person, excluding tax and tip.

| | |
|---|---|
| ★★★★ | An Extraordinary Experience |
| ★★★ | Excellent |
| ★★ | Very Good |
| ★ | Good |

| | |
|---|---|
| $$$$ | Big Bucks ($25 and up) |
| $$$ | Expensive ($15-$25) |
| $$ | Reasonable ($10-$15) |
| $ | The Price is Right (less that $10) |

### ★★★★

Acquerello $$$ **78**
Alfred Schilling $$$ **192**
Café Mozart $$$$ **83**
Farallon $$$$ **42**

★

## HOTELS

The hotels listed below are grouped according to their price ratings; they are also listed in the main index. The hotel price ratings reflect the base price of a standard room for two people for one night during the peak season.

$$$$ Big Bucks ($180 and up)
$$$ Expensive ($120-$180)
$$ Reasonable ($80-$120)
$ The Price is Right (less than $80)

## $$$$

## $$$

## $$

# CREDITS

*Writer and Researcher
for the Ninth Edition*

**Donna Peck**

---

*Writers and Researchers
for Gay San Francisco*

**David Appell
Paul Balido
Robert Adams**

---

*Editorial Director*

**Edwin Tan**

---

*Jacket Design*

**Chin-Yee Lai**

*Design Director*

**Leah Carlson-Stanisic**

---

*Design Supervisor*

**Iva Hacker-Delany**

---

*Designers*

**Nicola Ferguson
Elizabeth McCleery**

---

*Map Designer*

**Patricia Keelin**

---

*Associate Director of Production*

**Dianne Pinkowitz**

PRINTED IN HONG KONG

02